Barron's Review Course Series

Let's Review:

Sequential Mathematics, Course III

Second Edition

Lawrence S. Leff
Assistant Principal, Mathematics Supervision
Franklin D. Roosevelt High School
Brooklyn, New York

BARRON'S

┌─── TO RHONA ──────────────────────────┐
│   │
│   *For the gifts of*   │
│   *love and friendship.*   │
│   │
└──┘

© Copyright 1997 by Barron's Educational Series, Inc.

Prior edition © 1992 by Barron's Educational Series, Inc.

All inquiries should be addressed to:
Barron's Educational Series, Inc.
250 Wireless Boulevard
Hauppauge, New York 11788

Library of Congress Catalog Card No. 96-35975

International Standard Book No. 0-8120-9917-6

Library of Congress Cataloging-in-Publication Data

Leff, Lawrence S.
    Let's review. Sequential mathematics, course III / Lawrence S.
Leff.—2nd ed.
        p.   cm.—(Barron's review course series)
    Includes index.
    ISBN 0-8120-9917-6
    1. Mathematics. 2. Mathematics—Study and teaching (Secondary)
—New York (State) I. Title II. Series.
QA39.2.L423   1997
510'.76—dc20   96-35975
                                                         CIP

PRINTED IN THE UNITED STATES OF AMERICA

9876543

TABLE OF CONTENTS

PREFACE

For which course can this book be used?

This new edition reflects the latest trends in the Regents Examination for Course III of the New York State Three-Year Sequence in High School Mathematics, including the use of *scientific calculators* instead of logarithmic and trigonometric tables of values. Since this book offers complete topic coverage as well as systematic Regents Exam preparation for Course III, it can be used either as a supplementary study aid or as the main textbook in classes that follow the Course III curriculum.

What special features does this book have?

- *Discussion of Scientific Calculators*
  There is a special introductory section on what you need to know about scientific calculators. Throughout the text, the use of scientific calculators is explained whenever appropriate, and typical calculator-key-pressing sequences are displayed.

- *A Compact Format Designed for Self-Study and Rapid Learning*
  For easy reference, the major topics of the book are grouped by the appropriate branch of mathematics. The friendly, straightforward writing style quickly identifies essential ideas while avoiding unnecessary details.

- *Key Ideas*
  Each section of each chapter begins with KEY IDEAS that highlight and motivate the material that follows. The KEY IDEAS, together with the helpful diagrams and numerous step-by-step demonstration examples, aim to anticipate and answer students' "why" questions.

- *Regents Examination Preparation*
  The demonstration examples throughout and the practice exercises at the end of each section use Regents Exam types of questions. Each chapter closes with a set of REGENTS TUNE-UP exercises selected from actual past Course III Regents Examinations. These Regents problems provide a comprehensive review of the material covered in the chapter while previewing the types and the levels of difficulty of problems found on actual Regents Examinations. To provide a culminating activity, several full-length Course III Regents Examinations with answers appear at the end of the book.

- *Answers to Hundreds of Practice Exercises*
  The answers to all of the odd-numbered exercises and to selected even-numbered exercises are given at the end of each chapter. In addition, the answers to *all* of the Regents Tune-up exercises are provided.

- *Glossary of Course III Terms*
  Important Course III mathematical terms are collected for easy reference in a glossary at the end of the book.

Who should use this book?

Students who are having difficulty keeping up with their classroom lessons or who want to advance on their own, will find this book well suited to their special needs. Students who want to sharpen their understanding and improve their test grades will benefit greatly from the easily understood explanations, helpful examples, and past Regents Exam questions organized by topic. Students preparing for the Course III Regents Examination will find this book particularly useful whenever they need further explanation or more practice on a troublesome topic.

Since this new edition is designed to be compatible with all styles of classroom teaching and curriculum organization, classroom *teachers* will want to include the book in their personal and department libraries. Teachers will find that it is an ideal companion to any of the existing Course III textbooks, providing a valuable lesson-planning aid as well as a rich source of classroom exercises, homework problems, and test questions.

LAWRENCE S. LEFF
November 1996

SCIENTIFIC CALCULATORS:
WHAT YOU NEED TO KNOW

All students are required to have access to scientific calculators when they take the New York State Course III Regents Examination. This book assumes that you already have a scientific calculator and are familiar with its main features. Since logarithmic and trigonometric tables will not be provided in Regents Examination booklets, you will need to know how to use your scientific calculator to do the following:

- Find the values of logarithms of positive numbers.
- Find the antilogarithms of numbers to a stated level of accuracy.
- Find the values of trigonometric functions of angles expressed in degrees, degrees and minutes, and radians.
- Find the degree or radian measures of angles using inverse trigonometric functions. Answers may be required to the nearest degree, nearest minute, nearest 10 minutes, or nearest tenth or hundredth of a degree or radian.

Notation and Conventions

In this book, all calculator keys, except those for numbers, will be boxed. For example, the key-pressing sequence

$$16 \boxed{\div} 2 \boxed{=}$$

means enter 16, press the calculator key labeled with the division symbol, enter 2, and then press the calculator key labeled with the equals symbol.

To access the special functions, operations, or values that are printed directly *above* certain calculator keys, you must first press the $\boxed{\text{2nd}}$, $\boxed{\text{SHIFT}}$, or $\boxed{\text{INV}}$ key, depending on your particular calculator. To simplify matters, this book will always refer to this special key as the $\boxed{\text{2nd}}$ function key.

Optional Calculator Features You Need to Know

In taking the Regents Examination, you are permitted to use all of the special features of your scientific calculator. Therefore, it will be to your advantage to know how to do these things:

- Evaluate numbers with fractional exponents using the "x to y" $\boxed{x^y}$ function key. Some calculators label this key $\boxed{y^x}$.
- Evaluate expressions using keys that calculate factorials $x!$, permutations $_nP_r$, and combinations $_nC_r$ keys.
- Calculate the mean $\bar{x}$ and the standard deviation σ_n of a set of n data values for a stated level of accuracy.

Cautions

Unfortunately, all scientific calculators do not work in the same way, nor is the arrangement or labeling of the keys the same. If any calculator procedure described in this book does not work with your particular calculator, you will need to read the instruction manual that came with the calculator.

CALCULATOR TIPS

- Press the $\boxed{\text{AC}}$ or *All Clear* key before performing a new calculation.
- Make sure the angular mode of the calculator is set to the correct unit of angle measurement. For example, if you are working with angles measured in degrees but RADians appears in the display window, you will need to change the angular mode of the calculator from radians to degrees.
- Remember that, when performing a chain calculation involving a sequence of arithmetic operations, or when applying a special calculator function to an arithmetic computation, you may need to use parentheses. If in doubt, use parentheses. For example, to find the value of $8^{\frac{1}{3}}$ using the $\boxed{x^y}$ function key, let $x = 8$ and $y = (1 \div 3)$. Verify that the key sequence

$$8 \ \boxed{x^y} \ \boxed{(} \ 1 \ \boxed{\div} \ 3 \ \boxed{)} \ \boxed{=}$$

produces 2 in the display window. Thus, $8^{\frac{1}{3}} = 2$.
- First estimate an answer, then use your calculator to obtain the actual answer. If your calculator result varies greatly from the estimate, start over. You may have inadvertently pressed the wrong key.
- Reduce the chances of introducing round-off errors by keeping the results of intermediate calculations in your calculator. For example, to find the value of

$$\frac{19.30 \times \sin 50°}{34.60}$$

correct to the *nearest hundredth*, perform one long calculation using this key sequence:

$$19.3 \ \boxed{\times} \ 50 \ \boxed{\text{SIN}} \ \boxed{\div} \ 34.6 \ \boxed{=} \ .$$

If this keystroke sequence does not work with your calculator, press the $\boxed{\text{SIN}}$ key before entering 50. Since the display of a typical calculator shows 0.427302247, the answer is 0.43, correct to the *nearest hundredth*.

Unit
One

ALGEBRAIC METHODS AND COMPLEX NUMBERS

CHAPTER 1

REVIEW AND EXTENSION OF ALGEBRAIC METHODS

1.1 DEFINING ZERO, NEGATIVE INTEGER, AND FRACTIONAL EXPONENTS

$\wedge$ KEY IDEAS $\diagdown$

A positive **exponent** represents the number of times a quantity, called the **base**, appears as a factor. Thus, the exponent *4* in the expression 3^4 indicates that the base *3* is to be used as a factor 4 times, as in

$$3^4 = 3 \cdot 3 \cdot 3 \cdot 3.$$

The laws that apply to quantities raised to positive integer powers hold true also for zero, negative integer, and fractional exponents.

Zero and Negative Integer Exponents

Zero and negative integer exponents are so defined that:

- Any nonzero quantity raised to the zero power is 1.

  Example: $5^0 = 1$ and $(-5)^0 = \mathbf{1}$

- Any nonzero quantity raised to a negative integer power is equal to the reciprocal of the same quantity with the exponent changed from negative to positive.

  Examples: *1.* $\quad x^{-3} = \dfrac{1}{x^3} \quad (x \neq 0)$

  2. $\quad \dfrac{1}{y^{-5}} = y^5 \quad (y \neq 0)$

The Laws of Exponents summarized in Table 1.1 apply to all integer-valued exponents.

TABLE 1.1 LAWS OF INTEGER EXPONENTS

Law	Rule	Example
Product	$x^a \cdot x^b = x^{a+b}$	$x^3 \cdot x^2 = x^{2+3} = x^5$
Quotient	$\dfrac{x^a}{x^b} = x^{a-b}$	$\dfrac{x^3}{x^2} = x^{3-2} = x^1 = x$
Power	$\left(x^a\right)^b = x^{ab}$	$\left(x^3\right)^2 = x^{3 \cdot 2} = x^6$
Power of Product	$(xy)^a = x^a y^a$	$(xy)^3 = x^3 y^3$
Power of Quotient	$\left(\dfrac{x}{y}\right)^a = \dfrac{x^a}{y^a}$	$\left(\dfrac{x}{y}\right)^2 = \dfrac{x^2}{y^2} \quad (y \neq 0)$

A fraction raised to a negative integer power can be simplified by inverting the fraction and changing the sign of the exponent from negative to positive, as in

$$\left(\frac{5}{2}\right)^{-3} = \left(\frac{2}{5}\right)^3 = \frac{2^3}{5^3} = \frac{8}{125}.$$

MATH FACTS

ZERO AND NEGATIVE INTEGER EXPONENT RULES

- $x^0 = 1 \qquad (x \neq 0)$

- $x^{-n} = \dfrac{1}{x^n}$ and $x^n = \dfrac{1}{x^{-n}} \qquad (x \neq 0)$

- $\left(\dfrac{a}{b}\right)^{-n} = \left(\dfrac{b}{a}\right)^n \qquad (a, b \neq 0)$

Examples

1. Rewrite in simplest form, using a positive exponent:

(a) $2x^{-4}$ (b) $\dfrac{1}{2x^{-4}}$ (c) $(2x)^{-4}$

Solutions:

(a) $2x^{-4} = \dfrac{2}{x^4}$

(b) $\dfrac{1}{2x^{-4}} = \dfrac{x^4}{2}$

(c) $(2x)^{-4} = \dfrac{1}{(2x)^4}$

$= \dfrac{1}{2^4 x^4} = \dfrac{1}{16x^4}$

2. Rewrite in simplest form, using positive exponents:

(a) $\dfrac{3x^{-2}}{5y^{-3}}$ (b) $\left(\dfrac{r^3}{s^2}\right)^{-4}$ (c) $\dfrac{12x^{-5}y^7}{6y^3}$

Solutions:

(a) $\dfrac{3x^{-2}}{5y^{-3}} = \dfrac{3y^3}{5x^2}$ (c) $\dfrac{12x^{-5}y^7}{6y^3} = \dfrac{12y^{7-3}}{6x^5}$

(b) $\left(\dfrac{r^3}{s^2}\right)^{-4} = \left(\dfrac{s^2}{r^3}\right)^{4} = \dfrac{8^8}{r^{12}}$ $= \dfrac{2y^4}{x^5}$

3. If $x = 3$, find the value of each expression:

(a) $2x^0 + x^{-2}$ (b) $(2x)^0 - 6x^{-2}$

Solutions: Replace x by 3 and simplify:

(a) $2x^0 + x^{-2} = 2(3^0) + 3^{-2}$

$= 2 \cdot 1 + \dfrac{1}{3^2}$

$= 2 + \dfrac{1}{9}$

$= 2\dfrac{1}{9}$ or $\dfrac{19}{9}$

(b) $(2x)^0 - 6x^{-2} = (2 \cdot 3)^0 - 6(3)^{-2}$

$= 6^0 - \dfrac{6}{3^2}$

$= 1 - \dfrac{6}{9}$

$= \dfrac{3}{9}$ or $\dfrac{1}{3}$

Square Root

A **square root** of a nonnegative number is one of two identical factors whose product is the number. For example, a square root of 16 is 4 since $4^2 = 16$. Thus, $\sqrt{16} = 4$, where the symbol $\sqrt{\ }$ is called a **radical sign** and 16, the number underneath the radical sign, is the **radicand**. The expression $\sqrt{16}$ is read as "the square root of 16" or as "radical 16."

Every positive number has two square roots. For example, the two square roots of 16 are 4 and -4 since $4^2 = 16$ and $(-4)^2 = 16$. The positive square root is called the *principal* square root. If a number has more than one real root, the root that has the same sign as the original number is called the **principal root**. The expression $\sqrt{x}$ always names the *principal* square root of x. Thus, $\sqrt{16} = 4$ rather than $\sqrt{16} = -4$.

Not all real numbers have square roots. For example, $\sqrt{-9}$ does not name a real number since it is not possible to find two identical real numbers whose product is negative 9.

The *k*th Root of a Number

The **cube root** of a number is one of three identical factors whose product is the number. The principal cube root of 8 is 2 since $2^3 = 8$. The principal cube root of -8 is -2 since $(-2)^3 = -8$. Thus

$$\sqrt[3]{8} = 2 \quad \text{and} \quad \sqrt[3]{-8} = -2 \,.$$

A **fourth root** of a nonnegative number is one of four identical factors whose product is the number. There are two real fourth roots of 81, 3 and -3, since $3^4 = 81$ and $(-3)^4 = 81$. The principal fourth root, however, is 3 since it has the same sign as 81. Thus

$$\sqrt[4]{81} = 3 \,.$$

In general:

- The number k in $\sqrt[k]{x}$ is called the **index** of the radical and indicates what root is to be taken. Therefore, k represents some integer greater than or equal to 2. If the index does not appear, as in square root radicals, it is assumed to be 2. Thus, $\sqrt[2]{9}$ and $\sqrt{9}$ mean the same thing.

- If the index k is even and $x < 0$, then $\sqrt[k]{x}$ is not real.

Using Exponents to Indicate Roots

By extending Table 1.1 to include fractional exponents, the Product Law of Exponents may be used to give meaning to these exponents. Since

$$x^{\frac{1}{2}} \cdot x^{\frac{1}{2}} = x^{\frac{1}{2}+\frac{1}{2}} = x^1 \quad,$$

$x^{\frac{1}{2}}$ represents one of two identical factors whose product is x. Thus, $x^{\frac{1}{2}} = \sqrt[2]{x}$ or $\sqrt{x}$. Similarly, $x^{\frac{1}{3}} = \sqrt[3]{x}$. In general, $x^{\frac{1}{k}}$ represents the kth root of x.

===== **MATH FACTS** =====

MEANING OF $x^{\frac{1}{k}}$

$$x^{\frac{1}{k}} = \sqrt[k]{x}$$

where k is an integer ≥ 2 and $x \geq 0$ whenever k is even.

Interpreting Fractional Exponents

In giving meaning to $x^{\frac{n}{k}}$, assume that $k \neq 0$ and the fractional exponent $\frac{n}{k}$ is already in lowest terms. Since $x^{\frac{n}{k}} = \left(x^{\frac{1}{k}}\right)^n$, the quantity $x^{\frac{n}{k}}$ may be evaluated by finding the kth root of the base x, and then raising the result to the nth power. For example,

$$27^{\frac{2}{3}} = \left(\sqrt[3]{27}\right)^2 = (3)^2 = \mathbf{9}.$$

Since it is also true that $x^{\frac{n}{k}} = \left(x^n\right)^{\frac{1}{k}}$, the quantity $x^{\frac{n}{k}}$ may be evaluated by raising the base x to the nth power, and then finding the kth root of the result. For example,

$$27^{\frac{2}{3}} = \sqrt[3]{27^2} = \sqrt[3]{729} = \mathbf{9}.$$

MATH FACTS

MEANING OF $x^{\frac{n}{k}}$

$$x^{\frac{n}{k}} = \sqrt[k]{x^n} = \left(\sqrt[k]{x}\right)^n$$

where k is an integer ≥ 2 and $x \geq 0$ whenever k is even.

Examples

4. Rewrite with a fractional exponent and simplify:

(a) $\sqrt{y^8}$ **(b)** $\sqrt[3]{8x^6}$

Solutions: **(a)** $\sqrt{y^8} = \left(y^8\right)^{\frac{1}{2}} = y^{\frac{8}{2}} = \mathbf{y^4}$ **(b)** $\sqrt[3]{8x^6} = \left(8x^6\right)^{\frac{1}{3}}$

$$= (8)^{\frac{1}{3}}\left(x^6\right)^{\frac{1}{3}}$$

$$= 2 \cdot x^{\frac{6}{3}} = \mathbf{2x^2}$$

5. If $x = 16$, find the value of each expression:

(a) $2x^{\frac{1}{2}} - x^{\frac{3}{4}}$ **(b)** $\left(\dfrac{2}{x}\right)^{-\frac{3}{2}}$

Solutions: Replace x by 16 and simplify:

(a) $2x^{\frac{1}{2}} - x^{\frac{3}{4}} = 2(16)^{\frac{1}{2}} - 16^{\frac{3}{4}}$

$= 2\sqrt{16} - \left(\sqrt[4]{16}\right)^3$

$= 2 \cdot 4 \ - (2)^3$

$= 8 \quad - 8$

$= 0$

(b) $\left(\dfrac{2}{x}\right)^{-\frac{3}{2}} = \left(\dfrac{2}{16}\right)^{-\frac{3}{2}} = \left(\dfrac{16}{2}\right)^{\frac{2}{3}}$

$= 8^{\frac{2}{3}}$

$= \left(\sqrt[3]{8}\right)^2 = (2)^2 = 4$

Using a Scientific Calculator to Evaluate $x^{\frac{p}{k}}$

The $\boxed{x^y}$ key can be used to evaluate a number raised to a fractional power. For example, the value of $8^{-\frac{2}{3}}$ is found by keying in

$$8 \;\boxed{x^y}\; \boxed{(}\; 2 \;\boxed{\pm}\; \boxed{\div}\; 3 \;\boxed{)}\; \boxed{=} \;.$$

Since the display window shows 0.25, $8^{-\frac{2}{3}} = 0.25$. If your calculator does not have a "x to the y" function key look for a "y to the x" function key.

Exercise Set 1.1

1–6. Rewrite in simplest form, using a positive exponent.

1. $3y^{-2}$ **3.** $\dfrac{1}{3y^{-2}}$ **5.** $\left(x^{-2}y^{-3}\right)^2$

2. $\dfrac{(3y)^{-2}}{3}$ **4.** $\dfrac{2x^{-3}}{3y^{-2}}$ **6.** $\left(\dfrac{a^{-3}}{b^{-2}}\right)^{-2}$

7. If $10^x = m$, express each of the following in terms of m:
(a) 10^{x+3} (b) 10^{3x} (c) 10^{x-2} (d) $10^{\frac{x}{2}}$

8–11. Rewrite in simplest form, using positive exponents.

8. $\dfrac{15x^{-2}}{10x^4y^{-3}}$ **9.** $\left(\dfrac{p^3}{q^2}\right)^{-3}$ **10.** $\left(\dfrac{u^{-2}}{v^{-3}}\right)^{-1}$ **11.** $\dfrac{16a^5b^{-1}}{24a^{-3}b^2}$

12–19. If x = 4, find the value of each expression.

12. $2x^0 + x^{-2}$ **14.** $x^{-\frac{1}{2}}$ **16.** $(2x)^{\frac{1}{3}}$ **18.** $\left(x^{-3}\right)^{\frac{1}{2}}$

13. $2(x+1)^0 - 6x^{-2}$ **15.** $x^{\frac{3}{2}}$ **17.** $(16x)^{\frac{2}{3}}$ **19.** $\left(\dfrac{x}{3}\right)^{-2}$

20–23. Evaluate.

20. $64^{\frac{2}{3}}$ **21.** $64^{-\frac{3}{2}}$ **22.** $\left(\dfrac{25}{16}\right)^{\frac{3}{2}}$ **23.** $\left(\dfrac{25}{16}\right)^{-\frac{3}{2}}$

24–26. If x = 8, find the value of each expression.

24. $x^{\frac{2}{3}} - (x+1)^{\frac{3}{2}}$ **25.** $x^{-\frac{4}{3}} + (3x)^{0}$ **26.** $\dfrac{1}{x^2} + x^{-2}$

27–31. Write in exponential form, and then simplify.

27. $\sqrt{y^{10}}$ **28.** $\sqrt{a^2 b^6}$ **29.** $\sqrt[3]{27x^{12}}$ **30.** $\sqrt{4m^2 n}$ **31.** $\sqrt[3]{-8x^6 y^2}$

1.2 FACTORING ALGEBRAIC EXPRESSIONS

⌃ KEY IDEAS ⌃

The polynomial $x^2 + 5x$ is factored when it is written as $x(x + 5)$. The polynomials x and $x+5$ are factors of the original polynomial. **Factoring** a polynomial means writing it as the product of two or more other polynomials.

The distributive property can be used to check that an expression has been factored correctly. For example, to verify that $x^2 + 5x$ can be factored as $x(x + 5)$, multiply each term inside the parentheses by x. The result should be the original expression:

$$x(x + 5) = x \cdot x + x \cdot 5 = x^2 + 5x.$$

Factoring is usually performed "over the set of integers." This statement means that, if a polynomial has integer coefficients, then any factor of the polynomial must also have an integer coefficient.

Factoring can be used in simplifying algebraic fractions and in solving quadratic equations.

Factoring Polynomials

Some polynomials can be factored by recognizing that each term of the polynomial contains a common numerical factor, a common literal factor, or both.

Examples: 1. $2a - 8b = 2(a - 4b)$

2. $10y^2 + 15y = 5y(2y + 3)$

3. $6r^2 s - 9rs^2 + 12r^2 s^2 = 3rs(2r - 3s + 4rs)$

4. $-3x - 7y = -(3x + 7y)$

Factoring the Difference of Two Squares

The binomials $p + q$ and $p - q$ are called *conjugate* binomials since they take the sum and difference of the *same* two terms. Any binomial of the form $p^2 - q^2$ can be factored as the product of the conjugate binomials $p + q$ and $p - q$.

Examples: 1. $y^2 - 36 = (y + 6)(y - 6)$
  2. $4a^2 - 25b^2 = (2a + 5b)(2a - 5b)$

===== **MATH FACTS** =====

FACTORING THE DIFFERENCE OF TWO SQUARES

$$p^2 - q^2 = (p + q)(p - q)$$

Factoring $x^2 + bx + c$

Two binomials can be multiplied horizontally by using the familiar FOIL method, where F represents the product of the <u>F</u>irst terms of the binomials, O and I represent the products of the <u>O</u>utermost and <u>I</u>nnermost terms of the binomials, and L represents the product of the <u>L</u>ast terms of the binomials.

$$\overset{\text{F} \quad \text{O} \quad \text{I} \quad \text{L}}{}$$

Example: $(x + 5)(x - 2) = x^2 + (-2x + 5x) + [(5)(-2)]$
$$= x^2 + 3x - 10$$

Using the reverse of this process, begin factoring $x^2 + bx + c$ by writing

$$x^2 + bx + c = (x + \underline{\quad})(x + \underline{\quad}).$$

The blanks must be filled with two numbers whose product is c *and* whose sum is b. For example, start factoring $x^2 - 7x - 18$ by writing

$$x^2 - 7x - 18 = (x + \underline{\quad})(x + \underline{\quad}).$$

Next, identify the pairs of factors of -18. Although -18 has four pairs of factors (1, -18; -1, 18; 9, -2; -9, 2), only -9 and 2 have a sum of -7. Therefore fill in the blanks with -9 and 2. Hence

$$x^2 - 7x - 18 = (x - 9)(x + 2).$$

Factoring $ax^2 + bx + c$ ($a \neq 1$)

When determining the possible binomial factors of $ax^2 + bx + c$, where a is different from 1, the factors of a must be taken into consideration. For example, the binomial factors of $4x^2 - x - 5$ take the form

$$(\Box x + \underline{\quad})(\Box x + \underline{\quad}).$$

Since 4 has two pairs of positive factors (2, 2 and 4, 1), more than one pair of numbers can be entered in the boxes as coefficients of x:

$$4x^2 - x - 5 = (2x + \underline{\quad})(2x + \underline{\quad}) \text{ or } 4x^2 - x - 5 = (4x + \underline{\quad})(x + \underline{\quad})$$

Next, identify the pairs of factors of $-5(-5, 1$ and $5, -1)$. Each pair of factors must be tested by placing the factors in the blanks in each pair of possible binomial factors. By trial and error, you determine that the correct pair of factors is -5 and 1; position them in the binomials in such a way that the sum of the outermost and innermost products is $-x$:

$$4x^2 - x - 5 = (\mathbf{4x - 5})(\mathbf{x + 1}).$$

To check that this is the correct factorization, use FOIL to verify that the product $(4x - 5)(x + 1)$ equals $4x^2 - x - 5$.

Factoring $ax^2 + bx + c$ by Decomposing bx

If a quadratic trinomial of the form $ax^2 + bx + c$ can be factored, its binomial factors can be identified by rewriting the middle term, bx, as the sum of two other terms and then factoring. The numerical coefficients of these two terms must be chosen so that their sum is b and their product is $a \cdot c$. To factor $3x^2 + 10x + 8$ using this method the procedure is as follows:

Find two integers whose sum is $+10$ (the coefficient of x), and whose product is 24 (the product of 3 and 8). Since these integers are 4 and 6, write:

$$3x^2 + 10x + 8 = 3x^2 + \underbrace{4x + 6x}_{+10x} + 8$$

Group the first and last pairs of terms:

$$= \left(3x^2 + 4x\right) + \left(6x + 8\right)$$

Factor out the greatest common factor of each pair of terms:

$$= x(3x + 4) + 2(3x + 4)$$

Factor out the common *binomial* factors:

$$= (3x + 4)(x + 2)$$

Thus, $3x^2 + 10x + 8 = (\mathbf{3x + 4})(\mathbf{x + 2})$.

Factoring Completely

A polynomial is factored *completely* when each of its factors cannot be factored further. To factor completely, it may be necessary to apply more than one factoring technique. Typically, begin by removing a common monomial factor, if possible, and then factoring further, again if possible.

$$\textit{Examples:} \quad 1. \ 3x^3 - 12x = 3x(x^2 - 4)$$
$$= 3x(x + 2)(x - 2)$$
$$2. \ t^3 + 6t^2 - 16t = t(t^2 + 6t - 16)$$
$$= t(t + 8)(t - 2)$$

Simplifying Fractions

If the numerator and the denominator of a fraction have a factor in common, the fraction can be simplified by factoring the numerator and the denominator and then canceling pair(s) of common factors in the numerator and denominator since their quotient is 1. This technique is used in simplifying arithmetic as well as algebraic fractions.

$$\textit{Examples:} \quad 1. \ \frac{x^2 + 3x}{x^2 - 9} = \frac{x\cancel{(x+3)}}{(x-3)\cancel{(x+3)}} = \frac{x}{x-3}$$

$$2. \ \frac{s-t}{2t-2s} = \frac{s-t}{2(t-s)} = \frac{-\cancel{(t-s)}}{2\cancel{(t-s)}} = -\frac{1}{2}$$

Avoiding a Zero Denominator

Since division by 0 is not defined, the variable or variables that appear in an algebraic fraction are assumed to be restricted in value so that the denominator can never be equal to 0. To identify the particular value or values of the variable that make an algebraic fraction undefined, rewrite the denominator and set it equal to 0. The root or roots of this equation represent the value or values that the variable *cannot* equal.

For example, to find the value or values of x that make the fraction

$$\frac{x^2 + 1}{x^2 - x - 12}$$

undefined, set $x^2 - x - 12$ equal to 0, and solve the resulting equation:

Factor:

Apply the Zero Product Rule:

Solve each equation:

$$x^2 - x - 12 = 0$$
$$(x+3)(x-4) = 0$$
$$x + 3 = 0 \text{ or } x - 4 = 0$$
$$x = -3 \text{ or } x = 4$$

The fraction is undefined when $x = -3$ or $x = 4$.

Exercise Set 1.2

1–9. Factor if possible.

1. $24x^3y + 30x^2y^5$

2. $20a^2c - 32a^3b^2$

3. $21 + 2w$

4. $6a^3 - 9a^2b$

5. $x^3 - x^2 + x$

6. $-ab - b$

7. $8u^5w^2 - 40u^2w^5$

8. $p^2k^4 - p^3k^2 + (pk)^2$

9. $(x+a)^2 - a(x+a)$

10–18. Factor as the product of two binomials.

10. $a^2 - 100$

11. $\dfrac{x^2}{4} - 36$

12. $0.16 - b^2$

13. $t^2 + 4t - 21$

14. $x^2 + 2xy + y^2$

15. $2q^2 - q - 15$

16. $3x^2 - 2x - 21$

17. $5s^2 + 14s - 3$

18. $4x^2 + 3x - 7$

19–27. Factor completely.

19. $2y^2 - 50$

20. $81 - b^4$

21. $45 - 4x - x^2$

22. $10y^3 + 50y^2 - 500y$

23. $-5t^2 + 5$

24. $x^4 - y^4$

25. $2p^3 + p^2 - 15p$

26. $x^2 - (x+42)$

27. $c(c-4) - 45$

28–29. Cross-multiply, and then solve for x.

28. $\dfrac{x-4}{2} = \dfrac{3x}{x+4}$

29. $\dfrac{x-2}{x} = \dfrac{x+4}{3x}$

30–35. Write in lowest terms.

30. $\dfrac{-x-y}{x+y}$

31. $\dfrac{3x+15}{x^2+5x}$

32. $\dfrac{3x+6}{x^2-4}$

33. $\dfrac{b-a}{a^2-b^2}$

34. $\dfrac{2x^2-50}{2x^2+14x+20}$

35. $\dfrac{x^2-y^2}{x^2-2xy+y^2}$

36–38. State for which value(s) of x *the fraction is undefined.*

36. $\dfrac{3}{x^2+x-2}$

37. $\dfrac{x+2}{x^2-2x}$

38. $\dfrac{x+5}{5^x-1}$

1.3 MULTIPLYING AND DIVIDING ALGEBRAIC FRACTIONS

$$\wedge$$
=== KEY IDEAS ===
$$\angle \quad \searrow$$

Arithmetic fractions are multiplied by writing the product of their numerators over the product of their denominators. To have the product appear in simplest form, it is often easier to cancel common pairs of factors in the numerator and denominator *before* multiplying:

$$\frac{4}{9} \cdot \frac{3}{10} = \frac{\overset{2}{\cancel{4}}}{\underset{3}{\cancel{9}}} \cdot \frac{\overset{1}{\cancel{3}}}{\underset{5}{\cancel{10}}} = \frac{2}{15}.$$

Algebraic fractions are multiplied in much the same way.

To divide one fraction by another, invert the second fraction and then multiply.

Multiplying Algebraic Fractions

To multiply algebraic fractions, begin by factoring the numerator and denominator of each fraction, if possible. Then cancel common factors whose quotient is 1.

Example

1. Write the product in the simplest form:

$$\frac{x^2 - 9}{10} \cdot \frac{15}{(x+3)^2}.$$

Solution: Begin by factoring the numerators and denominators:

$$\frac{x^2 - 9}{10} \cdot \frac{15}{(x+3)^2} = \frac{(x-3)(x+3)}{2 \cdot 5} \cdot \frac{5 \cdot 3}{(x+3)(x+3)}$$

Cancel common factors whose quotient is 1:

$$= \frac{(x-3)\overset{1}{\cancel{(x+3)}}}{2 \cdot \cancel{5}} \cdot \frac{\overset{1}{\cancel{5}} \cdot 3}{\cancel{(x+3)}(x+3)}$$

Multiply the remaining factors:

$$= \frac{3(x-3)}{2(x+3)}$$

12

Dividing Algebraic Fractions

To divide algebraic fractions, change the example into an equivalent multiplication problem by inverting the second fraction. Example 2 illustrates that you may need to use a variety of factoring techniques to identify common pairs of factors in the numerators and denominators of the fractions.

Example

2. Express each quotient in simplest form:

(a) $\dfrac{6x - 3x^2}{9x^3 - x} \div \dfrac{x^2 - 4}{3x^2 + 5x - 2}$ (b) $\dfrac{x^2 + 2xy + y^2}{xy - x} \div \dfrac{x^2 - y^2}{y^2 - y}$

Solutions: (a) Invert the second fraction and multiply:

$$\frac{6x - 3x^2}{9x^3 - x} \div \frac{x^2 - 4}{3x^2 + 5x - 2} = \frac{6x - 3x^2}{9x^3 - x} \cdot \frac{3x^2 + 5x - 2}{x^2 - 4}$$

Factor the numerators and denominators completely:

$$= \frac{3x(2 - x)}{x(3x + 1)(3x - 1)} \cdot \frac{(3x - 1)(x + 2)}{(x - 2)(x + 2)}$$

Cancel common factors whose quotient is 1:

$$= \frac{3\cancel{x}(2 - x)}{\cancel{x}(3x + 1)\cancel{(3x - 1)}} \cdot \frac{\cancel{(3x - 1)}\cancel{(x + 2)}}{(x - 2)\cancel{(x + 2)}}$$

Since $(2 - x) = -(x - 2)$, cancel $(2 - x)$ over $(x - 2)$ as -1:

$$= \frac{3\overset{-1}{\cancel{(2 - x)}}}{3x + 1} \cdot \frac{1}{\cancel{(x - 2)}}$$

Multiply the remaining factors:

$$= \frac{-3}{3x + 1}$$

(b) $\dfrac{x^2 + 2xy + y^2}{xy - x} \div \dfrac{x^2 - y^2}{y^2 - y} = \dfrac{\overset{1}{\cancel{(x + y)^2}}}{x\cancel{(y - 1)}} \cdot \dfrac{y\cancel{(y - 1)}}{\cancel{(x + y)}(x - y)}$

$$= \frac{y(x + y)}{x(x - y)}$$

Exercise Set 1.3

1–12. Express each product or quotient in simplest form.

1. $\dfrac{12y^2}{x^2+7x} \cdot \dfrac{x^2-49}{2y^5}$

2. $\dfrac{8m^3}{3} \div \dfrac{6m^3}{3m-12}$

3. $\dfrac{x^2-2x-8}{x^2-25} \cdot \dfrac{2x+10}{x^2-4}$

4. $\dfrac{18}{x^2-y^2} \div \dfrac{9}{y-x}$

5. $\dfrac{(x-7)^2}{x^2-6x-7} \cdot \dfrac{5x+5}{x^2-49}$

6. $\dfrac{a^2-b^2}{2ab} \div \dfrac{a-b}{a^2}$

7. $\dfrac{x^2-9}{x^2-8x} \cdot \dfrac{x-8}{x^2-6x+9}$

8. $\dfrac{x^2-3x}{x^2+3x-10} \div \dfrac{x^2-x-6}{x^2-4}$

9. $\dfrac{3p+6}{p^2-9} \div \dfrac{p^2+4p+4}{p^2+3p}$

10. $\dfrac{6a^2b}{x^2-x-72} \div \dfrac{2ab^3}{x^2-64}$

11. $\dfrac{r^2-s^2}{2rs} \cdot \dfrac{6r^2}{3s-3r}$

12. $\dfrac{x^2+2x}{x^2+2x-15} \cdot \dfrac{2x-6}{4} \div \dfrac{x^2+x-2}{x^2+4x-5}$

13. $\dfrac{t^2-1}{t^2-4} \div \dfrac{9t+9}{4t+12} \cdot \dfrac{2-t}{t^2+2t-3}$

14. $\dfrac{x^2+4xy+3y^2}{x^2-y^2} \cdot \dfrac{x^2+xy}{x-y} \div \dfrac{x^2+3xy}{(x-y)^2}$

1.4 ADDING AND SUBTRACTING ALGEBRAIC FRACTIONS

═══════════ ⋀ **KEY IDEAS** ⋁ ═══════════

Arithmetic fractions that have the same denominator are combined by writing the sum or difference of their numerators over the common denominator:

$$\frac{2}{7}+\frac{3}{7}=\frac{2+3}{y}=\frac{5}{7}\ .$$

If the fractions have *different* denominators, each fraction must first be changed into an equivalent fraction having the LCD (Lowest Common Denominator) as its denominator.

Algebraic fractions are handled in much the same way.

Combining Fractions with the Same Denominator

To combine algebraic fractions having the same denominator, write the sum or difference of the numerators over the common denominator and then simplify.

Example 1 illustrates that it is sometimes necessary to remove a factor of -1 from the denominator of a fraction before it can be combined with another fraction.

Example

1. Express as a single fraction in lowest terms: $\dfrac{4x}{x^2-4}+\dfrac{x+6}{4-x^2}$.

Solution: Rewrite $4-x^2$ as $-x^2+4$. Then factor out -1 so that

$$-x^2+4=-\left(x^2-4\right).$$

Rewrite the given expression: $\quad\dfrac{4x}{x^2-4}+\dfrac{x+6}{4-x^2}=\dfrac{4x}{x^2-4}+\dfrac{x+6}{-\left(x^2-4\right)}$

Place the negative sign in front of the second fraction: $\quad=\dfrac{4x}{x^2-4}-\dfrac{x+6}{x^2-4}$

Write the numerators over the common denominator: $\quad=\dfrac{4x-(x+6)}{x^2-4}$

Simplify the numerator: $\quad=\dfrac{4x-x-6}{x^2-4}$

Write the fraction in lowest terms: $\quad=\dfrac{3x-6}{x^2-4}$

Factor, and cancel common factors: $\quad=\dfrac{3\cancel{(x-2)}}{\cancel{(x-2)}(x+2)}$

$\quad=\dfrac{3}{x+2}$

Combining Fractions with Unlike Denominators

To combine fractions having unlike denominators, write the fractions as equivalent fractions having a common denominator by (1) factoring each of the original denominators and then comparing them to find the lowest common denominator (LCD); and (2) multiplying the denominator *and* the numerator of each fraction by the factor or factors needed to change the denominator to the LCD. The fractions can now be added by following the rules for adding fractions having like denominators.

Examples

2. Express the sum in simplest form: $\dfrac{x}{x+1}+\dfrac{x}{x-1}$.

Solution: The Lowest Common Denominator must contain the denominators $x+1$ and $x-1$ as factors. Hence

$$LCD = (x+1)(x-1).$$

Multiply each fraction by 1 in the form of the factor(s) of the LCD that its denominator lacks divided by that factor or factors.

$$\frac{x}{x+1}\left(\frac{x-1}{x-1}\right)+\frac{x}{x-1}\left(\frac{x+1}{x+1}\right)=\frac{x(x-1)+x(x+1)}{(x+1)(x-1)}$$

$$=\frac{\left(x^2-x\right)+\left(x^2+x\right)}{(x+1)(x-1)}$$

$$=\frac{2x^2}{(x+1)(x-1)}$$

3. Express the difference in simplest form: $\dfrac{x}{x^2+3x-4}-\dfrac{x-4}{x^2-1}$.

Solution: Factor each denominator:

$$x^2+3x-4 = (x-1)(x+4)$$
$$x^2-1 = (x-1)(x+1)$$
$$LCD = (x-1)(x+4)(x+1)$$

Compare each of the factored denominators to the LCD. The denominator of the first fraction lacks the factor $(x + 1)$, while the second fraction's denominator does not include $(x + 4)$ as a factor. Therefore, multiply each fraction by multiplying the numerator and the denominator of the first fraction by $(x + 1)$, and multiplying the numerator and the denominator of the second fraction by $(x + 4)$.

$$\frac{x}{x^2+3x-4}-\frac{x-4}{x^2-1}=\frac{x}{(x-1)(x+4)}-\frac{x-4}{(x-1)(x+1)}$$

Multiply by a form of 1: $=\dfrac{x}{(x-1)(x+4)}\left(\dfrac{x+1}{x+1}\right)-\dfrac{x-4}{(x-1)(x+1)}\left(\dfrac{x+4}{x+4}\right)$

Combine over the LCD: $=\dfrac{x(x+1)-(x-4)(x+4)}{(x-1)(x+4)(x+1)}$

Simplify the numerator:
$$= \frac{x^2 + x - (x^2 - 16)}{(x-1)(x+4)(x+1)}$$

$$= \frac{x+16}{(x-1)(x+4)(x+1)}$$

Exercise Set 1.4

1–16. Write each expression as a single fraction in simplest form.

1. $\dfrac{2x+y}{x+2y} + \dfrac{x+5y}{x+2y}$

2. $\dfrac{p}{p^2-9} - \dfrac{3}{p^2-9}$

3. $\dfrac{a^2-5}{a-b} + \dfrac{b^2-5}{b-a}$

4. $\dfrac{8x}{3x+12} + \dfrac{2}{2x+8}$

5. $\dfrac{5}{b-3} - \dfrac{4}{b}$

6. $\dfrac{y}{y^2-16} - \dfrac{1}{y+4}$

7. $\dfrac{7}{x^2-1} + \dfrac{1}{2x+2}$

8. $\dfrac{a^2+1}{a^2-1} - \dfrac{a}{a+1}$

9. $\dfrac{a}{a-b} + \dfrac{b}{a+b}$

10. $\dfrac{6}{y^2-9} + \dfrac{4}{(y-3)^2}$

11. $\dfrac{3}{x^2-4} + \dfrac{2}{x^2+5x+6}$

12. $\dfrac{2x}{x^2+7x} - \dfrac{6x-5}{x^2-49}$

13. $\dfrac{5}{r^2-s^2} - \dfrac{3}{(r+s)^2}$

14. $w - y - \dfrac{1}{w+y}$

15. $\dfrac{x+2}{x^2-9} + \dfrac{2}{x^2+x-6}$

16. $\dfrac{5}{a^2-3a-10} + \dfrac{3a-2}{a^2-25} - \dfrac{3a}{3a+6}$

17–18. Find each product by first simplifying the expressions within the parentheses.

17. $\left(2 + \dfrac{2}{x}\right)\left(\dfrac{1}{x+1} - 1\right)$

18. $\left(\dfrac{1}{x+1} - \dfrac{1}{x-1}\right)^2$

1.5 SIMPLIFYING COMPLEX FRACTIONS

$$\bigwedge$$ **KEY IDEAS** $$\diagup\diagdown$$

Fractions such as

$$\frac{\dfrac{4}{5}}{6},\ \frac{2}{\dfrac{9}{10}},\ \frac{\dfrac{2}{7}}{\dfrac{3}{8}},\ \text{and}\ \frac{\dfrac{x}{2}+\dfrac{1}{x}}{\dfrac{1}{2x}}$$

are examples of *complex fractions*. A **complex fraction** is a fraction that has other fractions in its numerator, in its denominator, or in both its numerator and its denominator. Simplifying a complex fraction means writing it as a "simple" fraction that does not have another fraction in either its numerator or its denominator.

Simplifying a Complex Fraction by Dividing

A complex fraction can be simplified by dividing its numerator by its denominator:

$$\frac{\dfrac{2}{7}}{\dfrac{3}{5}}=\frac{2}{7}\div\frac{3}{5}=\frac{2}{7}\cdot\frac{5}{3}=\frac{10}{21}.$$

Example

1. Express in simplest form:

(a) $\dfrac{\dfrac{x}{2}+\dfrac{1}{x}}{\dfrac{1}{2x}}$ **(b)** $\dfrac{1-x^{-1}}{1-x^{-2}}$

Solutions: **(a)** Rewrite the complex fraction as a division example:

$$\frac{\dfrac{x}{2}+\dfrac{1}{x}}{\dfrac{1}{2x}}=\left[\frac{x}{2}+\frac{1}{x}\right]\div\frac{1}{2x}$$

Invert the last fraction and multiply: $= \left[\dfrac{x}{2} + \dfrac{1}{x} \right] \dfrac{2x}{1}$

Use the distributive law: $= \left(\dfrac{x}{2} \right) \cdot 2x + \left(\dfrac{1}{x} \right) \cdot 2x$

Simplify: $= x^2 + 2$

(b) Rewrite with positive exponents: $\dfrac{1 - x^{-1}}{1 - x^{-2}} = \dfrac{1 - \dfrac{1}{x}}{1 - \dfrac{1}{x^2}}$

Combine terms in the numerator and in the denominator:

$$= \dfrac{\dfrac{x}{x} - \dfrac{1}{x}}{\dfrac{x^2}{x^2} - \dfrac{1}{x^2}} = \dfrac{\dfrac{x-1}{x}}{\dfrac{x^2-1}{x^2}}$$

Divide: $= \left(\dfrac{x-1}{x} \right) \div \left(\dfrac{x^2-1}{x^2} \right)$

Invert the last fraction and multiply: $= \left(\dfrac{x-1}{x} \right) \cdot \left(\dfrac{x^2}{x^2-1} \right)$

Simplify: $= \dfrac{\overset{1}{\cancel{(x-1)}}}{\cancel{x}} \cdot \dfrac{\overset{x^1}{\cancel{x^2}}}{\cancel{(x-1)}(x+1)}$

Multiply the remaining factors: $= \dfrac{x}{x+1}$

Simplifying a Complex Fraction by Clearing Fractions

A complex fraction may also be simplified by (1) determining the LCD of the denominators, and (2) multiplying the complex fraction by 1 in the form of the LCD divided by itself:

Multiplying by 1

$$\dfrac{\dfrac{2}{7}}{\dfrac{3}{5}} \cdot \left[\dfrac{35}{35} \right] = \dfrac{35 \left(\dfrac{2}{7} \right)}{35 \left(\dfrac{3}{5} \right)} = \dfrac{10}{21}$$

35 is the LCD of 7 and 5.

19

Example

2. Express in simplest form: $\dfrac{1-\dfrac{1}{x}}{1-\dfrac{1}{x^2}}$.

Solution: The LCD of $\frac{1}{x}$ and $\frac{1}{x^2}$ is x^2. Therefore, multiply the numerator *and* the denominator of the complex fraction by 1 in the form of x^2 divided by itself:

$$\left[\frac{x^2}{x^2}\right] \cdot \frac{1-\dfrac{1}{x}}{1-\dfrac{1}{x^2}} = \frac{x^2\left(1-\dfrac{1}{x}\right)}{x^2\left(1-\dfrac{1}{x^2}\right)}$$

Use the distributive property:
$$= \frac{x^2 - \dfrac{x^2}{x}}{x^2 - \dfrac{x^2}{x^2}}$$

Simplify:
$$= \frac{x^2 - x}{x^2 - 1}$$

Factor and simplify:
$$= \frac{x(x-1)}{(x+1)(x-1)}$$

$$= \frac{x}{x+1}$$

Exercise Set 1.5

1–11. Write each complex fraction in simplest form.

1. $\dfrac{\dfrac{x}{x+1}}{1-\dfrac{x}{x+1}}$

2. $\dfrac{a-1}{\dfrac{1}{a}-1}$

3. $\dfrac{3-\dfrac{3}{x}}{x-1}$

4. $\dfrac{n-\dfrac{1}{n}}{\dfrac{1-n^2}{n}}$

5. $\dfrac{4-x^{-2}}{2-x^{-1}}$

6. $\dfrac{x^{-1}}{x^{-1}+y^{-1}}$

7. $\dfrac{\dfrac{y}{x}-\dfrac{x}{y}}{\dfrac{1}{x}+\dfrac{1}{y}}$

8. $\dfrac{1+\dfrac{b}{a-b}}{1-\dfrac{a}{a-b}}$

9. $\dfrac{\dfrac{a}{b}+1}{\dfrac{a}{b}-\dfrac{b}{a}}$

10. $\dfrac{m - \dfrac{1}{m}}{m - 2 + \dfrac{1}{m}}$ **11.** $\dfrac{a+b^{-1}}{b+a^{-1}}$

12. Express in simplest form the value of $\dfrac{r+s}{1-rs}$ when $r=\dfrac{1}{3}$ and $s=\dfrac{1}{7}$.

1.6   WORKING WITH RADICALS

Square root radicals may be multiplied and divided:

$$2\sqrt{3} \cdot 4\sqrt{7} = 2 \cdot 4\sqrt{3 \cdot 7} = \mathbf{8\sqrt{21}} \ .$$

Square root radicals with the same radicand may be combined by adding their numerical coefficients:

$$2\sqrt{5} + 6\sqrt{5} = \mathbf{8\sqrt{5}} \ .$$

A square root radical is not considered to be in simplest form until a perfect square factor greater than 1 or a fraction, if any, is removed from its radicand. A fraction that has a radical in its denominator is not considered to be in simplest form until the denominator is made rational.

Using Factoring to Simplify Radicals

If the radicand of a square root radical can be factored so that one of its factors is a perfect square other than 1, then the radical can be simplified by using the fact that

$$\sqrt{ab} = \sqrt{a} \cdot \sqrt{b} \qquad (a,b \geq 0).$$

For example, to simplify $\sqrt{75}$, write the radicand as the product of two numbers such that one of the numbers is the greatest perfect square factor of 75:

$$\sqrt{75} = \sqrt{25 \cdot 3} = \sqrt{25} \cdot \sqrt{3} = 5\sqrt{3} \ .$$

Example

1. Write each radical in simplest form:

(a) $\sqrt{72}$ (b) $\sqrt{x^5}$ (c) $\sqrt{18r^4s^3}$

Solutions: (a) $\sqrt{72} = \sqrt{36}\sqrt{2} = \mathbf{6\sqrt{2}}$

(b) $\sqrt{x^5} = \sqrt{x^4}\sqrt{x} = \mathbf{x^2\sqrt{x}}$

(c) $\sqrt{18r^4s^3} = \sqrt{9r^4s^2}\sqrt{2s} = \mathbf{3r^2s\sqrt{2s}}$

Multiplying and Dividing Radicals

Since $\sqrt{ab} = \sqrt{a}\sqrt{b}$, it must also be true that

$$\sqrt{a}\sqrt{b} = \sqrt{ab} \qquad (a, b \geq 0).$$

Thus, to multiply two radicals having the *same index*, write the product of their radicands underneath the same radical sign and then simplify, if possible. Also, note that the product of two identical square root radicals is the radicand:

$$\sqrt{a}\sqrt{a} = \sqrt{a^2} = a .$$

Examples: *1.* $\sqrt{8} \cdot \sqrt{6} = \sqrt{48}$

$$= \sqrt{16} \cdot \sqrt{3} = \mathbf{4\sqrt{3}}$$

2. $\left(2\sqrt{3}\right)^2 = \left(2\sqrt{3}\right)\left(2\sqrt{3}\right)$

$$= (2 \cdot 2)\left(\sqrt{3} \cdot \sqrt{3}\right)$$

$$= 4 \cdot 3 = \mathbf{12}$$

Radicals are divided in a similar way since it is true that

$$\frac{\sqrt{a}}{\sqrt{b}} = \sqrt{\frac{a}{b}} \qquad \text{where } a \geq 0, b > 0$$

Examples: *1.* $\dfrac{\sqrt{40}}{\sqrt{8}} = \sqrt{\dfrac{40}{8}} = \mathbf{\sqrt{5}}$

2. $\sqrt{\dfrac{3}{4}} = \dfrac{\sqrt{3}}{\sqrt{4}} = \dfrac{\mathbf{\sqrt{3}}}{\mathbf{2}}$

Combining Radicals

Some radicals must be simplified before they can be combined.

Examples: *1.* $5\sqrt{2} + \sqrt{18} = 5\sqrt{2} + \sqrt{9}\sqrt{2}$

$$= 5\sqrt{2} + 3\sqrt{2}$$

$$= (5+3)\sqrt{2} = \mathbf{8\sqrt{2}}$$

2. $2\sqrt{80} - 3\sqrt{20} = 2\sqrt{16}\sqrt{5} - 3\sqrt{4}\sqrt{5}$
$$= 2 \cdot 4\sqrt{5} - 3 \cdot 2\sqrt{5}$$
$$= 8\sqrt{5} - 6\sqrt{5}$$
$$= (8-6)\sqrt{5} = 2\sqrt{5}$$

Multiplying Radicals Using FOIL

To find the product of two radical expressions that take the form of a binomial, use FOIL:

Examples:

1. $\left(4 - 2\sqrt{3}\right)^2 = \left(4 - 2\sqrt{3}\right)\left(4 - 2\sqrt{3}\right)$

$$= \overset{F}{4 \cdot 4} + \overset{O}{(4)\left(-2\sqrt{3}\right)} + \overset{I}{\left(-2\sqrt{3}\right)(4)} + \overset{L}{\left(-2\sqrt{3}\right)\left(-2\sqrt{3}\right)}$$

$$= 16 - 8\sqrt{3} \qquad -8\sqrt{3} \qquad +(-2)^2\left(\sqrt{3}\right)^2$$

$$= 16 - 16\sqrt{3} \qquad\qquad\qquad + 4 \cdot 3$$

$$= \mathbf{28 - 16\sqrt{3}}$$

2. $\left(7 + 2\sqrt{3}\right)\left(7 - 2\sqrt{3}\right) = \overset{F}{7 \cdot 7} + \overset{O}{(7)\left(-2\sqrt{3}\right)} + \overset{I}{(7)\left(2\sqrt{3}\right)} - \overset{L}{\left(2\sqrt{3}\right)^2}$

$$= 49 - 14\sqrt{3} \qquad +14\sqrt{3} \qquad -\left(2\sqrt{3}\right)\left(2\sqrt{3}\right)$$

$$= 49 + 0 \qquad\qquad\qquad - 4 \cdot 3$$

$$= \mathbf{37}$$

In Example 2, *conjugate* radical expressions are being multiplied, so their product does not contain a radical. **Conjugate radical expressions** are two radical expressions that take the sum and the difference of the *same* two terms. If A, B, and C are rational and C is greater than 0, then $\left(A + B\sqrt{C}\right)$ and $\left(A - B\sqrt{C}\right)$ are conjugate radical expressions whose product is $A^2 - B^2C$. Thus, the product of two conjugate radical expressions is always rational.

═══════════════ **MATH FACTS** ═══════════════

PRODUCT OF CONJUGATE RADICAL EXPRESSIONS

$$\left(A + B\sqrt{C}\right)\left(A - B\sqrt{C}\right) = A^2 - B^2C$$

Example

2. Multiply: $\left(5 + 3\sqrt{2}\right)\left(5 - 3\sqrt{2}\right)$.

Solution: The factors have the form $A + B\sqrt{C}$ and $A - B\sqrt{C}$, where $A = 5$, $B = 3$, and $C = 2$. Since the product of $A + B\sqrt{C}$ and $A - B\sqrt{C}$ is $A^2 - B^2 C$,

$$\left(5 + 3\sqrt{2}\right)\left(5 - 3\sqrt{2}\right) = 5^2 - (3)^2 (2)$$
$$= 25 - 9 \cdot 2$$
$$= 7$$

Note: If you forget that $\left(A + B\sqrt{C}\right)\left(A - B\sqrt{C}\right) = A^2 - B^2 C$, then multiply using the FOIL method.

Rationalizing Denominators

A fraction whose denominator is a monomial or binomial radical expression can be changed into an equivalent fraction that does not have radicals in its denominator. To do this, multiply the original fraction by 1 in the form of an appropriate *rationalizing factor* divided by itself. The rationalizing factor is determined as follows:

- If the denominator is a monomial radical expression, then the rationalizing factor is the radical term. For example, to express the fraction $\frac{5}{\sqrt{3}}$ as an equivalent fraction with a rational denominator, multiply the numerator and the denominator of the fraction by the rationalizing factor of $\sqrt{3}$:

$$\frac{5}{\sqrt{3}} = \frac{5}{\sqrt{3}} \cdot \left(\frac{\sqrt{3}}{\sqrt{3}}\right) = \frac{5\sqrt{3}}{\left(\sqrt{3}\right)^2} = \frac{5\sqrt{3}}{3}.$$

- If the denominator is a binomial radical expression, then the rationalizing factor is its conjugate. For example, to change the fraction $\frac{3}{7 - 3\sqrt{5}}$ into an equivalent fraction with a rational denominator, multiply the numerator and the denominator of the fraction by the conjugate of $7 - 3\sqrt{5}$, which is $7 + 3\sqrt{5}$:

$$\frac{3}{7 - 3\sqrt{5}} = \frac{3}{7 - 3\sqrt{5}} \cdot \left(\frac{7 + 3\sqrt{5}}{7 + 3\sqrt{5}}\right)$$
$$= \frac{3\left(7 + 3\sqrt{5}\right)}{7^2 - 3^2 5}$$
$$= \frac{3\left(7 + 3\sqrt{5}\right)}{49 - 45}$$
$$= \frac{3\left(7 + 3\sqrt{5}\right)}{4} \text{ or } \frac{21 + 9\sqrt{5}}{4}$$

Examples

3. Combine, and express the result in simplest form: $\dfrac{24}{\sqrt{8}}+\sqrt{32}$

Solution: Rationalize the denominator of the fraction:

$$\frac{24}{\sqrt{8}}+\sqrt{32}=\frac{24}{\sqrt{8}}\cdot\left(\frac{\sqrt{8}}{\sqrt{8}}\right)+\sqrt{32}$$

$$=\frac{24\sqrt{8}}{\left(\sqrt{8}\right)^2}\quad+\sqrt{32}$$

Simplify:

$$=\frac{\overset{3}{\cancel{24}}\sqrt{4}\sqrt{2}}{\cancel{8}}+\sqrt{16}\sqrt{2}$$

$$=3\cdot2\sqrt{2}\quad+4\sqrt{2}$$

$$=\mathbf{10\sqrt{2}}$$

4. Express as an equivalent fraction with a rational denominator: $\dfrac{\sqrt{6}}{\sqrt{6}-2}$.

Solution: The rationalizing factor is the conjugate of $\sqrt{6}-2$, which is $\sqrt{6}+2$. Multiply the numerator and the denominator by $\sqrt{6}+2$:

$$\frac{\sqrt{6}}{\sqrt{6}-2}\cdot\left(\frac{\sqrt{6}+2}{\sqrt{6}+2}\right)=\frac{\sqrt{6}\left(\sqrt{6}+2\right)}{\left(\sqrt{6}\right)^2-2^2}$$

$$=\frac{6+2\sqrt{6}}{6-4}=\frac{\overset{1}{\cancel{2}}\left(3+\sqrt{6}\right)}{\cancel{2}}=\mathbf{3+\sqrt{6}}$$

Exercise Set 1.6

1–6. Write each radical in simplest form.

1. $\sqrt{98}$ **3.** $\sqrt{y^8}$ **5.** $\sqrt{28r^5s}$

2. $2\sqrt{84}$ **4.** $\sqrt{x^4y^3}$ **6.** $\sqrt[3]{w^6y^3}$

7–12. Express each product in simplest form.

7. $\sqrt{12}\cdot\sqrt{10}$ **9.** $\left(2\sqrt{3}\right)^2$ **11.** $\sqrt{t^7}\cdot\sqrt{t^3}$

8. $3\sqrt{8}\cdot2\sqrt{50}$ **10.** $\sqrt{x^5}\cdot\sqrt{x}$ **12.** $\sqrt{r^3}\cdot\sqrt{rs^2}$

13–18. Express each sum or difference in simplest form.

13. $2\sqrt{3} + \sqrt{27}$ **16.** $\sqrt{49x} + \sqrt{x}$

14. $\sqrt{56} - \sqrt{28}$ **17.** $\sqrt{108y} - \sqrt{12y}$

15. $\sqrt{48} - 2\sqrt{75}$ **18.** $2\sqrt{20} - 3\sqrt{5} + \sqrt{45}$

19–24. Express each product in simplest form.

19. $\sqrt{3}\left(\sqrt{12} - 2\sqrt{3}\right)$ **22.** $\left(3 + 2\sqrt{3}\right)\left(3 - \sqrt{12}\right)$

20. $\left(8 - \sqrt{5}\right)\left(8 + \sqrt{5}\right)$ **23.** $\left(1 - 2\sqrt{3}\right)^2$

21. $\left(\sqrt{3} - \sqrt{7}\right)\left(\sqrt{3} + \sqrt{7}\right)$ **24.** $\left(\sqrt{2} - \sqrt{3}\right)^2$

25–27. Combine, and express each result in simplest form.

25. $\dfrac{6}{\sqrt{12}} + \sqrt{27}$ **26.** $\dfrac{15}{\sqrt{20}} - \sqrt{45}$ **27.** $\dfrac{40}{\sqrt{8}} - \sqrt{50}$

28–33. Express each fraction as an equivalent fraction with a rational denominator.

28. $\dfrac{2}{\sqrt{3} - 1}$ **30.** $\dfrac{\sqrt{2}}{1 - 3\sqrt{2}}$ **32.** $\dfrac{1 - \sqrt{3}}{1 + \sqrt{3}}$

29. $\dfrac{24}{1 + \sqrt{7}}$ **31.** $\dfrac{1}{\sqrt{2} + \sqrt{3}}$ **33.** $\dfrac{\sqrt{5} + \sqrt{2}}{\sqrt{5} - \sqrt{2}}$

REGENTS TUNE UP: CHAPTER 1

Each of the questions in this section has appeared on a previous Course III Regents Examination. Here is an opportunity for you to review Chapter 1 and, at the same time, prepare for the Course III Regents Examination.

1. Evaluate: $a^0 + a^{-\frac{1}{2}}$, when $a = 9$.

2. Express as an equivalent fraction with a rational denominator: $\dfrac{2}{5 - 2\sqrt{3}}$.

3. Express in simplest form: $\dfrac{1 + \dfrac{1}{a}}{a - \dfrac{1}{a}}$.

4. Express the product $(y+1)\left(\dfrac{y}{1 - y^2}\right)$ as a fraction in lowest terms.

5. Perform the indicated operations and reduce to *lowest* terms:

$$\frac{x^2 + 2x}{x - 1} \div \frac{x^2 - x - 6}{x^2 + 2x - 3} .$$

6. Perform the indicated operations and reduce completely:

$$\frac{x^2 + 4x + 3}{x^2 + x} \cdot \frac{12 - 3x}{2x} \div \frac{x^2 - x - 12}{4x^3} .$$

7. Combine and reduce to lowest terms:

$$\frac{4x}{2x + 6} + \frac{x}{x + 3} .$$

8. The expression $\dfrac{3 + \sqrt{5}}{3 - \sqrt{5}}$ is equivalent to:

(1) $\dfrac{7}{2}$ **(2)** $\dfrac{7 + 3\sqrt{5}}{7}$ **(3)** $\dfrac{10\sqrt{5}}{7}$ **(4)** $\dfrac{7 + 3\sqrt{5}}{2}$

9. Express in simplest form:

$$\frac{9}{\sqrt{27}} + \sqrt{12} .$$

27

10. Express as a fraction in simplest form: $\dfrac{\dfrac{1}{n} - \dfrac{1}{3n^2}}{1 - \dfrac{1}{9n^2}}$.

11. Express $\dfrac{5}{4 - \sqrt{13}}$ as an equivalent fraction with a rational denominator.

12. Which fraction is defined for all real numbers?

(1) $\dfrac{x^2 - 1}{(x-1)^2}$ (2) $\dfrac{x^2 - 1}{x+1}$ (3) $\dfrac{x^2 - 1}{x^2}$ (4) $\dfrac{x^2 - 1}{x^2 + 1}$

ANSWERS TO SELECTED EXERCISES: CHAPTER 1

Section 1.1

1. $\dfrac{3}{y^2}$

3. $\dfrac{y^2}{3}$

5. $\dfrac{1}{x^4 y^6}$

7. (a) $1000m$

   (b) m^3

   (c) $\dfrac{m}{1000}$

   (d) $\sqrt{m}$

9. $\dfrac{q^6}{p^9}$

11. $\dfrac{2}{3} a^8 b$

13. $\dfrac{13}{8}$

15. 8

17. 16

19. $\dfrac{9}{16}$

21. $\dfrac{1}{512}$

23. $\dfrac{64}{125}$

25. $\dfrac{17}{16}$

27. y^5

29. $3x^4$

31. $-2x^2 y^{\frac{2}{3}}$

Section 1.2

1. $6x^2 y(4x + 5y^4)$

3. Not factorable

5. $x(x^2 - x + 1)$

7. $8u^2 w^2(u^3 - 5w^3)$

9. $x(x + a)$

11. $\left(\dfrac{x}{2} - 6\right)\left(\dfrac{x}{2} + 6\right)$

13. $(t + 7)(t - 3)$

15. $(2q + 5)(q - 3)$

17. $(5s - 1)(s + 3)$

19. $2(y - 5)(y + 5)$

21. $-(x + 9)(x - 5)$

23. $-5(t - 1)(t + 1)$

25. $p(2p - 5)(p + 3)$

27. $(c - 9)(c + 5)$

29. $x = 5$

31. $\dfrac{3}{x}$

33. $\dfrac{-1}{a + b}$

35. $\dfrac{x + y}{x - y}$ **37.** 0 and 2

Section 1.3

1. $\dfrac{6(x-7)}{xy^3}$

3. $\dfrac{2(x-4)}{(x-5)(x-2)}$

5. $\dfrac{5}{x+7}$

7. $\dfrac{x+3}{x(x-3)}$

9. $\dfrac{3p}{(p-3)(p+2)}$

11. $\dfrac{-r(r+s)}{s}$

13. $\dfrac{-4}{9(t+2)}$

Section 1.4

1. 3

3. $a+b$

5. $\dfrac{b+12}{b(b-3)}$

7. $\dfrac{x+13}{2(x-1)(x+1)}$

9. $\dfrac{a^2+2ab-b^2}{(a-b)(a+b)}$

11. $\dfrac{5(x+1)}{(x+3)(x-2)(x+2)}$

13. $\dfrac{2(r+4s)}{(r-s)(r+s)^2}$

15. $\dfrac{x^2-2x-6}{(x-3)(x+3)(x-2)}$

17. -2

Section 1.5

1. x

3. $\dfrac{3}{x}$

5. $\dfrac{2x+1}{x}$

7. $y-x$

9. $\dfrac{a}{a-b}$

11. $\dfrac{a}{b}$

Section 1.6

1. $7\sqrt{2}$

3. y^4

5. $2r^2\sqrt{7s}$

7. $2\sqrt{30}$

9. 12

11. t^5

13. $5\sqrt{3}$

15. $-6\sqrt{3}$

17. $4\sqrt{3y}$

19. 0

21. -4

23. $13-4\sqrt{3}$

25. $4\sqrt{3}$

27. $5\sqrt{2}$

29. $-4\left(1-\sqrt{7}\right)$

31. $\sqrt{3}-\sqrt{2}$

33. $\dfrac{7+2\sqrt{10}}{3}$

35. $-\dfrac{4+\sqrt{6}}{10}$

Regents Tune-Up: Chapter 1

1. $\frac{4}{3}$

2. $\dfrac{2\left(5+2\sqrt{3}\right)}{13}$

3. $\dfrac{1}{a-1}$

4. $\dfrac{y}{y-1}$

5. $\dfrac{x(x+3)}{x-3}$

6. $-6x$

7. $\dfrac{3x}{x+3}$

8. (4)

9. $3\sqrt{3}$

10. $\dfrac{3}{3n+1}$

11. $\dfrac{5\left(4+\sqrt{13}\right)}{3}$

12. $(4)\,15$

CHAPTER 2

REVIEW AND EXTENSION OF EQUATION SOLVING

2.1 SOLVING ABSOLUTE-VALUE EQUATIONS AND INEQUALITIES

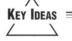

KEY IDEAS

The **absolute value** of a real number x, written as $|x|$, represents the *distance* of that number from 0 on a number line. Since distance cannot be negative,

$$|x| = x \text{ when } x \geq 0 \quad \text{and} \quad |x| = -x \text{ when } x < 0.$$

Equations and inequalities that involve absolute value are solved by writing equivalent statements using the following rules:

- If $|x| = d$, then $x = -d$ or $x = d$.

    Graph:

- If $|x| < d$, then $-d < x < d$.

    Graph:

- If $|x| > d$, then $x < -d$ or $x > d$.

    Graph:

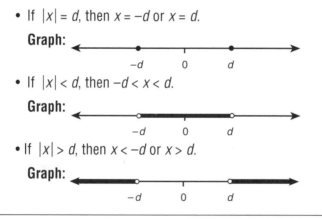

Solving Absolute-Value Equations

To solve a first-degree absolute-value equation of the form $|ax - b| = d$, write and then solve each equation in the disjunction

$$ax - b = -d \quad \text{or} \quad ax - b = d.$$

Examples

1. Find the solution set: $|2x + 3| = 1$.

Solution: If $|2x+3|=1$, then

$$
\begin{array}{r|r}
2x+3=-1 \quad \text{or} & 2x+3=1 \\
2x=-4 & 2x=-2 \\
\dfrac{2x}{2}=\dfrac{-4}{2} & \dfrac{2x}{2}=\dfrac{-2}{2} \\
x=-2 \quad \text{or} & x=-1
\end{array}
$$

The solution set is $\{-2, -1\}$. The check is left for you.

2. Solve and check: $|x+3|=2x$.

Solution: If $|x+3|=2x$, then

$$
\begin{array}{r|r}
x+3=-2x \quad \text{or} & x+3=2x \\
3x+3=0 & 3=x \\
3x=-3 & x=3 \\
x=-1 &
\end{array}
$$

$$
\begin{array}{c|c}
\textit{To check } x=-1: & \textit{To check } x=3: \\[4pt]
|x+3|=2x & |x+3|=2x \\
|-1+3| \;?\; 2(-1) & |3+3| \;?\; 2\cdot 3 \\
|2| \;?\; -2 & |6| \;?\; 6 \\
2 \neq -2 & 6=6
\end{array}
$$

Hence the only root of $|x+3|=2x$ is **$x=3$**.

Solving Absolute-Value Inequalities (Less Than)

To solve a first-degree absolute-value inequality of the form $|ax-b|<d$, write the compound inequality

$$-d < ax-b < d$$

and then solve for x. If $|ax-b| \le d$, remove the absolute-value sign by writing

$$-d \le ax-b \le d.$$

Example

3. Solve for x and graph the solution set:

(a) $|2x-1| \le 7$ **(b)** $|2x-1| < 7$

Solutions: **(a)** If $|2x-1| \le 7$, then

$$-7 \le 2x-1 \le 7$$

Add 1 to each member: $\quad +1-7 \le 2x-1+1 \le 7+1$

Simplify: $\qquad\qquad\quad -6 \le 2x \qquad\quad \le 8$

Divide each member by 2: $\quad \dfrac{-6}{2} \le \dfrac{2x}{2} \qquad \le \dfrac{8}{2}$

$$-3 \le x \qquad\qquad \le 4$$

31

The solution interval is $-3 \leq x \leq 4$. The graph is shown below.

As a check you should pick any convenient point in this interval, for example, 0, and verify that it satisfies the original absolute-value inequality.

(b) If $|2x - 1| < 7$, then $-7 \leq 2x - 1 < 7$. Using the result obtained in part (a), you find that the solution interval is $-3 < x < 4$. The graph is shown below.

Solving Absolute-Value Inequalities (Greater Than)

To solve a first-degree absolute-value inequality of the form $|ax - b| > d$, write and then solve the equations in the disjunction

$$ax - b < -d \quad \text{or} \quad ax - b > d.$$

If $|ax - b| \geq d$, then remove the absolute value sign by writing the disjunction

$$ax - b \leq -d \quad \text{or} \quad ax - b \geq d.$$

Example

4. Solve for x and graph the solution set:
(a) $|3x + 1| \geq 7$ (b) $|3x + 1| > 7$

Solutions: **(a)** If $|3x + 1| \geq 7$, then

$$3x + 1 \leq -7 \quad \text{or} \quad 3x + 1 \geq 7.$$

Solve each inequality:

$3x \leq -8$	$3x \geq 6$
$\dfrac{3x}{3} \leq -\dfrac{8}{3}$	$\dfrac{3x}{3} \geq \dfrac{6}{3}$
$x \leq -\dfrac{8}{3}$	$x \geq 2$

The solution intervals are $x \leq -\frac{8}{3}$ and $x \geq 2$. The graph shown below.

(b) If $|3x + 1| > 7$, then $3x + 1 < -7$ or $3x + 1 > 7$. Using the result obtained in part (a), you find that the solution intervals are $x < -\frac{8}{3}$ and $x > 2$. The graph is shown below.

Exercise Set 2.1

1–15. Find and then graph the solution set.

1. $|x| = 5$

2. $|x| + 4 = 0$

3. $|x - 3| \le 2$

4. $4 > |x + 1|$

5. $\dfrac{|x + 1|}{2} > 3$

6. $|2 - y| \le 1$

7. $|2x - 5| \le 7$

8. $|3 - x| > 1$

9. $|4x + 1| \ge 9$

10. $\dfrac{|2x - 1|}{3} > 5$

11. $3 + |x + 5| \le 6$

12. $-2|4x - 1| > 10$

13. $|3 - 2x| < 7$

14. $11 < |4 - 3x|$

15. $\dfrac{|2 - n|}{5} - 1 \le 0$

16–17. Solve for y and check.

16. $|1 - y| = y + 2$

17. $|y + 3| \le 2y$

2.2 SOLVING QUADRATIC INEQUALITIES ALGEBRAICALLY

KEY IDEAS

Inequalities such as

$$x^2 - 2x - 3 < 0 \quad \text{and} \quad x^2 - 2x - 3 > 0$$

are **quadratic inequalities** that are in standard form since the nonzero terms appear on the left side of the inequality symbol. To solve either inequality, factor the quadratic polynomial.

The set of all values of x that make the two factors have different signs, so that their product is negative, is the solution to $x^2 - 2x - 3 < 0$. The set of all values of x that make the two binomial factors have the same sign, so that their product is positive, is the solution to $x^2 - 2x - 3 > 0$.

If the inequality is "$\ge$" or "$\le$," the solution set also includes the values of x for which the quadratic polynomial is 0.

Solving Quadratic Inequalities by Factoring

To solve a quadratic inequality such as $x^2 - 2x < 3$, follow these steps:

Step 1: Write the quadratic inequality in standard form and factor:

$$x^2 - 2x - 3 < 0$$
$$(x + 1)(x - 3) < 0$$

Step 2: Find the roots of the related quadratic equation. If $(x+1)(x-3)=0$, then

$$x = -1 \quad \text{or} \quad x = 3.$$

Step 3: Locate the roots on a number line. The two roots divide the number line (Figure 2.1) into three possible solution intervals:
(I) $x < -1$,
(II) $-1 < x < 3$,
and (III) $x > 3$.

Figure 2.1 Locating Roots on a Number Line

Step 4: Determine the sign of the product of the two factors on each interval.

Interval	Select a Test Value	Value of Factors		$(x+1)(x-3)<0$?
		$(x+1)$	$(x-3)$	
$x<-1$	$x=-2$	(-1)	(-5)	No, since $(-1)(-5)>0$.
$-1<x<3$	$x=0$	(1)	(-3)	Yes, since $(1)(-3)<0$.
$x>3$	$x=4$	(5)	(1)	No, since $(5)(1)>0$.

Step 5: Write and graph the solution set. The solution set is $\{x: -1 < x < 3\}$. The graph is shown below.

General Form of the Solution Intervals

If r_1 and r_2 $(r_1 < r_2)$ represent the roots of $ax^2 + bx + c = 0\,(a>0)$, then the solution intervals to the related set of quadratic inequalities are given in Table 2.1. Knowing these general forms can greatly simplify matters. For example, the solution interval to the quadratic inequality $x^2 + x - 6 < 0$ has the form $r_1 < x < r_2$, where r_1 and r_2 are the roots of the related quadratic equation $x^2 + x - 6 = 0$. You can verify that the roots of this equation are $x = -3$ and $x = 2$. Since -3 is less than 2, let $r_1 = -3$ and $r_2 = 2$. The solution interval is, therefore, $-3 < x < 2$. If the original quadratic inequality was $x^2 + x - 6 \geq 0$, the solution intervals would be $x \leq -3$ or $x \geq 2$.

TABLE 2.1 GENERAL SOLUTIONS TO QUADRATIC INEQUALITIES ($a > 0$)

Inequality	Solution Interval(s)	Graph
$ax^2 + bx + c < 0$	$r_1 < x < r_2$	
$ax^2 + bx + c \leq 0$	$r_1 \leq x \leq r_2$	
$ax^2 + bx + c > 0$	$x < r_1$ or $x > r_2$	
$ax^2 + bx + c \geq 0$	$x \leq r_1$ or $x \geq r_2$	

Examples

1. Solve, and graph the solution set: $8 - 2x \leq x^2$.

Solution: $8 - 2x \leq x^2$
Collect terms on the same side: $0 \leq x^2 + 2x - 8$
Write in standard form: $x^2 + 2x - 8 \geq 0$
Write the related equation: $x^2 + 2x - 8 = 0$
Solve by factoring: $(x + 4)(x - 2) = 0$
                    $x = -4$ or $x = 2$

Let $r_1 = -4$ and $r_2 = 2$. The general form of the solution to $x^2 + 2x - 8 \geq 0$ is $x \leq r_1$ or $x \geq r_2$. Hence the solution set is $\{x: x \leq -4$ or $x \geq 2\}$. The graph is shown below.

-4 2

2. Solve, and graph the solution set: $4x \geq x^2$.

Solution: If $4x > x^2$, then $0 > x^2 - 4x$ or, equivalently, $x^2 - 4x < 0$. Find r_1 and r_2, the roots of the related quadratic equation.

$$x^2 - 4x = 0$$
$$x(x - 4) = 0$$
$$x = 0 \quad \text{or} \quad x - 4 = 0$$
$$x = 0 \quad | \quad x = 4$$

The solution interval for $x^2 - 4x < 0$ has the form $r_1 < x < r_2$. Since $r_1 = 0$ and $r_2 = 4$, the solution set is $\{x: 0 < x < 4\}$. The graph is shown below.

0 4

Exercise Set 2.2

1–15. Solve, and graph the solution set.

1. $x^2 + 4x - 5 \geq 0$
2. $n^2 - 6n \leq 27$
3. $x^2 - 5x \geq 0$
4. $y^2 + 9y \leq 36$
5. $b^2 - 25 \leq 0$

6. $x^2 + 4 \leq 4x$
7. $7x \geq x^2$
8. $2x^2 > 5x + 3$
9. $6 \leq t^2 - t$
10. $x^2 - 4x + 4 \geq 0$

11. $4m \leq m^2$
12. $6h^2 < 7h + 3$
13. $0 \leq -(x^2 + 2x - 63)$
14. $(x - 2)(x + 1) \geq 10$
15. $x^2 - 6x + 9 < 0$

2.3 SOLVING FRACTIONAL EQUATIONS

⌃ KEY IDEAS

An equation such as

$$\frac{2}{y} - \frac{9}{10} = \frac{1}{5y}$$

is called a **fractional equation** since at least one of the fractions in the equation contains a variable in the denominator. A fractional equation can be cleared of its fractions by multiplying each term of the equation, right and left sides, by the lowest common denominator (LCD) of its fractions.

The solution of the new equation may include *extra* roots that are *not* roots of the fractional equation. These extra roots are called **extraneous roots**. Extraneous roots may be introduced whenever the original equation is multiplied by a variable expression.

To solve the fractional equation

$$\frac{2}{y} - \frac{9}{10} = \frac{1}{5y}$$

multiply each term by the LCD, $10y$, and then solve the resulting equation.

$$10y\left(\frac{2}{y}\right) - 10y\left(\frac{9}{10}\right) = 10y\left(\frac{1}{5y}\right)$$

$$10\overset{1}{\cancel{y}}\left(\frac{2}{\cancel{y}}\right) - \overset{1}{\cancel{10}}y\left(\frac{9}{\cancel{10}}\right) = \overset{2}{\cancel{10}}\cancel{y}\left(\frac{1}{\cancel{5y}}\right)$$

$$20 - 9y = 2$$
$$-9y = 2 - 20$$
$$y = \frac{-18}{-9}$$
$$y = 2$$

It is left to you to check that $y = 2$ is a root.

Example

Solve for x and check:

$$\frac{x}{x+2} - \frac{1}{x-2} = \frac{8}{x^2-4}.$$

Solution: Rewrite the equation with its denominator(s) factored:

$$\frac{x}{x+2} - \frac{1}{x-2} = \frac{8}{(x+2)(x-2)}$$

The LCD of the denominators is $(x-2)(x+2)$. Hence each term of the fractional equation must be multiplied by $(x-2)(x+2)$:

$$(x-2)(x+2)\left(\frac{x}{x+2}\right) - (x-2)(x+2)\left(\frac{1}{x-2}\right) = (x-2)(x+2)\left[\frac{8}{(x+2)(x-2)}\right]$$

$$(x-2)\cancel{(x+2)}\frac{x}{\cancel{x+2}} - \cancel{(x-2)}(x+2)\frac{1}{\cancel{x-2}} = \cancel{(x-2)}\cancel{(x+2)}\frac{8}{\cancel{(x+2)}\cancel{(x-2)}}$$

$$x(x-2) - (x+2) = 8$$
$$x^2 - 2x - x - 2 = 8$$
$$x^2 - 3x - 10 = 0$$
$$(x+2)(x-5) = 0$$
$$x+2 = 0 \quad \text{or} \quad x-5 = 0$$
$$x = -2 \ | \qquad x = 5$$

Check: If $x = -2$, then denominators $x+2$ and x^2-4 in the original equations will be equal to 0, which is not permitted. Hence $x = -2$ is an *extraneous root* and is, therefore, rejected. You should verify that $x = 5$ satisfies the original fractional equation. The fractional equation has the single root $x = 5$.

Exercise Set 2.3

1–16. Solve for the variable and check.

1. $\dfrac{1}{5} - \dfrac{1}{3x} = \dfrac{1}{15x}$

2. $\dfrac{3}{5r} - \dfrac{2}{6r} = \dfrac{1}{15}$

3. $\dfrac{1}{x} + \dfrac{3}{2x} = \dfrac{x-4}{2}$

4. $\dfrac{5}{w} + 3w = \dfrac{17}{w}$

5. $\dfrac{x+2}{4x} - \dfrac{1}{x} = \dfrac{1}{12}$

6. $\dfrac{1}{y} - \dfrac{y+1}{8} = \dfrac{y-1}{4y}$

7. $\dfrac{x+15}{5x} - \dfrac{1}{2} = \dfrac{x-2}{2x}$

8. $\dfrac{3}{5} + \dfrac{n-2}{3} = \dfrac{14}{5n}$

9. $\dfrac{x}{5} - \dfrac{6}{x+2} = \dfrac{7x-16}{5x+10}$

10. $\dfrac{t}{t-3} + \dfrac{t-2}{2} = \dfrac{5t-3}{4t-12}$

11. $\dfrac{8}{y^2-25} + \dfrac{2}{y+5} = \dfrac{y}{y-5}$

12. $\dfrac{2}{n-3} + \dfrac{n-2}{n^2-2n-3} = \dfrac{2n+1}{n+1}$

13. $\dfrac{1}{b-3} - \dfrac{3}{2b+6} = \dfrac{b}{b^2-9}$

14. $\dfrac{1}{x-2} + \dfrac{x+2}{x+5} = \dfrac{3}{x^2+3x-10}$

15. $\dfrac{4}{m^2-16} + \dfrac{m-3}{m+4} = \dfrac{1}{m-4}$

16. $\dfrac{2}{r-6} = \dfrac{10}{r^2-7r+6} - \dfrac{r}{r-1}$

2.4 SOLVING RADICAL EQUATIONS AND EQUATIONS WITH RATIONAL EXPONENTS

KEY IDEAS

Equations such as

$$\sqrt{2x+3} = 7, \quad \sqrt{1-3x} = 8, \quad \text{and} \quad \sqrt{x+2} - 3 = 2x$$

are examples of **radical equations**, since the variable is included in the radicand. An equation having a square root radical is solved by isolating the radical and then squaring both sides of the equation. If the radical is a cube root, it is eliminated by cubing both sides of the equation.

If $x^{\frac{p}{k}} = c$, where c is some nonzero constant, then

$$x = c^{\frac{k}{p}}.$$

Solving Radical Equations

An equation containing a radical is solved by isolating the radical and then raising *both* sides of the equation to the power that eliminates the radical. This procedure may introduce *extraneous roots*—roots of the new equation that do not satisfy the original radical equation. Hence be sure to check all roots of the transformed equation in the original radical equation.

Examples

1. Solve for n: $\qquad \sqrt{2n} = 4\sqrt{5}.$

Solution: Square both sides:

$$\left(\sqrt{2n}\right)^2 = \left(4\sqrt{5}\right)^2$$

$$2n = 4^2\left(\sqrt{5}\right)^2$$

38

$$2n = 16 \cdot 5$$
$$n = \frac{80}{2}$$
$$n = \mathbf{40} \qquad \text{The check is left for you.}$$

2. Solve for x: $\sqrt{4-x} - 8 = x$.

Solution:

$$\sqrt{4-x} - 8 = x$$

Isolate the radical: $\qquad\qquad \sqrt{4-x} = x + 8$

Square both sides: $\qquad\qquad \left(\sqrt{4-x}\right)^2 = (x+8)^2$

$$4 - x = x^2 + 16x + 64$$

Combine like terms: $\qquad\qquad 0 = x^2 + 16x + x + 64 - 4$

Write in standard form: $\qquad x^2 + 17x + 60 = 0$

Factor: $\qquad\qquad\qquad (x+5)(x+12) = 0$

$$x + 5 = 0 \quad \text{or} \quad x + 12 = 0$$
$$x = -5 \quad | \qquad x = -12$$

To check x = –5:

$$\sqrt{4-x} - 8 \overset{?}{=} x$$
$$\sqrt{4-(-5)} - 8 \,\Big|\, -5$$
$$\sqrt{4+5} - 8 \,\Big|\, -5$$
$$3 - 8 \,\Big|\, -5$$
$$-5 = -5$$

To check x = –12:

$$\sqrt{4-x} - 8 \overset{?}{=} x$$
$$\sqrt{4-(-12)} - 8 \,\Big|\, -12$$
$$\sqrt{4+12} - 8 \,\Big|\, -12$$
$$4 - 8 \,\Big|\, -12$$
$$-4 \ne -12$$

Therefore, –5 is a root and –12 is an *extraneous root* that must be rejected.
The solution of $\sqrt{4-x} - 8 = x$ is the single root $\boldsymbol{x = -5}$.

3. Solve for x: $\sqrt[3]{3x-4} = 2$.

Solution: Raise both members of the equation to the third power:

$$\left(\sqrt[3]{3x-4}\right)^3 = 2^3$$
$$3x - 4 = 8$$
$$3x = 12$$
$$x = \mathbf{4} \qquad \text{The check is left for you.}$$

Solving Equations with Rational Exponents

Equations in which the variable has a rational exponent of the form $\frac{p}{k}$ are solved by isolating the variable and then raising both sides of the equation to the $\frac{k}{p}$ power.

Example

4. Solve for x:

(a) $x^{\frac{3}{2}} - 3 = 5$

(b) $x^{-\frac{4}{3}} = \dfrac{81}{16}$

Solutions: (a) $x^{\frac{3}{2}} - 3 = 5$

(b) $x^{-\frac{4}{3}} = \dfrac{81}{16}$

$$x^{\frac{3}{2}} = 8$$

$$\left(x^{-\frac{4}{3}}\right)^{-\frac{3}{4}} = \left(\dfrac{81}{16}\right)^{-\frac{3}{4}}$$

$$\left(x^{\frac{3}{2}}\right)^{\frac{2}{3}} = 8^{\frac{2}{3}}$$

$$x = \left(\dfrac{16}{81}\right)^{\frac{3}{4}}$$

$$x = 4$$

$$x = \left(\dfrac{2}{3}\right)^{3} = \dfrac{8}{27}$$

Exercise Set 2.4

1–15. Solve for the variable and check.

1. $\sqrt{x^2 - 25} = x - 1$

2. $\sqrt{5x + 1} = 25 - 3x$

3. $\sqrt{x - 1} = x - 7$

4. $\sqrt{3 - x} = 3 + x$

5. $2\sqrt{3y} = 5\sqrt{12}$

6. $\sqrt{13 - 3x} + x = 1$

7. $n - \sqrt{3n + 4} = 2$

8. $\sqrt{1 - 2x} = \sqrt{x^2 - 7}$

9. $2\sqrt{1 - 3p} = 3 - p$

10. $t - 2\sqrt{4t - 7} = 0$

11. $x^{\frac{2}{3}} = 25$

12. $2x^{\frac{3}{2}} = 54$

13. $x^{-\frac{4}{3}} = 16$

14. $x^{-\frac{3}{4}} = \dfrac{27}{8}$

15. $x^{-\frac{2}{3}} = 16^{-\frac{1}{2}}$

REGENTS TUNE UP: CHAPTER 2

Each of the questions in this section has appeared on a previous Course III Regents Examination. Here is an opportunity for you to review Chapter 2 and, at the same time, prepare for the Course III Regents Examination.

1. What is the solution set of the equation $\sqrt{9x^2 - 11} = 5$?

2. Solve for x: $x^{\frac{3}{2}} = 64$.

3. What is the solution set of the equation $2x - |x + 3| = 9$?
(1) $\{12\}$ (2) $\{2\}$ (3) $\{2, 12\}$ (4) $\{\ \}$

4. What is the solution set of the inequality $x^2 - 6x - 7 > 0$?

5. Solve for x: $\sqrt{x^2 + 7} = x + 1$.

6. What is the solution set of $|3 - 2x| = 5$?

7. What is the solution set of $(x + 3)(x - 2) > 0$?

(1)   (3)

(2)   (4)

8. What is the graph of the solution set of $|2x - 1| < 9$?

(1)   (3)

(2)   (4)

9. What is the solution set of $x^2 - x - 6 < 0$?
(1) $\{x \mid x < -2 \text{ or } x > 3\}$ (3) $\{x \mid -3 < x < 2\}$
(2) $\{x \mid x < -3 \text{ or } x > 2\}$ (4) $\{x \mid -2 < x < 3\}$

10. What is the solution set of the equation $|3x - 1| = x + 5$?
(1) $\{-1\}$ (3) $\{3\}$
(2) $\{-1, 3\}$ (4) $\{1, -3\}$

11. What is the solution set of $x^2 - 3x - 28 \geq 0$?
(1) $x \geq 7 \text{ or } x \leq -4$ (3) $-4 \leq x \leq 7$
(2) $x \leq 7 \text{ or } x \geq -4$ (4) $-4 < x < 7$

41

12. Solve for x:

$$\frac{x}{x-2} - \frac{8}{x+3} = \frac{10}{x^2 + x - 6}.$$

ANSWERS TO SELECTED EXERCISES: CHAPTER 2

Section 2.1
1. $\{-5, 5\}$

2. $\{\ \}$

3. $\{x : 1 \le x \le 5\}$

4. $\{x : -5 < x < 3\}$

5. $\{x : x < -7 \text{ or } x > 5\}$

6. $\{y : 1 \le y \le 3\}$

7. $\{x : -1 < x \le 6\}$

8. $\{x : x < 2 \text{ or } x > 4\}$

9. $\{x : x \le -\frac{5}{2} \text{ or } x \ge 2\}$

10. $\{x : x < -7 \text{ or } x > 8\}$

11. $\{x : -5 \le x \le 1\}$

12. $\{\ \}$

13. $\{x : 2 < x < 5\}$

14. $\{x : x < -\frac{7}{3} \text{ or } x > 5\}$

15. $\{n : -3 \le n \le 7\}$

16. $-\frac{1}{2}$

17. $y \ge 3$

Section 2.2
1. $x \le -5 \text{ or } x \ge 1$

2. $-3 \le n \le 9$

3. $x \le 0 \text{ or } x \ge 5$

4. $-12 \le y \le 3$

5. $-5 \le b \le 5$

6. 2

7. $0 \le x \le 7$

8. $x < -\frac{1}{2} \text{ or } x > 3$

9. $t \le -2 \text{ or } t \ge 3$

10. All real numbers

11. $m \le 0 \text{ or } m \ge 4$

12. $-\frac{1}{3} < h < \frac{3}{2}$

13. $-7 \le x \le 9$

14. $x \le -3 \text{ or } x \ge 4$

15. No real numbers

Section 2.3
1. 2

3. -1 or 5

5. 3

7. $\frac{5}{2}$

9. 7

11. -2 or -1

13. 5

15. 2 or 6

Section 2.4
1. 13

3. 10

5. 25

7. 7

9. -5 or -1

11. 125

12. 9

13. $\frac{1}{8}$

14. $\frac{16}{81}$

15. 8

Regents Tune-Up: Chapter 2
1. -2 or 2

2. 16

3. (2)

4. $x < -1 \text{ or } x > 7$

5. 3

6. -1 or 4

7. (4)

8. (3)

9. (4)

10. (2)

11. (1)

12. 3

CHAPTER 3
COMPLEX NUMBERS

3.1 CLASSIFYING NUMBERS

KEY IDEAS

The numbers of arithmetic—whole numbers, integers, rational numbers (fractions), and irrational numbers—form the set of **real numbers**. A number such as $\sqrt{-4}$ is *not* real. A new type of number called *imaginary*, was invented to make it possible to work with square roots of negative numbers. The set of **imaginary numbers** is based on the **imaginary unit** *i*, which is so defined that

$$i^2 = -1 \text{ and } i = \sqrt{-1}.$$

Square roots of negative numbers other than −1 can be expressed in terms of *i* by factoring out $\sqrt{-1}$ and replacing it with *i*. For example,

$$\sqrt{-4} = \sqrt{4} \cdot \sqrt{-1} = 2i.$$

The sum of a real number and an imaginary number, such as $3 + 2i$, is called a **complex number.**

Field Properties

A set of numbers S and two operations, such as addition and multiplication, form a **field** (*F*) if each of the field properties listed in Table 3.1 is true for any numbers a, b, and c that are in set S.

TABLE 3.1 FIELD PROPERTIES

Field Property	Addition	Multiplication
F_1: Closure	$a + b$ is in S.	$a \cdot b$ is in S.
F_2: Commutative	$a + b = b + a$	$a \cdot b = b \cdot a$
F_3: Associative	$(a + b) + c = a + (b + c)$	$(a \cdot b)c = a(b \cdot c)$
F_4: Identity	0 is in S: $a + 0 = 0 + a = a$	1 is in S: $a \cdot 1 = 1 \cdot a = a$
F_5: Inverse	$-a$ is in S: $a + (-a) = (-a) + a = 0$	$\dfrac{1}{a}$ is in S ($a \neq 0$) $a \cdot \dfrac{1}{a} = \dfrac{1}{a} \cdot a = 1$
F_6: Distributive	$a(b + c) = ab + ac$ and $(b + c)a = ba + ca$	

43

Properties F_1 through F_6 in Table 3.1 hold for *all* real numbers so that the set of real numbers is a field. A subset of the real numbers, however, may not be a field. For example, to determine whether the set of integers forms a field under the operations of addition and multiplication, determine whether each of the field properties holds:

F_1: The set of integers is *closed* under addition and multiplication because the sum or product of any two integers is an integer.

F_2: For any two integers, the order in which they are added or multiplied does not matter, so the commutative property holds.

F_3: For any three integers, the way in which the numbers are grouped when added or multiplied does not matter, so the associative property holds.

F_4: Adding the integer 0 to any integer a gives a, so that the additive identity is 0. Multiplying any integer a by the integer 1 gives a, so that the multiplicative identity is 1.

F_5: Adding a and its opposite, $-a$, gives the identity 0, so that each integer has an additive inverse. However, each nonzero integer does *not* have a multiplicative inverse (reciprocal) that is an integer. For example, if $a = 2$, then $2(\frac{1}{2}) = 1$. Since $\frac{1}{2}$ is not an integer, $a = 2$ does *not* have a multiplicative inverse.

Hence the set of integers is *not* a field, since it lacks property F_5 in Table 3.1 for the operation of multiplication.

The Set of Complex Numbers

An even root of a negative real number is called a **pure imaginary number.** The square roots of negative numbers may be expressed in terms of the imaginary unit i, where $i = \sqrt{-1}$.

Examples: 1. $\sqrt{-9} = \sqrt{9}\sqrt{-1} = \mathbf{3i}$

2. $-\sqrt{-6} = -\sqrt{6}\sqrt{-1} = \mathbf{-i\sqrt{6}}$

3. $\sqrt{-50} = \sqrt{25}\sqrt{-2} = 5\sqrt{2}\sqrt{-1} = \mathbf{5i\sqrt{2}}$

A **complex number** is the sum of a real number a and a pure imaginary number. When a complex number is written in the form $a + bi$, where $i = \sqrt{-1}$, it is said to be in **standard form.** Numbers such as $4 + 2i$ and $-5 + \sqrt{3}i$ are examples of complex numbers written in standard form. The complex number $\frac{2 + i}{3}$ is *not* in standard form unless it is written as

$$\frac{2}{3} + \frac{1}{3}i, \text{ so that } a = \frac{2}{3} \quad \text{and} \quad b = \frac{1}{3}.$$

Every real number is a complex number. If $b = 0$ in $a + bi$, then the complex number simplifies to a real number, since $a + bi = a + 0i = a$. Therefore, the set of real numbers is a *subset* of the set of complex numbers.

Arithmetic operations involving complex numbers are defined so that the set of complex numbers is a field. In performing arithmetic operations, terms involving i are treated as if they are monomials. Here are four examples:

(1) $3i + 5i = 8i$;   (2) $6i - i = 5i$;   (3) $i \cdot i = i^2$;   (4) $i^{13} \div i^4 = i^9$.

Examples

1. Find the sum of $2 + 3i$ and $4 - 5i$.

Solution: The sum of two complex numbers is the sum of their real parts and the sum of their imaginary parts. Treat the imaginary parts of complex numbers as monomials involving i:

$$(2 + 3i) + (4 - 5i) = (2 + 4) + (3i - 5i) = \mathbf{6 - 2i}.$$

2. Subtract $-4 + 6i$ from $1 - 2i$.

Solution: $(1 - 2i) - (-4 + 6i) = (1 - 2i) + (4 - 6i)$
$$= (1 + 4) + (-2i - 6i) = \mathbf{5 - 8i}$$

3. Find the additive inverse of $-1 + 2i$.

Solution: The sum of a complex number and its additive inverse is 0. since $(-1 + 2i) + (1 - 2i) = 0$, the additive inverse of $-1 + 2i$ is $\mathbf{1 - 2i}$.

4. Express as a monomial in terms of i:

(a) $\sqrt{-45}$ **(b)** $3\sqrt{-16} + \sqrt{-36}$ **(c)** $\sqrt{-18} + \sqrt{-32}$

Solutions: Factor out $\sqrt{-1}$ from each radical and simplify.

(a) $\sqrt{-45} = \sqrt{45}\sqrt{-1} = \sqrt{9}\sqrt{5}i = \mathbf{3\sqrt{5}i}$

(b) $3\sqrt{-16} + \sqrt{-36}\ = 3\sqrt{16}\sqrt{-1} + \sqrt{36}\sqrt{-1}$
$$= 12i \qquad\quad + 6i = \mathbf{18i}$$

(c) $\sqrt{-18} + \sqrt{-32}\ = \sqrt{9}\sqrt{2}i \ +\sqrt{16}\sqrt{2}i$
$$= 3\sqrt{2}i \quad\ +4\sqrt{2}i = \mathbf{7\sqrt{2}i}$$

Graphing Complex Numbers

A complex number of the form $a + bi$ can be graphed in the *complex* coordinate plane by using the ordered pair (a, b). The value of a is measured horizontally along the **real axis**, and the value of b is measured vertically along the **imaginary axis**. In Figure 3.1, the complex number $3+5i$ is graphed by drawing a directed segment from the origin O to the ordered pair (3, 5).

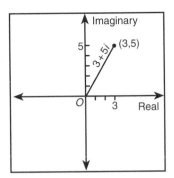

Figure 3.1 Graphing a Complex Number

Example

5. In which quadrant is the sum of $2+5i$ and $-6-2i$ located?

Solution: Since $(2+5i)+(-6-2i)=-4+3i$, $a=-4$ and $b=3$. The ordered pair $(-4, 3)$ is located in **Quadrant II**. Notice in the diagram that the sum is the diagonal of the parallelogram whose adjacent sides are the directed segments from the origin to each of the complex ordered pairs.

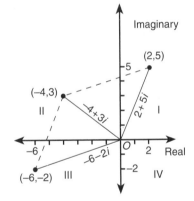

Simplifying Powers of *i*.

Any nonnegative integer power of i can be reduced to either ± 1 or $\pm i$, as the following list suggests:

$$i^0 = 1 \qquad i^4 = i^2 \cdot i^2 = 1 \qquad i^8 = i^4 \cdot i^4 = 1$$
$$i^1 = i \qquad i^5 = i^4 \cdot i = i \qquad i^9 = i^8 \cdot i = i$$
$$i^2 = -1 \qquad i^6 = i^4 \cdot i^2 = i^2 = -1 \quad i^{10} = i^8 \cdot i^2 = i^2 = -1$$
$$i^3 = i^2 \cdot i = -i \quad i^7 = i^4 \cdot i^3 = i^3 = -i \quad i^{11} = i^8 \cdot i^3 = i^3 = -i$$

Observe that consecutive integer powers of i greater than 3 follow a cyclic pattern that repeats every four integers. Since integer powers of i that are multiples of 4 are equal to 1, powers of i can be simplified by dividing the exponent by 4 and using the remainder as the new power of i. For example, i^{14} is equivalent to i^2, since $14 \div 4 = 3$, remainder 2.

Examples

6. Solve for x: $x^2 + 16 = 0$.

Solution: $x^2 = -16$
$$x = \pm\sqrt{-16}$$
$$= \pm 4i$$

7. Simplify:
(a) i^{52} **(b)** i^{25} **(c)** $i^7 \cdot i^{27}$

Solutions: To simplify i^n: (1) Divide n by 4 and note the remainder, R; then (2) write $i^n = i^R$.
(a) Divide: $52 \div 4 = 13$, remainder 0. Hence $i^{52} = i^0 = $ **1**.
(b) Divide: $25 \div 4 = 6$, remainder 1. Hence $i^{25} = i^1 = i$.
(c) $i^7 \cdot i^{27} = i^{34}$. Divide: $34 \div 4 = 8$, remainder 2. Hence $i^{34} = i^2 = $ **−1**.

Exercise Set 3.1

1–6. Determine whether each set of numbers forms a field under the operations of addition and multiplication. If the system does not form a field, state a field property the system lacks and illustrate, using specific numbers.

1. {rationals} **2.** {irrationals} **3.** {−1, 0, 1}
4. {pure imaginary numbers}
5. {all real numbers between −5 and 5, inclusive}
6. {all numbers of the form $q\sqrt{2}$, q is rational}

7–8. Subtract.

7. $3 - 3i$ from $-2 + 2i$ **8.** $-5 - 2i$ from $-8 + 2i$

9–14. Determine the sum and the quadrant in which it is located.

9. -4 and $1 + 5i$ **11.** $2 - 5i$ and $5 - 2i$ **13.** $5 - 2i$ and $-1 + 3i$
10. $-3i$ and $-2-i$ **12.** $-3-9i$ and $1+i$ **14.** $-7+3i$ and $8-8i$

15. Find the additive inverse of:
(a) $5 - 3i$ **(b)** $-1 - 2i$ **(c)** $3 + 7i$

16–24. Express in simplest form.

16. $\sqrt{-36}$ **17.** $2\sqrt{-16}$ **18.** $\sqrt{-28}$

19. $2\sqrt{-9} + 3\sqrt{-25}$ **20.** $3\sqrt{-1} - 2\sqrt{-4}$ **21.** $\sqrt{-12} + \sqrt{-27}$

22. $2\sqrt{-8} - 3\sqrt{-18}$ **23.** $-3\sqrt{-48} - 2\sqrt{-3}$ **24.** $2\sqrt{-50} - \sqrt{-2} + \sqrt{-8}$

25–27. Solve each equation for x. *Express complex roots in terms of* i.

25. $x^2 + 25 = 0$ **26.** $2x^2 + 3 = -5$ **27.** $3x^2 + 41 = 5$

28–32. Express in simplest form.

28. i^{60} **29.** i^{99} **30.** $i^{18} + i^0$ **31.** $i^3 \cdot i^{11}$ **32.** $(i^4)^6$

3.2   MULTIPLYING AND DIVIDING COMPLEX NUMBERS

KEY IDEAS

Complex numbers in $a + bi$ form may be multiplied and divided in much the same way that binomials that contain radicals are multiplied and divided. There is, however, one exception. If a and b are *both* negative numbers, then $\sqrt{a}\sqrt{b} \neq \sqrt{ab}$. For example, $\sqrt{-4}\sqrt{-9} \neq \sqrt{36}$. Rather,

$$\sqrt{-4}\sqrt{-9} = 2i \cdot 3i = 6i^2 = -6.$$

Multiplying Pure Imaginary Numbers

In general, if b and d are real numbers, then

$$bi \cdot di = (bd)(i^2) = bd(-1) = -bd$$

Hence the product of two pure imaginary numbers is real, since i^2 can be replaced by -1.

Examples: *1.* $2i \cdot 5i = 10i^2 = -10$

          2. $\sqrt{-16}\sqrt{-9} = 4i \cdot 3i = 12i^2 = -12$

          3. $(4i)^2 = 4i \cdot 4i = 16i^2 = -16$

          4. $2i(3 - 5i) = 6i + (2i)(-5i)$

$$= 6i - 10i^2$$
$$= 6i - 10(-1)$$
$$= 6i + 10 \text{ or } 10 + 6i$$

Multiplying Complex Numbers

Complex numbers are treated as if they are binomials and are multiplied using FOIL.

$$\underbrace{\text{F} \quad \text{O} \quad \text{I} \quad \text{L}}$$

Examples: 1. $(2+3i)(4+5i) = 2 \cdot 4 + (2 \cdot 5i + 3i \cdot 4) + 3i \cdot 5i$
$$= \ 8 \ + (10i + 12i) \ + \ 15i^2$$
$$= \ 8 \ + \qquad 22i \qquad - \ 15$$
$$= \ -7 + 22i$$

2. $(3+4i)(3-4i) = 3 \cdot 3 + [2(-4i) + 2(4i)] + (4i)(-4i)$
$$= 3^2 + \qquad 0 \qquad + \ 4^2(-i^2)$$
$$= \ 9 \ + \qquad\qquad\qquad 16$$
$$= 25$$

Notice in Example 2 that the product of $(3+4i)$ and $(3-4i)$ equals $3^2 + 4^2$ or 25. The product does not contain i. This happens whenever the two complex numbers form a *conjugate pair*. Two complex numbers are **complex conjugates** if they take the sum and difference of the same two terms. The complex conjugate of $a + bi$ is $a - bi$. The product of a pair of complex conjugates is *always* a positive real number.

=== **MATH FACTS** ===

MULTIPLYING COMPLEX CONJUGATES

$$(a + bi)(a - bi) = a^2 + b^2$$

Example

1. Express each product in simplest form:
(a) $(4+2i)(4-2i)$ (b) $(-3+i)(-3-i)$

Solutions: (a) Since $4 + 2i$ and $4 - 2i$ are complex conjugates, their product is $a^2 + b^2$, where $a = 4$ and $b = 2$:

$$(4+2i)(4-2i) = 4^2 + 2^2 = 20.$$

(b) Since $-3 + i$ and $-3 - i$ are complex conjugates, their product is $a^2 + b^2$, where $a = -3$ and $b = 1$:

$$(-3 + i)(-3 - i) = (-3)^2 + (1)^2 = 10.$$

Dividing Complex Numbers

If the denominator of a fraction is a complex number, then the quotient can be expressed in standard $a + bi$ form by multiplying the fraction by 1 in the form of the complex conjugate of the denominator divided by itself. For example,

$$\frac{3+i}{1-2i} = \frac{3+i}{1-2i}\left(\frac{1+2i}{1+2i}\right) = \frac{(3+1)(1+2i)}{1^2+2^2}$$

Use FOIL:
$$= \frac{3+(6i+i)+2i^2}{1+4}$$

Simplify:
$$= \frac{3+7i-2}{5}$$

Put into $a + bi$ form:
$$= \frac{1}{5} + \frac{7}{5}i$$

Example

2. Write the multiplicative inverse of $3 + 4i$ in standard form.

Solution: The multiplicative inverse of a complex number is its reciprocal. Thus, the multiplicative inverse of $3 + 4i$ is $\frac{1}{3+4i}$, which can be expressed in standard form by multiplying the numerator and the denominator by the complex conjugate of $3 + 4i$:

$$\frac{1}{3+4i}\left(\frac{3-4i}{3-4i}\right) = \frac{3-4i}{3^2+4^2} = \frac{3-4i}{9+16}$$

$$= \frac{3-4i}{25} = \frac{3}{25} - \frac{4}{25}i$$

Exercise Set 3.2

1–15. Express each product in simplest form.

1. $3i \cdot 5i$

2. $-2i \cdot 4i$

3. $(-5i)(-6i)$

4. $3i(-2+i)$

5. $-2i(-1-3i)$

6. $(3+2i)(1+i)$

7. $(2-i)(1-2i)$

8. $(-3+5i)(-2+i)$

9. $(1+3i)^2$

10. $(-2+4i)^2$

11. $(2-5i)(2+5i)$

12. $(-2+5i)(-2-5i)$

13. $(4-2i)(4+2i)$

14. $(\sqrt{3}-i)(\sqrt{3}+i)$

15. $(\sqrt{5}+i\sqrt{2})(\sqrt{5}-i\sqrt{2})$

16–20. Find each multiplicative inverse, and write it in standard $a + bi$ *form.*

16. $1-3i$ **17.** $2+7i$ **18.** $-3+5i$ **19.** $\sqrt{3}-i$ **20.** $\sqrt{7}+i\sqrt{2}$

21–26. Express each quotient in simplest a + bi *form.*

21. $\dfrac{2-5i}{i}$ **23.** $\dfrac{2-i}{2+i}$ **25.** $\dfrac{4+\sqrt{-9}}{4-\sqrt{-9}}$

22. $\dfrac{3i}{1-i}$ **24.** $\dfrac{3+2i}{1-2i}$ **26.** $\dfrac{\sqrt{5}-i}{\sqrt{5}}$

3.3 SOLVING QUADRATIC EQUATIONS HAVING IMAGINARY ROOTS

KEY IDEAS

With the introduction of complex numbers, it is possible to find the roots of *any* quadratic equation of the form

$$ax^2 + bx + c = 0 \quad (a \neq 0)$$

by using the quadratic formula

$$x = \frac{-b \pm \sqrt{b^2 - 4ac}}{2a}.$$

The radicand $b^2 - 4ac$ is called the **discriminant**. If the discriminant is negative, then the roots of the quadratic equation are imaginary and can be represented in terms of the imaginary unit, i.

The graph of a quadratic equation with imaginary roots is a parabola that has no x-intercepts.

Quadratic Equations and Parabolas

The graph of $y = ax^2 + bx + c$, where a, b, and c are real numbers and $a \neq 0$, is a parabola and may intersect the x-axis in two points, one point, or no point, depending on the nature of the roots of the related quadratic equation $ax^2 + bx + c = 0$. The possibilities are given in Table 3.2.

TABLE 3.2 RELATING THE PARABOLA $y = ax^2 + bx + c$ TO THE NATURE OF THE ROOTS OF $ax^2 + bx + c = 0$ $(a \neq 0)$

A Possible Graph of $y = ax^2 + bx + c$ $(a > 0)$	$ax^2 + bx + c = 0$ $(a \neq 0)$	
	Discriminant	Nature of Roots
	$b^2 - 4ac > 0$ (Two x-intercepts)	Real and unequal. If $b^2 - 4ac$ is a perfect square, roots are rational; otherwise, roots are irrational.
	$b^2 - 4ac = 0$ (One x-intercept, so graph is tangent to the x-axis.)	Real, rational, and equal.
	$b^2 - 4ac < 0$ (No x-intercept)	Imaginary and unequal.

Solving Quadratic Equations

Imaginary roots of quadratic equations arise when the discriminant is less than 0 and always occur in conjugate pairs. If $a + bi$ is a root of a quadratic equation, then $a - bi$ must be the other root.

Example

1. Express the roots of $x^2 + 5 = 2x$ in $a + bi$ form.

Solution: Put the equation into standard form:

$$x^2 - 2x + 5 = 0.$$

Write the quadratic formula: $x = \dfrac{-b \pm \sqrt{b^2 - 4ac}}{2a}$

Let $a = 1$, $b = -2$, $c = 5$: $\quad x = \dfrac{-(-2) \pm \sqrt{(-2)^2 - 4(1)(5)}}{2(1)}$

$$= \frac{2 \pm \sqrt{4 - 20}}{2}$$

$$= \frac{2 \pm \sqrt{-16}}{2}$$

$$= \frac{2 \pm 4i}{2}$$

$$= \frac{2}{2} \pm \frac{4i}{2} = 1 \pm 2i$$

The roots of $x^2 + 5 = 2x$ are **$1 + 2i$** and **$1 - 2i$**.

Describing the Type of Roots

It is not necessary to solve a quadratic equation in order to determine the *nature* of its roots. The value of the discriminant tells us the type of roots (see Table 3.2).

Example

2. Find the discriminant and describe the nature of the roots:
(a) $3x^2 - 11x = 4$ **(b)** $-2x^2 + 3x - 4 = 0$

Solutions: **(a)** Write the equation in standard form:

$$3x^2 - 11x - 4 = 0.$$

Let $a = 3$, $b = -11$, and $c = -4$. Next, evaluate the discriminant:

$$b^2 - 4ac = (-11)^2 - 4(3)(-4)$$
$$= 121 + 48 = \mathbf{169}$$

Since the discriminant is a perfect square ($169 = 13 \times 13$), the roots of $3x^2 - 11x = 4$ are **real**, **rational**, and **equal**.

(b) Since $-2x^2 + 3x - 4 = 0$, let $a = -2$, $b = 3$, and $c = -4$. Then

$$b^2 - 4ac = 32 - 4(-2)(-4)$$
$$= 9 - 32 = -23$$

Since the discriminant is less than 0, the roots of $-2x^2 + 3x - 4 = 0$ are **imaginary** and, as a result, unequal.

Finding an Unknown Coefficient (*a, b,* or *c*)

The discriminant can be used to determine the value that an unknown coefficient in a quadratic equation must have in order for the roots to be of a given type.

Examples

3. Find the *smallest* integer value of k that makes the roots of the equation $x^2 - 5x + k = 0$ imaginary.

Solution: For the equation $x^2 - 5x + k = 0$, let $a = 1$, $b = -5$, and $c = k$. If the roots are imaginary, the discriminant is less than 0.

$$b^2 - 4ac < 0$$
$$(-5)^2 - 4(1)(k) < 0$$
$$25 - 4k < 0$$
$$-4k < -25$$

Divide by -4 and reverse the direction of the inequality:

$$\frac{-4k}{-4} > \frac{-25}{-4}$$
$$k > 6\frac{1}{4}$$

The *smallest* integer value of k that makes the inequality a true statement is 7. Hence $k = \mathbf{7}$.

4. For what value of k is the graph of $y = kx^2 - 12x + 9$ tangent to the x-axis?

Solution: A parabola is tangent to the x-axis if it intersects the x-axis in exactly one point. This situation corresponds to the one in which the roots of the related quadratic equation $kx^2 - 12x + 9 = 0$ are real and *equal.* Let $a = k$, $b = -12$, and $c = 9$. If the roots are real and equal, the value of the discriminant must be 0.

$$b^2 - 4ac = -0$$
$$(-12)^2 - 4k(9) = 0$$
$$144 - 36k = 0$$
$$-36k = -144$$
$$k = \frac{-144}{-36} = 4$$

Exercise Set 3.3

1–9. Solve each equation, and express its roots in a + bi *form.*

1. $x^2 + 13 = 4x$ **4.** $-x^2 = 4(2x+5)$ **7.** $3(x^2+1) = 5x$

2. $x^2 = 6x - 25$ **5.** $-x^2 + 2x = 10$ **8.** $2x^2 + 5 = 6x$

3. $\dfrac{x^2}{2} = x - 1$ **6.** $x + \dfrac{5}{x} = 2$ **9.** $2(x+2) = -\dfrac{5}{x}$

10. For the graph of $y = x^2 - 2kx + 16$, determine the value of k such that:
    (a) the graph is tangent to the x-axis and k is positive.
    (b) k is the largest integer for which the graph has no x-intercept.

11–14. For each equation find the discriminant and describe the nature of the roots.

11. $3x^2 + 5x + 2 = 0$ **13.** $-2x^2 + 3x = 2$

12. $2x^2 - 1 = 5x$ **14.** $x - 1 = x^2 - 2x + 1$

15–18. For each equation find the value or values of k *that make the roots real and equal.*

15. $x^2 + kx + 25 = 0$ **17.** $kx^2 - 14x + 49 = 0$

16. $9x^2 + 6x + k = 0$ **18.** $kx^2 - 11kx + 121 = 0$

19–22. For each equation find the largest integral value of k *that makes the roots real.*

19. $x^2 - 4x + k = 0$ **21.** $2x^2 - 7x + k = 0$

20. $kx^2 - 9x + 3 = 0$ **22.** $kx^2 - 10x + k = 0$

23. What is the *smallest* integral value of k that makes the roots of the equation $2x^2 - 5x + k = 0$ imaginary?

3.4 APPLYING THE SUM AND THE PRODUCT OF THE ROOTS FORMULAS

═══════════════ ⌃ **KEY IDEAS** ═══════════════

If $ax^2 + bx + c = 0$ $(a \neq 0)$, then the sum and the product of the roots may be determined without solving the equation by using these formulas:

$$\text{Sum of roots} = -\frac{b}{a} \quad \text{and} \quad \text{Product of roots} = \frac{c}{a}$$

A quadratic equation can be formed when only its roots are known by writing

$$x^2 - (\text{sum of roots})\, x + (\text{product of roots}) = 0$$

Checking Roots of Quadratic Equations

Rather than substituting into the original equation, the roots obtained by solving a quadratic equation of the form $ax^2 + bx + c = 0$ $(a \neq 0)$ can be checked by verifying that their sum equals $-\frac{b}{a}$ and their product equals $\frac{c}{a}$.

Example

1. Determine whether $3 \pm \sqrt{10}$ are the roots of $x^2 - 6x = 1$.

Solution: If $x^2 - 6x = 1$, then $x^2 - 6x - 1 = 0$, where $a = 1$, $b = -6$, and $c = -1$.

$$\text{Sum} = -\frac{b}{a} = -\frac{(-6)}{1} = 6 \quad \text{Product} = \frac{c}{a} = \frac{-1}{1} = -1$$

The roots to be checked are $3 - \sqrt{10}$ and $3 + \sqrt{10}$. If their sum is 6 and their product is -1, then these must be the roots of the given equation.

$$\text{Sum} = (3 - \sqrt{10}) + (3 + \sqrt{10}) \quad \text{Product} = (3 - \sqrt{10})(3 + \sqrt{10})$$
$$= 6 \qquad\qquad\qquad = (3)^2 - (\sqrt{10})^2$$
$$= 9 - 10$$
$$= -1$$

Since the sums agree and the products agree, $3 \pm \sqrt{10}$ **are the roots** of $x^2 - 6x = 1$.

Forming Quadratic Equations Whose Roots Are Given

A quadratic equation having a given pair of numbers r_1 and r_2 as its roots can be formed by writing

$$x^2 - (r_1 + r_2) x + r_1 \cdot r_2 = 0$$

Keep in mind that irrational and imaginary roots must occur in conjugate pairs.

Examples

2. Find a quadratic equation that has $5 + 2i$ as one of its roots.

Solution: Imaginary roots always occur in conjugate pairs. Let $r_1 = 5 + 2i$ and $r_2 = 5 - 2i$. Then

$$\text{Sum} = r_1 + r_2 = (5 + 2i) + (5 - 2i) = 10$$
$$\begin{aligned} \text{Product} = \ r_1 r_2 &= (5 + 2i)(5 - 2i) \\ &= 5^2 + 2^2 = 29 \end{aligned}$$

In general, $x^2 - (r_1 + r_2)x + r_1 r_2 = 0$. Substituting for the sum and product gives $x^2 - 10x + 29 = 0$.

3. The roots of the equation $x^2 + px + q = 0$ are $1 \pm \sqrt{3}i$. Find the value of: **(a)** p　**(b)** q

Solutions: The value of p equals the negative of the sum of the roots, and the value of q equals the product of the roots. Let $r_1 = 1 + \sqrt{3}i$ and $r_2 = 1 - \sqrt{3}i$.

(a) $\begin{aligned} p = -(r_1 + r_2) &= -[(1 + \sqrt{3}i) + (1 - \sqrt{3}i)] \\ &= -(2 + 0) = -2 \end{aligned}$

(b) $\begin{aligned} q = r_1 r_2 &= (1 + \sqrt{3}i)(1 - \sqrt{3}i) \\ &= 1^2 + (\sqrt{3})^2 \\ &= 1 + 3 = 4 \end{aligned}$

Exercise Set 3.4

1. Given the equation $x^2 - x + q = 0$, one of whose roots is 3.
   (a) Find the sum of the roots.
   (b) Using your answer to part (a), find the value of q.
   (c) Find the value of q by replacing x by 3 in the original equation.

2. One root of the equation $6x^2 + kx + 5 = 0$ is 1.
   (a) What is the other root?　**(b)** What is the value of k?

3. By what amount does the sum of the roots of the equation $3x^2 - 6x + 3 = 0$ exceed the product of the roots?

4–5. Given the equation $x^2 + px + q = 0$.

4. If the roots are $\pm i$, find the values of p and q.

5. If the roots are $2 \pm \sqrt{6}$, find the values of p and q.

6. In the equation $ax^2 + bx + a = 0$, a and b are integers. If one root is $\frac{1}{2}$, find:
   (a) the other root   **(b)** the sum and product of the roots

7–14. Write a quadratic equation with integer coefficients whose roots are given.

7. $\{1, -2\}$

8. $\{\sqrt{5}, -\sqrt{5}\}$

9. $\{2i, -2i\}$

10. $\left\{\dfrac{1}{2}, \dfrac{1}{3}\right\}$

11. $\left\{\dfrac{1}{4}, -\dfrac{1}{2}\right\}$

12. $\{2 \pm 3i\}$

13. $\{1 \pm \sqrt{7}\}$

14. $\{1 \pm i\sqrt{2}\}$

REGENTS TUNE-UP: CHAPTER 3

Each of the questions in this section has appeared on a previous Course III Regents Examination. Here is an opportunity for you to review Chapter 3 and, at the same time, prepare for the Course III Regents Examination.

1. Express $3i(1-i)$ in $a + bi$ form.

2. Express the product $(3-i)(4+i)$ in the form $a + bi$.

3. Expressed in simplest form, $2\sqrt{-50} - 3\sqrt{-8}$ is equivalent to:
 (1) $16i\sqrt{2}$ (2) $3i\sqrt{2}$ (3) $4i\sqrt{2}$ (4) $-\sqrt{-42}$

4. The roots of the equation $x^2 + x + 1 = 0$ are
 (1) real, rational, and unequal (3) real, rational, and equal
 (2) real, irrational, and unequal (4) imaginary

5. What is the sum of the roots of the equation $3x^2 = 9x + 1$?

6. Solve the equation $3x^2 - 4x = -2$, and express the roots in $a + bi$ form.

7. If the equation $9x^2 - 12x + k = 0$ has equal roots, find the value of k.

8. Express the roots of the equation $3x^2 = -2(2x + 3)$ in $a + bi$ form.

9. If the sum of the roots of the equation $2x^2 - 5x - 3 = 0$ is added to the product of the roots, the result is

 (1) 1 (2) $-\dfrac{1}{4}$ (3) -1 (4) 4

10. Solve the equation

$$\frac{x+8}{5} + \frac{x+5}{x} = 1,$$

and express the roots in the form $a + bi$.

11. What is the product of the roots of the equation $2x^2 - 9x + 6 = 0$?
 (1) $\dfrac{9}{2}$ (2) $-\dfrac{9}{2}$ (3) 3 (4) $\dfrac{1}{3}$

12. The expression $\dfrac{1}{5+2i}$ is equivalent to

(1) $\dfrac{5+2i}{21}$ (3) $\dfrac{5-2i}{21}$

(2) $\dfrac{5+2i}{29}$ (4) $\dfrac{5-2i}{29}$

13. If $4 + 2i - (a + 4i) = 9 - 2i$, find the value of a.

14. If $Z_1 = -1 + 6i$ and $Z_2 = 4 + 2i$, graphically represent Z_1, Z_2, and $Z_1 + Z_2$.

ANSWERS TO SELECTED EXERCISES: CHAPTER 3

Section 3.1
1. System is a field.
3. Since $1 + 1 = 2$ and 2 is not an element of $\{-1, 0, 1\}$, the system is not closed under addition, so it does not form a field.
5. Since $-5 \times 5 = -25$ and -25 is not an element of the set of all real numbers from -5 to 5, inclusive, the system is not closed under multiplication, so it does not form a field.

7. $-5+5i$ **15. (a)** $-5+3i$ **25.** $x = \pm 5i$
9. $-3+5i$, Quadrant II   **(b)** $1+2i$ **(c)** $-3-7i$ **27.** $x = \pm 2i\sqrt{3}$
10. $-2-4i$, Quadrant III   **17.** $8i$ **28.** 1
11. $7-7i$, Quadrant IV   **19.** $21i$ **29.** $-i$
13. $4+i$, Quadrant I   **21.** $5i\sqrt{3}$ **30.** 0
14. $1-5i$, Quadrant IV   **22.** $-5i\sqrt{2}$ **31.** -1
                       23. $-14i\sqrt{3}$ **32.** 1

Section 3.2
1. -15 **9.** $-8+6i$ **17.** $\dfrac{2}{53} - \dfrac{7}{53}i$ **23.** $\dfrac{3}{5} - \dfrac{4}{5}i$
3. -30 **11.** 29
5. $-6+2i$ **13.** 20   **19.** $\dfrac{\sqrt{3}}{4} + \dfrac{1}{4}i$ **25.** $\dfrac{7}{25} + \dfrac{24}{25}i$
7. $-5i$ **15.** 7   **21.** $-5-2i$

Section 3.3
1. $2 \pm 3i$ **3.** $1 \pm i$ **5.** $1 \pm 3i$
2. $3 \pm 4i$ **4.** $-4 \pm 2i$ **6.** $1 \pm 2i$

7. $\dfrac{5}{6} \pm \dfrac{\sqrt{11}}{6}\, i$

8. $\dfrac{3}{2} \pm \dfrac{1}{2}\, i$

9. $-1 \pm \dfrac{\sqrt{6}}{2}\, i$

10. **(a)** 4   **(b)** 3

11. Discriminant is 1, so roots are real, rational, and unequal.

13. Discriminant is –7, so roots are imaginary.

15. $\pm\, 10$

17. 1

19. 3

21. 6

23. 4

Section 3.4

1. **(a)** –2   **(b)** –6

2. **(a)** $\frac{5}{6}$ **(b)** –11

3. 1

4. $p = 0,\, q = 1$

5. $p = -4,\, q = -2$

6. **(a)** 2

  (b) Sum $= \frac{5}{2}$,
  product $= 1$

7. $x^2 + x - 2 = 0$

9. $x^2 + 4 = 0$

11. $8x^2 + 2x - 1 = 0$

13. $x^2 - 2x - 6 = 0$

Regents Tune–Up: Chapter 3

1. $3 + 3i$

2. $13 - i$

3. (3)

4. (4)

5. 3

6. $\dfrac{2}{3} \pm \dfrac{\sqrt{2}}{3}\, i$

7. 4

8. $-\dfrac{2}{3} \pm \dfrac{\sqrt{14}}{3}\, i$

9. (1)

10. $-4 \pm 3i$

11. (3)

12. (4)

13. –5

14.

61

Unit Two

FUNCTIONS AND CIRCLES

CHAPTER 4

RELATIONS, FUNCTIONS, AND TRANSFORMATIONS

4.1 DEFINING RELATIONS AND FUNCTIONS

=== KEY IDEAS ===

A **function** in two variables describes how two quantities are related to each other. A function may take the form of a set of ordered pairs, an equation in two variables, or a graph. Regardless of the form it takes, a function must obey the condition that no two of its ordered pairs have the same first member (x) but different second members (y).

Definition of Relations

A **relation** is a set of ordered pairs. The set of all first members of the ordered pairs is called the **domain**. The set of all second members of the ordered pairs is called the **range**. For example, here is a relation that pairs three pupils with their heights:

{(John, 70 inches), (Maria, 68 inches), (George, 66 inches)}

The domain and range of this relation are as follows:

Domain = {John, Maria, George}
Range = {70, 68, 66}

Definition of Function

A function is a special type of relation. A **function** is a set of ordered pairs of the form (x, y) in which no two ordered pairs have the same value of x but different values of y. The ordered pairs that comprise a function may appear as a list, an equation, or a graph. If

$$f = \{(-1, 1), (0, 0), (1, 1), (2, 4)\},$$

then relation f is a function. However, if

$$g = \{(1, 2), (2, 1), (1, 3)\},$$

then relation g is *not* a function since the ordered pairs (1, 2) and (1, 3) have the same value of x but different values of y.

Describing Functions Using Equations

Some functions consist of a set of ordered pairs in which the values of y can be obtained from the corresponding values of x by using an equation. For example, the equation $y = x + 1$ defines a function consisting of the set of all ordered pairs whose second member, y, is one more than its first member, x. Notice that the value of y *depends* on the value of x. If $x = 3$, then $y = 4$; if $x = 7.5$, then $y = 8.5$; and so forth. For this reason, the variable y is sometimes referred to as the **dependent** variable, while the variable x is called the **independent** variable.

An equation that describes a function may be thought of as a *rule* that tells how the elements of the domain are paired or assigned to the elements of the range. For example, suppose that function g is described by the equation $y = 3x$. If the domain of g is $\{1, 2, 3\}$, then the function rule $y = 3x$ tells us to pair the numbers 1, 2, and 3 with numbers that are three times as great. Thus, $g = \{(1, 3), (2, 6), (3, 9)\}$.

Example

1. Determine whether each set of ordered pairs or sentences describes a function:

   (a) $\{(4, 4), (4, 0), (2, 2)\}$ **(c)** $y = x^3$ **(e)** $y = |x|$

   (b) $\{(1, 5), (0, 5), (2, 3)\}$ **(d)** $y > x$ **(f)** $x = y^2$

Solutions: **(a)** The set of ordered pairs is *not* a function since two ordered pairs, (4, 4) and (4, 0), have the same first member but different second members.
(b) The set of ordered pairs is a function.
(c) For each value of x, the equation produces exactly one value of y. Hence, the equation $y = x^3$ describes a function.
(d) The relation $y > x$ is *not* a function since it includes ordered pairs such as (1, 2) and (1, 3) that have the same value of x paired with different values of y.
(e) The equation $y = |x|$ describes a function since each value of x (positive, negative, or zero) determines exactly one value of y.
(f) The equation $x = y^2$ does *not* describe a function since ordered pairs such as (4, 2) and (4, –2) satisfy the equation but have different values of y for the same value of x.

Describing a Function as a Mapping

In Figure 4.1, the elements -1, 0, 1, and 2 of the domain of function f are paired with or "mapped onto" the corresponding elements of the range, using the function rule $y = x^2$. Since each element x of the domain is paired with x^2 in the range, the *mapping* that describes this function may be represented in symbols as $\mathbf{f: x \rightarrow x^2}$.

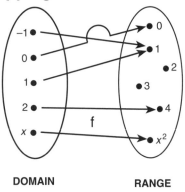

DOMAIN　　　　　　**RANGE**

Figure 4.1 Domain and Range

Function Notation

Functions are usually designated by lower-case letters such as f and g. For any function f the value of y that corresponds to a *particular* value of x is denoted by $f(x)$. If function f is described by the equation $y = 4x$, then the notation $f(2)$ represents the value of y when $x = 2$. If $x = 2$, then $y = 4 \cdot 2 = 8$. Hence $f(2) = 8$. The expression $f(2)$ is read as "f of 2." Similarly, $f(3) = 12$ since, when $x = 3$, $y = 4 \cdot 3 = 12$.

Since y and $f(x)$ mean the same thing, $y = f(x)$. The equation $y = 4x$ may be written as $f(x) = 4x$.

Examples

2. If $y = x^2 + 1$, find f(5).

Solution: The notation $f(5)$ tells us to find the value of y when $x = 5$.

Let $y = f(x)$:　　　$y = f(x) = x^2 + 1$
Replace x by 5:　　$f(5) = 5^2 + 1$
Simplify:　　　　　　$= \mathbf{26}$

3. If $f(x) = x^{\frac{3}{2}} - (x-1)^0$, find f(9).

Solution: Replace x by 9 and simplify:

$$
\begin{aligned}
f(9) &= 9^{\frac{3}{2}} & -(9-1)^0 \\
&= (\sqrt{9})^3 & -8^0 \\
&= 3^3 & -1 \\
&= 27 & -1 \\
&= \mathbf{26}
\end{aligned}
$$

4. If g = {(–2, 5), (–1, 2), (0, 1), (1, 2), (2, 5)}, find g(1).

Solution: The notation g(1) tells us to find the value of *y* in the ordered pair in which *x* = 1. In the ordered pair (1, 2), *x* = 1 and *y* = 2. Hence g(1) = **2**.

5. If $g(t) = t^2$, find:
(a) 3g(2)   **(b)** $[g(-3)]^2$ **(c)** g(4n)   **(d)** g(x + 1)

Solutions:
(a) Let *t* = 2. Since g(2) = 2^2 = 4, then 3[g(2)] = 3[4] = **12**.
(b) Let *t* = –3. Since g(–3) = $(-3)^2$ = 9, then $[g(-3)]^2 = [9]^2 = $ **81**.
(c) Let *t* = 4n and simplify.

$$g(t) = t^2$$
$$g(4n) = (4n)^2$$
$$= 16n^2$$

(d) Let *t* = x + 1 and simplify.

$$g(t) = t^2$$
$$g(x + 1) = (x + 1)^2$$
$$= x^2 + 2x + 1$$

Restricting the Domain and Range

Unless otherwise indicated, the domain and range of a function are the largest possible sets of real numbers. In order that a real-valued function be defined for each number in its domain, it may be necessary to exclude one or more real numbers from the domain. For example, if $y = \frac{x}{x-5}$, then *x* cannot equal 5 since this value makes the denominator 0. Hence the domain of this function consists of all real numbers *except* 5.

To illustrate further, if $y = \sqrt{x-1}$, then *x* must take on values greater than or equal to 1 in order for the radicand to remain nonnegative. Hence the domain of this function consists of all real numbers greater than or equal to 1. Since *y* is equal to the square root of a nonnegative number, *y* is also non-negative. The domain and range of this function can be expressed using set notation as follows:

$$\text{Domain} = \{x: x \geq 1\}$$
$$\text{Range} = \{y: y \geq 0\}$$

Exercise Set 4.1

1–8. For each relation, find the domain and the range.

1. {(–2, 2), (3, 2), (0, 3)}

2. {(–4, 0), (–1, 0), (1, 1)}

3. y = 1 – x

4. $y = \sqrt{x+3}$

5. $y = \sqrt{x-3}$

6. $y = \sqrt{3-x}$

7. $y = \sqrt{x+3}$

8. $y = \dfrac{x}{x^2-1}$

9. Which of the following relations is *not* a function?

    (1) $x = |y|$ (2) $2x + 3y = 6$ (3) $x = \sqrt{y}$ (4) $x = y^3$

10. For each function, express f(4) in simplest form.

    (a) $f(x) = x^2 - 4x + 1$ **(d)** $f(t) = (2t)^{\frac{2}{3}}$

    (b) $f(x) = x^2 - x^{\frac{1}{2}}$ **(e)** $f(x) = \sqrt{x^2 + 9} + \sqrt{9x}$

    (c) $f(s) = (2s)^0 + 2s^0 + 2^s$ **(f)** $y = x^{\frac{3}{2}} + x^{-\frac{1}{2}}$

11. If $s = \{(-2, 4), (-1, 1), (0, 6), (1, -1), (2, 8)\}$, find:

    (a) $s(-2) + s(2)$ **(b)** $3s(0)$ **(c)** $[s(2)]^{\frac{1}{3}}$

12. If $f(x) = x + 2$ and $g(x) = x^2 + 2x - 4$, for which values of x is $f(x) = g(x)$?

13. If $h(t) = (t + 1)^2$, find:

    (a) $h(-1)$ **(b)** $[h(3)]^2$ **(c)** $2h(-4)$ **(d)** $h(2y)$ **(e)** $h(x - 1)$

4.2 RECOGNIZING WHEN A GRAPH IS A FUNCTION

KEY IDEAS

Since a graph consists of a set of ordered pairs, it describes a relation that may or may not be a function.

Vertical-Line Test

In Figure 4.2, a vertical line intersects the graph in more than one point. The graph contains two points that have the same *x*-value but different *y*-values. Thus, the graph does not represent a function.

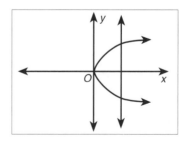

Figure 4.2 Vertical-Line Test

VERTICAL-LINE TEST

A graph represents a function if *no* vertical line intersects it in more than one point. The graph at the right represents a function since it passes the vertical-line test.

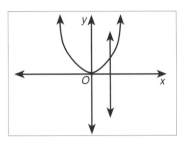

Recognizing Graphs of Quadratic Relations

The graphs of equations of the form

$$ax^2 + by^2 = c \quad (a, b, \text{ and } c \neq 0)$$

are given special names, which are summarized in Table 4.1. In each case the graphs fail the vertical-line test, so they do not represent functions.

Example

Name the graph of each equation:
(a) $4y^2 = 3 + 4x^2$ **(b)** $3x^2 = 18 - 3y^2$ **(c)** $-3x^2 - 5y^2 + 15 = 0$

Solutions: Rewrite each equation in the form $ax^2 + by^2 = c$.
(a) If $4y^2 = 3 + 4x^2$, then $-4x^2 + 4y^2 = 3$. This equation corresponds to the general form $ax^2 + by^2 = c$, where a and b have opposite signs. Hence the graph is a **hyperbola**.
(b) If $3x^2 = 18 - 3y^2$, then $3x^2 + 3y^2 = 18$. This equation corresponds to the general form $ax^2 + by^2 = c$, where a and b are equal and a, b, and c have the same sign. Hence the graph is a **circle**. Notice that dividing each member of the equation by 3 gives $x^2 + y^2 = 6$. Hence the radius of this circle is $\sqrt{6}$.
(c) If $-3x^2 - 5y^2 + 15 = 0$, then $15 = 3x^2 + 5y^2$, which also can be written as $3x^2 + 5y^2 = 15$. This equation corresponds to the general form $ax^2 + by^2 = c$, where $a \neq b$ and a, b, and c have the same sign. Hence the graph is an **ellipse**.

TABLE 4.1 EQUATIONS OF GRAPHS OF QUADRATIC RELATIONS

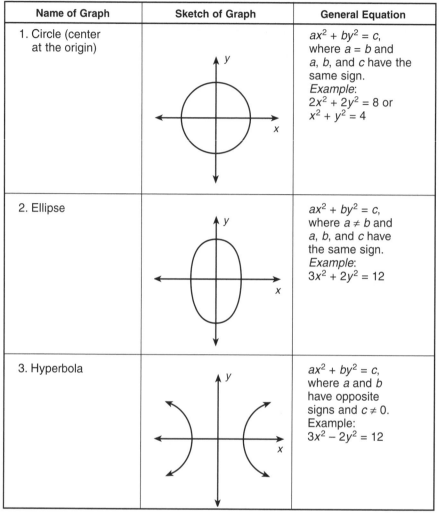

Name of Graph	Sketch of Graph	General Equation
1. Circle (center at the origin)		$ax^2 + by^2 = c$, where $a = b$ and a, b, and c have the same sign. *Example*: $2x^2 + 2y^2 = 8$ or $x^2 + y^2 = 4$
2. Ellipse		$ax^2 + by^2 = c$, where $a \neq b$ and a, b, and c have the same sign. *Example*: $3x^2 + 2y^2 = 12$
3. Hyperbola		$ax^2 + by^2 = c$, where a and b have opposite signs and $c \neq 0$. Example: $3x^2 - 2y^2 = 12$

Exercise Set 4.2

1–9. Name the graph of each relation, and state whether the graph represents a function.

1. $3x^2 = 12 - 3y^2$

2. $4x^2 + 8 = 2y^2$

3. $18 = 3y^2 + 3x^2$

4. $2x^2 - 13 = y$

5. $2x + 2y = 32$

6. $5y^2 = 3 - x^2$

7. $15 - 4x^2 = 4y^2$

8. $x^2 = 2y$

9. $0 = x^2 - (y^2 + 10)$

10–13. State whether each graph represents a function.

10.

12.

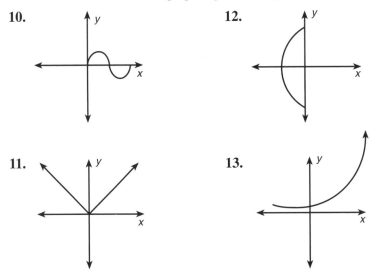

11.

13.

4.3   COMPOSING TWO FUNCTIONS

KEY IDEAS

Functions f and g may be linked together to form a *composite function* by using the output of function g as the input of function f:

The new function is called the **composition** of function g *followed by* function f and is denoted by **f ∘ g**. The function value for this composite function is represented by (f ∘ g) (x) or, equivalently, by f(g(x)).

The composite function that puts the output of function f into function g is called the **composition** of function f *followed by* function g and is denoted by **g ∘ f**. The function value for this composite function is represented by (g ∘ f)(x) or, equivalently, by g(f(x)).

Evaluating Composite Functions

If $f(x) = x^2$ and $g(x) = 3x$, then f(g(2)) is determined by evaluating function g at $x = 2$ and putting the result into function f. Since $g(2) = 3 \cdot 2 = 6$,

$$f(g(2)) = f(6) = 6^2 = \mathbf{36}.$$

If $x = 2$ $g(f(2))$ is determined by evaluating function f at $x = 2$ and putting the result into function g. Since $f(2) = 2^2 = 4$,

$$g(f(2)) = g(4) = 3 \cdot 4 = \mathbf{12}.$$

Notice that $f(g(2))$ and $g(f(2))$ are not equal. *The order in which two functions are composed matters.*

Examples

1. If $f(x) = 2x + 1$ and $g(x) = |x|$, find:
(a) $f(g(-3))$ **(b)** $(g \circ f)(-3)$

Solutions: **(a)** Since $g(-3) = |-3| = 3$,

$$f(g(-3)) = f(3) = 2 \cdot 3 + 1 = \mathbf{7}$$

(b) The expression $(g \circ f)(-3)$ means $g(f(-3))$. If $f(x) = 2x + 1$, then $f(-3)$ $= 2(-3) + 1 = -5$. Since $g(x) = |x|$,

$$g(f(-3)) = g(-5) = |-5| = \mathbf{5.}$$

2. Let $f = \{(1, 2), (3, 8), (5, 4), (7, 8)\}$, and $g = \{(1, 3), (2, 6), (8, 5)\}$. Find:
(a) $f(g(1))$ **(b)** $g(f(7))$ **(c)** $f(g(2))$ **(d)** $g(f(5))$

Solutions: Evaluate by starting with the "inside" function.
(a) Since function g includes the ordered pair $(1, 3)$, then $g(1) = 3$, so $f(g(1)) = f(3)$. Function f includes the ordered pair $(3, 8)$, so $f(3) = 8$. Hence $f(g(1)) = \mathbf{8}$.
(b) $g(f(7)) = g(8) = \mathbf{5}$.
(c) $f(g(2)) = f(6)$. Since 6 is not in the domain of function f, $f(g(2))$ is not defined. In general, in order for $f(g(x))$ to be defined, $g(x)$ must be in the domain of function f.
(d) $g(f(5)) = g(4)$. Since 4 is not in the domain of function g, $g(f(5))$ is not defined. In general, in order for $g(f(x))$ to be defined, $f(x)$ must be in the domain of function g.

Finding an Equation for a Composite Function

If $f(x) = x^2$ and $g(x) = 3x$, then a single equation that defines $f(g(x))$ can be determined as follows:

Write the "outside" function:	$f(x) = [x]^2$
Replace x by the "inside" function:	$f(g(x)) = [g(x)]^2$
Express the right side in terms of x:	$= [3x]^2$
Simplify:	$= \mathbf{9x^2}$

To find an equation for $g(f(x))$, proceed as follows:

Write the "outside" function:	$g(x) = 3[x]$
Replace x by the "inside" function:	$g(f(x)) = 3[f(x)]$
Express the right side in terms of x:	$= 3[x^2]$
Simplify:	$= \mathbf{3x^2}$

Once again, notice that the composition of two functions is *not* a commutative operation since $f(g(x))$ and $g(f(x))$ produce different equations.

Examples

3. Let $f(x) = x^2 + 1$ and $g(x) = \sqrt{x}$, where $x \geq 0$. Find:
(a) $g(f(x))$ **(b)** $f(g(x))$

Solutions: **(a)**
$$g(x) = \sqrt{x}$$
$$g(f(x)) = \sqrt{[f(x)]}$$
$$= \sqrt{x^2 + 1}$$

(b)
$$f(x) = x^2 + 1$$
$$f(g(x)) = [g(x)]^2 + 1$$
$$= [\sqrt{x}]^2 + 1$$
$$= x + 1$$

4. If $f(x) = 2x$, find $f(f(x))$.

Solution: $f(f(x)) = f(2x) = 2[2x] = \mathbf{4x}$.

Exercise Set 4.3

1–6. For the given definitions of functions f and g, find:

(a) $f(g(x))$ **(b)** $g(f(x))$ **(c)** $f(f(x))$ **(d)** $g(g(x))$

1. $f(x) = x^2; g(x) = \dfrac{x}{2}$

2. $f(x) = 2x + 3; g(x) = 3x + 2$

3. $f(x) = \sqrt{x}; g(x) = x^2$

4. $f(x) = x + 1; g(x) = \dfrac{1}{x}$ $(x \neq 0)$

5. $f(x) = x^2; g(x) = 1 - x$

6. $f(x) = 4x - 1; g(x) = \dfrac{x + 1}{4}$

7. If $f(x) = x^3$, find:

(a) $f(f(2))$ **(b)** $f(f(\dfrac{x}{2}))$ **(c)** $f(f(a^2))$.

8. If $f(x) = 2x$ and $g(x) = x^2 + 8$, find all values of x such that $f(g(x)) = g(f(x))$.

9. If $f(x) = 2x + k$ and $g(x) = \dfrac{x-5}{2}$, for what value of k are $f(g(x))$ and $g(f(x))$ always equal?

10. If $f = \{(1, -1), (4, 6), (6, 1)\}$ and $g = \{(-1, 6), (4, 1), (1, 3)\}$, evaluate each of the following, provided that it exists:
(a) $f(g(4))$ **(c)** $g(f(6))$ **(e)** $(f \circ g)(4)$
(b) $g(g(4))$ **(d)** $(g \circ f)(4)$ **(f)** $(f \circ f \circ f)(4)$

4.4 VIEWING TRANSFORMATIONS AS FUNCTIONS

KEY IDEAS

Mathematical functions can be used to describe how objects are flipped (reflected), turned (rotated), slid (translated), and changed in size (dilated). These types of functions are called **transformations**. The set of points of the original figure is in the *domain*, and the corresponding set of points of the new figure is in the *range*. Each point of the new figure is the **image** of exactly one point of the original figure, called the **preimage**.

Transformations as Functions

Under a transformation, each point of a figure is "moved" according to some given rule that may be expressed as a function. This function maps the set of points of the original figure onto the set of image points in such a way that each point of the original figure is paired with exactly one point of the new figure. Furthermore, each point of the new figure (range) corresponds to exactly one point of the original figure (domain). Each type of transformation uses a different function rule for "transforming" the original figure into the new figure.

MATH FACTS

DEFINITION OF TRANSFORMATION

A **transformation** is a one-to-one function whose domain and range are the set of points in the plane.

Line Reflections

Reflecting a figure in a line means flipping it over the line so that its mirror image lies across the line and is the same distance from the line. In Figure 4.3, the reflection of $\triangle ABC$ in line k is $\triangle A'B'C'$. This may be written in function notation as

$$r_k(\triangle ABC) = \triangle A'B'C'.$$

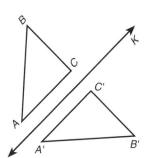

Figure 4.3 Reflecting a Figure in a Line

The function rule associated with this mapping imposes the condition that the image points be located so that line k is the perpendicular bisector of segments $\overline{AA'}$, $\overline{BB'}$, and $\overline{CC'}$. As a result, each angle and each side of $\triangle ABC$ have the same measure as the corresponding parts of $\triangle A'B'C'$. The two triangles are, therefore, congruent. Thus, under a line reflection, segment length and angle measure are unchanged.

If you point to vertex A of $\triangle ABC$, then to vertex B, and then to vertex C, in that order, your finger is moving in a *clockwise* direction. Doing the same with the corresponding vertices of $\triangle A'B'C'$, your finger moves in a *counterclockwise* (reverse) direction. The *orientations* of the two triangles are reversed. It is this property of reflections that accounts for mirror images of objects appearing "backward" in comparison to the original figure.

MATH FACTS

PROPERTIES OF LINE REFLECTIONS

- Preserve collinearity and betweenness (ordering) of points.
- Preserve distance and angle measure.
- Produce an image congruent to the original figure.
- Do *not* preserve orientation.

Rotations

Rotating a figure means turning it a specified number of degrees about some fixed point, called the **center of rotation**. The amount of turn is called the

angle of rotation. *Positive* angles of rotation turn figures in a *counterclockwise* direction. *Negative* angles of rotation produce *clockwise* turns. In Figure 4.4, the image of $\triangle ABC$ after it is rotated $x°$ in the counterclockwise direction about center O is $\triangle A'B'C'$. Triangle $A'B'C'$ is located in such a way that:

$m\angle AOA' = x$ and $OA = OA'$
$m\angle BOB' = x$ and $OB = OB'$
$m\angle COC' = x$ and $OC = OC'$

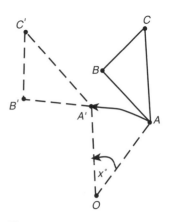

Figure 4.4 Rotating a Figure

In symbols,

$$R_{O,x°}(\triangle ABC) = \triangle A'B'C'.$$

Notice that a rotation is represented by a capital R. The center and the amount of rotation are written as subscripts after the letter R and one-half line below it. Sometimes $R_{O,x°}$ is written as $\text{Rot}_{O,x°}$. When a particular point is understood to be the center of rotation, it may be convenient to omit it and to write $R_{x°}$ instead of $R_{O,x°}$.

Translations

A translation "moves" a figure a fixed distance in a specified direction. A figure and its translated image are congruent. If point (x, y) is translated h units in the horizontal direction and k units in the vertical direction, as shown in Figure 4.5, then its image is determined according to the function rule:

$$T_{h,k}(x,y) = (x + h, y + k).$$

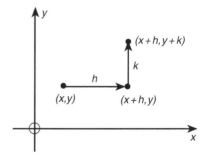

Figure 4.5 Translating a Figure

Examples

1. What is the image of point $(-3, 4)$ under the translation $T_{5,-1}$?

Solution: $T_{5,-1}(-3, 4) = (-3 + 5, 4 + (-1)) = \mathbf{(2, 3)}$

2. If the image of $(-4, 1)$ under a translation is $(0, -4)$, what are the coordinates of the image of $(2, 3)$ under the same translation?

Solution: Since $T_{h,k}(-4, 1) = (-4 + h, 1 + k) = (0, -4)$,

$$-4 + h = 0 \quad \text{or} \quad h = 4, \quad \text{and} \quad 1 + k = -4 \quad \text{or} \quad k = -5.$$

Hence $T_{4,-5}(2, 3) = (2 + 4, 3 - 5) = \textbf{(6, -2)}$.

Dilations

A **dilation** of a figure is a size transformation that changes distance while preserving angle measure. The size transformation of a figure that results from viewing it with a magnifying glass is an example of a dilation. Reflections, rotations, and translations produce images *congruent* to the original figures, while dilations produce *similar* figures.

Under a dilation with center $O\,(0, 0)$ and magnitude k, the image of $A(x, y)$ is $A'(kx, ky)$, as can be indicated by writing

$$D_k A(x, y) = A'(kx, ky).$$

The scale factor k can be any nonzero real number. As shown in Figure 4.6, if $k < 0$, then A' is located on the ray opposite $\overrightarrow{OA}$.

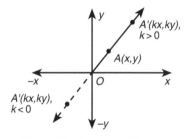

Figure 4.6 Dilating a Figure

=== **MATH FACTS** ===

SIZE TRANSFORMATIONS OF GRAPHS

To find an equation of the dilation of a graph with positive scale factor k, replace x by $\frac{x}{k}$ and y by $\frac{y}{k}$ in the original equation of the graph. For example, the image of the circle $x^2 + y^2 = 9$ under a dilation with a scale factor of 2 is the circle $\left(\frac{x}{2}\right)^2 + \left(\frac{y}{2}\right)^2 = 9$ or, in simpler form, $x^2 + y^2 = 36$.

Examples

3. What are the coordinates of the image of $(-3, 1)$ under dilation D_2?

Solution: In general, $D_2(x, y) = (2x, 2y)$. Hence

$$D_2(-3, 1) = [2 \cdot (-3), 2 \cdot 1] = \textbf{(-6, 2)}.$$

4. If $D_k(9, 3) = (6, 2)$, what is the constant of dilation?

Solution: In general, $D_k (a, b) = (ka, kb)$. Since $D_k (9, 3) = (9k, 3k) = (6, 2)$ then $9k = 6$ and $3k = 2$. Solve either equation for k:

$$3k = 2$$
$$k = \frac{2}{3}$$

5. What is an equation of the image of the graph of the circle $x^2 + y^2 = 64$ under a size transformation of magnitude $\frac{1}{2}$?

Solution: An equation of the image of the original circle has the general form

$$\left(\frac{x}{k}\right)^2 + \left(\frac{y}{k}\right)^2 = 64.$$

Since the magnitude of the transformation is $\frac{1}{2}$, let $k = \frac{1}{2}$.

$$\left(\frac{x}{\frac{1}{2}}\right)^2 + \left(\frac{y}{\frac{1}{2}}\right)^2 = 64$$
$$(2x)^2 + (2y)^2 = 64$$
$$4x^2 + 4y^2 = 64$$
$$x^2 + y^2 = \frac{64}{4} = 16$$

Hence an equation of the image of the original circle is $x^2 + y^2 = 16$.

Exercise Set 4.4

1. Determine the coordinates of the image of point $(2, -1)$ under each of the following translations:
(a) $T_{0,3}$ (b) $T_{-3,0}$ (c) $T_{-2,4}$ (d) $T_{-5,1}$ (e) $T_{-4,-2}$

2. If the image of $(-1, 5)$ under a translation is $(2, 1)$, find the coordinates of the image of each point under the same translation:
(a) $(-1, 2)$ (b) $(1, -5)$ (c) $(3, 4)$ (d) $(4, 3)$ (e) $(-6, -2)$

3. Find the coordinates of the image of $(-8, -6)$ under each of the following dilations:
(a) D_2 (b) $D_{\frac{1}{2}}$ (c) D_1 (d) D_{-3}

4. If the image of $(4, 6)$ under a certain dilation is $(6, 9)$, find the coordinates of the image of each point under the same dilation:
(a) $(0, 2)$ (b) $(8, 0)$ (c) $(10, 4)$ (d) $(-2, -4)$ (e) $(6, 9)$

4.5 REFLECTING AND ROTATING USING COORDINATES

$$\wedge \atop \text{KEY IDEAS} \atop /\qquad\backslash$$

The coordinates of the images of certain types of reflections and rotations in the coordinate plane can be easily located using special function mapping rules.

Reflecting Using Coordinates

In Figure 4.7, point $A(a, b)$ is reflected in the origin. Its image is determined according to the mapping

$$A(a, b) \rightarrow A'(-a, -b).$$

When this mapping is used, the origin is the midpoint of $\overline{AA'}$.

The mapping rules for reflecting points in special lines in the coordinate plane are summarized in Table 4.2 and illustrated in Figure 4.8.

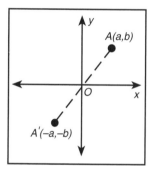

Figure 4.7 Reflecting Using Coordinates

TABLE 4.2 REFLECTING POINTS IN SPECIAL LINES IN THE COORDINATE PLANE

Line of Reflection	Mapping Rule
1. x-axis 2. y-axis	1. $(a, b) \rightarrow (a, -b)$ 2. $(a, b) \rightarrow (-a, b)$
3. $y = k$ 4. $x = h$	3. $(a, b) \rightarrow [a, (2k - b)]$ 4. $(a, b) \rightarrow [(2h - a), b]$
5. $y = x$ 6. $y = -x$	5. $(a, b) \rightarrow (b, a)$ 6. $(a, b) \rightarrow (-b, -a)$

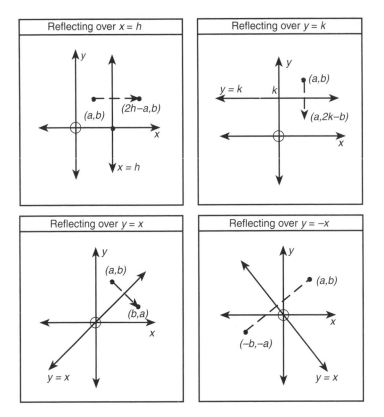

Figure 4.8 Graphing Reflections of (a, b) over the Lines $x = h$, $y = k$, $y = x$, and $y = -x$. If $h = 0$, the line of reflection is the y-axis and the coordinates of the image point simplify to $(-a, b)$. If $k = 0$, the line of reflection is the x-axis and the coordinates of the image point simplify to $(a, -b)$.

Example

1. Find the image of a reflection of $A(3, 4)$ in each of the following lines:
(a) $y = -x$ **(b)** $x = 2$ **(c)** $y = -1$

Solutions: **(a)** If (a, b) is reflected in the line $y = -x$, its image is $(-b, -a)$. Let $a = 3$ and $b = 4$. Then

$$(3, 4) \xrightarrow{\;r_{y=-x}\;} (-4, -3).$$

(b) If (a, b) is reflected in the vertical line $x = h$, its image is $[2h - a), b]$. Let $h = 2$, $a = 3$, and $b = 4$. Then

$$(3, 4) \xrightarrow{\;r_{x=2}\;} [(2 \cdot 2 - 3), 4)] = (1, 4).$$

(c) If (a, b) is reflected in the horizontal line $y = k$, its image is $[(a, (2k - b)]$. Let $k = -1$, $a = 3$, and $b = 4$. Then

$$(3, 4) \xrightarrow{\;r_{y=-1}\;} [3, (2(-1) - 4)] = (3, -6).$$

Rotating Using Coordinates

In Figure 4.9, rectangle $AB'C'D'$ is the image of rectangle $ABCD$ under a 90° counterclockwise rotation about the origin. Compare the coordinates of corresponding vertices of the two rectangles. For example,

$$C(6, 3) \rightarrow C'(-3, 6).$$

In general, under a 90° rotation (a, b) is mapped onto $(-b, a)$.

The coordinates of the images of points rotated about the origin through angles that are multiples of 90° can be determined using the function rules given in Table 4.3.

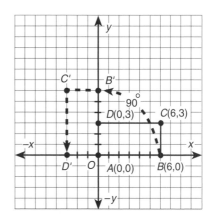

Figure 4.9 Rotation Through Angles That Are Multiples of 90°

TABLE 4.3 FUNCTION RULES FOR SPECIAL ROTATIONS

$$R_{90°}(a, b) = (-b, a)$$
$$R_{180°}(a, b) = (-a, -b)$$
$$R_{270°}(a, b) = (b, -a)$$

You should verify the following:

- Rotating a point 360° about the origin produces an image that coincides with the original point.
- Rotating a point –90° about the origin is equivalent to rotating the point 270° about the origin. In general, a rotation of x degrees in the clockwise direction ($x < 0$) is equivalent to a rotation of $360 - |x|$ degrees in the counterclockwise direction.

Examples

2. What is the image of point $(-1, 5)$ under a rotation of 90° about the origin in the counterclockwise direction?

Solution: In general, $R_{90°}(x, y) = (-y, x)$. Hence **(–1, 5) → (–5, –1)**.

3. Under a counterclockwise rotation about the origin, the image of $(-2, 4)$ is $(4, 2)$. What is the smallest possible measure of the angle of rotation?

Solution: The coordinates of the image of $(-2, 4)$ are determined according to the rule $(x, y) \rightarrow (y, -x)$, where $x = -2$ and $y = 4$. This mapping rule defines a counterclockwise rotation of **270°** about the origin.

79

4. Which rotation is equivalent to $R_{-150°}$?
(1) $R_{150°}$ (2) $R_{-210°}$ (3) $R_{210°}$ (4) $R_{510°}$

Solution: A rotation of $-150°$ is equivalent to a rotation of $360 - |-150|$ $= 360 - 150 = 210°$. The correct choice is (3).

Half-Turns

Rotating point $A(a, b)$ $180°$ about the origin and reflecting point A in the origin produce images having the same coordinates, namely, $(-a, -b)$. These two transformations are, therefore, equivalent. A rotation of $180°$ about any point P is called a **half-turn** and is equivalent to a reflection in point P.

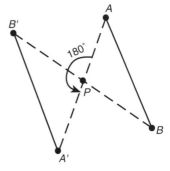

In Figure 4.10, the image of a half-turn of $\overline{AB}$ about center P is the line segment whose endpoints are the reflections of points A and B in point P. Points A' and B' are determined to that P is the midpoint of $\overline{AA'}$ and $\overline{BB'}$.

Figure 4.10 A Half-Turn
$R_{P,180°}: \overline{AB} \to \overline{A'B'}$

Exercise Set 4.5

1. Find the image of a reflection of $P(-1, 3)$ in each of the following:
(a) $(0, 0)$ (c) y-axis (e) $y = -1$
(b) x-axis (d) $y = x$ (f) $x = 2$

2. Find the image of a reflection of $A(1, 4)$ in each line:
(a) $x = 0$ (c) $y = x$ (e) $y = 2$
(b) $y = 0$ (d) $y = -x$ (f) $x = -1$

3. Find the image of each point after a reflection in the line $x = 3$ followed by a reflection in the origin:
(a) $(1, 1)$ (b) $(-1, 2)$ (c) $(3, -1)$ (d) $(2, 0)$ (e) $(0, 0)$

4. Find the image of each point after a reflection in the line $y = 1$ followed by a reflection in the line $y = x$:
(a) $(3, 3)$ (b) $(2, -1)$ (c) $(-1, 4)$ (d) $(0, 1)$ (e) $(0, 0)$

5. For each rotation, find the *smallest* positive angle of rotation that produces an equivalent rotation about the same center:
(a) $R_{-180°}$ (b) $R_{-230°}$ (c) $R_{-65°}$

6. Find the image of point $(3, -2)$ under each rotation about the origin:
   (a) $R_{90°}$ (b) $R_{180°}$ (c) $R_{270°}$ (d) $R_{360°}$

7. Find the image of point $(-4, 1)$ under each rotation about the origin:
   (a) $R_{-90°}$ (b) $R_{-180°}$ (c) $R_{-270°}$ (d) $R_{-360°}$

8. Which transformation does *not* preserve distance?
   (1) dilation   (2) translation   (3) rotation   (4) reflection

9. Which transformation of $P(x, y)$ is *not* equivalent to the other three transformations?
   (1) a reflection of $P(x, y)$ in the origin
   (2) the translation $P(x, y) \rightarrow P'(x - 1, y - 1)$
   (3) a dilation of $P(x, y)$ with center at the origin and a scale factor of -1
   (4) a rotation of $P(x, y)$ $180°$ about the origin

10. What is an equation of the line that passes through the origin and contains the image of $T_{2,3}(1, 3)$?

11. A sequence of transformations that reflect point P through the origin, over the x-axis, and then over the line $y = x$ is equivalent to a rotation about the origin. What is the amount of the rotation?

12. (a) On graph paper, draw and label the line segment determined by $A(4, 1)$ and $B(5, 4)$.
    (b) Graph $\overline{A'B'}$, the image of $\overline{AB}$, after a reflection over line $y = x$.
    (c) Graph $\overline{A''B''}$, the image of $\overline{A'B'}$, after the transformation defined by the mapping $(x, y) \rightarrow (x - 5, y - 5)$.
    (d) Graph $\overline{A'''B'''}$, the image of $\overline{A''B''}$, after a reflection through the origin.
    (e) Write a translation that will map $\overline{A'B'}$ onto $\overline{B'''A'''}$.

13. (a) On graph paper, draw and label $\triangle ABC$, whose vertices are $A(3, 1)$, $B(4, 3)$, and $C(6, 1)$.
    (b) Draw the image of $\triangle ABC$ under a reflection in the line $y = x$. What are the coordinates of $\triangle A'B'C'$, the image of $\triangle ABC$?
    (c) Draw the image of $\triangle A'B'C'$ under a rotation about the origin of $90°$ in the counterclockwise direction. What are the coordinates of $\triangle A''B''C''$, the image of $\triangle A'B'C'$?
    (d) Draw the image $\triangle A''B''C''$ under a reflection in the origin. What are the coordinates of $\triangle A'''B'''C'''$, the image of $\triangle A''B''C''$?

4.6 COMPOSING TRANSFORMATIONS

∧
=== KEY IDEAS ===
╱   ╲

Geometric transformations, like algebraic functions, may be composed. A composite transformation is evaluated by working from right to left. For example, to evaluate $r_{x\text{-axis}} \circ r_{y\text{-axis}}$ begin by reflecting in the y-axis:

$$(x, y) \xrightarrow{\ r_{y-\text{axis}}\ } (-x, y) \xrightarrow{\ r_{x-\text{axis}}\ } (-x, -y).$$

Some composite transformations produce familiar transformations. For example, the image point $(-x, -y)$ is also obtained by reflecting (x, y) in the origin. Hence the composite of reflections in the coordinate axes is equivalent to a reflection in the origin.

Evaluating Composite Transformations

In composing transformations, the order in which the transformations are performed matters, as Example 1 illustrates. Example 2 shows that more than two functions may be composed.

Examples

1. Find the coordinates of the image of $P(-2, 4)$ under each composite transformation:

(a) $r_{y=x} \circ r_{y\text{-axis}}$ **(b)** $r_{y\text{-axis}} \circ r_{y=x}$

Solutions: **(a)** In general,

$$r_{y\text{-axis}}(x, y) = (-x, y) \quad \text{and} \quad r_{y=x}(x, y) = (y, x).$$

Perform $r_{y\text{-axis}}$ first, followed by $r_{y=x}$:

$$(-2, 4) \xrightarrow{\ r_{y-\text{axis}}\ } (2, 4) \xrightarrow{\ r_{y=x}\ } (4, 2).$$

Under the composite transformation, the coordinates of the image of $P(-2, 4)$ are **(−4, −2)**.

(b) Perform $r_{y=x}$, followed by $r_{y\text{-axis}}$:

$$(-2, 4) \xrightarrow{\ r_{y=x}\ } (4, -2) \xrightarrow{\ r_{y-\text{axis}}\ } (-4, -2).$$

Under the composite transformation, the coordinates of the image of $P(-2, 4)$ are **(−4, −2)**.

2. In the accompanying figure, p and q are lines of symmetry for regular hexagon $ABCDEF$ intersecting at point O, the center of the hexagon. Determine the image of each composite transformation:

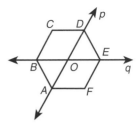

(a) $r_p \circ r_q \, (\overline{AB})$ (b) $r_q \circ r_p \circ r_q \, (D)$

Solutions: **(a)** Reflect $\overline{AB}$ in line q, followed by the reflection of its image in line p.

$$\overline{AB} \xrightarrow{\;r_q\;} \overline{CB} \xrightarrow{\;r_p\;} \overline{EF}$$

(b) When the composite is evaluated from right to left, point D is reflected in line q, followed by a reflection in line p, followed by a reflection in line q.

$$D \xrightarrow{\;r_q\;} F \xrightarrow{\;r_p\;} B \xrightarrow{\;r_q\;}$$

Consecutive Rotations and Translations

Composing two rotations or two translations results in a transformation of the same type.

- *Consecutive Rotations.* A rotation of x degrees followed by a rotation of y degrees about the same center produces a rotation of $x + y$ degrees with the same center:

$$R_y \circ R_x = R_{x+y}.$$

  For example, a rotation of $30°$ about point O followed by a rotation of $40°$ about the same point is equivalent to a single rotation of $70°$ about point O.

- *Consecutive Translations.* Translation $T_{a,b}$ followed by translation $T_{c,d}$ produces a translation that maps point (x, y) of the original figure onto point $(x + a + c, y + b + d)$. In general,

$$T_{c,d} \circ T_{a,b}(x,y) = (x + a + c, \, y + b + d).$$

  For example, translation $T_{1,2}$ followed by translation $T_{3,4}$ is equivalent to the single translation $T_{4,6}$.

Consecutive Reflections

Composing two line reflections produces familiar types of transformations.

- *Parallel Reflecting Lines.* Consecutive reflections in lines that are parallel *translate* the original figure. In Figure 4.11, lines p and q are parallel. Triangle ABC is reflected in line p and its image is then reflected in line q, producing $\triangle A''B''C''$. Comparing the positions of $\triangle ABC$ and $A''B''C''$ reveals that $\triangle ABC$ is "moved" over line p and then over line q in a direction that is perpendicular to lines p and q. Furthermore, the distance that $\triangle ABC$ is moved is twice the distance between the parallel lines.
- *Intersecting Reflecting Lines.* Consecutive reflections in lines that intersect *rotate* the original figure so that:
  (1) The center of rotation is the point at which reflecting lines intersect.
  (2) The amount of rotation is twice the measure of the angle formed by the lines of reflection. This is illustrated in Figure 4.12.

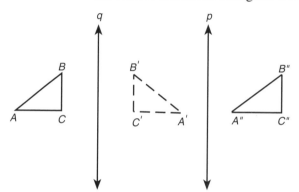

Figure 4.11 Composing Two Line Reflections in Parallel Lines

$$r_p \circ r_q (\triangle ABC) = \triangle A''B''C''$$

Direction of Translation

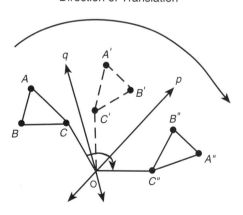

Figure 4.11 Composing Two Line Reflections in Intersecting Lines

$$r_p \circ r_q (\triangle ABC) = \triangle A''B''C''$$

COMPOSING TWO LINE REFLECTIONS

- If lines p and q are parallel, $r_p \circ r_q$ is a *translation*.
- If lines p and q intersect, $r_p \circ r_q$ is a *rotation*.

Example

3. If $(9, -1)$ is the image under the composite transformation $T_{h,k} \circ T_{4,3}$ $(2, -2)$, find the values of h and k.

Solution:

$$(2, -2) \xrightarrow{T_{4,3}} (6, 1) \xrightarrow{T_{h,k}} (6 + h, 1 + k) = (9, -1)$$

Hence $6 + h = 9$ and $1 + k = -1$, so $h = \mathbf{3}$ and $k = \mathbf{-2}$.

Glide Reflections

Sliding a reflected image in a direction parallel to the line of reflection produces a *glide reflection*, as shown in Figure 4.13.

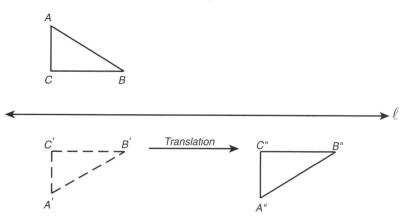

Figure 4.13 Glide Reflection   Triangle $A''B''C''$ is the image of $\triangle ABC$ after a reflection in line ℓ followed by a translation in a direction parallel to line ℓ. Triangle $A''B''C''$ is also the image of $\triangle ABC$ when the reflection follows the translation.

DEFINITION OF GLIDE REFLECTION

A **glide reflection** is the composite of a line reflection and of a translation whose direction is parallel to the reflecting line.

Since any translation may be expressed as the composition of reflections in parallel lines, a glide reflection may be thought of as the composition of reflections in parallel lines and a third reflection in a line that is perpendicular to the parallel lines.

Isometry

A line reflection, a rotation, and a translation each preserves distance and is, therefore, an *isometry* (plural: *isometries*). A dilation, however, is *not* an isometry since it does *not* preserve distance.

DEFINITION OF ISOMETRY

An **isometry** is a transformation that preserves distance.

If an isometry preserves orientation, it is called a **direct isometry**. Rotations and translations preserve orientation and are, therefore, direct isometries. An **opposite isometry** is an isometry in which orientation changes. A line reflection reverses orientation and is, therefore, an opposite isometry.

Examples

4. Which transformation is *not* an isometry?

(1) $(x, y) \rightarrow (x - 1, y + 2)$ (3) $(x, y) \rightarrow \left(\dfrac{1}{2}x, \dfrac{1}{2}y \right)$

(2) $(x, y) \rightarrow (x, -y)$ (4) $(x, y) \rightarrow (-y, -x)$

Solution: An isometry preserves distance. Choice (1) is a translation, choice (2) is a reflection in the x-axis, choice (4) is a reflection in the line $y = -x$. Each of these transformations preserves distance.

The transformation described by the mapping $(x, y) \rightarrow \left(\dfrac{1}{2}x, \dfrac{1}{2}y\right)$ is a dilation, which does *not* preserve distance since the scale factor is $\dfrac{1}{2}$. The correct choice is **(3)**.

5. Which of the following transformations is *not* a direct isometry?
(1) composite of two translations
(2) composite of two reflections in parallel lines
(3) composite of two reflections in intersecting lines
(4) glide reflection

Solution: A direct isometry preserves orientation. Each of choices (1) and (2) produces a translation, which preserves orientation and therefore is a direct isometry. Choice (3) produces a rotation, and a rotation is a direct isometry.
   A glide reflection is the composite of a reflection and a translation. Since a translation preserves orientation while a reflection reverses it, a glide reflection reverses orientation and therefore is not a direct isometry. The correct choice is **(4)**.

Exercise Set 4.6

1. Find the coordinates of the image of each point under the composite transformation $r_{y=x} \circ r_{x\text{-axis}}$:
(a) $(4, 7)$ (b) $(5, -2)$ (c) $(0, 3)$ (d) $(-4, 0)$ (e) $(-2, -3)$

2. Find the coordinates of the image of each point under the composite transformation $r_{y=1} \circ r_{y\text{-axis}}$:
(a) $(2, 0)$ (b) $(0, -1)$ (c) $(5, -1)$ (d) $(-2, 5)$ (e) $(-3, -4)$

3. Given point $A(-2, 5)$, find the coordinates of the image of each composite transformation:
(a) $T_{2,2} \circ T_{-1,3}(A)$ (d) $r_{x\text{-axis}} \circ T_{2,-4}(A)$
(b) $T_{-1,0} \circ T_{0,-1}(A)$ (e) $T_{2,-3} \circ r_{y=1}(A)$
(c) $R_{90°} \circ r_{y=x}(A)$ (f) $r_{x\text{-axis}} \circ r_{y=x} \circ r_{y\text{-axis}}(A)$

4. If $(-4, 8)$ is the image under the composite transformation $T_{h,3} \circ T_{-2,k}(-3, 0)$, find the values of h and k.

5. Which transformation is *not* an isometry?
(1) $J: (x, y) \rightarrow (x + 2, y + 2)$ (3) $L: (x, y) \rightarrow (y, -x)$
(2) $K: (x, y) \rightarrow (2x, 2y)$ (4) $M: (x, y) \rightarrow (-x, -y)$

6. Which transformation is an opposite isometry?
(1) $S: (x, y) \rightarrow (x - 2, y - 2)$ (3) $U: (x, y) \rightarrow (-y, x)$
(2) $T: (x, y) \rightarrow (y, x)$ (4) $W: (x, y) \rightarrow (y, -x)$

7. Which composite transformation does *not* represent a glide reflection?
   (1) $r_{x\text{-axis}} \circ T_{4,0}$ (3) $r_{y=x} \circ T_{2,4}$
   (2) $r_{y\text{-axis}} \circ T_{0,4}$ (4) $r_{x=1} \circ r_{y=3} \circ r_{x=5}$

8. In the accompanying figure, lines ℓ and m are lines of symmetry. Find:
   (a) $r_m \circ r_\ell(\overline{FG})$ **(b)** $r_\ell \circ r_m(\overline{BC})$ **(c)** $r_m \circ r_\ell \circ r_m(H)$

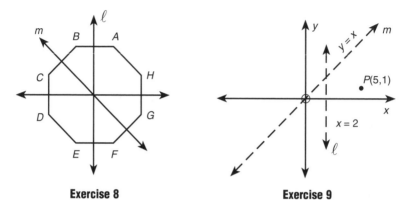

Exercise 8   Exercise 9

9. In the accompanying figure, lines ℓ and m are lines of symmetry
   where line m refers to the line $y = x$. Find:
   (a) $r_\ell \circ r_m(P)$ **(b)** $r_m \circ r_\ell(P)$ **(c)** $r_\ell \circ r_m \circ r_{x\text{-axis}}(P)$

10. **(a)** On graph paper, graph and label the triangle whose vertices are
    $A(6, 1)$, $B(8, 5)$, and $C(5, 4)$.
    (b) Graph and state the coordinates of $\triangle A'B'C'$, the image of $\triangle ABC$ in
    a reflection over the line $y = x$.
    (c) Graph and state the coordinates of $\triangle A''B''C''$, the image of $\triangle ABC$
    after the composite transformation $r_{y\text{-axis}} \circ r_{x\text{-axis}}$ $(\triangle ABC)$.
    (d) Find the coordinates of $\triangle A'''B'''C'''$, the image of $\triangle ABC$ after a
    translation that maps $P(0,0)$ onto $P'(3, -1)$.

11. **(a)** On graph paper, graph and label the triangle whose vertices are
    $A(4, 0)$, $B(8, 1)$ and $C(8, 4)$.
    (b) Graph and state the coordinates of $\triangle A'B'C'$, the image of $\triangle ABC$
    after the composite transformation $r_{x=0} \circ r_{y=x}(\triangle ABC)$.
    (c) Which single type of transformation maps $\triangle ABC$ onto $\triangle A'B'C'$?
    (1) rotation   (3) glide reflection
    (2) dilation   (4) translation
    (d) Graph and state the coordinates of $\triangle A''B''C''$, the image of $\triangle ABC$
    after the composite transformation $r_{y=-4} \circ r_{y=0}(\triangle ABC)$.
    (e) Which single type of transformation maps $\triangle ABC$ onto $\triangle A''B''C''$?
    (1) rotation   (3) glide reflection
    (2) dilation   (4) translation

4.7 FINDING THE INVERSE OF A FUNCTION

$$\wedge$$
$$=\!=\!=\!=\!=\!=\!=\!=\!=\!=\!=\!=\!= \text{KEY IDEAS} =\!=\!=\!=\!=\!=\!=\!=\!=\!=\!=\!=$$
$$/\quad\quad\backslash$$

In each ordered pair of the function

$$f = \{(1,2),(2,4),(3,6),(4,8)\}.$$

the y-value is two times the x-value. To undo or reverse the effect of this function, start with the y-value, and halve it to get back the original x-value. The result is the function

$$f^{-1} = \{(2,1), (4,2), (6,3),(8,4)\}$$

The -1 in f^{-1} is *not* an exponent. The expression f^{-1} is read as "the **inverse** of function f." The inverse of a function is formed by interchanging the x- and y-members of each ordered pair of the function.

Forming Inverse Functions

If a function is described by a set of ordered pairs, its inverse is formed by switching the positions of the x-and y-values in each ordered pair. Thus, if $f = \{(-1, 0), (0, 1), (1, 2)\}$, then the inverse of function f is the function

$$f^{-1} = \{(0, -1), (1, 0), (2, 1)\}.$$

If a function is described by an equation, its inverse is formed by (1) interchanging x and y; and then (2) solving for y in terms of x. To find the inverse of $2x - y = 3$, proceed as follows:

Interchange x and y: $2y - x = 3$
Solve for y: $2y = x + 3$
$$y = \frac{x+3}{2}$$

Example

1. Find the inverse of $f(x) = x - 2$.

Solution:
Replace f(x) by y: $y = x - 2$
Interchange x and y: $x = y - 2$
Solve for y: $y = x + 2$
Replace y by $f^{-1}(x)$: $f^{-1}(x) = x + 2$ or $y = x + 2$

One-to-One Functions

If f = {(2, 4), (3, 9)}, then its inverse is f^{-1} = {(4, 2), (9, 3)}. Since function f has the property that no two of its ordered pairs have the same *y*-value, its inverse f^{-1} is a function. The inverse of a function, however, is not always a function. For example, if g = {(1, 5), (3, 5)}, then its inverse is {(5, 1), (5, 3)}. Although g is a function, its inverse is not a function.

Functions that have inverses that are functions are called *one-to-one functions*. Function f is a one-to-one function, but function g is *not* a one-to-one function.

MATH FACTS

DEFINITION OF ONE-TO-ONE FUNCTION

A **one-to-one function** is a function in which no two ordered pairs have the same *y*-value.

It follows that:

- If a function is one-to-one, then its inverse is also a function.
- If a function is not one-to-one, then its inverse is *not* a function.

Example

2. Determine whether each function is a one-to-one function. If the function is one-to-one, determine its inverse.
(a) $y = 4x$ **(b)** $y = |x|$

Solutions: **(a)** The function described by the equation $y = 4x$ is one-to-one, since no value of x that is substituted into the equation $y = 4x$ ever produces two different values for y. The inverse is formed by interchanging x and y and then solving for y:

$$x = 4y$$
$$y = \frac{x}{4}$$

(b) The absolute-value function includes ordered pairs such as (2, 2) and (–2, 2). Hence $y = |x|$ does *not* describe a one-to-one function, so its inverse is *not* a function.

Horizontal-Line Test

Since, in Figure 4.14, a horizontal line intersects the accompanying parabola in two different points, the graph contains two ordered pairs with the same y-value. Thus, the graph does not represent a one-to-one function.

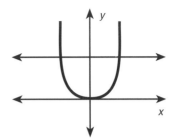

Figure 4.14 Horizontal-Line Test

MATH FACTS

HORIZONTAL-LINE TEST

A function is a one-to-one function if no horizontal line intersects its graph in more than one point. The graph at the right passes the horizontal-line test and therefore has an inverse function.

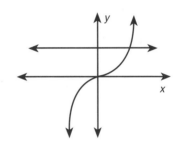

Symmetry and Inverse Functions

For every point (a, b) contained on the graph of a one-to-one function, the corresponding point (b, a) is found on the graph of its inverse, as shown in Figure 4.15. Also, the reflection of point (a, b) in the line $y = x$ is point (b, a). Thus, the graphs of a function and its inverse are symmetric with respect to the line $y = x$, and either graph may be obtained by reflecting the other graph in the line $y = x$.

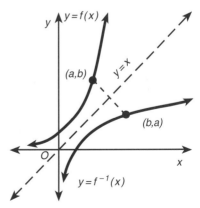

Figure 4.15 Symmetry and Inverse Functions

Example

3. If $f(x) = x^2$ and $x \geq 0$, find $f^{-1}(x)$.

Solution: Since the domain is restricted to nonnegative values, the graph of $f(x) = x^2$ is confined to Quadrant I, as shown in the acompany-
ing diagram. The graph passes the
horizontal-line test, so proceed to
find the inverse function.

Write original equation: $y = x^2$
Interchange x and y: $x = y^2$
Solve for y: $y = \pm\sqrt{x}$
   Since the domain of the original
function (nonnegative numbers) becomes the range of the inverse function, y must also be nonnegative. Hence drop the $\pm$ sign in front of $\sqrt{x}$
and write $y = \mathbf{f^{-1}(x)} = \sqrt{x}$.

The Identity Function

If $i(x) = x$, the composition of function i with any other function f gives back
the original function f. Hence $i(x) = x$ is called the **identity function.** For
example, if f = $\{(1, 1), (2, 4), (3, 9)\}$, and $i(x) = x$, then:

$f(i(x))$	$i(f(x))$
$f(i(1)) = f(1) = 1$	$i(f(1)) = i(1) = 1$
$f(i(2)) = f(2) = 4$	$i(f(2)) = i(4) = 4$
$f(i(3)) = f(3) = 9$	$i(f(3)) = i(9) = 9$

Notice that, for all x for which f is defined,

$$f(i(x)) = i(f(x)) = y = f(x).$$

Composing Inverse Functions

Performing an arithmetic operation with a number and its inverse under that
operation always produces the identity element for that operation. For example,

$$4 + (-4) = 0 \quad \text{and} \quad 4 \times \frac{1}{4} = 1.$$

Similarly, composing a function and its inverse, in any order, produces the
identity function $i(x) = x$. Thus functions f and g are inverses if $f(g(x)) = x$
and $g(f(x)) = x$.

Examples

4. Prove that $f(x) = 1 - x^3$ and $g(x) = \sqrt{1-x}$ are inverse functions.

Solution: Show that $f(g(x)) = x$ and $g(f(x)) = x$.

$$f(g(x)) = 1 - [g(x)]^3 \qquad\qquad g(f(x)) = \sqrt[3]{1 - f(x)}$$
$$= 1 - (\sqrt[3]{1-x})^3 \qquad\qquad\quad = \sqrt[3]{1 - (1 - x^3)}$$
$$= 1 - (1 - x) \qquad\qquad\qquad\quad = \sqrt[3]{x^3}$$
$$= x \qquad\qquad\qquad\qquad\qquad\quad = x$$

Since $f(g(x)) = g(f(x)) = x$, **f and g are inverses**.

5. If $f(x) = 1.9x^3 - 17$, find $f(f^{-1}(6.4))$.

Solution: Since $f(f^{-1}(x)) = x$, then $f(f^{-1}(6.4)) = $ **6.4**.

Exercise Set 4.7

1–8. For each function, find its inverse, provided that it exists. If it does not exist, tell why.

1. $f = \{(-1, 2), (2, 3), (4, 5), (-2, 3)\}$
2. $g = \{(-2, 5), (5, -2), (1, 2)\}$
3. $y = 3 - x$
4. $g(x) = x^3 + 1$

5. $f(x) = 3x + 2$
6. $h(x) = \sqrt{x^2 + 1}$
7. $2x + 3y = 5$
8. $f(x) = \dfrac{x^2}{2} + 4$

9–10. For each pair, prove that the functions are inverse.

9. $f(x) = 7x + 1$ and $g(x) = \dfrac{x-1}{7}$

10. $f(x) = 2 - \dfrac{1}{x}$ and $g(x) = \dfrac{1}{x-2}$

11. Which transformation can be used to find the set of ordered pairs of the inverse of a one-to-one function?

12–14. Determine whether the function represented by each graph has an inverse function.

12. **13.** **14.**

4.8 GRAPHING AN INVERSE VARIATION

KEY IDEAS

If $xy = 48$, then, as *x increases* from 1 to 2 to 3 to 4 . . . , the corresponding value of *y decreases* from 48 to 24 to 16 to 12 . . . . Variables *x* and *y* are said to be *inversely* related since, as the value of one variable gets larger, the value of the other variable gets smaller. This happens whenever the product of *x* and *y* remains constant.

Definition of Inverse Variation

An **inverse variation** between two nonzero variables, say x and y, is a relation in which their product remains constant. If k is some nonzero constant, then y varies inversely as x if

$$xy = k \quad \text{or, equivalently,} \quad y = \frac{k}{x} \quad (k \neq 0).$$

In these equations, k is called the **constant of variation.**

Example

1. If y varies inversely as x, and $y = 32$ when $x = 6$, find y when $x = 9$.

Solution: If y varies inversely as x, then the product of x and y must be the same for any two ordered pairs (x_1, y_1) and (x_2, y_2). Thus

$$x_1 \cdot y_1 = x_2 \cdot y_2$$

Let $x_1 = 6$, $y_1 = 32$, and $x_2 = 9$: $\quad (6)(32) = (9)(y)$

Simplify: $\quad 198 = 9y$

Divide both sides by 9: $\quad \dfrac{198}{9} = \dfrac{9y}{9}$

$$22 = y \quad \text{or} \quad y = \mathbf{22}$$

Graph of an Inverse Variation

The graph of $xy = 4$, shown in Figure 4.16, is called an **equilateral** or **rectangular hyperbola**. The hyperbola consists of two different branches located in opposite quadrants. Since the graph passes the vertical-line test, the equation $xy = 4$ describes a function.

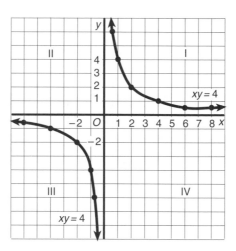

Figure 4.16 Graph of an Inverse Variation

In general, the graph of $xy = k$ has these additional features:

- The coordinate axes are *asymptotes*—lines that frame the graph and to which the graph gets closer and closer but never touches.
- If $k > 0$, the branches of the graph are located in Quadrants I and III, since in these quadrants the x- and y-coordinates have the same sign, so their product is positive.
- If $k < 0$, the branches of the graph are located in Quadrants II and IV, since in these quadrants the x- and y-coordinates have opposite signs, so their product is negative.
- Each branch of the hyperbola is a reflection of the other branch in the origin. If point (a, b) lies on a branch of the hyperbola, then its image on the other branch is point $(-a, -b)$.

Examples

2. (a) Draw the graph of $xy = 6$ in the interval $-6 \le x \le 6$ ($x \ne 0$).
    (b) On the same set of axes, sketch the graph of the image of $xy = 6$ after a rotation of $90°$.

Solutions: **(a)** On the closed interval $-6 \le x \le 6$ ($x \ne 0$), the graph of $xy = 6$ is in Quadrants I and III and has the y-axis as an asymptote, $x = 6$ as an endpoint in Quadrant I, and $x = -6$ as an endpoint in Quadrant III. Construct a table of ordered pairs, using all integer values of x between -6 and 6, inclusive (except $x \ne 0$). Find the corresponding value of y such that $xy = 6$.

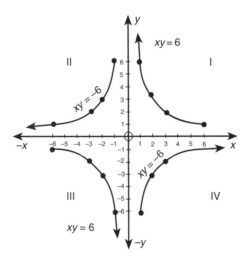

(b) Under a counterclockwise rotation of 90° about the origin, each point (x, y) of the graph is mapped onto $(-y, x)$. Replacing x by $-y$ and y by x in $xy = 6$ gives $(-y)(x) = 6$ or, equivalently, $xy = -6$. The graph of $xy = -6$ is located in Quadrants II and IV and has the restricted range $-6 \leq y \leq 6$ ($y \neq 0$).

	Quadrant I			Quadrant III			
x	1	2	3	6	−1	−2	−3	−6
y	6	3	2	1	−6	−3	−2	−1

You can easily verify this fact by actually rotating the page that contains the graph of $xy = 6$ counterclockwise 90°. When you do this, the image of the x-axis is vertical, and the image of the positive y-axis lies horizontally at the left side of the page.

3. In Example 2, what is the equation of the image of the graph of $xy = 6$ after it is dilated using a scale factor of 2?

Solution: Under a dilation having a scale factor of 2, the image of each point (x, y) of the graph is mapped onto $(2x, 2y)$. The coordinates of each point on the original graph are one-half the coordinates of the corresponding image point. Thus, replacing x by $\frac{x}{2}$ and y by $\frac{y}{2}$ in the original equation gives the equation of the dilated graph:

$$xy = 6 \xrightarrow{D_2} \left(\frac{x}{2}\right)\left(\frac{y}{2}\right) = 6 \quad \text{or} \quad xy = 24$$

Hence the image of $xy = 6$ is the graph whose equation is **$xy = 24$.** If the domain of the original graph is $-6 \leq x \leq 6$, then the domain of the dilated graph is $-12 \leq x \leq 12$ ($x \neq 0$), since each value of x is doubled.

Exercise Set 4.8

1. If y varies inversely as x, and $y = 24$ when $x = 3$, find x when $y = 8$.

2. If y varies inversely as x, and $y = 80$ when $x = 5$, find x when $y = 100$.

3. If y varies inversely as x, and $x = 4$ when $y = 21$, find y when $x = 6$.

4. The number of hours required to complete a certain job varies inversely as the number of people assigned to the job. It is known that 8 people take 24 hours to complete the job. How many hours will 12 people need to complete the same job, assuming that each person does the same amount of work?

5. (a) Using graph paper, draw the graph of $xy = 12$, where $-12 \le x \le 12$ ($x \ne 0$).
   (b) What is an equation of the image of $xy = 12$ under a dilation having a scale factor of $\frac{1}{2}$?
   (c) Sketch the image of $xy = 12$ after a reflection in the x-axis. What is an equation of this graph?

6. (a) Using graph paper, draw the graph of $xy = -10$ in the interval $-10 \le x \le 10$ ($x \ne 0$).
   (b) On the same set of axes, draw and label the graph of the image of $xy = -10$ after a rotation of $90°$. What is an equation of this graph?

REGENTS TUNE-UP: CHAPTER 4

Each of the questions in this section has appeared on a previous Course III Regents Examination. Here is an opportunity for you to review Chapter 4 and, at the same time, prepare for the Course III Regents Examination.

---

1. What is the image of $R_{-180°}(-4, -7)$?

2. If $f(x) = 3x$ and $g(x) = 7x - 1$, what is $(f \circ g)(4)$?

3. If $M(-2, 8)$ is reflected in the y-axis, what are the coordinates of M', the image of M?

4. If $f(x) = x^{\frac{3}{4}}$, find $f(16)$.

5. If $f(x) = 4x^{-2} - 2x^0$, find the value of $f(2)$.

6. A translation maps $A(-2, 1)$ onto $A'(2, 2)$. Find the coordinates of B', the image of $B(-4, -5)$ under the same translation.

7. In the accompanying diagram of a regular octagon, ℓ, m, and p are lines of symmetry. What is $r_p \circ r_m(E)$?

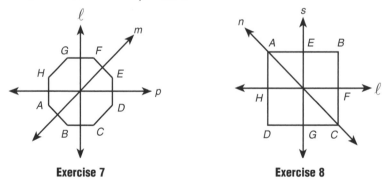

Exercise 7   **Exercise 8**

8. In the accompanying diagram, $ABCD$ is a square with symmetry lines n, s, and ℓ. What is $r_n \circ r_s(\overline{BF})$?

9. In the accompanying figure, p and q are symmetry lines for the figure $ABCDEF$. Find $r_q \circ r_p \circ r_q(A)$.

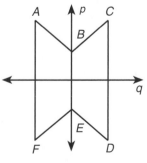

Exercise 9

10. The rate at which a man travels from city A to city B varies inversely as the time it takes to make the trip. If the man can make the trip in $3\frac{1}{2}$ hours at 60 kilometers per hour, how many kilometers per hour must he travel to make the trip in 3 hours?

11. Find the image of $A(4, -3)$ under the transformation $r_{x = 2}$.

12. The diameter of a wheel varies inversely as the number of revolutions that the wheel makes to cover a certain distance. If a wheel with a 26-inch diameter makes 10 revolutions in covering a certain distance, how many revolutions will a wheel with a diameter of 20 inches make in covering the same distance?

13. For any point (x, y), which transformation is equivalent to $R_{45°} \circ R_{-135°}$?
  (1) $R_{-90°}$ (3) $r_{y = x}$
  (2) $R_{90°}$ (4) $r_{x\text{-axis}}$

14. Which transformation is *not* an isometry?
  (1) $(x, y) \rightarrow (x + 6, y - 2)$ (3) $(x, y) \rightarrow \left(\dfrac{x}{2}, \dfrac{y}{2}\right)$
  (2) $(x, y) \rightarrow (y, -x)$ (4) $(x, y) \rightarrow (-y, -x)$

15. The domain for $g(x) = 5x - 1$ is $-2 \leq x \leq 2$. The *smallest* value in the range of $g(x)$ is
  (1) -11 (2) 9   (3) 11   (4) -9

16. The graph of the equation $4x^2 + 16y^2 = 25$ is
  (1) a circle   (3) an ellipse
  (2) a hyperbola   (4) a parabola

17. If $f(x) = x^2 - 3$, then $f(a - b)$ is equivalent to:
  (1) $a^2 - b^2 - 3$
  (2) $a^2 - 2ab - b^2 - 3$
  (3) $a^2 - 2ab + b^2 - 3$
  (4) $a^2 + b^2 - 3$

18. Given: points $A(3, 0)$ and $B(-4, 6)$. Write the letters (a) through (e), and next to *each* letter write the coordinates of the images of points A and B after each transformation described.
  (a) the images of points A and B after a reflection in the line $y = x$
  (b) the images of points A and B after a rotation of 90° counterclockwise about the origin
  (c) the images of points A and B after a reflection in the line $x = 2$
  (d) the images of points A and B after a reflection through the origin
  (e) the images of points A and B after a dilation $D_{\frac{1}{2}}$

19. Triangle ABC has coordinates $A(-1, 4)$, $B(3, 7)$, and $C(5, 1)$.
  (a) On graph paper, draw and label $\triangle ABC$.
  (b) Graph and state the coordinates of $\triangle A'B'C'$, the image of $\triangle ABC$ under the composition $R_{0, 90} \circ r_{x\text{-axis}}$.
  (c) State the single transformation equivalent to $R_{0, 90} \circ r_{x\text{-axis}}$.

ANSWERS TO SELECTED EXERCISES: CHAPTER 4

Section 4.1
  1. Domain = $\{-2, 0, 3\}$, range = $\{2, 3\}$
  3. Domain = range = {all real numbers}
  5. Domain = $\{x: x \geq 3\}$, range = $\{y: y \geq 0\}$
  7. Domain = $\{x: x \geq 0\}$, range = $\{y: y \geq 3\}$
  9. (1)
  10. (a) 1   **(c)** 19   **(e)** 11
  11. (a) 12   **(b)** 18   **(c)** 2
  12. -3 and 2
  13. (a) 0   **(b)** 16   **(c)** 18   **(d)** $4y^2 + 4y + 1$ **(e)** x^2

Section 4.2
  1. Circle is not a function.
  2. Hyperbola is not a function.
  3. Circle is not a function.
  4. Parabola is a function.
  5. Line is a function.
  6. Ellipse is not a function.
  7. Circle is not a function.
  8. Parabola is a function.
  9. Hyperbola is not a function.
  10. Graph represents a function.
  11. Graph represents a function.
  12. Graph does not represent a function.
  13. Graph represents a function.

Section 4.3
  1. (a) $\dfrac{x^2}{4}$ **(b)** $\dfrac{x^2}{2}$ **(c)** $\dfrac{x^4}{4}$ **(d)** $\dfrac{x}{4}$

  3. (a) x **(b)** x **(c)** $x^{\frac{1}{4}}$ **(d)** x^4

  5. (a) $x^2 - 2x + 1$ **(b)** $1 - x^2$ **(c)** x^4 **(d)** x

  7. (a) 512   **(b)** $\dfrac{x^9}{512}$ **(c)** a^{18} **9.** 5

  10. (a) -1 **(b)** 3   **(c)** 3   **(d)** Does not exist.   **(e)** -1 **(f)** -1

Section 4.4
  1. (a) $(2, 2)$ **(b)** $(-1, -1)$ **(c)** $(0, 3)$ **(d)** $(-3, 0)$ **(e)** $(-2, -3)$
  2. (a) $(2, -2)$ **(b)** $(4, -9)$ **(c)** $(6, 0)$ **(d)** $(7, -1)$ **(e)** $(-3, -6)$
  3. (a) $(-16, -12)$ **(b)** $(-4, -3)$ **(c)** $(-8, -6)$ **(d)** $(24, 18)$
  4. (a) $(0, 3)$ **(b)** $(12, 0)$ **(c)** $(15, 6)$ **(d)** $(-3, -6)$ **(e)** $\left(9, \dfrac{27}{2}\right)$

Section 4.5

1. (a) $(1,-3)$ **(b)** $(-1,-3)$ **(c)** $(1,3)$ **(d)** $(3,-1)$ **(e)** $(-1,-5)$ **(f)** $(5,3)$
3. (a) $(-5,-1)$ **(b)** $(-7,-2)$ **(c)** $(-3,-1)$ **(d)** $(-4,0)$ **(e)** $(-6,0)$
5. (a) $180°$ **(b)** $130°$ **(c)** $295°$
7. (a) $(1,4)$ **(b)** $(4,-1)$ **(c)** $(-1,-4)$ **(d)** $(-4,1)$
9. (2)
11. $270°$
12. (b) Coordinates of endpoints are: $A'(1,4)$, $B'(4,5)$
      (c) Coordinates of endpoints are: $A''(-4,-1)$, $B''(-1,0)$
      (d) Coordinates of endpoints are: $A'''(4,1)$, $B'''(1,0)$
      (e) $T_{0,-4}(x,y)$
13. (b) Coordinates of vertices are: $A'(1,3)$, $B'(3,4)$, $C'(1,6)$
      (c) Coordinates of vertices are: $A''(-3,1)$, $B''(-4,3)$, $C''(-6,1)$
      (d) Coordinates of vertices are: $A'''(3,-1)$, $B'''(4,-3)$, $C'''(6,-1)$

Section 4.6

1. (a) $(-7,4)$ **(b)** $(2,5)$ **(c)** $(-3,0)$ **(d)** $(0,-4)$ **(e)** $(3,-2)$
2. (a) $(-2,2)$ **(b)** $(0,3)$ **(c)** $(-5,3)$ **(d)** $(2,-3)$ **(e)** $(3,6)$
3. (a) $(-1,10)$ **(c)** $(2,5)$ **(e)** $(4,-6)$
      (b) $(-3,4)$ **(d)** $(0,-1)$ **(f)** $(-5,-2)$
4. $h=1, k=5$ **5.** (2) **6.** (2) **7.** (3)
8. (a) $\overline{AH}$ **(b)** $\overline{AH}$ **(c)** G
9. (a) $(3,5)$ **(b)** $(1,-1)$ **(c)** $(5,5)$
10. (b) Coordinates of vertices are: $A'(1,6)$, $B'(5,8)$, $C'(4,5)$
      (c) Coordinates of vertices are: $A''(-6,-1)$, $B''(-8,-5)$, $C''(-5,-4)$
      (d) Coordinates of vertices are: $A'''(9,0)$, $B'''(11,4)$, $C'''(8,3)$
11. (b) Coordinates of vertices are: $A'(0,4)$, $B'(-1,8)$, $C'(-4,8)$
      (c) (1)
      (d) Coordinates of vertices are: $A''(4,-8)$, $B''(8,-7)$, $C''(8,-4)$
      (e) (4)

Section 4.7

1. Does not exist since the inverse relation is not a function.

2. $g^{-1} = \{5,-2), (-2,5),(2,1)\}$ **5.** $y = \dfrac{x}{3} - \dfrac{2}{3}$

3. $y = 3 - x$ **6.** $y = \sqrt{x^2 - 1}$

4. $y = \sqrt[3]{x-1}$ **7.** $y = -\dfrac{3}{2}x + \dfrac{5}{2}$

8. Does not exist since the inverse relation, $y = \pm\sqrt{2x-8}$, is not a function.
9. Show that $f(g(x)) = x$ and $g(f(x)) = x$.
11. Reflection in the line $y = x$.
13. Fails the horizontal-line test, so no inverse function exists.
14. Passes the horizontal-line test, so an inverse function exists.

Section 4.8
1. 9   2. 4   3. 14   4. 16
5. **(b)** $xy = 3$ **(c)** $xy = -12$
6. **(b)** $xy = 10$

Regents Tune-Up: Chapter 4
1. (4, 7)   7. C 13. (1)
2. 81   8. $\overline{AE}$ 14. (3)
3. (2, 8)   9. C 15. (1)
4. 8   10. 70   16. (3)
5. −1   11. (0, −3)   17. (3)
6. (0, −4)   12. 13
18. **(a)** $A'(0, 3), B'(6, -4)$
    (b) $A'(0, 3), B'(-6, -4)$
    (c) $A'(1, 0), B'(8, 6)$
    (d) $A'(-3, 0), B'(4, -6)$
    (e) $A'\left(\dfrac{3}{2}, 0\right), B'(-2, 3)$

19. **(b)** Coordinates of vertices are: $A'(4, -1), B'(7, 3), C'(1, 5)$
    (c) Reflection in the line $y = x$

CHAPTER 5

EXPONENTIAL AND LOGARITHMIC FUNCTIONS

5.1 GRAPHING $y = b^x$ AND ITS INVERSE

An **exponential function** raises a positive constant other than 1 to a variable power. The function $y = 2^x$ is an exponential function. Its inverse is $x = 2^y$.

In order to solve for y in terms of x, the **logarithm function** was invented. If $x = 2^y$, then $y = \log_2 x$, which is read as "logarithm of x to base 2 is y." A logarithm is an *exponent* since, if $y = \log_b x$, then $x = b^y$.

Graphing $y = b^x$ ($b > 0$)

In Figure 5.1, the graphs of $y = 2^x$, $y = 10^x$, and $y = \left(\frac{1}{2}\right)^x$ are drawn on the same set of axes. The graph of $y = \left(\frac{1}{2}\right)^x$ is a reflection of the graph of $y = 2^x$ in the y-axis, since replacing x by $-x$ in $y = 2^x$ gives

$$y = 2^{-x} = (2^{-1})^x = \left(\frac{1}{2}\right)^x.$$

Thus, graphs of the forms

$$y = b^x \quad \text{and} \quad y = \left(\frac{1}{b}\right)^x$$

are reflections of each other in the y-axis. Furthermore, the graph of any exponential function $y = b^x$, where $b > 0$ and $b \neq 1$, has the x-axis as an asymptote, lies in Quadrants I

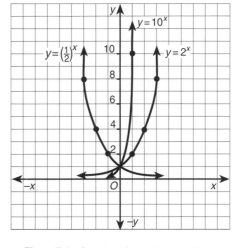

Figure 5.1 Graphs of $y = 2^x$, $y = 10^x$ and $y = \left(\frac{1}{2}\right)^x$

and II, and contains point $(0, 1)$. If $0 < b < 1$, the graph falls. If $b > 1$, the graph rises, with its steepness increasing as b gets larger. Notice, for example, that the graph of $y = 10^x$ in Figure 5.1 is steeper than the graph of $y = 2^x$.

The graph passes the vertical- and horizontal-line tests, so $y = b^x$ is a one-to-one function.

103

Graphing the Inverse of $y = b^x$ ($b > 0$ and $b \neq 1$)

The inverse of the exponential function $y = b^x$ is $x = b^y$, which may also be written as $y = \log_b x$, where "log" is an abbreviation for *logarithm*.

MATH FACTS

DEFINITION OF LOGARITHM

The **logarithm** of a positive number x to a given base b is the power to which b must be raised to obtain x, provided that $b > 0$ and $b \neq 1$. Thus

$$y = \log_b x \quad \text{means} \quad b^y = x.$$

The graphs of the exponential and logarithmic functions are shown in Figure 5.2. Since $y = \log_b x$ is the inverse of $y = b^x$, either graph is a reflection of the other in the line $y = x$. The key features of these graphs are compared in Table 5.1.

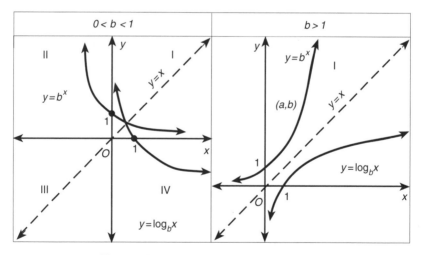

Figure 5.2 Graphs of $y = b^x$ and $y = \log_b x$

TABLE 5.1 COMPARISON OF THE FEATURES OF THE GRAPHS OF
$y = b^x$ **AND** $y = \log_b x$

Feature	Graph of $y = b^x$	Graph of $y = \log_b x$
Quadrants where located	I and II	I and IV
Domain	All real numbers	Positive real numbers
Range	Positive real numbers	All real numbers
x-intercept	None	(1, 0)
y-intercept	(0, 1)	None
Asymptote	x-axis	y-axis
$0 < b < 1$	Falls	Falls
$b > 1$	Rises	Rises

Note: The graph of every logarithmic function passes through (1, 0), and the graph of every exponential function passes through (0, 1).

Example

1. On the same set of axes, sketch and label the graphs of:
(a) $y = 3^x$ and its inverse
(b) the reflection of $y = 3^x$ in the y-axis

Solution: **(a)** To sketch the graph of $y = 3x$, use the sample points shown in the table at the right. The graph is shown below.

x	−1	0	1	2
$y = 3^x$	$\frac{1}{3}$	1	3	9

The inverse of $y = 3^x$ is the logarithmic function whose equation is $y = \log_3 x$. To obtain some sample points, inter-change the x- and y-values in the given table. Notice in the accompanying figure that the graph of $y = \log_3 x$ is the reflec-tion of the graph of $y = 3^x$ in the line $y = x$.

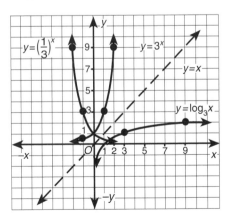

(b) In general, the graphs of $y = b^x$ and $y = \left(\frac{1}{b}\right)^x$ are reflec-tions of each other in the y-axis. In this example, $b = 3$ so that $y = \left(\frac{1}{3}\right)^x$ is the reflection of $y = 3^x$ in the y-axis. Some sample points are given in the accom-panying table. See the figure for part **(a)**.

x	−2	−1	0	1
$y = \left(\frac{1}{3}\right)^x$	9	3	1	$\frac{1}{3}$

Equivalent Exponential and Logarithmic Forms

The fact that $y = \log_b x$ means $x = b^y$ makes it possible to write equivalent exponential and logarithmic equations, as illustrated in Table 5.2.

TABLE 5.2 EQUIVALENT EXPONENTIAL AND LOGARITHMIC EQUATIONS

Exponential Form	Logarithmic Form
$4^3 = 64$	$\log_4 64 = 3$
$10^2 = 100$	$\log_{10} 100 = 2$
$5^0 = 1$	$\log_5 1 = 0$
$3^{-2} = \dfrac{1}{9}$	$\log_3 \left(\dfrac{1}{9}\right) = -2$

Examples

2. For each logarithmic equation, find x:
(a) $\log_2 x = 5$ **(b)** $\log_7 49 = x$ **(c)** $\log_x 8 = \dfrac{3}{4}$

Solutions: In each case change to exponential form.
(a) If $\log_2 x = 5$, then $2^5 = x$. Hence $x = \mathbf{32}$.
(b) If $\log_7 49 = x$, then $7^x = 49$. Since $7^x = 49 = 7^2$, $x = \mathbf{2}$.
(c) If $\log_x 8 = \frac{3}{4}$, then $x^{\frac{3}{4}} = 8$. Solve for x by raising both members of the equation to the $\frac{4}{3}$ power.

$$x = 8^{\frac{4}{3}} = \left(\sqrt[3]{8}\right)^4 = (2)^4 = \mathbf{16}$$

3. If $\log_x 5 = 3$, solve for x correct to the *nearest tenth*.

Solution: If $\log_x 5 = 3$, then $x^3 = 5$, so $x = 5^{\frac{1}{3}}$. Using your calculator, press

$$5 \boxed{x^y} \boxed{(} 1 \boxed{\div} 3 \boxed{)} \boxed{=} .$$

Thus, correct to the *nearest tenth*, x is **1.7**.

Common Logarithms

A logarithm whose base is 10 is called a **common logarithm**. A common logarithm is indicated when the base is omitted. Thus, $\log x$ is understood to mean $\log_{10} x$.

The common logarithm of any power of 10 can be determined by sight. Thus, $\log 10 = 1$ since $10^1 = 10$; $\log 100 = 2$ since $10^2 = 100$; $\log 1000 = 3$ since $10^3 = 1000$; and so forth.

Exercise Set 5.1

1–4. Change from exponential into logarithmic form.

1. $2^4 = 16$ **2.** $8^{\frac{2}{3}} = 4$ **3.** $6^0 = 1$ **4.** $5^{-2} = \dfrac{1}{25}$

5–13. Change from logarithmic into exponential form, and find x.

5. $\log_6 36 = x$ **8.** $\log_5 \dfrac{1}{5} = x$ **11.** $\log_x 16 = \dfrac{4}{3}$

6. $\log x = -1$ **9.** $\log_9 x = \dfrac{3}{2}$ **12.** $\log_x 16 = \dfrac{2}{3}$

7. $\log_x 0.01 = -2$ **10.** $\log_3(2 - x) = 2$ **13.** $\log_x 8 = -\dfrac{3}{2}$

14. If $f(x) = \log x$, find:
   (a) $f(10)$ **(b)** $f(100)$ **(c)** $f(1000)$ **(d)** $f(0.1)$

15. Find the value of k if the following points lie on the graph of $y = \log_{10} x$:
   (a) $(k, 0)$ **(b)** $(10, k)$ **(c)** $(k, -1)$

16. At which point do the graphs of $y = 5^x$ and $y = 5^{-x}$ intersect?

17. At which point do the graphs of $y = \log_4 x$ and $y = \log_{\frac{1}{4}} x$ intersect?

18. Sketch the graph of $y = 2^x$. On the same set of axes, sketch the reflection of $y = 2^x$ in:
   (a) the y-axis   **(b)** the line $y = x$

19. Solve for x correct to the nearest *tenth*.

   (a) $\log_x 17 = 5$ **(b)** $\log_x 7 = \dfrac{3}{4}$ **(c)** $\log_3 x = \dfrac{8}{5}$

20. Graph and label the function $y = 2^x$ for the domain $-2 \le x \le 3$. On the same set of axes, sketch:
   (a) the reflection in the x-axis of $y = 2^x$, and label the graph **a**
   (b) the reflection in the origin of $y = 2^x$, and label the graph **b**
   (c) the translation of $y = 2^x$ under $T_{(6,2)}$, and label the graph **c**

21. On the same set of axes, sketch the graphs of $y = \left(\dfrac{1}{2}\right)^x$ and $y = \log_{\frac{1}{2}} x$.
   Label each graph with its equation.

107

5.2 USING LOGARITHM LAWS

$$\bigwedge$$
KEY IDEAS

Since logarithms are exponents, the laws for finding the logarithms of a product, quotient, and power are consistent with the laws of exponents for these operations.

Power Property	Logarithm Property
$b^m \cdot b^n = b^{m+n}$	$\log_b(xy) = \log_b x + \log_b y$
$\dfrac{b^m}{b^n} = b^{m-n}$	$\log_b \dfrac{x}{y} = \log_b x - \log_b y$
$(b^m)^n = b^{mn}$	$\log_b x^n = n \log_b x$

Logarithm Laws

Logarithms of products, quotients, powers, and roots can be simplified by using one or more of the following logarithm laws:

- *Product Law.* The logarithm of a product equals the sum of the logarithms of its factors.

$$\log_b(xy) = \log_b x + \log_b y$$

  Examples: 1. $\log 21 = \log(7 \cdot 3) = \log 7 + \log 3$
  2. $\log_b 5mn = \log_b 5 + \log_b m + \log_b n$
  3. $\log 100x = \log 100 + \log x = 2 + \log x$

- *Quotient Law.* The logarithm of a quotient equals the logarithm of the numerator minus the logarithm of the denominator.

$$\log_b \frac{x}{y} = \log_b x - \log_b y$$

  Examples: 1. $\log \dfrac{67}{13} = \log 67 - \log 13$

  2. $\log \dfrac{x}{10} = \log x - \log 10 = \log x - 1$

- *Power Law.* The logarithm of a quantity raised to a power equals the product of the exponent and the logarithm of the quantity.

$$\log_b x^n = n \log_b x$$

  Examples: 1. $\log_b x^5 = 5\log_b x$

  2. $\log_b \sqrt{x} = \log_b x^{\frac{1}{2}} = \frac{1}{2}\log_b x$

$$3.\ \log 10x^2 = \log 10 + \log x^2$$

Use Power Law of Logs: $= \mathbf{1} + \mathbf{2\log x}$

$$4.\ \log \sqrt[3]{\frac{m}{n}} = \log\left(\frac{m}{n}\right)^{\frac{1}{3}}$$

Use Power Law of Logs: $= \dfrac{1}{3}\log\dfrac{m}{n}$

Use Quotient Law of Logs: $= \dfrac{1}{3}(\log m - \log n)$

Sometimes it is necessary to reverse the steps that were taken in expanding a logarithmic expression. For example, to write $\frac{1}{2}(\log r - \log s)$ as the logarithm of a *single* expression, work from inside the parentheses outside in applying the "reverse" of the logarithm laws:

Use Quotient Law: $\dfrac{1}{2}(\log r - \log s) = \dfrac{1}{2}\log\left(\dfrac{r}{s}\right)$

Use Power Law: $= \log\left(\dfrac{r}{s}\right)^{\frac{1}{2}}$

$= \log\sqrt{\dfrac{r}{s}}$

Examples

1. If $\log x = n$, express $\log\left(\dfrac{x^3}{100}\right)$ in terms of n.

Solution:

Use Quotient Law: $\log\left(\dfrac{x^3}{100}\right) = \log x^3 - \log 100$

Use Power Law: $= 3\log x - \log 100$
Simplify common log: $= 3\log x - 2$
Replace $\log x$ by n: $= 3n - 2$

2. If $\log 2 = x$ and $\log 3 = y$, express each of the following in terms of x and y:
(a) $\log \sqrt{6}$ **(b)** $\log 24$ **(c)** $\log 1.5$

Solution: **(a)** $\log \sqrt{6} = \log 6^{\frac{1}{2}}$

Use Power Law: $= \dfrac{1}{2}\log 6$

Factor 6: $= \dfrac{1}{2}\log(2\cdot 3)$

109

Use Product Law: $\qquad\qquad\qquad = \dfrac{1}{2}(\log 2 + \log 3)$

Let log 2 = x and log 3 = y: $\qquad\quad = \dfrac{1}{2}(x + y)$

(b) Since 24 can be factored as $8 \cdot 3$ or $2^3 \cdot 3$,

$$\log 24 = \log (2^3 \cdot 3)$$

Use Product Law: $\qquad\qquad\quad = \log 2^3 + \log 3$

Use Power Law: $\qquad\qquad\quad = 3\log 2 + \log 3$

$\qquad\qquad\qquad\qquad\qquad = 3x + y$

(c) $\log 1.5 = \log \left(\dfrac{3}{2}\right)$

$\qquad\qquad = \log 3 - \log 2$

$\qquad\qquad = y \qquad - x$

3. If log A = 0.4262, find log $\sqrt{A}$.

Solution: Use the Power Law:

$$\log \sqrt{A} = \log A^{\frac{1}{2}} = \frac{1}{2}\log A = \frac{1}{2}(0.4262) = \mathbf{0.2131}$$

4. If $x = \dfrac{a\sqrt{b}}{c}$, express log x in terms of log a, log b, and log c.

Solution: $\qquad\quad \log x = \log \left(\dfrac{a\sqrt{b}}{c}\right)$

Use Quotient Law: $\qquad = \log(a\sqrt{b}) \quad - \log c$

Use Product Law: $\qquad = \log a + \log \sqrt{b} - \log c$

Use Power Law: $\qquad\; = \log a + \log b^{\frac{1}{2}} - \log c$

$\qquad\qquad\qquad\quad\; = \boldsymbol{\log a + \dfrac{1}{2}\log b - \log c}$

5. If log N = 2log x + log y, express N in terms of x and y.

Solution: Write the right side of the equation as the logarithm of a single expression:

$$\log N = 2\log x + \log y$$
$$= \log x^2 + \log y$$
$$= \log x^2 y$$

If the *logarithms* of two expressions are equal, then the two expressions are equal, provided that the bases are the same. Thus

$$N = x^2 y.$$

Solving Logarithmic Equations

An equation in which each term is a logarithm is solved by putting the equation in the form

$$\log_b N = \log_b M.$$

If $\log_b N = \log_b M$, then $N = M$ since the bases are the same.

Example

6. Solve for x: $\log x - \dfrac{1}{3}\log 8 = \log 7$.

Solution:

Use Power Law:	$\log x - \log 8^{\frac{1}{3}} = \log 7$
Simplify:	$\log x - \log 2 = \log 7$
Use Quotient Law:	$\log\dfrac{x}{2} = \log 7$
Equate numbers since their logs are equal:	$\dfrac{x}{2} = 7$
	$x = 14$ The check is left for you.

Some logarithmic equations are solved by forming and then solving the equivalent exponential equation.

Example

7. Find x if $\log_4(x - 3) + \log_4(x + 3) = 2$.

Solution:

Use Product Law:	$\log_4[(x - 3)(x + 3)] = 2$
Put into exponential form:	$(x - 3)(x + 3) = 4^2$
Multiply:	$x^2 - 9 = 16$
Take square roots:	$x^2 = 25$
	$x = 5$ or $x = -5$

Checking the root $x = -5$ in the original equation leads to the sum $\log_4(-8)$ + $\log_4(-2)$ on the left side of the equation. Since logarithms of negative numbers are undefined, reject $x = -5$. The solution is $x = 5$. The check for this root is left for you.

Exercise Set 5.2

1–4. If log x *= n, express in terms of* n:

1. $\log\dfrac{x^2}{10}$ **2.** $\log\dfrac{100}{\sqrt{x}}$ **3.** $\log x\sqrt{x}$ **4.** $\log\sqrt{1000x}$

5. If log 3 = x and log 5 = y, express in terms of x and y:

(a) log 15   (b) log 45   (c) log 75   (d) log 0.6   (e) log $\dfrac{5}{9}$

6. If log 2 = 0.3010 and log 7 and 0.8451, find:
(a) log 49   (b) log 3.5   (c) log 70   (d) log 28   (e) log $\sqrt{2}$

7–13. Express log x *in terms of log* m, *log* n, *and log* p.

7. $x = \sqrt{mnp}$

10. $x = \dfrac{p}{\sqrt{mn}}$

12. $x = \dfrac{n\sqrt{m}}{p}$

8. $x = m\sqrt{np}$

11. $x = \dfrac{np}{\sqrt{m}}$

13. $x = \dfrac{(mp)^2}{n}$

9. $x = \dfrac{mp}{n^2}$

14. If $V = \pi r^2 h$, write log V in terms of log π, log r, and log h.

15–20. Write each logarithmic expression as the logarithm of a single expression.

15. $2\log r - \dfrac{1}{3}\log s$

18. $\dfrac{1}{3}(\log r - 2\log t) + \log s$

16. $\dfrac{1}{2}\log r + 3\log s$

19. $3\left(\log s + \dfrac{1}{2}\log t\right) - \log r$

17. $\log r + 2\log s - \log t$

20. $2\log t - \left(\log s + \dfrac{1}{3}\log r\right)$

21–22. Express N *in terms of* x *and* y.

21. $\log N = 2\log x - 3\log y$

22. $\log N = x\log y + 2\log y$

23–30. Solve for x:

23. $2\log_5 x = \log_5 16$

27. $\log x + \dfrac{1}{2}\log 25 = 2\log 10$

24. $\log_x 4 + \log_x 16 = 2$

28. $\log_3(x - 4) + \log_3 (x + 4) = 2$

25. $\log_3(7x + 4) - \log_3 2 = 2\log_3 x$

29. $\log_6(x + 5) + \log_6 x = 2$

26. $\log_x 2 + \log_x 4 = \dfrac{3}{2}$

30. $\log_9 x + \log_9 (x - 6) = \dfrac{3}{2}$

5.3 COMPUTING WITH LOGARITHMS

$$\bigwedge_{\text{KEY IDEAS}}$$

Before computers and calculators became widely available, common logarithm values were obtained from tables and then used to perform complicated arithmetic calculations applying the properties of logarithms. Instead of working with tables, a scientific calculator can be used to find a common logarithm of any positive number.

Parts of a Common Logarithm

Since 32.6 is between 10 and 100, $10^1 < 32.6 < 10^2$. This means that 32.6 is equal to 10 raised to a power that is between 1 and 2.

$$32.6 = 10^{1.\underline{}} \quad \text{and} \quad \log 32.6 = 1.\underline{}.$$

Each underlined space is reserved for the decimal part of the logarithm, which is called the **mantissa**. The integer part of the logarithm is the **characteristic**. If log 32.6 = 1.5132, the *characteristic* of $\underline{1}$.5132 is 1. The *mantissa* of 1.$\underline{5132}$ is .5132.

In general, the logarithm of a number N takes the form

$$\log N = \underline{\text{Characteristic}.\underline{}\ \underline{}\ \underline{}\ \underline{}}$$
$$\leftarrow Mantissa \rightarrow$$

Finding Common Logarithms Using a Calculator

To find the value of log x, enter x and then press the $\boxed{\text{LOG}}$ key. Some calculators require you to press the $\boxed{\text{LOG}}$ key before entering the number. To evaluate log 100, key in

$$\boxed{\text{LOG}} \ 100 \ \boxed{=} \quad \text{or} \quad 100 \ \boxed{\text{LOG}}.$$

Usually, the logarithm of a number that is not a power of 10 must be rounded off to four decimal places. Use your calculator to verify that log 24, correct to four decimal places, is 1.3802. In other words, log 24 ≈ 1.3802, where the symbol ≈ is read as "is approximately equal to."

Logarithms of Numbers Between 0 and 1

The graphs of the two logarithm functions in Figure 5.2 on page 104 illustrate that, for all x-values between 0 and 1, the curves fall below the x-axis, so the corresponding *y*-values are negative. These observations indicate that the logarithm of a number between 0 and 1 will always be a negative number. Use your calculator to verify that log 0.01 = −2. This means that point (0.01, −2) is on the graph of *y* = log *x*. As another example, use your calculator to verify that log 0.0326 ≈ −1.4868.

Finding Antilogarithms of Numbers

If you know the logarithm of a number *N* (the exponent of 10 that produces *N*), you can use your scientific calculator to find *N* by finding the **antilogarithm** of the exponent. Thus, if log *N* = 1.7657, then

$$N = 10^{1.7657} = \text{antilogarithm of } 1.7657.$$

Since finding logarithms and finding antilogarithms are inverse operations, use the key on your scientific calculator labeled 10^x, the inverse of log *x*, to find an antilogarithm. For example, to find the antilogarithm of 1.7657 correct to the *nearest hundredth*:

- Locate 10^x on your calculator. Since 10^x is usually printed directly *above* the $\boxed{\text{LOG}}$ key, you will probably have to press the $\boxed{\text{2nd}}$ function key before pressing the key that accesses the 10^x function.
- Use 1.7657 for the value of *x* and one of the following key sequences:

$$\boxed{\text{2nd}}\ 10^x\ 1.7657\ \boxed{=} \quad \text{or} \quad 1.7657\ \boxed{\text{2nd}}\ 10^x$$

- Round off the displayed value to the required level of accuracy. Thus, the antilogarithm of 1.7657, correct to the *nearest hundredth*, is 58.3. .

MATH FACTS

FINDING ANTILOGARITHMS

If log *N* = *k*, then *N* = antilogarithm of *k*. To find *N* when *k* is given, key in

$$\boxed{\text{2nd}}\ \boxed{10^x}\ k\ \boxed{=} \quad \text{or} \quad k\ \boxed{\text{2nd}}\ \boxed{10^x}$$

Examples

1. If log *N* = −1.1302, find *N* correct to the *nearest one-thousandth*.

Solution: Since the logarithm value (exponent of 10) is a negative number, enter it *without* its sign and then press the change-of-sign key, $\boxed{+/-}$, as in

$$\boxed{\text{2nd}}\ \boxed{10^x}\ 1.1302\ \boxed{+/-}\ \boxed{=} \quad \text{or} \quad 1.1302\ \boxed{+/-}\ \boxed{\text{2nd}}\ \boxed{10^x}$$

Since *N* ≈ 0.074096893, *N* correct to the *nearest one-thousandth* is **0.074.**

2. If $\log\left(\dfrac{x}{4}\right) = 1.5$, find x correct to the *nearest tenth*.

Solution: If $\log\left(\dfrac{x}{4}\right) = 1.5$, then $\dfrac{x}{4}$ = antilogarithm of 1.5, so

$$x = 4 \times \text{antilogarithm of 1.5.}$$

Using your scientific calculator, key in

$$\boxed{4}\;\boxed{\times}\;\boxed{\text{2nd}}\;\boxed{10^x}\;\boxed{1.5}\;\boxed{=}\quad\text{or}\quad\boxed{4}\;\boxed{\times}\;\boxed{1.5}\;\boxed{\text{2nd}}\;\boxed{10^x}\;\boxed{=}.$$

Since $x \approx 126.4911$, the value of x correct to the *nearest tenth* is **126.5**.

Exercise Set 5.3

1. Given $\log 2.45 = 0.3892$, find:
   (a) $\log 245$ **(b)** $\log 0.0245$ **(c)** $\log(2.45)^3$ **(d)** $\log \sqrt[3]{0.245}$

2–4. Estimate x *to the nearest hundredth.*

2. $\log x = 0.8131$ **3.** $\log x = 0.6100$ **4.** $\log x = 0.7040$

5. Find the integer whose logarithm is between 1.5611 and 1.5466.

6. Find the number correct to the *nearest hundredth* whose logarithm is closest to:
   (a) -0.8041 **(b)** -1.4949

7. If $\log 100x = 1.3488$, find x correct to the *nearest hundredth*.

8. If $(\log x)^2 = 3.7812$, find x correct to the *nearest hundredth*.

9. If $\log \sqrt{x} = -0.6419$, find x correct to the *nearest hundreth*.

10. If $\log(x - 3) = 1.0317$, find x correct to the *nearest tenth*.

11. If $\log N = \dfrac{\log 13.4}{\log 100}$, find N correct to the *nearest tenth*.

12. If $\log\left(\dfrac{1}{N}\right) = \dfrac{1}{\log 56.2}$, find N correct to the *nearest hundredth*.

5.4   SOLVING EXPONENTIAL EQUATIONS

KEY IDEAS

Equations such as

$$5^{x+1} = 25^x, \quad 3^{x-4} = 9, \quad \text{and} \quad 2^{3x} = 6$$

are called *exponential* equations. An **exponential equation** is an equation in which the variable is contained in one or more exponents. Some exponential equations can be solved by writing each side of the equation as a power of the same base and then equating the exponents. For example, if $3^{x-4} = 9$, then $3^{x-4} = 3^2$, implying that the exponents $x - 4$ and 2 are equal so that $x - 4 = 2$ or $x = 6$.

When both sides of an exponential equation cannot be expressed as a power of the same base, as in $2^{3x} = 6$, logarithms are needed.

Exponential Equations Having a Common Base

If $b^m = b^n$, then $m = n$ (provided that $b \neq 1$). This principle is used to solve exponential equations in which both sides can be expressed as powers of the same base.

Example

1. Solve for x:
(a) $9^{x+1} = 27^x$ (b) $64^{1-x} = \dfrac{1}{16}$

Solutions:

(a)

	$9^{x+1} = 27^x$
Write each side as a power of 3:	$(3^2)^{x+1} = (3^3)^x$
Use Power Law of Exponents:	$3^{2(x+1)} = 3^{3x}$
Equate exponents:	$2(x + 1) = 3x$
Solve for x:	$2x + 2 = 3x$
	$x = 2$

(b)

	$64^{1-x} = \dfrac{1}{16}$
Write each side as a power of 4:	$(4^3)^{1-x} = 4^{-2}$
Use Power Law of Exponents:	$4^{3(1-x)} = 4^{-2}$
Equate exponents:	$3(1 - x) = -2$
Solve for x:	$3 - 3x = -2$
	$-3x = -5$
	$x = \dfrac{5}{3}$

Note: In each part the check is left for you.

Exponential Equations Lacking a Common Base

Exponential equations for which it is not possible to express both sides as rational powers of the same base are solved by taking the logarithm of each side of the equation. In general, if $a^x = b$, then

$$x \log a = \log b \quad \text{so that} \quad x = \frac{\log b}{\log a}.$$

Examples

2. Solve the equation $2^{3x} = 6$ for x to the *nearest hundredth*.

Solution: Solve by using logarithms.

Take log of each side: $\qquad \log (2^{3x}) = \log 6$
Use Power Law of Logs: $\qquad 3x \log 2 = \log 6$

Solve for x: $\qquad\qquad\qquad x = \dfrac{1}{3}\left(\dfrac{\log 6}{\log 2}\right)$

Evaluate common logs: $\qquad\quad = \dfrac{1}{3}\left(\dfrac{0.7782}{0.3010}\right)$

Divide: $\qquad\qquad\qquad\quad = \dfrac{0.7782}{0.9030} = 0.8618$

Round to the nearest hundredth. $\quad = \mathbf{0.86}$

3. Solve the equation $\log_3 21 = x$ to the *nearest tenth*.

Solution: If $\log_3 21 = x$, then $3^x = 21$.

Take log of each side: $\qquad x \log 3 = \log 21$

Solve for x: $\qquad\qquad\qquad x = \dfrac{\log 21}{\log 3}$

Evaluate common logs: $\qquad\quad = \dfrac{1.3222}{0.4771}$

Divide: $\qquad\qquad\qquad\quad = 2.77$
Round to the nearest tenth: $\quad = \mathbf{2.8}$

Exercise Set 5.4

1–9. Solve each equation for x.

1. $2^{x-3} = 64$ $\qquad$ **4.** $27^x = 3^{2x-1}$ $\qquad$ **7.** $9^{2x} = \dfrac{1}{81}$

2. $4^{2x+1} = 8^x$ $\qquad$ **5.** $64 = 16^{7x-2}$ $\qquad$ **8.** $\left(\dfrac{1}{8}\right)^{2x+1} = 4$

3. $6^{1-4x} = \dfrac{1}{6}$ $\qquad$ **6.** $2^{1-3x} - \dfrac{1}{4} = 0$ $\qquad$ **9.** $7^{x^2-2x} = 1$

10–15. Using logarithms, solve each equation for x *to the nearest tenth.*

10. $4^x = 12$

12. $\left(\dfrac{1}{3}\right)^{-x} = 7$

14. $\log_6 10 = x$

11. $3^{2x} = 75$

13. $27^x = 500$

15. $3\log_3 2 = x$

REGENTS TUNE-UP: CHAPTER 5

Each of the questions in this section has appeared on a previous Course III Regents Examination. Here is an opportunity for you to review Chapter 5 and, at the same time, prepare for the Course III Regents Examination.

---

1. The graph of the function $f(x) = 3^x$ lies in which quadrant(s)?

2. Find the value of x: $\log_3(x - 2) = 2$.

3. If $\log_x\left(\dfrac{1}{4}\right) = -1$, find x.

4. Using logarithms, solve the equation $(1.95)^x = 54$ for x to the *nearest integer*.

5. If $\log_3 5 = x$, find x to the *nearest tenth*.

6. If $x = \dfrac{\sqrt{r}}{s}$, which expression is equivalent to $\log x$?

(1) $2\log r$

(3) $\dfrac{1}{2}\log r - \log s$

(2) $2\log r - \log s$

(4) $\dfrac{\log r - \log s}{2}$

7. If $\log 3 = a$ and $\log 5 = b$, then $\log 45$ is equal to:
(1) $a^2 + b$ (2) $2a + b$ (3) $2ab$ (4) a^2b

8. Solve for x: $4^{3x} = 8^{x+1}$.

9. The expression $3\log x - \dfrac{1}{2}\log y$ is equal to:

(1) $\log\left(\dfrac{x^3}{y^2}\right)$ (2) $\log\left(\dfrac{x^3}{\sqrt{y}}\right)$ (3) $\log\sqrt{\dfrac{3x}{y}}$ (4) $\dfrac{\log 3x}{\frac{1}{2}\log y}$

10. If $\log_9 x = \dfrac{3}{2}$, what is the value of x?

(1) $\dfrac{3}{2}$ (2) 8   (3) $\dfrac{27}{2}$ (4) 27

11. **(a)** Solve for x, and express the roots in terms of i: $2x^2 = 6x - 5$.
    (b) Using logarithms, find x to the *nearest tenth*: $3^{2x} = 100$.

12. Given: $f(x) = 2^x$.
    (a) On graph paper, sketch the graph of $f(x)$ in the interval $-1 \leq x \leq 3$. Label the graph (a).
    (b) On the same set of axes, sketch the image of the graph drawn in part **(a)** after $(T_{2,-1} \circ r_{x\text{-axis}})$. Label the graph (b).
    (c) On the same set of axes, sketch the image of the graph drawn in part **(b)** after D_{-1}. Label the graph (c).

13. **(a)** Given: $\log_b 2 = 0.6931$ and $\log_b 3 = 1.0986$.
    Find: $\log_b \sqrt{12}$.

    (b) Solve for x: $\log_8 (x - 6) + \log_8 (x + 6) = 2$.

ANSWERS TO SELECTED EXERCISES: CHAPTER 5

Section 5.1
1. $\log_2 16 = 4$
3. $\log_8 4 = 0$
5. 2
7. 10
9. 27
11. 8
13. $\dfrac{1}{4}$
15. **(a)** 1
    (b) 1
    (c) 0.1
17. $(1, 0)$
19. **(a)** 1.8
    (b) 13.4
    (c) 5.8

21.

Section 5.2
1. $2n - 1$
3. $\dfrac{3}{2}n$
5. **(a)** $x + y$
   (b) $2x + y$
   (c) $x + 2y$
   (d) $x - y$
   (e) $y - 2x$

7. $\dfrac{1}{2}(\log m + \log n + \log p)$
9. $\log m + \log p - 2\log n$
11. $\log n + \log p - \dfrac{1}{2}\log m$
13. $2(\log m + \log p) - \log n$
15. $\dfrac{r^2}{\sqrt[3]{s}}$

16. $\dfrac{\sqrt{r}}{s^3}$
17. $\dfrac{rs^2}{t}$
18. $\sqrt[3]{\dfrac{r}{t^2}}\, s$

119

19. $\dfrac{\left(s\sqrt{t}\right)^3}{r}$

22. y^{x+2}

25. 4

28. 5

20. $\dfrac{t^2}{s\sqrt[3]{r}}$

23. 4

26. 4

29. 4

21. $\dfrac{x^2}{y^3}$

24. 8

27. 20

30. 9

Section 5.3

1. **(a)** 2.3892   **2.** 6.50   **6.** **(a)** 0.16   **9.** 0.05
    (b) −1.6108   **3.** 4.07   **(b)** 0.03   **10.** 13.8
    (c) 1.1676   **4.** 5.06   **7.** 0.22   **11.** 3.7
    (d) 0.1297   **5.** 36   **8.** 88.00 or 0.01   **12.** 0.27

Section 5.4

1. 9

5. $\dfrac{1}{2}$

9. 0 or 2

13. 1.9

2. −2

6. 1

10. 1.8

14. 1.3

3. $\dfrac{1}{2}$

7. −1

11. 2.0

15. 1.9

4. −1

8. $-\dfrac{5}{6}$

12. 1.8

Regents Tune-Up: Chapter 5

1. Quadrants I and II   **12.**
2. 11
3. 4
4. 6
5. 1.5
6. (3)
7. (2)
8. 1
9. (2)
10. (4)

11. **(a)** $\dfrac{3\pm i}{2}$
    (b) 2.1

13. **(a)** 1.2424
    (b) 10

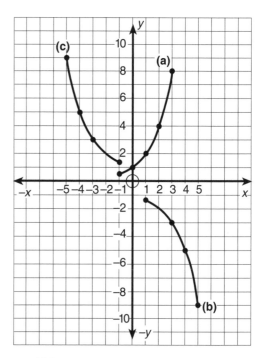

CHAPTER 6

CIRCLES

6.1 BEGINNING DEFINITIONS AND CIRCLE RELATIONSHIPS

===== △ KEY IDEAS △ =====

An important branch of geometry is concerned with measuring angles and special segments that intersect a circle. Before this subject can be discussed, however, some terms and relationships must be introduced. To simplify the discussion, the terms *equal* and *congruent* will be used interchangeably.

Special Segments and Lines of a Circle

A **circle** (Figure 6.1) is the set of all points that are the same distance from a fixed point in the plane, called the **center**. You should also know these facts:

- A **radius** of a circle is a segment whose endpoints are the center and a point on the circle. The plural of *radius* is *radii*. Radii of the same circle are congruent. Circles that have equal radii are congruent.

- A **chord** is a line segment whose endpoints are on the circle.

- A **diameter** is a chord that passes through the center of a circle. The length of a diameter is two times the length of a radius of the circle.

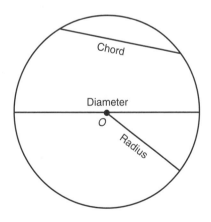

Figure 6.1 Circle *O*

- A **secant** is a line that intersects a circle in two different points. Every secant contains a chord of the circle. In Figure 6.2, $\overleftrightarrow{SEC}$ is a secant and $\overline{CES}$ is a *secant segment*. Since $\overline{CE}$ is the part of secant segment $\overline{CES}$ that lies outside the circle, it is called an *external secant segment*.

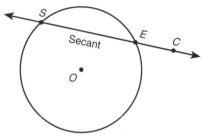

Figure 6.2 Secant and Secant Segment

- A **tangent** is a line that intersects a circle in exactly one point. The point of contact is called the *point of tangency*. In Figure 6.3, $\overrightarrow{TA}$ is a tangent and $\overline{TA}$ is a *tangent segment* since one of its endpoints, point *A*, is the point of tangency of $\overrightarrow{TA}$. Notice that radius $\overline{OA}$ is shown to be perpendicular to tangent $\overleftrightarrow{TA}$. This relationship between radii and tangents is always true.

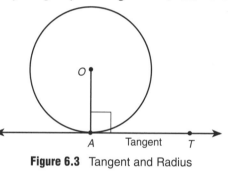

Figure 6.3 Tangent and Radius

MATH FACTS

=======

RADIUS ⊥ TANGENT

A radius drawn to the point of tangency is perpendicular to the tangent at this point.

Congruent Triangles and Circles

Congruent triangles can be used to help establish important circle relationships. For example, in Figure 6.4, radii $\overline{OA}$ and $\overline{OB}$ are drawn to tangency points *A* and *B*. Right triangles *OAP* and *OBP* are congruent by the hypotenuse-leg theorem since $\overline{OP} \cong \overline{OP}$ (hypotenuse) and $\overline{OA} \cong \overline{OB}$ (leg).

Since corresponding parts of congruent triangles are equal, $PA = PB$. This proves that tangent segments drawn to a circle from the same point have the same length.

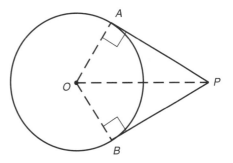

Figure 6.4 Equal Tangent Segments

MATH FACTS

EQUAL TANGENT SEGMENTS

If two tangent segments are drawn to a circle from the same point, they have the same length.

Example

1. In the accompanying diagram, $\overleftrightarrow{PAB}$ is tangent to circle R at A and tangent to circle S at B. $\overleftrightarrow{PCD}$ is tangent to circle R at C and tangent to circle S at D. Chord $\overline{BD}$ is drawn.
(a) If m$\angle PBD = 70$, find m$\angle P$.   **(b)** If $PA = 4$ and $PCD = 7$, find AB.

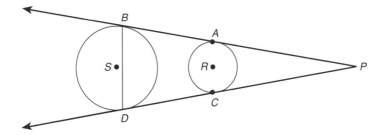

Solutions: Line segments PAB and PCD are drawn from the same point, P, and both are tangent to circle S, so they have the same length.
(a) Triangle BPD is isosceles with $PAB = PCD$. Since the measures of the base angles of an isosceles triangle are equal, m$\angle PDB = 70$. Hence

$$70 + 70 + m\angle P = 180$$
$$m\angle P = \mathbf{40}$$

(b) If $PCD = 7$, then $PAB = 7$. Since $AB + PA = PAB$ and $PA = 4$,

$$AB + 4 = 7$$
$$AB = \mathbf{3}$$

Polygons and Circles

If a polygon is **inscribed** in a circle, as in Figure 6.5, then each vertex of the polygon is a point on the circle. The circle is said to be *circumscribed* about the polygon.

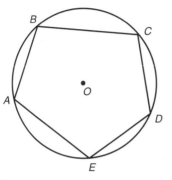

Figure 6.5 Polygon Inscribed in Circle

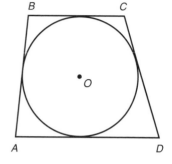

Figure 6.6 Polygon Circumscribed about Circle

If a polygon is **circumscribed** about a circle, as in Figure 6.6, then each of its sides is tangent to the circle. The circle is said to be *inscribed* in the polygon.

Arcs of a Circle

There are 360° in one complete revolution. Thus, the degree measure of a circle is 360. An **arc** of a circle is a curved portion of the circle whose degree measure is between 0 and 360.

- A **semicircle** is an arc that is one-half of the circle. A diameter of a circle divides the circle into two semicircles. The degree measure of a semicircle is 180.
- A **minor arc** is an arc that is less than a semicircle. The degree measure of a minor arc is between 0 and 180. Minor arcs are named by their endpoints, as $\overarc{AB}$ in Figure 6.7.
- A **major arc** is an arc that is greater than a semicircle. The degree measure of a major arc is between 180 and 360. Since, as in Figure 6.7, major arc AB and minor arc AB have the same endpoints, a major arc is named by using a third point on the circle, as $\overarc{APB}$. If $m\overarc{AB} = 70$, then

$$m\overarc{APB} = 360 - 70 = 290.$$

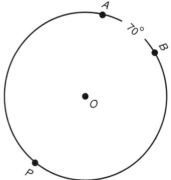

Figure 6.7 Major and Minor Arcs

In general, the degree measure of a major arc is 360 minus the measure of the minor arc that has the same endpoints.
- **Congruent arcs** are arcs in the same circle, or in congruent circles, that have the same degree measure.

Central Angles

Drawing two radii of a circle forms a *central* angle whose sides intercept a minor arc on the circle.

- A **central angle** is an angle whose vertex is at the center of a circle. In Figure 6.8, $\angle AOB$ is a central angle.
- The **degree measure of a minor arc** is the degree measure of the central angle that intercepts it. In Figure 6.8, $\text{m}\widehat{AB} = \text{m}\angle AOB$. If two central angles of a circle have the same measure, then their intercepted arcs will also have the same measure and will, therefore, be equal. Hence, if $\text{m}\angle AOB = \text{m}\angle COD$, then $\text{m}\widehat{AB} = \text{m}\widehat{CD}$.

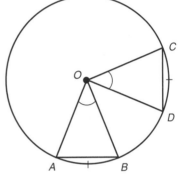

Figure 6.8 Measure of Minor Arc

Congruent Arcs and Chords

In Figure 6.9, if chord $\overline{AB}$ = chord $\overline{CD}$, then $\text{m}\widehat{AB} = \text{m}\widehat{CD}$. Conversely, if arcs AB and CD are equal, then chord $\overline{AB}$ = chord $\overline{CD}$. If $\overline{AB}$ is parallel to $\overline{CD}$, then $\text{m}\widehat{AB} = \text{m}\widehat{BD}$.

- Equal chords have equal arcs.
- Equal arcs have equal chords.
- Arcs between parallel chords are equal.

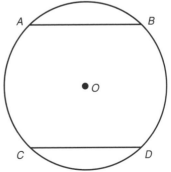

Figure 6.9 Congruent Arcs and Circles

Examples

2. In the accompanying diagram, $\overline{AB}$ is parallel to $\overline{CD}$. If m$\widehat{AB}$ = 110 and m$\widehat{CD}$ = 90, what is the measure of central angle *BOD*?

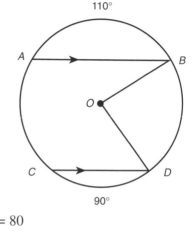

Solution: Since parallel chords intercept equal arcs, let x = m$\widehat{BD}$ = m$\widehat{AC}$. The sum of the measures of the arcs that comprise a circle is 360. Thus

$$\text{m}\widehat{AB} + \text{m}\widehat{BD} + \text{m}\widehat{CD} + \text{m}\widehat{AC} = 360$$
$$110 + \quad x \quad + \quad 90 \quad + \quad x \quad = 360$$
$$2x \quad + \quad 200 \quad = 360$$
$$x = \frac{160}{2} = 80$$

Hence, m$\widehat{BD}$ = 80. Since a central angle and its intercepted arc have the same measure, m∠*BOD* = **80.**

3. In the accompanying diagram, regular hexagon *ABCDEF* is inscribed in circle *O*. Line *p* is a line of symmetry. What is the image of $r_p \circ R_{-240°}(F)$?

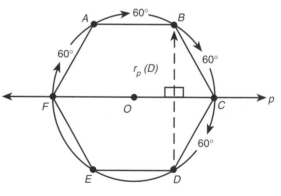

Solution: The given notation $r_p \circ R_{-240°}(F)$ means that point *F* must be rotated 240° in the *clockwise* direction, followed by a reflection of the image point in line *p*. In a *regular* hexagon, each of the six sides has the same length and, therefore, circle *O* is divided into six equal arcs.

Since a circle measures 360°, the measure of each of the six arcs is $\frac{360°}{6}$, or 60°. Thus "moving" from one vertex to an adjacent vertex corresponds to a rotation of 60° about center *O*. Hence

$$r_p \circ R_{-240°}(F) = F \xrightarrow{\quad R_{-240} \quad} D \xrightarrow{\quad r_p \quad} \textbf{B.}$$

4. In Example 3, does *ABCDEF* have *rotational* symmetry?

Solution: A figure has rotational symmetry if it is its own image under some rotation about its center. If *ABCDEF* is rotated 60° in either direction, as in the accompanying diagram, each vertex of the image will coincide with a vertex of the original figure. Hence a regular hexagon has **60° rotational symmetry**.

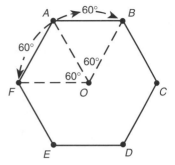

Diameters and Chords

In Figure 6.10, diameter $\overline{AOB}$ is drawn perpendicular to chord $\overline{CD}$ at *M*. As a result, chord segments $\overline{CM}$ and $\overline{DM}$ are congruent, as are the corresponding pairs of arcs on either side of the diameter. This can be proved by showing that right triangles *COM* and *DOM* are congruent.

Since $\overline{OC} \cong \overline{OD}$ (hyp) and $\overline{OM} \cong \overline{OM}$ (leg), right triangles *COM* and *DOM* are congruent by the hyp-leg theorem. Thus

$$\overline{CM} \cong \overline{DM} \quad \text{and} \quad \angle 1 \cong \angle 2$$

since corresponding parts of congruent triangles are congruent (CPCTC). since congruent central angles intercept congruent arcs, $\overset{\frown}{CB} \cong \overset{\frown}{DB}$. Subtracting these arcs from semicircles $\overset{\frown}{ACB}$ and $\overset{\frown}{ADB}$, respectively, gives $\overset{\frown}{AC} \cong \overset{\frown}{AD}$.

Referring to Figure 6.10, if it is known that $\overline{OB}$ bisects $\overline{CD}$, it may be concluded that $\overline{OB}$ is perpendicular to $\overline{CD}$.

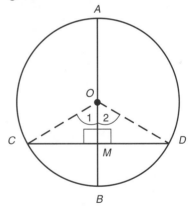

Figure 6.10 Diameters and Chords

MATH FACTS

DIAMETER ⊥ CHORD

If a diameter (or a line passing through the center of a circle is perpendicular to a chord, then it bisects the chord and its arcs. Conversely, if a line passing through the center of a circle bisects a chord that is not a diameter, then it is perpendicular to the chord.

Equidistant Chords

In Figure 6.11, the lengths of perpendicular segments $\overline{OP}$ and $\overline{OQ}$ represent the distances between the center O and line segments $\overline{AB}$ and $\overline{CD}$, respectively. If $AB = CD$, then $OP = OQ$. Conversely, if $OP = OQ$, then $AB = CD$.

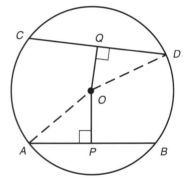

Figure 6.11 Equidistant Chords

MATH FACTS

EQUIDISTANT CHORDS

In a circle:

- Equal chords are the same distance from the center.
- Chords that are the same distance from the center are equal.

Example

5. A chord is 3 inches from the center of a circle whose radius is 5 inches. What is the length of the chord?

Solution: In the accompanying diagram, radius $\overline{OA}$ is 5 and OE, the distance of chord $\overline{AB}$ from center O, is 3. Thus, $\triangle OEA$ is a 3-4-5 right triangle, with $AE = 4$. Since $\overline{OE}$ is perpendicular to chord $\overline{AB}$ and passes through the center O, it lies on a diameter, so that it bisects the chord.

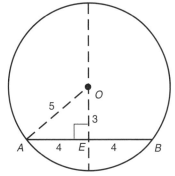

Hence $AE = BE = 4$.

The length of the chord is, therefore, $4 + 4$ or **8** inches.

SUMMARY

1. In the same circle, two **arcs** are equal if any one of the following statements is true:

- The central angles that intercept the arcs are equal.
- The chords that the arcs determine are equal.
- The arcs are between parallel chords.
- The arcs are formed by a chord and a diameter drawn perpendicular to the chord.
- The arcs are semicircles.

2. In the same circle, two **chords** are equal if any one of the following statements is true:

- The arcs that the chords intercept are equal.
- The chords are the same distance from the center.

Exercise Set 6.1

1–4. In the accompanying diagram, $\overline{AB}$ *is parallel to* $\overline{CD}$ *in circle* O.

1. If m∠AOB = 80 and m∠COD = 70, find m$\widehat{ADB}$.

2. If m$\widehat{BD}$ = 75 and m$\widehat{CD}$ = 90, find m∠AOB.

3. If m∠BAO = 40 and m$\widehat{CD}$ = 70, find m$\widehat{BD}$.

4. If $OC = CD$ and m$\widehat{AC}$ = 79, find m∠AOB.

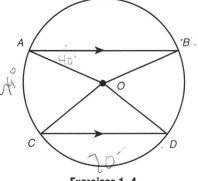

Exercises 1–4

5. If regular pentagon *ABCDE* is inscribed in circle *O*, what is the image of $R_{216°} \circ R_{-72°}(A)$?

6. In the accompanying diagram, line *p* is a line of symmetry of regular hexagon *ABCDEF*. Find the image of:
   (a) $R_{120°} \circ r_p(C)$
   (b) $r_p \circ R_{-240°}(B)$
   (c) $R_{120°} \circ r_p \circ R_{-60°}(A)$
   (d) $r_p \circ R_{-240°} \circ r_p(F)$

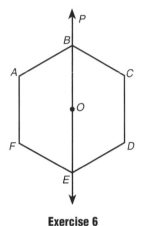

Exercise 6

7. Which of the following geometric figures has 45° rotational symmetry?
   (1) equilateral triangle   (3) rhombus
   (2) square   (4) regular octagon

8. A chord 48 centimeters in length is 7 centimeters from the center of a circle. What is the length of a radius of this circle?

9. A chord is 5 inches from the center of a circle whose diameter is 26 inches. What is the length of the chord?

10. How far from the center of a circle whose radius is 17 inches is a 30-inch chord?

11. In the accompanying figure, $\overline{JK}$, $\overline{JL}$, and $\overline{LK}$ are tangent to circle *O*. What is the length, *x*, of $\overline{JTL}$?

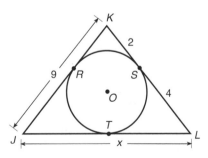

Exercise 11

130

6.2 MEASURING ANGLES OF CIRCLES

The vertex of an angle whose sides are chords, secants, or tangents may lie on the circle, inside the circle, or outside the circle. In each case there is a relationship between the measure of the angle and the measure(s) of the arc(s) it intercepts.

Vertex on the Circle: Inscribed Angles

In Figure 6.12, $\angle ABC$ is an *inscribed* angle that intercepts arc AC. An inscribed **angle** is an angle whose vertex is on the circle and whose sides are chords. If the measure of $\widehat{AC}$ is 50°, for example, then the measure of $\angle ABC$ is one-half of 50° or **25°**. Thus

$$m\angle ABC = \frac{1}{2}m\widehat{AC}.$$

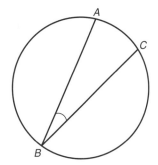

Figure 6.12 Inscribed Angles

INSCRIBED ANGLE THEOREM

The measure of an inscribed angle is one-half the measure of its intercepted arc.

As a result of the inscribed angle relationship:

• If two inscribed angles intercept the same (or congruent) arcs, then the angles must have the same measure and are, therefore, congruent. In Figure 6.13, inscribed angles B and D are congruent since they intercept the same arc, $\widehat{AC}$.

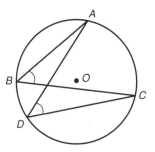

Figure 6.13 Angles that Intercept the Same Arcs. $\angle B \cong \angle D$

- An angle inscribed in a semicircle is a right angle since its intercepted arc is also a semicircle and $\frac{1}{2}(180°)$ is 90°. In Figure 6.14, $\angle AHB$ is a right angle since it is inscribed in semi-circle AHB.

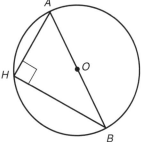

Figure 6.14 Angle Inscribed in a Semicircle

- The opposite angles of an inscribed quadrilateral are supplementary. In Figure 6.15,

$$a + c = 180$$

and

$$b + d = 180.$$

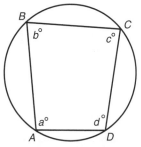

Figure 6.15 Opposite Angles of an Inscribed Quadrilateral

Examples

1. In each case, find the value of x:

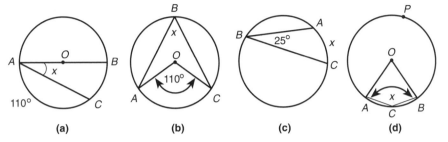

| (a) | (b) | (c) | (d) |

Solutions: **(a)** $A\widehat{BC}$ is a semicircle, so $m\widehat{BC} = 180 - 110 = 70$.

$$x = \frac{1}{2} \, m\widehat{BC} = \frac{1}{2} (70)$$
$$= \mathbf{35}$$

(b) $\angle AOC$ is a central angle, so $m\widehat{AC} = 110$.

$$m\angle ABC = \frac{1}{2} \, m\widehat{AC} = \frac{1}{2} (110)$$
$$= \mathbf{55}$$

(c) The measure of an arc intercepted by an inscribed angle must be twice the measure of the inscribed angle. Hence

$$x = 2(m\angle ABC) = 2(25)$$
$$= \mathbf{50}$$

(d) $\angle AOB$ is a central angle, so $m\widehat{ACB} = 70$.

$$m\widehat{APB} = 360 - 70 = 290$$
$$x = \frac{1}{2} \, m\widehat{APB} = \frac{1}{2} (290)$$
$$= \mathbf{145}$$

2. Given: In circle O, $\overline{AB}$ is a diameter, $A\widehat{M} \cong D\widehat{M}$.
  Prove: $\triangle AMB \cong \triangle CMB$

Solution: The triangles can be proved congruent by using the ASA postulate. Here is the formal proof.

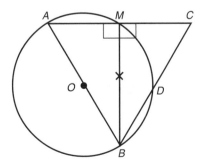

PROOF

Statement	Reason
1. In circle O, $\overline{AB}$ is a diameter.	1. Given.
2. $\angle AMB$ is a right angle.	2. An angle inscribed in a semicircle is a right angle.
3. $\angle CMB$ is a right angle.	3. The supplement of a right angle is a right angle.
4. $\angle AMB \cong \angle CMB$ (A)	4. All right angles are congruent.
5. $\overline{MB} \cong \overline{MB}$ (S)	5. Reflexive property.
6. $\overset{\frown}{AM} \cong \overset{\frown}{DM}$	6. Given.
7. $\angle ABM \cong \angle CBM$ (A)	7. Inscribed angles that intercept congruent arcs are congruent.
8. $\triangle AMB \cong \triangle CMB$	8. ASA postulate.

Vertex on the Circle: Chord-Tangent Angle

In Figure 6.16, $\angle ABC$ is formed by chord $\overline{AB}$ and tangent $\overrightarrow{BC}$ and intercepts arc AB. If the measure of $\overset{\frown}{AB}$ is 110°, for example, then the measure of $\angle ABC$ is one-half of 110° or 55°. Thus

$$m\angle ABC = \frac{1}{2} m\overset{\frown}{AB}.$$

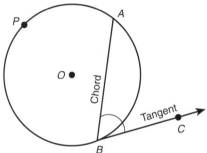

Figure 6.16 Chord-Tangent Angle

MATH FACTS

CHORD-TANGENT ANGLE THEOREM

The measure of an angle formed by a tangent and a chord drawn to the point of tangency is one-half the measure of its intercepted arc.

Example

3. In the accompanying diagram, $\overrightarrow{DE}$ is tangent to circle O, at D, $\overline{AOB}$ is a diameter, and $\overline{CD}$ is parallel to $\overline{AOB}$. If m∠DAB = 21, find m∠CDE.

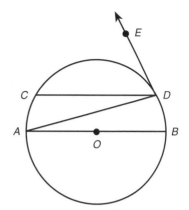

Solution: Angle CDE intercepts arc CD, so the measure of this arc is needed. Since the sum of the measures of the arcs of a semicircle is 180,

$$\text{m}\overset{\frown}{AC} + \text{m}\overset{\frown}{CD} + \text{m}\overset{\frown}{DB} = 180.$$

The measure of inscribed angle DAB is 21. The measure of its intercepted arc, $\overset{\frown}{DB}$, must be twice as great, or 42. Since parallel chords intercept equal arcs, m$\overset{\frown}{AC}$ = m$\overset{\frown}{DB}$ = 42. Hence:

$$42 + \text{m}\overset{\frown}{CD} + 42 = 180$$
$$\text{m}\overset{\frown}{CD} = 180 - 84$$
$$= 96$$

Since ∠CDE is formed by a chord and a tangent,

$$\text{m}\angle CDE = \frac{1}{2}\,\text{m}\overset{\frown}{CD}$$
$$= \frac{1}{2}\,(96)$$
$$= \mathbf{48}$$

Vertex Inside the Circle: Angles Formed by Intersecting Chords

In Figure 6.17, ∠AEC is formed by chords $\overline{AB}$ and $\overline{CD}$ intersecting at point E inside the circle. Angle AEC intercepts *two* arcs: arc AC and arc BD, which lies opposite its equal vertical angle. The measure of ∠AEC is found by taking the average of the measures of its two intercepted arcs. Thus

$$\text{m}\angle AEC = \frac{1}{2}\,(\text{m}\overset{\frown}{AC} + \text{m}\overset{\frown}{BD}).$$

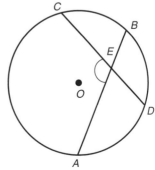

Figure 6.17 Angle Formed by Intersecting Chords

MATH FACTS

CHORD-CHORD ANGLE THEOREM

The measure of the angle formed by two chords intersecting inside a circle is one-half of the sum of the measures of its two intercepted arcs.

Examples

4. In the accompanying diagram, find the value of x.

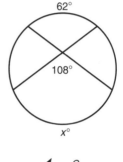

Solution: $108 = \dfrac{1}{2}(x + 62)$

or $\quad 2(108) = x + 62$
$\qquad 216 = x + 62$
$\qquad\quad x = 216 - 62 = \mathbf{154}$

5. In the accompanying diagram, regular pentagon *ABCDE* is inscribed in circle *O*. Chords $\overline{AD}$ and $\overline{BE}$ intersect at *F*, and $\overleftrightarrow{BT}$ is tangent to circle *O* at *B*. Find:
(a) m∠*ABT* **(b)** m∠*AFE*

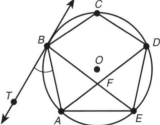

Solutions: **(a)** In a regular pentagon all of the five sides have the same length, and therefore circle *O* is divided into five equal arcs. The measure of each arc is, therefore, $\frac{360}{5}$ or 72. Hence

$$m\angle ABT = \frac{1}{2}\,m\widehat{AB} = \frac{1}{2}(72) = \mathbf{36}.$$

(b) Angle *AFE* intercepts arcs *BCD* and *AE*. Since

$$m\widehat{AE} = 72 \text{ and } m\widehat{BCD} = m\widehat{BC} + m\widehat{CD} = 72 + 72 = 144,$$

$$m\angle AFE = \frac{1}{2}(m\widehat{BCD} + m\widehat{AE})$$

$$= \frac{1}{2}(144 + 72)$$

$$= \frac{1}{2}(216)$$

$$= \mathbf{108}$$

6. In the accompanying diagram, chord $\overline{BE}$ bisects $\angle ABC$. If m$\angle ABC =$ 70 and m$\widehat{BAE} = 200$, find m$\angle AFE$.

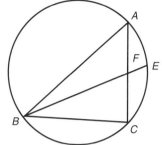

Solution: Angle *AFE* intercepts arcs *AE* and *BC*, whose measures must be determined. Since $\overline{BE}$ bisects inscribed angle *ABC*, m$\angle ABE = 35$, so m$\widehat{AE} = 2 \times 35$ or 70. Similarly, m$\angle CBE = 35$, so m$\widehat{CE} = 70$. Since the sum of the degree measures of the arcs of a circle is 360,

$$m\widehat{BC} + m\widehat{BAE} + m\widehat{CE} = 360$$
$$m\widehat{BC} + 200\ \ \ \ + 70\ \ = 360$$
$$m\widehat{BC}\ \ = 90$$

The measure of $\angle AFE$ is one-half the sum of the measures of its intercepted arcs. Hence

$$m\angle AFE = \frac{1}{2}\,(m\widehat{AE} + m\widehat{BC})$$
$$= \frac{1}{2}\,(70 + 90)$$
$$= \textbf{80}$$

Vertex Outside the Circle: Angles Formed by Two Secants, Two Tangents, or a Secant and a Tangent

If the vertex of an angle lies outside the circle, the sides of the angle may be two secants, two tangents, or a secant and a tangent. In each case the measure of the angle is one-half the difference of the measures of the two arcs that lie between the sides of the angle (see Figure 6.18).

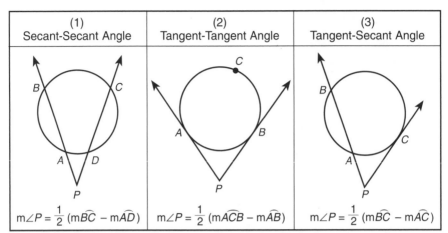

(1) Secant-Secant Angle	(2) Tangent-Tangent Angle	(3) Tangent-Secant Angle
$m\angle P = \frac{1}{2}(m\overset{\frown}{BC} - m\overset{\frown}{AD})$	$m\angle P = \frac{1}{2}(m\overset{\frown}{ACB} - m\overset{\frown}{AB})$	$m\angle P = \frac{1}{2}(m\overset{\frown}{BC} - m\overset{\frown}{AC})$

Figure 6.18 Angles Whose Vertices are Outside the Circle. In each case the measure of the angle is found by taking one-half the difference of the measures of the intercepted arcs.

MATH FACTS

SEC-SEC, TAN-TAN, TAN-SEC THEOREM

The measure of an angle formed by two secants, two tangents, or a tangent and a secant intersecting outside a circle is one-half the difference of the measures of its two intercepted arcs.

Examples

7. In each case, find the value of x:

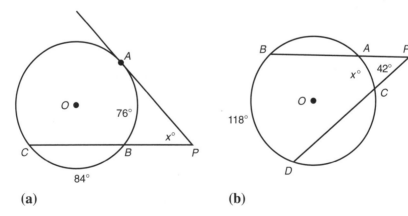

(a)   **(b)**

Solutions:

(a) $m\widehat{AC} + 76 + 84 = 360$

$$m\widehat{AC} = 360 - 160$$

$$= 200$$

Hence

$$x = \frac{1}{2}(m\widehat{AC} - m\widehat{AB})$$

$$= \frac{1}{2}(200 - 76)$$

$$= \frac{1}{2}(124)$$

$$= \mathbf{62}$$

(b) $m\angle P = \frac{1}{2}(m\widehat{BD} - m\widehat{AC})$

$$42 = \frac{1}{2}(118 - x)$$

$$84 = 118 - x$$

$$x = 118 - 84$$

$$= \mathbf{34}$$

8. In the accompanying diagram, $\overrightarrow{PA}$ is tangent to circle O at point A. Secant $\overline{PBC}$ is drawn. Chords $\overline{CA}$ and $\overline{BD}$ intersect at point E. If

$$m\widehat{AD} : m\widehat{AB} : m\widehat{DC} : m\widehat{BC}$$
$$= 2 : 3 : 4 : 6,$$

find the measure of each of the numbered angles.

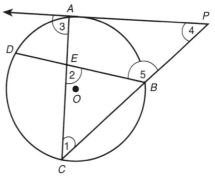

Solution: First find the degree measures of the arcs of the circle. Let $2x = m\widehat{AD}$. Then

$$3x = m\widehat{AB}, \quad 4x = m\widehat{CD}, \quad \text{and} \quad 6x = m\widehat{BC}.$$

Since the sum of the degree measures of the arcs of a circle is 360,

$$m\widehat{AD} + m\widehat{AB} + m\widehat{DC} + m\widehat{BC} = 360$$
$$2x \quad + 3x \quad + 4x \quad + 6x \quad = 360$$
$$15x = 360$$
$$x = \frac{360}{15} = 24$$

Hence

$$m\widehat{AD} = 2x = 2(24) = 48$$
$$m\widehat{AB} = 3x = 3(24) = 72$$
$$m\widehat{DC} = 4x = 4(24) = 96$$
$$m\widehat{BC} = 6x = 6(24) = 144$$

∠1 is an inscribed angle:

$$m\angle 1 = \frac{1}{2}\,m\widehat{AB}$$
$$= \frac{1}{2}(72)$$
$$= \mathbf{36}$$

∠3 is a tangent-chord angle:

$$m\angle 3 = \frac{1}{2}\,m\widehat{AC} = \frac{1}{2}(m\widehat{AD} + m\widehat{DC})$$
$$= \frac{1}{2}(48 + 96)$$
$$= \mathbf{72}$$

∠2 is a chord-chord angle:

$$m\angle 2 = \frac{1}{2}(m\widehat{AD} + m\widehat{BC})$$
$$= \frac{1}{2}(48 + 144)$$
$$= \mathbf{96}$$

∠4 is a secant-tangent angle:

$$m\angle 4 = \frac{1}{2}(m\widehat{AC} - m\widehat{AB})$$
$$= \frac{1}{2}(144 - 72)$$
$$= \mathbf{36}$$

∠5: Angles 5 and *CBD* are supplementary. The measure of ∠5 may be found indirectly by first finding m∠*CBD*.

$$m\angle CBD = \frac{1}{2}\,m\widehat{DC} = \frac{1}{2}(96) = 48$$

$$m\angle 5 = 180 - m\angle CBD$$
$$= 180 - 48$$
$$= \mathbf{132}$$

Exercise Set 6.2

1–8. Find the value of x.

1.

$\overline{AB} \parallel \overline{CD}$

2.

3.

295°

4.

110°

125°

5.

54°

6.

29°

7.

54°

38°

8.

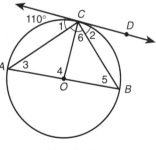

120°

4x

2x

9. In the accompanying diagram, $\overleftrightarrow{CD}$ is tangent to circle O at C. $\overline{AOB}$ is a diameter, and $\overline{OC}$ is a radius. Chords $\overline{AC}$ and $\overline{BC}$ are drawn. Find the measure of each of the numbered angles.

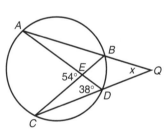

110°

Exercise 9

10. Regular hexagon *ABCDEF* is inscribed in circle *O*. Chords $\overline{AD}$ and $\overline{CE}$ intersect at *H*. Tangents drawn to circle *O* at *A* and *F* intersect at point *P*. Find:

(a) m∠*CED* (b) m∠*BAF* (c) m∠*AHE* (d) m∠*APF*

11. In the accompanying diagram, $\overline{CD}$ is tangent to circle *O*, $\overline{AB} \cong \overline{AD}$, m$\widehat{AB}$ = 150, and $\overline{EOD}$ is a diameter. Find:

(a) m$\widehat{BD}$ (c) m∠*EFB*
(b) m∠*ACD* (d) m∠*EDA*

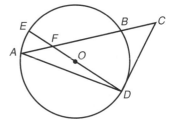

Exercise 11

12. In the accompanying diagram, $\overline{PCD}$ and $\overline{PBA}$ are secants from external point *P* to circle *O*. Chords $\overline{DA}$, $\overline{DEB}$, $\overline{CEA}$, and $\overline{C}$ and drawn. $\overline{AB} \cong \overline{DC}$, m$\widehat{BC}$ is twice m$\widehat{AB}$, and m$\widehat{AD}$ is 60 more than m$\widehat{BC}$. Find:

(a) m$\widehat{AB}$
(b) m∠*P*
(c) m∠*DAC*
(d) m∠*DEA*
(e) m∠*PCB*

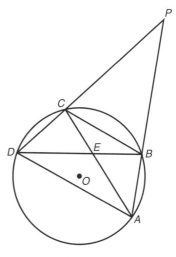

Exercise 12

13. In circle *O*, tangent $\overrightarrow{PW}$ and $\overline{PST}$ are drawn. Chord $\overline{WA}$ is parallel to chord $\overline{ST}$. Chords $\overline{AS}$ and $\overline{WT}$ intersect at point *B*. If m$\widehat{WA}$: m$\widehat{AT}$: m$\widehat{ST}$ = 1 : 3 : 5, find:

(a) m$\widehat{WA}$, m$\widehat{AT}$, m$\widehat{ST}$, m$\widehat{SW}$
(b) m∠*WTS*
(c) m∠*TBS*
(d) m∠*TWP*
(e) m∠*WPT*
(f) m∠*ASP*

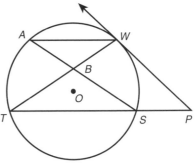

142

6.3 FINDING CHORD, TANGENT, AND SECANT-SEGMENT LENGTHS

KEY IDEAS

If two angles of one triangle are congruent to two angles of another triangle, then the triangles are similar and the lengths of their corresponding sides are in proportion. If triangles that have chord, tangent, or secant segments as sides can be proved similar, some useful proportions involving the lengths of these segments can be formed.

Similar Triangles and Circles

The following angle measurement relationships are often used in obtaining the congruent pairs of angles needed to prove that triangles are similar:

- Inscribed angles (or angles formed by a tangent and a chord) that intercept the same (or congruent) arcs are congruent.
- Angles that are inscribed in a semicircle, are formed by a radius drawn to a point of tangency, or are formed by perpendicular lines are right angles and are, therefore, congruent.

Example

1. Given: In circle P, $\overline{AB}$ is a diameter, $\overline{DB}$ is a tangent to circle P at B, $\overline{CD} \perp \overline{DB}$.

Prove: $\dfrac{AB}{BC} = \dfrac{BC}{CD}$

Solution: To prove that a proportion is true, first identify the triangles that have these segments as sides, and then prove that the triangles are similar. In this example, it is necessary to prove that triangles ABC and CBD are similar since $\overline{AB}$ and $\overline{BC}$ (reading "across" the *top* of the proportion) are sides of $\triangle ABC$, and $\overline{BC}$ and $\overline{CD}$ (reading "across" the *bottom* of the proportion) are sides of $\triangle CBD$.

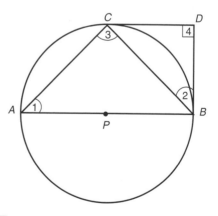

143

Proof: Angle 1 is an inscribed angle, and $\angle 2$ is formed by a tangent and a chord. Since the measure of each angle is one-half the measure of the same arc, $\overset{\frown}{BC}$, angles 1 and 2 are congruent. Angle 3 is inscribed in a semicircle, and $\angle 4$ is formed by perpendicular lines. Since each angle is a right angle, angles 3 and 4 are congruent. Hence

$$\angle 1 \cong \angle 2 \quad \text{and} \quad \angle 3 \cong \angle 4,$$

so triangles ABC and CBD are similar by the AA Theorem of Similarity. The lengths of corresponding sides of similar triangles are in proportion, so

$$\frac{AB}{BC} = \frac{BC}{CD}.$$

Products of Segments of Intersecting Chords

In Figure 6.19, chords $\overline{AB}$ and $\overline{CD}$ intersect at E, forming segments p, q, r, and s as shown. Triangles AED and CEB are similar since (1) the vertical angles at E are congruent, and (2) inscribed angles D and B are congruent because they intercept the same arc.

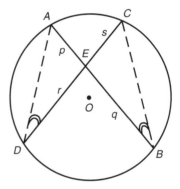

Since the lengths of corresponding sides of similar triangles are in proportion,

$$\frac{p}{r} = \frac{s}{q} \quad \text{or} \quad p \cdot q = r \cdot s.$$

Figure 6.19 Products of Intersecting-Chord Segments

MATH FACTS

CHORD SEGMENTS THEOREM

If two chords intersect, the product of the segment lengths of one chord is equal to the product of the segment lengths of the other chord.

Examples

2. In the accompanying diagram, chords $\overline{AB}$ and $\overline{CD}$ of circle O intersect in E so that $CE = 5$ centimeters and $ED = 16$ centimeters. If the length of $\overline{AE}$ exceeds the length of $\overline{EB}$ by 2 centimeters, find the length of $\overline{EB}$.

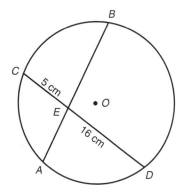

Solution: Let $EB = x$. Then $AE = x + 2$.

$$EB \cdot AE = CE \cdot ED$$
$$x(x+2) = 5 \cdot 16$$
$$x^2 + 2x - 80 = 0$$
$$(x + 10)(x - 8) = 0$$

| $x + 10 = 0$ | or | $x - 8 = 0$ |

$x = -10$ $x = 8$

Reject -10 since x must be positive. $EB = x = 8$ and $AE = x + 2 = 8 + 2 = 10$

The length of $\overline{EB}$ is **8 cm.**

3. In circle O, chord $\overline{AB}$ bisects chord $\overline{DC}$ at E. If $AE = 4$ and $EB = 89$, find the length of $\overline{DC}$.

Solution: Since $\overline{AB}$ bisects $\overline{DC}$ at E, point E is the midpoint of $\overline{DC}$. Let $x = CE = ED$.

$$CE \cdot ED = EB \cdot AE$$
$$x \cdot \quad x = \quad 9 \cdot 4$$
$$x^2 = 36$$
$$x = \sqrt{36} = 6$$

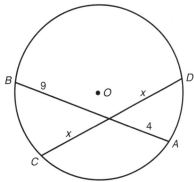

Hence $CE = ED = 6$. Since $CD = CE + ED = 12$, the length of $\overline{CD}$ is **12.**

Tangent-Secant Segments

In Figure 6.20, tangent $\overline{PT}$ and secant $\overline{PAB}$ are drawn from the same point, P. Secant segment $\overline{PA}$ falls outside the circle and is called an *external secant segment*. By drawing $\overline{AT}$ and $\overline{BT}$, triangles PAT and PTB are formed. These triangles are similar since (1) $\angle P \cong \angle P$, and (2) the measures of angles PTA and B are each one-half the measure of $\overparen{AT}$, and the angles are, therefore, congruent. Hence

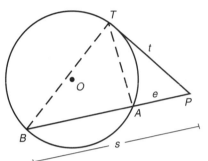

$$\frac{t}{e} = \frac{s}{t} \quad \text{and} \quad t^2 = s \cdot e.$$

Figure 6.20 Tangent-Secant Segments

TAN-SEC SEGMENTS THEOREM

If a tangent and a secant are drawn to a circle from the same point, then the square of the length of the tangent equals the product of the lengths of the secant and its external segment.

Example

4. In the accompanying diagram. $\overline{PT}$ is tangent to circle O at T and $\overline{PAB}$ is a secant.
(a) If $PT = 6$ and $PAB = 12$, find PA.
(b) If $PA = 4$ and $AB = 12$, find PT.
(c) If $PT = 12$ and $AB = 7$, find PAB.

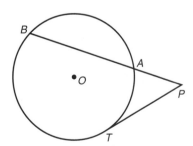

Solutions: **(a)** $(PT)^2 = PAB \cdot PA$
$$6^2 = 12(PA)$$
$$36 = 12(PA)$$
$$\text{or} \quad PA = \frac{36}{12}$$
$$= 3$$

(b) Since $PA = 4$ and $AB = 12$, $PAB = 4 + 12 = 16$.

$$(PT)^2 = PAB \cdot PA$$
$$= (16)(4)$$
$$= 64$$
$$PT = \sqrt{64}$$
$$= \mathbf{8}$$

(c) Let $PAB = x$. Then $PA = x - 7$.

$$(PT)^2 = PAB \cdot PA$$
$$(12)^2 = x(x - 7)$$
$$144 = x^2 - 7x$$
$$0 = x^2 - 7x - 144 \quad \text{or} \quad x^2 - 7x - 144 = 0$$
$$(x - 16)(x + 9) = 0$$
$$x - 16 = 0 \quad \text{or} \quad x + 9 = 0$$
$$x = 16 \quad \bigg| \quad x = -9. \text{ Reject since length}$$
$$\text{cannot be negative.}$$

$PAB = \mathbf{16}$

Segment of Two Secants

If in Figure 6.21, two secants are drawn to a circle from the same point, then

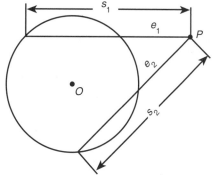

$$s_1 \times e_1 = s_2 \times e_2.$$

Figure 6.21 Segments of Two Secants

MATH FACTS

SEC-SEC SEGMENTS THEOREM

If two secants are drawn to a circle from the same point, the product of the lengths of one secant and its external segment is equal to the product of the lengths of the other secant and its external segment.

Example

5. In each case find the value of *x*:

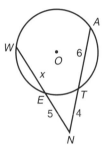

(a)   **(b)**

Solutions:

(a) $PA \cdot PB = PC \cdot PD$
$$3 \cdot 8 \ = 2 \ \cdot x$$
$$24 = 2x$$
$$\mathbf{12} = x$$

(b) $NE \cdot NW = NT \cdot NA$, where $NE = 5$,
$NW = x + 5$, $NT = 4$, $NA = 6 + 4 = 10$
$$5(x + 5) = 4 \cdot 10$$
$$5x + 25 = 40$$
$$5x = 15$$
$$x = \mathbf{3}$$

Exercise Set 6.3

1. If $RK = 5$, $KH = 9$, and $PK = 15$, find *KN*.

2. If $PK = 27$, $KN = 3$, and *K* is the midpoint of *RH*, find *RK*.

3. If $RH = 16$, $RK = 4$, and $PK = 8$, find *PN*.

4. If $RH = 22$, $PK = 7$, and $KN = 3$, find *RK*.

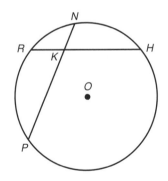

Exercises 1–4

5. If $PW = 5$, $PG = 8$, and $PH = 2$, find *KH*.

6. If $GW = 7$, $PW = 3$, and $PK = 15$, find *PH*.

7. If *W* is the midpoint of $\overline{GP}$ and $PH = 5$, and $KH = 35$, find *PG*.

8. If $PW = 6$, $WG = 9$, and $PH = 9$, find *KH*.

9. If $GW = 11$, $PH = 5$, and $KH = 7$, find *PW*.

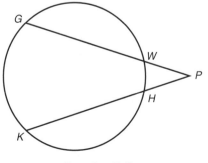

Exercises 5–9

10. If $RV = 9$ and $RM = 3$, find RT.

11. If $MT = 24$ and $RM = 1$, find RV.

12. If $RV = 8$ and $RM = 4$, find MT.

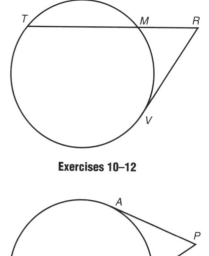

Exercises 10–12

13. Given: circle O with tangent $\overline{PA}$ and secant $\overline{PBC}$; chord $\overline{DE}$ bisects chord $\overline{BC}$ at M; $PA = 3$; $PB = 1$.
   (a) Find BC.
   (b) If $DE = 10$ and $DM > EM$, find EM.

Exercise 13

14. (a) If $NA = 4$, $JA = 8$, and $WA = 11$, find OK.
   (b) If A is the midpoint of $\overline{JW}$, $AK = 32$, and $NA = 18$, find JW and OA.
   (c) If $JA = 12$, $AW = 9$, and AK is three times the length of $\overline{NA}$, find OK.

Exercise 14

15. A circle divides a secant segment into an internal segment having a length of 30 and an external segment having a length of 2. Find the length of a tangent segment drawn to the circle from the same exterior point.

16. From a point 2 units from a circle, a tangent segment is drawn. If the radius of the circle is 8, find the length of the tangent segment.

17. Secant $\overline{PAB}$ and tangent $\overline{PA}$ are drawn to circle O from point P. If the ratio of PA to AB is 1 to 4 and the length of $\overline{PC}$ is 80, find the length of secant $\overline{PAB}$.

18. Given: Triangle HBW is inscribed in circle O, tangent segment $\overline{AB}$ is tangent at point B, $ABLM$ is a parallelogram.

Prove: $\dfrac{BL}{BW} = \dfrac{BM}{BH}$

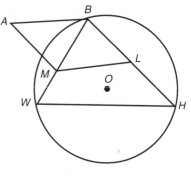

Exercise 18

19. Given: In circle O, $\overline{KJ}$ is a diameter, $\overleftrightarrow{MJ}$ is tangent at point J, N is the midpoint of $\overarc{LNJ}$.

Prove: $\dfrac{KL}{KJ} = \dfrac{KP}{KM}$

20. Given: In circle O, $\overleftrightarrow{KJ}$ is a diameter, $\overleftrightarrow{MJ}$ is tangent at point J, $\overline{JP} \cong \overline{JM}$.

Prove: $\dfrac{KL}{KJ} = \dfrac{LP}{KM}$

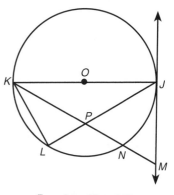

Exercises 19 and 20

REGENTS TUNE-UP: CHAPTER 6

Each of the questions in this section has appeared on a previous Course III Regents Examination. Here is an opportunity for you to review Chapter 6 and, at the same time, prepare for the Course III Regents Examination.

1. In the accompanying diagram, $\overrightarrow{PA}$ is tangent to circle O at A and $\overline{PBC}$ is a secant. If $CB = 9$ and $PB = 3$, find the length of $\overline{PA}$.

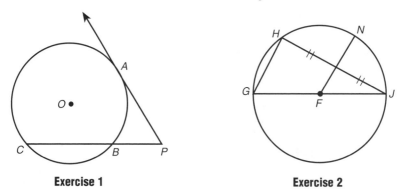

Exercise 1   **Exercise 2**

2. In the accompanying diagram of circle F, $\overline{FN}$ bisects $\overline{HJ}$ and $m\widehat{NJ} = 68$. Find $m\widehat{HG}$.

3. In circle O, diameter $\overline{AB}$ is perpendicular to chord $\overline{CD}$ at E. If $AE = 16$ and $EB = 4$, find CD.

4. Two secants, $\overline{ABC}$ and $\overline{ADE}$, are drawn to a circle from external point A. If $AB = 4$, $BC = 6$, and $AD = 5$, find DE.

5. In the accompanying diagram of circle O, diameter $\overline{AB}$ is perpendicular to chord $\overline{CD}$ at point E. What is the image of $\overline{AC}$ in $\overline{AB}$?
(1) $\overline{AD}$ (3) $\overline{ED}$
(2) $\overline{BD}$ (4) $\overline{AE}$

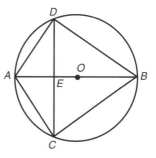

6. Quadrilateral $ABCD$ is inscribed in circle O. If $m\widehat{AB} = 132$ and $m\widehat{BC} = 82$, find $m\angle ADC$.

151

7. In circle O, chord $\overline{CD}$ is parallel to diameter $\overline{AB}$ with radii $\overline{OC}$ and $\overline{OD}$ drawn. If m$\overarc{AC}$ = 25, what is m$\angle COD$?

8. In a circle, chords $\overline{AB}$ and $\overline{CD}$ intersect at point E. If $AE = x + 1$, $EB = x$, $CE = 2$, and $ED = 3$, find the value of x.

9. In the accompanying diagram, $\overrightarrow{PC}$ is tangent to circle O at point C. If m$\overarc{AD}$ = 122 and m$\angle BAC$ = 73, find:
   (a) m$\overarc{BC}$ **(b)** m$\angle ABC$ **(c)** m$\angle P$ **(d)** m$\angle BEA$ **(e)** m$\angle PDA$

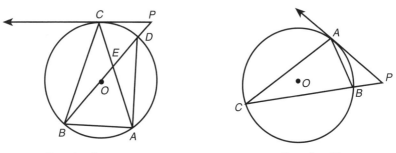

Exercise 9   Exercise 10

10. In the accompanying diagram, $\overrightarrow{PA}$ is tangent to circle O at A, $\overline{PBC}$ is a secant, m$\angle P$ = 42, and m$\overarc{AC}$: m$\overarc{AB}$ = 5 : 2. Find:
   (a) m$\overarc{AC}$ **(b)** m$\overarc{BC}$ **(c)** m$\angle ACB$ **(d)** m$\angle ABP$

ANSWERS TO SELECTED EXERCISES: CHAPTER 6

Section 6.1
1. 210   **5.** C **9.** 24 inches
3. 95   **7.** (4)   **11.** 11

Section 6.2
1. 66   **9.** m$\angle 1$ = 55, m$\angle 2$ = 35, m$\angle 3$ = 35,
3. 115   m$\angle 4$ = 110, m$\angle 5$ = 55, m$\angle 6$ = 55
5. 232   **11. (a)** 60   **(b)** 45   **(c)** 135   **(d)** 15
7. 22   **13. (a)** m$\overarc{WA}$ = 30, m$\overarc{AT}$ = 90, m$\overarc{ST}$ = 150, m$\overarc{SW}$ = 90
                     (b) 45   **(c)** 90   **(d)** 120   **(e)** 15   **(f)** 135

Section 6.3
1. 3   **5.** 18   **9.** 4   **13. (a)** 8   **15.** 8
3. 6   **7.** 20   **11.** 5   **(b)** 2   **17.** 20

18. Prove $\triangle BLM \sim \triangle BWH$ by using the AA Theorem of Similarity:

- $\angle MBL \cong HBW$ (Reflexive property)
- $\angle ABM \cong \angle BML$ (Alternate interior angles formed by parallel lines are congruent.)
- $\triangle BLM \sim \triangle BWH$, so $\frac{BL}{BW} = \frac{BM}{BH}$ (The lengths of corresponding sides of similar triangles are in proportion.)

19. Prove $\triangle KLP \sim \triangle KJM$ by using the AA Theorem of Similarity:

- $\angle L \cong \angle KJM$ (All right angles are congruent.)
- $m\angle LKP = \frac{1}{2} m\widehat{NC}$, $m\angle JKM = \frac{1}{2} m\widehat{JN}$, and $\widehat{JN} \cong \widehat{NL}$, so $\angle LKP \cong \angle JKM$.
- $\triangle KLP \sim \triangle KJM$, so $\frac{KL}{KJ} = \frac{KP}{KM}$ (The lengths of corresponding sides of similar triangles are in proportion.)

20. Prove $\triangle KLP \sim \triangle KJM$ by using the AA Theorem of Similarity:

- $\angle L \cong \angle KJM$ (All right angles are congruent.)
- Since $\overline{JP} \cong \overline{JM}$, then $\angle M \cong \angle JPM \cong \angle KPL$.
- $\triangle KLP \sim \triangle KJM$, so $\frac{KL}{KJ} = \frac{LP}{KM}$ (The lengths of corresponding sides of similar triangles are in proportion.)

Regents Tune-Up: Chapter 6

1. 6	**5.** (1)	**9. (a)** 146	**10. (a)** 140
2. 44	**6.** 107	**(b)** 78	**(b)** 164
3. 16	**7.** 130	**(c)** 56	**(c)** 28
4. 3	**8.** 2	**(d)** 46	**(d)** 110
		(e) 151	

TRIGONOMETRY AND SOLVING TRIANGLES

CHAPTER 7

TRIGONOMETRIC FUNCTIONS: THE GENERAL ANGLE

7.1 REVIEWING RIGHT-TRIANGLE TRIGONOMETRY

KEY IDEAS

In a right triangle, the ratios of the length of selected pairs of sides can be related to the measure of either of the acute angles, using the sine, cosine, and tangent trigonometric ratios:

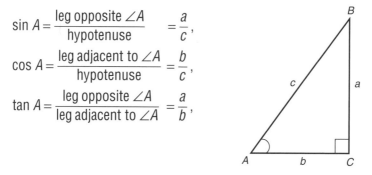

$$\sin A = \frac{\text{leg opposite } \angle A}{\text{hypotenuse}} = \frac{a}{c},$$

$$\cos A = \frac{\text{leg adjacent to } \angle A}{\text{hypotenuse}} = \frac{b}{c},$$

$$\tan A = \frac{\text{leg opposite } \angle A}{\text{leg adjacent to } \angle A} = \frac{a}{b},$$

where *sin, cos,* and *tan* are abbreviations for *sine, cosine,* and *tangent,* respectively.

Writing Trigonometric Ratios

If the lengths of two sides of a right triangle are known, the trigonometric function values of either acute angle can be determined.

Example

1. In right triangle *ACB*, hypotenuse *AB* = 5 and *BC* = 3. Find the value of:
(a) sin *A*   **(b)** cos *A*   **(c)** tan *A*

Solutions: Since $\triangle ACB$ is a 3-4-5 right triangle, $AC = 4$.

(a) $\sin A = \dfrac{\text{leg opposite } \angle A}{\text{hypotenuse}}$

$= \dfrac{BC}{AB} = \dfrac{3}{5} \text{ or } \mathbf{0.6}$

(b) $\cos A = \dfrac{\text{leg adjacent to } \angle A}{\text{hypotenuse}}$

$= \dfrac{AC}{AB} = \dfrac{4}{5} \text{ or } \mathbf{0.8}$

(c) $\tan A = \dfrac{\text{leg opposite } \angle A}{\text{leg adjacent to } \angle A}$

$= \dfrac{BC}{AC} = \dfrac{3}{4} \text{ or } \mathbf{0.75}$

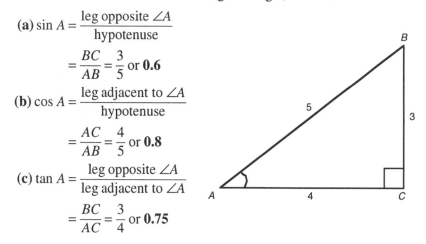

Finding Trigonometric Function Values

To use a scientific calculator to find the value of sin x, cos x, or tan x, where x is measured in degrees, proceed as follows:

- Set the angular mode of your calculator to DEGrees, if necessary. If you see RADians instead of DEGrees in the display window, press the DRG or MODE key until DEG appears in the display window.
- Press the key labeled with the name of the appropriate trigonometric function, enter the number x, and then press the $\boxed{=}$ key. Some calculators require that you enter the measure of the angle before pressing the trignometric function key. For example, to find the value of sin 54°, use the key sequence

$$\boxed{\text{SIN}} \quad 54 \quad \boxed{=} \qquad or \qquad 54 \quad \boxed{\text{SIN}}.$$

Thus, sin 54° ≈ 0.8090169.

Converting Minutes to Degrees

Each of the 60 equal parts of a degree is called a **minute**. The angle 28°30′ is read as "28 degrees, 30 minutes." Since there are 60 minutes in 1 degree, dividing 30 minutes by 60 changes 30 minutes to a fractional part of a degree. Thus

$$28°30' = 28° + \left(\frac{30}{60}\right)^{\circ} = \mathbf{28.5°}.$$

MATH FACTS

CHANGING FROM MINUTES TO DEGREES

To convert $n°m'$ to an equivalent number of degrees, divide m by 60 and then add the result to n. Some scientific calculators have a function key that converts degrees and minutes into degrees and decimal parts of a degree.

Example

2. Find the value of cos 37°20′ correct to *four decimal places.*

Solution: If your calculator does not have a key that converts a minute into a decimal part of a degree, change 37°20′ into an equivalent number of degrees by dividing 20 by 60, adding the quotient to 37, and then evaluating the cosine of the resulting angle:

$$20 \boxed{\div} 60 \boxed{+} 37 \boxed{=} \boxed{\text{COS}}.$$

If this key sequence does not work with your calculator, try this sequence:

$$\boxed{\text{COS}} \boxed{(} 20 \boxed{\div} 60 \boxed{+} 37 \boxed{)} \boxed{=}.$$

Finding Angles Using Inverse Trigonometric Functions

Most scientific calculators have sin⁻¹ printed directly above the $\boxed{\text{SIN}}$ key, cos⁻¹ printed directly above the $\boxed{\text{COS}}$ key, and tan⁻¹ printed directly above the $\boxed{\text{TAN}}$ key. These second or *inverse* calculator functions are used to find the measure of an angle when you know the value of a particular trigonometric function of that angle. For example, if tan x = 2.197, then x = tan⁻¹ 2.197, which is read as "x is an angle whose tangent is 2.197."

To find the degree measure of $\angle x$, make sure the angular mode of the calculator is set to degrees. Then key in

$$2.197 \boxed{\text{2nd}} \boxed{\text{TAN}^{-1}} \quad \text{or} \quad \boxed{\text{2nd}} \boxed{\text{TAN}^{-1}} 2.197 \boxed{=}.$$

Since $x \approx 65.526579°$, $\angle x$, correct to the *nearest degree,* is **66°**.

Note: One way to change 65.526579° to an angle expressed to the *nearest minute* is to multiply the first three digits of the decimal part by 60, round off the product, and then add the result to 65. Since .526 × 60′ ≈ 32′, 65.526579° ≈ 65°32′. Some calculators have a special function key that does this operation automatically.

Angles of Elevation and Depression

A person sometimes has to look up or down to sight a distant object. The **angle of elevation** is the angle through which an observer must *raise* his or her line of sight in order to see an object *above* the observer's horizontal line of vision. The **angle of depression** is the angle through which an observer must *lower* his or her line of sight in order to see an object *below* the observer's horizontal line of vision. As shown in Figure 7.1, the measures of the angles of elevation and depression are equal, since they are alternate interior angles formed by parallel lines.

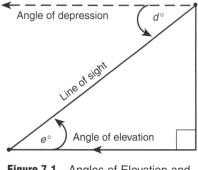

Figure 7.1 Angles of Elevation and Depression

Examples

3. A man standing 30 feet from a flagpole observes the angle of elevation of its top to be 48°30′. Find the height of the flagpole, correct to the *nearest tenth of a foot*.

Solution: If x = the height of the flagpole, then

$$\tan 48°30' = \frac{x}{30}$$
$$x = 30 \tan 48°30'$$
$$= 30(1.1303)$$
$$= 33.909$$

The height of the flagpole, correct to the *nearest tenth of a foot,* is **33.9**.

4. When the altitude of a plane is 800 meters, the pilot spots a target at a distance of 1200 meters. Find, correct to the *nearest 10 minutes,* the angle of depression at which the pilot observes the target.

Solution: If x = measure of angle of depression, then

$$\sin x° = \frac{800}{1200} = \frac{2}{3} = 0.6667$$
$$x = \sin^{-1} 0.6667$$
$$\approx 41.813°$$
$$\approx 41°49'$$

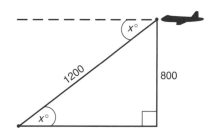

157

The angle of depression, correct to the *nearest 10 minutes,* is **41°50′**.

Exercise Set 7.1

1. Find to four decimal places:
   (a) sin 30°   (c) cos 67°10′   (e) tan 18°20′
   (b) tan 45°   (d) sin 55°40′   (f) $(\sin 60°)^2 + (\cos 60°)^2$

2. Find the complement of each of the following angles:
   (a) 19°20′   (b) 35°42′   (c) 64°52′

3. Find the supplement of each of the following angles:
   (a) 64°25′   (b) 113°38′   (c) 126°08′

4. Find the degree measure of angle x, correct to the *nearest 10 minutes:*
   (a) $\cos x = 0.8700$ (c) $\tan x = 1.2110$ (e) $\tan x = 0.5036$

   (b) $\sin x = 0.9298$ (d) $\cos x = \dfrac{3}{5}$ (f) $\sin x = \dfrac{5}{8}$

5. In right triangle RTS, $\angle T$ is the right angle. If $\sin R = \dfrac{5}{13}$, express as a fraction:
   (a) $\cos R$ and $\tan R$ (b) $\sin S$, $\cos S$, and $\tan S$

6. If the length of a diagonal of a rectangle is 41 and the length of its longest side is 40, find, correct to the *nearest 10 minutes,* the measure of the angle formed by the diagonal and the
   (a) shortest side   (b) longest side

7. In an isosceles right triangle, the length of the hypotenuse is 2. Find:
   (a) the length of each leg
   (b) the values of the sine, cosine, and tangent of either acute angle of the triangle

8. The perimeter of an equilateral triangle is 6. If an altitude is drawn to the base of the triangle, find:
   (a) the length of the altitude
   (b) the values of the sine, cosine, and tangent of the angle formed by the base and a side of the triangle. (Answers may be left in radical form.)

9. In right triangle ACB, $\angle C$ is the right angle, $AB = 25$, and $AC = 24$. Find the values of the sine, cosine, and tangent of the acute angle having the *smallest* measure.

10. At noon, a tree having a height of 10 feet casts a shadow 14 feet in length. Find, to the *nearest tenth of a degree,* the angle of elevation of the sun at this time.

11. Find, to the *nearest tenth of a foot,* the height of a building that casts a shadow 80.4 feet when the angle of elevation of the sun is 42°40′.

12. A man observes that the angle of depression from the top of a cliff overlooking the ocean to a ship is 37°30′. If at this moment the ship is 500 meters from the foot of the cliff, find, to the *nearest tenth of a meter,* the height of the cliff.

13. When the altitude of a plane is 950 meters, the pilot spots a target at a distance of 1275 meters. At what angle of depression, correct to the *nearest 10 minutes,* does the pilot observe the target?

14. In the diagram shown, *ACB* is an isosceles right triangle, $m\angle C = 90$, $AC = 10$, and $\overline{AD}$ bisects $\angle BAC$. Find to the *nearest tenth* the length of:
(a) $\overline{CD}$ (b) $\overline{BD}$

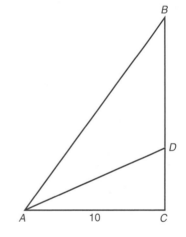

7.2 PLACING ANGLES IN STANDARD POSITION

KEY IDEAS

The use of coordinates gives meaning to trigonometric functions of angles of rotation greater than 90° or less than 0°. The Greek letter θ (theta) is commonly used in mathematics to represent an angle whose measure is not known.

Standard Position

An angle is in **standard position** when its vertex is at the origin (O) and one of its sides, called the **initial side,** remains fixed on the x-axis (see Figure 7.2). The other side of the angle, called the **terminal** side, moves in a counterclockwise direction for positive angles of rotation.

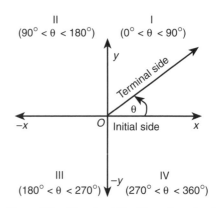

Figure 7.2 Standard Position of an Angle

Angles Greater Than 360°

An angle in standard position whose measure is greater than 360° will complete more than one full rotation. For example, an angle of rotation of 410° will complete one full rotation and its terminal side will lie in Quadrant I, making an angle of 410°–360° or 50° with the positive x-axis.

Although the angles 50° and 410° have different measures, they are *coterminal.* **Coterminal angles** (see Figure 7.3) are angles whose terminal sides coincide. To reduce an angle greater than 360° to a coterminal angle between 0° and 360°, successively subtract 360° from the given angle until the difference is between 0 and 360. For example, to find an angle that is coterminal with an angle of 860°, proceed as follows:

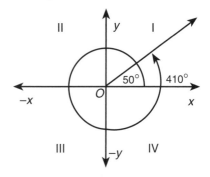

Figure 7.3 Coterminal Angles

Subtract 360 from 860: 860 – 360 = 500
Subtract 360 from 500: 500 – 360 = **140**

Hence angles of 860° and 140° are coterminal.

Negative Angles

A *negative* angle indicates a clockwise rotation about the origin. For example, the terminal side of an angle measuring –150° lies in Quadrant III, as shown in Figure 7.4. Notice that angles of –150° and 210° are coterminal.

A positive and negative angle are coterminal if the sum of the absolute values of their measures is 360° (or a multiple of 360°).

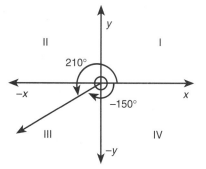

Figure 7.4 Negative Angles

Arc Length and Radian Measure

A *radian,* like a degree, is a unit of angle measure. The radian measure of a central angle of a circle compares the length of its intercepted arc with the length of the radius of the circle.

=== MATH FACTS ===

DEFINITION OF RADIAN AND ARC-LENGTH FORMULA

One **radian** is the measure of a central angle of a circle that intercepts an arc whose length equals the radius of the circle.

If θ represents the measure of a central angle in radians and s represents the length of its intercepted arc, then, in a circle whose radius is r,

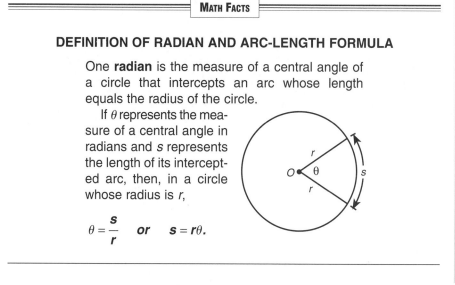

$$\theta = \frac{s}{r} \quad \textit{or} \quad s = r\theta.$$

Example

If the measure of a central angle of a circle is 2 radians and the radius of the circle is 5 centimeters, then the length of the intercepted arc s is

$$s = r\theta = 5 \times 2 = \textbf{10 cm.}$$

Converting Between Radians and Degrees

Since angles may be measured in degrees or in radians, it is sometimes necessary to be able to express the degree measure of a given angle in radians, or the radian measure of a given angle in degrees.

- To change from degrees to radians:

  Multiple the number of degrees by $\dfrac{\pi}{180°}$.

  Example: $60° = \overset{1}{\cancel{60°}} \times \left(\dfrac{\pi}{\underset{3}{\cancel{180°}}} \right) = \dfrac{\pi}{3}$ **radians**

- To change from radians to degrees:

  Multiply the number of radians by $\dfrac{180°}{\pi}$.

  Example: $\dfrac{\pi}{2}$ radians $= \dfrac{\overset{1}{\cancel{\pi}}}{\underset{}{\cancel{2}}} \times \dfrac{\overset{90}{\cancel{180°}}}{\cancel{\pi}} = \mathbf{90°}$

Examples

1. Find the measure of a central angle that intercepts an arc of length 3π in a circle whose radius is 9 centimeters.

Solution: In a circle, the length of an arc s equals the product of its radius r and the radian measure of its central angle θ. Since $s = r\theta$ and $s = 3\pi$, and $r = 9$:

$3\pi = 9\theta$ or $\theta = \dfrac{3\pi}{9} = \dfrac{\pi}{3}$ **radians**

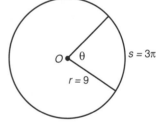

2. Change from degrees to radians:
(a) 45° **(b)** 300°

Solutions: To convert from degrees to radians, multiply by $\dfrac{\pi}{180°}$.

In each case leave the answer in terms of π as this form gives an *exact* value.

(a) $\overset{}{\cancel{45°}} \times \dfrac{\pi}{\underset{4}{\cancel{180}}} = \dfrac{\pi}{4}$ **radians**   **(b)** $\overset{5}{\cancel{300°}} \times \dfrac{\pi}{\underset{3}{\cancel{180°}}} = \dfrac{5\pi}{3}$ **radians**

3. Change from radians to degrees:

(a) $\dfrac{7}{12}\pi$ (b) $-\dfrac{5\pi}{9}$

Solutions: To convert from radians to degrees, multiply by $\dfrac{180°}{\pi}$.

(a) $\dfrac{\overset{}{7\pi}}{\cancel{12}}\times\dfrac{\overset{30°}{\cancel{180°}}}{\cancel{\pi}}=\mathbf{210°}$ (b) $-\dfrac{\overset{}{5\pi}}{\cancel{9}}\times\dfrac{\overset{20°}{\cancel{180°}}}{\cancel{\pi}}=\mathbf{-100°}$

Scientific Calculators and Radian Measure

To evaluate trigonometric functions of angles expressed in radians, first set the angular mode of the calculator to RADians. Then proceed as usual by entering the angle in terms of π. Angles that are expressed as fractional parts of π need to be enclosed in parentheses. For example, to find the value of $\sin\frac{\pi}{3}$, use one of the following key sequences:

$\boxed{\text{SIN}}\ \boxed{(}\ \boxed{\pi}\ \boxed{\div}\ \boxed{3}\ \boxed{)}\ \boxed{=}$ or $\boxed{(}\ \boxed{\pi}\ \boxed{\div}\ \boxed{3}\ \boxed{)}\ \boxed{\text{SIN}}$

Thus, correct to four decimal places, $\sin\frac{\pi}{3}\approx\mathbf{0.8660.}$

Reciprocal Functions

Secant, cosecant, and *cotangent* (abbreviated as *sec, csc,* and *cot*) are the names given to the functions that are the reciprocals of cosine, sine, and tangent, respectively. Thus, for all values of θ except those that make the denominator 0, the formulas for the reciprocal functions are as follows:

$$\sec\theta=\frac{1}{\cos\theta},\ \ \csc\theta=\frac{1}{\sin\theta},\ \text{and}\ \cot\theta=\frac{1}{\tan\theta}.$$

To find the value of the secant, cosecant, or cotangent of an angle, use a scientific calculator to find the value of the reciprocal function (cosine, sine, or tangent). Then find the reciprocal of the computed value in the calculator display window by using the calculator's reciprocal key, $\boxed{1/x}$. For example:

- Since $\sec 50°=\dfrac{1}{\cos 50°}$, you can find the value of sec 50° correct to four decimal places by using a key sequence similar to this one:

$$50\ \boxed{\text{COS}}\ \boxed{1/x}.$$

Thus, sec 50° $\approx\mathbf{1.5557.}$

- Since $\csc 35°20' = \dfrac{1}{\sin 35°20'}$, you can find the value of $\csc 35°20'$ correct to four decimal places by using a key sequence similar to this one:

$$35.3333 \quad \boxed{\text{SIN}} \quad \boxed{1/x}.$$

Thus, $\csc 35°20' \approx \mathbf{1.7291}$.

Coordinate Definitions of the Six Trigonometric Functions

The six trigonometric functions of an angle in standard position can be defined in terms of the coordinates of *any* point $P(x, y)$ on its terminal side and its distance r from the origin. In the accompanying chart, it is understood that x and y cannot be 0 when either appears in the denominator of a fraction.

	Function		Reciprocal
	$\sin \theta = \dfrac{y}{r}$	and	$\csc \theta = \dfrac{r}{y}$
	$\cos \theta = \dfrac{x}{r}$	and	$\sec \theta = \dfrac{r}{x}$
	$\tan \theta = \dfrac{y}{x}$	and	$\cot \theta = \dfrac{x}{y}$

Since these definitions do not depend on a right triangle, trigonometric functions of angles *greater* than 90° may be determined if the values of x, y, and r are known. Notice that, as the terminal side rotates 360°, $P(x, y)$ determines a circle whose center is at the origin and whose radius is $OP = r$. Thus the values of x, y, and r must satisfy the relationship

$$x^2 + y^2 = r^2.$$

Example

4. If $P(\sqrt{7}, -3)$ lies on a terminal ray of an angle θ, find the exact value of each of the six trigonometric functions of θ.

Solution: Since $P(\sqrt{7}, -3) = P(x, y)$, let $x = \sqrt{7}$ and $y = -3$.

Since $x > 0$ and $y < 0$, $\angle\theta$ terminates in Quadrant IV.

Find r:

$$x^2 + y^2 = r^2$$
$$(\sqrt{7})^2 + (-3)^2 = r^2$$
$$7 + 9 = r^2$$
$$16 = r^2$$

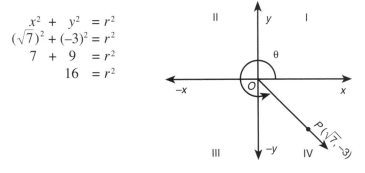

Since r is always positive, $r = +\sqrt{16} = 4$. Applying the coordinate definitions where $x = \sqrt{7}$, $y = -3$, and $r = 4$ gives

$$\sin\theta = \frac{y}{r} = -\frac{3}{4} \quad \text{and} \quad \csc\theta = \frac{r}{y} = \frac{4}{-3} \quad \text{or} \quad -\frac{4}{3}$$

$$\cos\theta = \frac{x}{r} = \frac{\sqrt{7}}{4} \quad \text{and} \quad \sec\theta = \frac{r}{x} = \frac{4}{\sqrt{7}}$$

$$\tan\theta = \frac{x}{y} = -\frac{3}{7} \quad \text{and} \quad \cot\theta = \frac{x}{y} = -\frac{\sqrt{7}}{-3} \quad \text{or} \quad -\frac{\sqrt{7}}{3}$$

Finding the Signs of Trigonometric Functions

If $P(x, y)$ is any point of the terminal side of an angle θ in standard position ($x, y \neq 0$), then the values of the trigonometric functions of $\angle\theta$ are positive or negative, depending on the signs of x and y in the quadrant in which the angle lies. The possibilities are listed in the accompanying table. Notice that Quadrant I is the only quadrant in which all of the six trigonometric functions are positive at the same time. In each of the other quadrants, only one of the basic trigonometric functions and its reciprocal function are positive.

Trigonometric Function	Quadrant in Which θ Lies			
	I	II	III	IV
$\sin\theta$ and $\csc\theta$	+	+	–	–
$\cos\theta$ and $\sec\theta$	+	–	–	+
$\tan\theta$ and $\cot\theta$	+	–	+	–

The first letter in each word of the sentence

*A*ll *S*tudents *T*ake *C*alculus

is helpful in remembering the quadrants in which the different trigonometric functions are positive. Note that:

$A = A$ll functions are positive in Quadrant I.
$S = S$ine and cosecant are positive in Quadrant II.
$T = T$angent and cotangent are positive in Quadrant III.
$C = C$osine and secant are positive in Quadrant IV.

Example

5. If $\cos \theta = -\dfrac{4}{5}$ and $\tan \theta$ is positive, what is the value of $\sin \theta$?

Solution: Cosine is negative in the second and *third* quadrants. Tangent is positive in the first and *third* quadrants. Hence in Quadrant III cosine is negative and, at the same time, tangent is positive.

Let $P(x, y)$ be a point on the terminal side of $\angle\theta$ such that, if $\cos \theta = -\dfrac{4}{5} = \dfrac{x}{r}$,

then $x = -4$ and $r = 5$. Find y:

$$x^2 + y^2 = r^2$$
$$(-4)^2 + y^2 = 5^2$$
$$16 + y^2 = 25$$
$$y^2 = 9$$
$$y = \pm\sqrt{9} = \pm 3$$

Since $\angle\theta$ is in Quadrant III, $y = -3$. Thus, $x = -4$, $y = -3$, $r = 5$, and

$$\sin \theta = \frac{y}{r} = -\frac{3}{5}.$$

Cofunction Relationships

The use of the prefix *co-* in *cosine, cosecant,* and *cotangent* is not accidental. The prefix represents "complementary." Each of these functions has the same value as its "complementary" function when the angles are complementary. Thus:

| $\sin \theta = \cos (90 - \theta)$ |
| $\sec \theta = \csc (90 - \theta)$ |
| $\tan \theta = \cot (90 - \theta)$ |

Examples: *1.* $\sin 60° = \cos 30°$
2. $\sec 15° = \csc 75°$
3. $\tan 20°50' = \cot 69°10'$

Exercise Set 7.2

1. Change from degrees to radians:
(a) 90° (c) 330° (e) −225°
(b) 100° (d) 198° (f) 120°

2. Change from radians to degrees:

(a) $\dfrac{\pi}{3}$ (b) $\dfrac{4}{9}\pi$ (c) $\dfrac{7}{6}\pi$ (d) $-\dfrac{5}{12}\pi$ (e) $\dfrac{7}{4}\pi$ (f) -2π

3. Find the number of radians in a central angle of a circle that intercepts an arc of 2 feet in a circle whose radius is 3 feet.

4. In a circle whose radius is 4 inches, find the length of an arc intercepted by a central angle of 2 radians.

5. Find x correct to four decimal places:
(a) cot 50° (b) csc 72°30′ (c) sec 19°40′

6. Find x correct to the *nearest 10 minutes* if:

(a) sec $x = 3.1708$ (c) csc $x = 1.0790$ (e) sec $x = \dfrac{\pi}{2}$

(b) cot $x = 1.6971$ (d) cot $x = \pi$ (f) csc $x = \dfrac{\pi}{3}$

7. Find the number of inches in the radius of a circle in which a central angle of 2.5 radians intercepts an arc of 15 inches.

8. Find the number of inches in the length of an arc of a circle intercepted by a central angle of $\dfrac{1}{2}$ radian, if the circumference of the circle is 8π inches.

9. If point $P(-2, \sqrt{5})$ lies on the terminal ray of obtuse angle θ, find the value of each of the six trigonometric functions.

10. Find the exact value of each of the five other trigonometric functions if:

(a) tan $\theta = -\dfrac{5}{12}$ and sin θ is negative

(b) sin $\theta = -\dfrac{1}{\sqrt{5}}$ and cos θ is negative

11. Find the exact value of cos θ if cot $\theta = \dfrac{-15}{8}$ and csc θ is positive.

12. Find the exact value of sin θ if tan $\theta = 4$ and cos θ is negative.

13–15. Find the value of positive acute angle x.

13. $\tan (2x)° = \cot (3x)°$

14. $\sin (4x - 15)° = \cos (x + 15)°$

15. $\csc (3x + 16)° = \sec (29 - 2x)°$

16. Find each value correct to four decimal places:

(a) $\sin \dfrac{\pi}{5}$ (c) $\tan \dfrac{2\pi}{3}$ (e) $\cot \dfrac{9\pi}{8}$

(b) $\cos \dfrac{\pi}{8}$ (d) $\sec \dfrac{7\pi}{5}$ (f) $\csc \dfrac{15\pi}{13}$

7.3 WRITING TRIGONOMETRIC FUNCTIONS USING REFERENCE ANGLES

KEY IDEAS

In working with trigonometric functions, it is useful to be able to express the functions of an angle in Quadrant II, III, or IV as trigonometric functions of a positive acute angle.

Finding Reference Angles

For any angle θ in standard position, the **reference angle** is the *acute* angle θ_R, whose vertex is the origin and whose sides are the terminal side of $\angle\theta$ and the *x*-axis. For a Quadrant I angle, the original angle and the reference angle are the same. The reference angles in the other quadrants are shown in Figure 7.5.

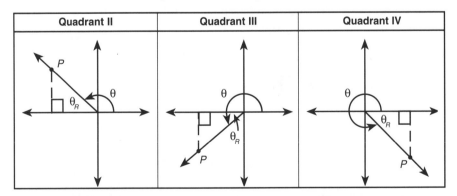

Figure 7.5 Reference Angles in Quadrants II, III, IV

The right triangle that contains the reference angle is called the **reference triangle.** The value of a trigonometric function of *any* angle θ can be expressed as either plus or minus the value of the *same* trigonometric function of its reference angle θ_R:

$$\text{Trig function of } \theta = \pm\text{Trig function of } \theta_R.$$

The sign is positive or negative, depending on the sign of the trigonometric function in the quadrant in which the terminal side of the angle lies. For example, if $\theta = 135°$, as in Figure 7.6, then $\theta_R = 45°$ since $180° - 135° = 45°$. Since sine is positive in Quadrant II, $\sin 135° = \sin 45°$. Since cosine and tangent are negative in this quadrant,

$$\cos 135° = -\cos 45°$$
$$\text{and } \tan 135° = -\tan 45°.$$

Figure 7.6 Writing Functions of Reference Angles

Table 7.1 summarizes how to *reduce* a function of any angle θ between 90° and 360° to a function of a positive acute angle θ_R.

TABLE 7.1 REDUCTION FORMULAS

Quadrant	θ_R	$\sin \theta$	$\cos \theta$	$\tan \theta$
II	$180° - \theta$	$\sin \theta = \sin \theta_R$	$\cos \theta = -\cos \theta_R$	$\tan \theta = -\tan \theta_R$
III	$\theta - 180°$	$\sin \theta = -\sin \theta_R$	$\cos \theta = -\cos \theta_R$	$\tan \theta = \tan \theta_R$
IV	$360° - \theta$	$\sin \theta = -\sin \theta_R$	$\cos \theta = \cos \theta_R$	$\tan \theta = -\tan \theta_R$

Example

1. Express as an equivalent function of a positive acute angle:

(a) $\tan 130°$ **(b)** $\sin (-110°)$ **(c)** $\sec 485°$ **(d)** $\cos \dfrac{7\pi}{9}$

Solutions: **(a)** An angle of 130° is located in Quadrant II. The reference angle is $180° - 130°$ or 50°. Since tangent is negative in Quadrant II,

$$\tan 130° = -\mathbf{tan\ 50°}.$$

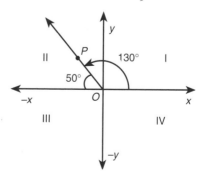

169

(b) An angle of $-110°$ represents a *clockwise* rotation of $110°$, so that the terminal side of the angle lies in Quadrant III, forming an angle of $70°$ with the negative x-axis. Since $\theta_R = 70°$ and sine is negative in Quadrant III,

$$\sin(-110°) = -\textbf{sin } 70°.$$

(c) An angle of $485°$ is coterminal with an angle of $485° - 360°$ or $125°$, which lies in Quadrant II. Since the reference angle is $180° - 125°$ or $55°$, and secant is negative in Quadrant II,

$\sec 485° = \sec 125° = -\textbf{sec } 55°.$

(d) Since $\dfrac{7\pi}{9} > \dfrac{\pi}{2}$ but $\dfrac{7\pi}{9} > \pi$, θ lies in Quadrant II. Hence

$$\theta_R = \pi - \frac{7\pi}{9} = \frac{9\pi}{9} - \frac{7\pi}{9} = \frac{2\pi}{9}.$$

Since cosine is negative in the second quadrant,

$$\cos\frac{7\pi}{9} = -\textbf{cos}\,\frac{2\pi}{9}.$$

Functions of Special Angles

Finding the exact values of trigonometric functions of angles measuring $30°$, $60°$, and $45°$ is sometimes required. The values of the trigonometric functions of $30°$ and $60°$ are summarized in the following table, which should be memorized:

x	Sin x	Cos x	Tan x
$30°$	$\dfrac{1}{2}$	$\dfrac{\sqrt{3}}{2}$	$\dfrac{1}{\sqrt{3}}$ or $\dfrac{\sqrt{3}}{3}$
$60°$	$\dfrac{\sqrt{3}}{2}$	$\dfrac{1}{2}$	$\sqrt{3}$

The next table summarizes values of trigonometric functions of 45°, which should also be memorized:

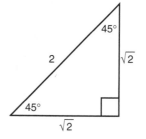

x	Sin x	Cos x	Tan x
45°	$\dfrac{\sqrt{2}}{2}$	$\dfrac{\sqrt{2}}{2}$	1

Example

2. Find the exact value:
(a) cos 120°   **(b)** tan 225°   **(c)** sin 300°   **(d)** cos (–30°)

Solutions: In each case, you should first determine the quadrant in which the angle terminates. If a diagram will help, draw it.
(a) An angle measuring 120° is located in Quadrant II. The measure of the reference angle is 180° – 120° = 60°. Since cosine is negative in the second quadrant,

$$\cos 120° = -\cos 60° = -\frac{1}{2}.$$

(b) An angle measuring 225° is located in Quadrant III. Since $\theta_R = 225°$ – 180° = 45° and tangent is positive in the third quadrant,

$$\tan 225° = \tan 45° = \mathbf{1}.$$

(c) An angle measuring 300° is located in Quadrant IV. Since $\theta_R = 360°$ – 300° = 60° and sine is negative in the fourth quadrant,

$$\sin 300° = -\sin 60° = -\frac{\sqrt{3}}{2}.$$

(d) An angle of –30° represents a *clockwise* rotation of 30°, so the terminal side of the angle lies in Quadrant IV, forming an angle of 30° with the positive x-axis. Since $\theta_R = 30°$ and cosine is positive in Quadrant IV,

$$\cos (-30°) = \cos 30° = \frac{\sqrt{3}}{2}.$$

Quadrantal Angles

An angle whose terminal side coincides with a coordinate axis, as in Figure 7.7, is called a **quadrantal angle.** An angle of rotation whose measure is 0°,

90°, 180°, 270°, or 360° is a *quadrantal* angle. If $P(x, y)$ is on the terminal side of an angle of rotation of 90°, then $P(x, y)$ falls on the positive y-axis so that $x = 0$ and $y = r$. Hence

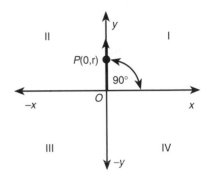

$$\sin 90° = \frac{y}{r} = \frac{r}{r} = 1$$

and

$$\cos 90° = \frac{x}{r} = \frac{0}{r} = 0.$$

Figure 7.7 Quadrantal Angles

Since $\tan 90° = y \div x$ and $x = 0$, $\tan 90°$ is not defined.

A similar analysis makes it possible to find the values of the other quadrantal angles listed in Table 7.2. By inverting the values of sine, cosine, and tangent, the values of the corresponding reciprocal functions (cosecant, secant, and cotangent) can be determined, provided that a zero denominator does not result. For example, since

$$\sec 90° = \frac{1}{\cos 90°} = \frac{1}{0},$$

$\sec 90°$ is not defined.

You can also use your scientific calculator to find the values of the sine, cosine, and tangent of the quadrantal angles, provided that they exist.

TABLE 7.2 EVALUATING FUNCTIONS OF QUADRANTAL ANGLES

	$\dfrac{\pi}{2}$	π	$\dfrac{3\pi}{2}$	2π
Trig Function	$\theta = 90°$	$\theta = 180°$	$\theta = 270°$	$\theta = 360°$ (or 0°)
Sin θ	1	0	−1	0
Cos θ	0	−1	0	1
Tan θ	*Undefined*	0	*Undefined*	0

Note: Since 0° and 360° (2π) are coterminal angles, they are listed together.

Example

3. If $f(x) = 2 \sin x + \cos 2x$, find $f\left(\dfrac{\pi}{2}\right)$.

Solution: Let $x = \dfrac{\pi}{2}$. Then:

$$f\left(\frac{\pi}{2}\right) = 2 \sin \frac{\pi}{2} + \cos 2\left(\frac{\pi}{2}\right)$$
$$= 2(1) \qquad + \cos \pi$$
$$= 2 \qquad\quad + (-1)$$
$$= \mathbf{1}$$

Exercise Set 7.3

1–8. Express each as an equivalent function of a positive acute angle.

1. cos 105°   **3.** sin 250°   **5.** $\sin \dfrac{5\pi}{3}$ **7.** $\tan \dfrac{5\pi}{4}$

2. tan (−110°)   **4.** csc 490°   **6.** $\cos \dfrac{7\pi}{6}$ **8.** sec 505°

9–20. Find the exact value.

9. sin 120°   **12.** cos 300°   **15.** cos 135°   **18.** sin 300°

10. tan 315°   **13.** csc (−30°)   **16.** tan 150°   **19.** cot (−135°)

11. $\sin \dfrac{4}{3}\pi$ **14.** $\cot \dfrac{5\pi}{4}$ **17.** $\sec \dfrac{7\pi}{6}$ **20.** $\csc \dfrac{11\pi}{3}$

21–26. If $0° \le x < 360°$, find possible values for x that satisfy each equation.

21. $\sin x = \dfrac{\sqrt{2}}{2}$ **23.** tan x = −1   **25.** $\cot x = \sqrt{3}$

22. $\sin x = -\dfrac{1}{2}$ **24.** $\cos x = -\dfrac{\sqrt{3}}{2}$ **26.** sec x = 2

27–28. In each of the following, find $f\left(\dfrac{\pi}{4}\right)$.
27. $f(x) = 2 \tan x - \sin 2x$

28. $f(x) = \cot x - \tan 3x$

29–30. In each of the following find $f\left(\dfrac{\pi}{2}\right)$.
29. $f(x) = 2 \sin 3x + \cos x$

30. $f(x) = \cos 4x - \cos 2x + \sin x$

31–35. If $0° \le x < 360°$, for which value of x is the given expression not *defined?*

31. sec x   **32.** csc x   **33.** $\dfrac{1}{1+\sin x}$ **34.** $\dfrac{1}{1+\tan x}$ **35.** $\dfrac{1}{1-2\cos x}$

173

7.4 SKETCHING $y = a \sin bx$ and $y = a \cos bx$

========== $\wedge$ KEY IDEAS ==========

The function values of sine and cosine repeat ever 360°. For example,

$$\sin 40° = \sin (40 + 360)° = \sin (40 + 720)° = \ldots$$

As a result, sine and cosine are examples of *periodic functions*. The graphs of the sine and cosine functions have fundamentally the same wavelike appearance, which repeats their shape every 360° or 2π radians. Each repetition of the graph is called a *cycle*.

Comparing Sine and Cosine Curves

Table 7.3 and 7.4 summarize the key features of the graphs of $y = \sin x$ and $y = \cos x$. The sine and cosine curves have the same basic shape, but the cosine curve is translated horizontally 90°.

The sine and cosine functions have the same *amplitude, period,* and *frequency*. The **amplitude** of sin x and cos x is their maximum value, which is 1. The **period** of the sine and cosine curves is 2π radians or 360°, since their shapes are repeated every 2π radians. In an interval of 2π radians, the graphs of sin x and cos x each complete one full cycle, so their **frequency** is 1.

TABLE 7.3 FEATURES OF $y = \sin x$ ($-2\pi \leq x \leq 2\pi$)

Feature	$y = \sin x$	Graph ($-2\pi \leq x \leq 2\pi$)
Amplitude	1	
Frequency	1	
Period	2π	
y-intercept	$y = 0$	
x-intercepts	multiples of π	
Symmetric to:	origin	

TABLE 7.4 FEATURES OF $y = \cos x$ $(-2\pi \le x \le 2\pi)$

Feature	$y = \cos x$	Graph $(-2\pi \le x \le 2\pi)$
Amplitude	1	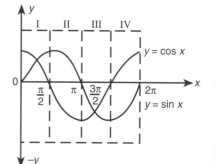
Frequency	1	
Period	2π	
y-intercept	$y = 1$	
x-intercepts	odd multiples of $\dfrac{\pi}{2}$	
Symmetric to:	y-axis	

Examples

1. On the interval $0 \le x \le 2\pi$, sketch the graphs of $y = \sin x$ and $y = \cos x$ on the same set of axes. In which quadrant is sin x decreasing and cos x increasing?

Solution: In Quadrant III, the graph of $y = \sin x$ falls while the graph of $y = \cos x$ rises. Thus sin x is decreasing and cos x is increasing in Quadrant **III.**

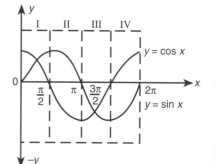

2. On the interval $-\pi \le x \le \pi$, sketch the graph of $y = \sin x$ and its image under the transformation $T_{\pi,0}$.

Solution: The solid curve is the graph of $y = \sin x$ on the interval $-\pi \le x \le \pi$. The broken curve is the image of $y = \sin x$ under the transformation $T_{\pi,0}$, which translates the graph in the horizontal direction π radians to the right.

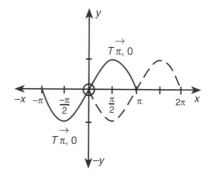

Curves with Different Amplitudes and Periods

In an equation of the form

$$y = a \sin bx \quad \text{or} \quad y = a \cos bx,$$

175

a multiplies the value of the function so that a determines the maximum height of amplitude of the graph. The value of b multiplies the angle x so that its value affects the frequency with which the graph repeats itself in an interval of 2π radians. If $y = a \sin bx$ or $y = a \cos bx$, then

$$\textbf{amplitude} = |a|, \quad \textbf{frequency} = |b|, \quad \textbf{period} = \frac{2\pi}{|b|}.$$

To sketch the graph of $y = 3 \sin 2x$ on $0 \le x \le 2\pi$, follow these steps:

Step 1: Determine the amplitude and the period. For the equation $y = 3 \sin 2x$, $a = 3$ and $b = 2$. Therefore the amplitude is 3, and the period is $\frac{2\pi}{2}$ or π radians.

Step 2: Frame the graph, using rectangles. Since the period is π radians, the graph will complete one cycle from 0 to π radians and another full cycle from π to 2π radians. Label the x-axis with these points. You may also reason that, since the coefficient of x in $y = 3 \sin 2x$ is 2, the frequency is 2, so that the curve completes *two* full cycles in an interval of 2π radians.

The amplitude is 3, so the graph does not rise above $y = 3$ or fall below $y = -3$. Indicate this fact by drawing two horizontal boundary lines through $y = 3$ and $y = -3$, stopping at $x = 2\pi$. Then form two rectangles by drawing vertical lines through $x = \pi$ and $x = 2\pi$. Each of these rectangles will contain one complete cycle of the graph. Next, divide the x-axis from 0 to π into four intervals of equal length, and do the same for the interval from π to 2π. At these key points, the curve either passes through the x-axis, achieves a maximum height, or reaches a minimum height.

Step 3: Sketch the curve. Knowing the basic shape of the sine curve, draw on complete cycle from 0 to π radians, starting at $(0, 0)$ (see Figure 7.8). Use the points marked off on the x-axis and the rectangular boundary lines as guideposts. Then draw another complete cycle from π to 2π radians.

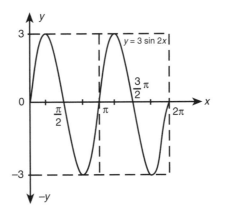

Figure 7.8 Graph of $y = 3 \sin 2x$ ($0 \le x \le 2\pi$)

176

Examples

3. Determine the equation of each graph:

(a)

(b)

Solutions: **(a)** The curve has the basic shape of a cosine curve whose amplitude is 1. The curve completes one-half of a complete cycle in 2π radians, so its frequency is $\frac{1}{2}$. Since $a = 1$ and $b = \frac{1}{2}$, the equation of the curve is

$$y = \cos \frac{1}{2}x.$$

(b) The curve has the basic shape of a sine curve whose amplitude is 2, except that it has been reflected in the *x*-axis. The equation of the original curve is, therefore, $y = 2 \sin x$. To reflect the graph of this equation in the *x*-axis, replace *y* by *–y*, resulting in $-y = 2 \sin x$ or

$$y = -2 \sin x.$$

4. On the same set of axes, sketch and label the graph of the equations $y = 2 \sin \frac{1}{2}x$ and $y = \cos 2x$ in the interval $0 \le x \le 2\pi$.

(b) What is a value of *x* in the interval $0 \le x \le 2\pi$ for which $2 \sin \frac{1}{2}x - \cos 2x = 1$?

Solutions: **(a)** The equation $y = 2 \sin \frac{1}{2}x$ has the form $y = a \sin bx$, where $a = 2$ and $b = \frac{1}{2}$. Hence the amplitude of this graph is 2, and its frequency is $\frac{1}{2}$. Since the amplitude is 2, the sine curve achieves a maximum height of 2 and reaches a minimum height of –2. A frequency of $\frac{1}{2}$ means that in the interval specified by the question, 0 to 2π, the curve will complete one-half of a full cycle. This represents one arch of the sine curve, which appears in the accompanying graph.

The equation $y = \cos 2x$ has the form $y = a \cos bx$, where $a = 1$ and $b = 2$. The amplitude of the curve is 1, and its frequency is 2.

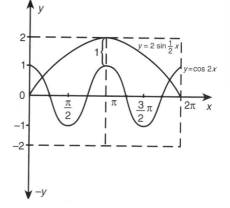

The curve reaches a maximum height of 1 and a minimum height of –1. Mark off on the x-axis four intervals of equal length from 0 to π radians, and four intervals of equal length from π to 2π radians. Knowing the basic shape of the cosine curve, draw one complete cycle from 0 to π radians, and another complete cycle from π to 2π radians.

(b) For $2 \sin \frac{1}{2}x - \cos 2x = 1$, the height of the sine curve must be exactly one unit greater than the height of the cosine curve. Looking at the curves, you see that at $x = \pi$ the height of $y = 2 \sin \frac{1}{2}x$ is 2 and the height of $y = \cos 2x$ is 1. Therefore

$$2 \sin \frac{1}{2}x - \cos 2x = 1 \quad \text{at } x = \pi.$$

Exercise Set 7.4

1. Write an equation of the cosine curve if the amplitude is 3 and the frequency is:

   (a) 1   **(b)** 2   **(c)** $\dfrac{1}{2}$

2. Write an equation of the sine curve if the amplitude is 2 and the period is:

   (a) 2π **(b)** π **(c)** 4π

3. Write an equation of the horizontal line that is above the x-axis and tangent to the graph of:

   (a) $y = 3 \sin 2x$ **(b)** $y = 2 \cos \dfrac{1}{2}x$

4. If $0 \leq x < 2\pi$, for what value of x does the graph of each function reach its *maximum* (highest point)?

   (a) $y = 3 \sin \dfrac{1}{2}x$ **(b)** $y = -\cos 2x$

5. If $y = 2 \cos 3x$, what is the *minimum* value of y?

6. Determine the number of times the graph of $y = \sin 2x$ crosses the x-axis as x increases from $45°$ to $315°$.

7. In which quadrant is $\angle x$ located if the graphs of $y = \sin x$ and $y = \cos x$ are both decreasing when $\angle x$ is increasing?

8. The graph of which function passes through the point whose coordinates are $(\pi, 2)$?

   (1) $y = 2 \cos \dfrac{x}{2}$ (3) $y = 2 \sin \dfrac{x}{2}$

   (2) $y = \dfrac{1}{2} \cos 2x$ (4) $y = \dfrac{1}{2} \sin 2x$

9. The graph of which equation has a period of π radians and passes through the origin?

   (1) $y = \cos 2x$ (2) $y = \sin 2x$ (3) $y = \cos \dfrac{x}{2}$ (4) $y = \sin \dfrac{x}{2}$

10. As θ increases from π to 2π radians, the graph of $y = \sin \theta$
    (1) increases throughout the interval
    (2) decreases throughout the interval
    (3) decreases, then increases
    (4) increases, then decreases

11. (a) On the same set of axes, draw and label the graphs of $y = \sin \dfrac{1}{2}x$ and $y = 2 \cos x$, as x varies from 0 to 2π radians.
    (b) From the graphs made in answer to part (a), find the number of values of x greater than 0 and less than 2π for which $2 \cos x - \sin \dfrac{1}{2}x = 0$.

12. (a) On the same set of axes, draw and label the graphs of $y = 2 \sin x$ and $y = \cos 2x$ in the interval $-\pi \le x \le \pi$.
    (b) Answer the following from the graph made in part (a):

    (1) What is the value of the difference $2 \sin x - \cos 2x$ at $x = \dfrac{x}{2}$?
    (2) How many values in the interval $-\pi \le x \le \pi$ satisfy the equation $2 \sin x - \cos 2x = 0$?

13. (a) On the same set of axes, draw and label the graphs of the equations $y = 2 \sin x$ and $y = \cos \dfrac{1}{2}x$ for the values in the interval $0 \le x \le 2\pi$.

    (b) Each graph drawn in part (a) is symmetric about which of the following?
    (1) line $x = \pi$ (2) x-axis   (3) point $(\pi, 0)$ (4) origin

14–16. On the same set of axes, sketch and label the graph of each function and its image under the given transformation.

	Function	Interval	Transformation
14.	$y = \cos x$	$0 \le x \le 2\pi$	$r_{x\text{-axis}}$
15.	$y = 2 \sin x$	$0 \le x \le 2\pi$	$r_{x\text{-axis}}$
16.	$y = 2 \cos \dfrac{1}{2} x$	$-2\pi \le x \le 2\pi$	$D_{\frac{1}{2}}$

7.5   SKETCHING y = TAN x

KEY IDEAS

The graph of $y = \tan x$, unlike the sine and cosine curves, has no amplitude, has breaks in continuity, and repeats every π radians rather than every 2π radians.

Basic Features of the Tangent Curve

The function $y = \tan x$ is not defined at $x = 90°$ $\left(=\frac{\pi}{2}\right)$ or at $x = 270°$ $\left(=\frac{3\pi}{2}\right)$ or at any other odd multiple of $\pm \frac{\pi}{2}$. As x approaches an odd multiple of $\pm \frac{\pi}{2}$, the value of $\tan x$ becomes unbounded. The graph of the tangent function, shown

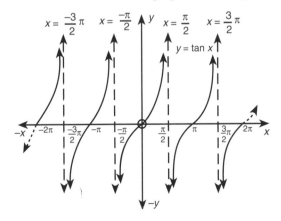

Figure 7.9   Graph of $y = \tan x$ $(-2\pi \le x \le 2\pi)$

in Figure 7.9, has these special features:

- The graph has no amplitude. Instead, vertical lines through odd multiples of $\pm\frac{\pi}{2}$ serve as asymptotes to the graph.
- The *period* of the graph is π radians, with the graph completing one full cycle between consecutive pairs of vertical asymptotes.
- The graph has *x*-intercepts at integer multiples of π.

Exercise Set 7.5

1. As x increases from $0°$ to $360°$, the graph of $y = \tan x$ rises in
   (1) no quadrant
   (2) all four quadrants
   (3) the first and third quadrants, only
   (4) the second and fourth quadrants, only

2. (a) On the same set of axes, sketch the graphs of $y = 3 \sin x$ and $y = \tan x$ as x varies from $-\pi$ to π radians.
   (b) From the graphs made in answer to part (a), determine the number of roots of $3 \sin x - \tan x = 0$ that lie between $-\frac{\pi}{2}$ and $\frac{\pi}{2}$ radians.

3. (a) On the same set of axes, sketch the graphs of $y = \cos 2x$ and $y = \tan x$ as x varies from $-\frac{\pi}{2}$ to $\frac{\pi}{2}$ radians.
   (b) From the graph made in answer to part (a), determine the number of points between $-\frac{\pi}{2}$ and $\frac{\pi}{2}$ radians for which $\tan x - \cos 2x = 0$.

7.6 FINDING INVERSE TRIGONOMETRIC FUNCTIONS

KEY IDEAS

Since the graphs of

$$y = \sin x, \quad y = \cos x, \quad \text{and} \quad y = \tan x$$

do not pass the horizontal-line test, their inverses are not functions. If, however, the domains of the original trigonometric functions are restricted so that their graphs pass the horizontal-line test, then their inverses are functions.

Using Inverse Trigonometric Notation

To form the inverse of $y = \sin x$, interchange x and y to obtain $x = \sin y$. Since there is no algebraic method that can be used to solve for y in terms of x, a new notation must be introduced.

If $y = \sin x$, then its inverse is written as

$$y = \textbf{arc sin } x.$$

When you read "arc sin x" think "the *angle* whose sine has the value x." For example, if $y = $ arc sin $\frac{1}{2}$, then y is the angle whose sine is one-half. Since $\sin 30° = \sin 150° = \frac{1}{2}$, then $y = 30°$ or $150°$; that is, the ordered pairs ($\frac{1}{2}$, $30°$) and ($\frac{1}{2}$, $150°$) satisfy the inverse relation. The inverse is not a function since the same value of x is paired with two different values of y.

The expression arc sin x may also be written, using inverse function notation, as $\sin^{-1} x$. Do not confuse the inverse notation $\sin^{-1} x$ with $(\sin x)^{-1}$, which means $\frac{1}{\sin x}$, or with $\sin x^{-1}$, which means $\sin \frac{1}{x}$.

Similarly, the inverse of $y = \cos x$ is

$$y = \textbf{arc cos } x \qquad \text{or} \qquad y = \textbf{cos}^{-1} x,$$

and the inverse of $y = \tan x$ is

$$y = \textbf{arc tan } x \qquad \text{or} \qquad y = \textbf{tan}^{-1} x.$$

Example

1. In the interval $0 \le \theta < 2\pi$, find:

(a) arc cos $\dfrac{1}{2}$ **(b)** arc tan (-1)

Solutions: **(a)** Finding arc cos $\dfrac{1}{2}$ means finding the angle (or angles) whose cosine is $\dfrac{1}{2}$. In the interval $0 \le \theta < 2\pi$, cosine is positive in Quadrants I and IV, so that $\cos 60° = \cos 300° = \dfrac{1}{2}$. Hence

$$\text{arc cos } \frac{1}{2} = \textbf{60}° \text{ or } \textbf{300}°.$$

(b) Finding arc tan (-1) means finding the angle (or angles) whose tangent is -1. In the interval $0 \le \theta < 2\pi$, tangent is negative in Quadrants II and IV, so that $\tan 135° = \tan 315° = -1$. Hence

$$\text{arc tan } (-1) = \textbf{45}° \text{ or } \textbf{315}°.$$

Forming Inverse Trigonometric Functions

Figure 7.10 shows that in the interval $-\frac{\pi}{2} \leq x \leq \frac{\pi}{2}$ the graph of $y = \sin x$ passes the horizontal-line test while $\sin x$ takes on its full range of values from -1 to 1. Hence, if the domain of $y = \sin x$ is restricted to $-\frac{\pi}{2} \leq x \leq \frac{\pi}{2}$, then its inverse is a function on this interval and has the restricted range $-\frac{\pi}{2} \leq y \leq \frac{\pi}{2}$.

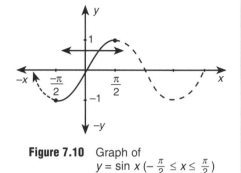

Figure 7.10 Graph of $y = \sin x \left(-\frac{\pi}{2} \leq x \leq \frac{\pi}{2}\right)$

The angle measures in the restricted range are called **principal values.** The principal values of the inverse *function* for sine are indicated by capitalizing the first letter of arc sin x or $\sin^{-1} x$, as in Arc sin x or $\text{Sin}^{-1} x$.

As is shown in Table 7.5, the domains of $y = \cos x$ and $y = \tan x$ may also be restricted so that their inverses are functions. Notice that the principal values (range) of Arc sin x and Arc tan x are restricted to the first and *fourth* quadrants, while the principal values (range) of Arc cos x are in the first and *second* quadrants.

TABLE 7.5 INVERSE TRIGONOMETRIC FUNCTIONS

Original Function	Restricted Domain	Inverse Function	Principal Values
$y = \sin x$	$-90° \leq x \leq 90°$	$y = $ Arc sin x	$-90° \leq y \leq 90°$
$y = \cos x$	$0° \leq x \leq 180°$	$y = $ Arc cos x	$0° \leq y \leq 180°$
$y = \tan x$	$-90° < x < 90°$	$y = $ Arc tan x	$-90° < y < 90°$

Examples

2. Find:

(a) Arc cos $\dfrac{1}{2}$ **(b)** Arc cos $\left(-\dfrac{1}{2}\right)$

Solution: **(a)** Let $\theta = $ Arc cos $\dfrac{1}{2}$. Then $\cos \theta = \dfrac{1}{2}$. The reference angle is $60°$. Since the principal value of θ is restricted to Quadrants I and II and cosine is positive in Quadrant I, $\theta = 60°$. Hence

$$\text{Arc cos } \frac{1}{2} = \mathbf{60°}.$$

(b) Let $\theta = $ Arc cos $\left(-\dfrac{1}{2}\right)$. Then cos $\theta = -\dfrac{1}{2}$. Since the principal value of θ is restricted to Quadrants I and II, and cosine is negative in Quadrant II, $\theta = 120°$. Hence

$$\text{Arc cos }\left(-\frac{1}{2}\right) = \mathbf{120°}.$$

3. Find Arc tan $(-\sqrt{3})$.

Solution: Let $\theta = $ Arc tan $(-\sqrt{3})$. Then tan $\theta = \sqrt{3}$. The reference angle is $60°$. Since the principal value of θ is restricted to Quadrants I and IV, and tangent is negative in Quadrant IV, $\theta = -60°$. Hence

$$\text{Arc tan }(-\sqrt{3}) = \mathbf{-60°}.$$

4. Find:
(a) Arc csc 2   **(b)** Arc csc (-2)

Solutions: **(a)** Let $\theta = $ Arc csc 2. Then csc $\theta = 2$ or, equivalently, sin $\theta = \dfrac{1}{2}$. The reference angle is $30°$. Since the principal value of θ is restricted to Quadrants I and IV, $\theta = 30°$. Hence

$$\text{Arc csc } 2 = \mathbf{30°}.$$

(b) Let $\theta = $ Arc csc (-2). Then csc $\theta = -2$, so that sin $\theta = -\dfrac{1}{2}$. Since the principal value of θ is restricted to Quadrants I and IV, and sine is negative in Quadrant IV, $\theta = -30°$. Hence

$$\text{Arc csc }(-2) = \mathbf{-30°}.$$

5. Find y:

(a) $y = \sin$ (Arc tan 1)   **(b)** $y = \tan\left[\text{Arc cos}\left(-\dfrac{\sqrt{3}}{2}\right)\right]$

Solutions: Begin by evaluating the inverse function.
(a) Let $\theta = $ Arc tan 1. Then tan $\theta = 1$. The reference angle is $45°$. Since the principal value θ lies only in Quadrants I and IV, $\theta = 45°$. Hence

$$y = \sin \text{ (Arc tan 1)} = \sin 45° = \frac{\sqrt{2}}{2}.$$

(b) Let $\theta = $ Arc cos $\left(-\dfrac{\sqrt{3}}{2}\right)$. Then cos $\theta = -\dfrac{\sqrt{3}}{2}$. The reference angle is $30°$. The principal value of θ lies only in Quadrants I and II. Since cos θ is negative in Quadrant II, $\theta = 180° - 30° = 150°$. Thus

$$y = \tan\left[\text{Arc cos}\left(-\frac{\sqrt{3}}{2}\right)\right]$$

$$= \tan(150°) = -\tan 30°$$

$$= -\frac{\sqrt{3}}{3}$$

6. Find the value of $\cot\left[\text{Arc sin}\left(-\frac{3}{\sqrt{13}}\right)\right]$.

Solution: Let $\theta = \text{Arc sin}\left(-\frac{3}{\sqrt{13}}\right)$. Then $\sin\theta = -\frac{3}{\sqrt{13}} = \frac{y}{r}$. The principal value of θ lies only in Quadrants I and IV. Since $\sin\theta$ is negative in Quadrant IV, θ lies in Quadrant IV. The value of x can be determined from the relationship $x^2 + y^2 = r^2$ by letting $y = -3$ and $r = \sqrt{13}$:

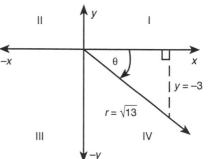

$$x^2 + (-3)^2 = (\sqrt{13})^2$$
$$x^2 + 9 = 13$$
$$x^2 = 4$$
$$x = \pm 2$$

Since θ is in Quadrant IV, $x = 2$ and $\cot\theta = \dfrac{x}{y} = \dfrac{2}{-3}$ or $-\dfrac{2}{3}$. Thus

$$\cot\left[\text{Arc sin}\left(-\frac{3}{\sqrt{3}}\right)\right] = -\frac{2}{3}.$$

7. Find the value of $\text{Cos}^{-1}(-0.8515)$ correct to the:
(a) *nearest tenth of a degree* (b) *nearest 10 minutes*

Solution: Here is a typical calculator key sequence for finding the number of degrees in the Quadrant II angle whose cosine is -0.8515:

$$0.8515 \quad \boxed{+/-} \quad \boxed{2nd} \quad \boxed{COS}$$

(a) Since $\text{Cos}^{-1}(-0.8515) \approx 148.375$, the unknown angle, correct to the *nearest tenth of a degree,* is 148.4°.
(b) Since there are 60 minutes per degree and

$$0.376 \text{ degree} \times 60 \ \frac{\text{minutes}}{\text{degree}} = 22.5 \text{ minutes,}$$

the unknown angle, correct to the *nearest 10 minutes,* is 148° 20′.

Exercise Set 7.6

1–10. Find the indicated angle correct to the: (a) nearest tenth of a degree (b) nearest 10 minutes

1. Arc sin 1

2. Arc tan $\sqrt{3}$

3. Arc cos 0

4. Arc sin $\left(-\dfrac{1}{2}\right)$

5. $\cos^{-1}\dfrac{\sqrt{2}}{2}$

6. $\tan^{-1}$ (0.4699)

7. Arc sin (–1) – Arc cos (–1)

8. Arc tan $\left(-\dfrac{\sqrt{3}}{3}\right)$

9. $\sin^{-1}$ (–0.9520)

10. $\sec^{-1}$ (–1.4059)

11–19. Find the exact value.

11. Arc sin (–1)

12. Arc cos $\dfrac{\sqrt{3}}{2}$

13. Arc tan $(-\sqrt{3})$

14. Arc sec (–2)

15. Arc csc $\sqrt{2}$

16. Arc cot $\dfrac{\sqrt{3}}{3}$

17. $\sec^{-1} 1 + \csc^{-1}$ (–1)

18. Arc sin $\dfrac{\sqrt{2}}{2}$ + Arc cos $\dfrac{\sqrt{2}}{2}$

19. $\tan^{-1} \sqrt{3} - \cot^{-1} (-\sqrt{3})$

20–36. Find the exact value.

20. sin (Arc cos 1)

21. cos (Arc tan 1)

22. $\tan\left(\text{Arc} \sin\dfrac{\sqrt{2}}{2}\right)$

23. $\sin\left[\text{Arc} \cos\left(-\dfrac{\sqrt{3}}{2}\right)\right]$

24. sin (Arc tan 3)

25. $\cos\left[\text{Sin}^{-1}\left(\dfrac{5}{13}\right)\right]$

26. $\cot\left(\text{Arc} \sin\dfrac{3}{5}\right)$

27. $\tan\left(\text{Arc} \cot\dfrac{1}{2}\right)$

28. tan (Arc tan $\sqrt{7}$)

29. $\tan\left[\text{Arc} \cos\left(-\dfrac{24}{25}\right)\right]$

30. $\cos\left(\text{Arc} \sin\dfrac{2}{3}\right)$

31. $\sin\left(\text{Arc} \tan\dfrac{1}{3}\right)$

32. $\sec\left(\text{Arc} \cos\dfrac{12}{13}\right)$

33. sec [Arc csc (–2)]

34. $\cos^{-1}\left(\sin\dfrac{7\pi}{6}\right)$

35. $\sin\left(\text{Arc} \sin\dfrac{\sqrt{2}}{2} + \text{Arc} \cos\dfrac{\sqrt{2}}{2}\right)$

36. cos [Arc cos (–1) + Arc tan $(-\sqrt{3})$]

Each of the questions in this section has appeared on a previous Course III Regents Examination. Here is an opportunity for you to review Chapter 7 and, at the same time, prepare for the Course III Regents Examination.

1. Express 3π radians in degrees.

2. If $\sin \theta = -\dfrac{4}{5}$ and θ is in Quadrant IV, find $\tan \theta$.

3. Express $\sin (-230°)$ as a function of a positive acute angle.

4. What is the exact value of $(\sin 60°)(\cos 60°)$?

5. As θ increases from π to $\dfrac{3\pi}{2}$, the value of $\cos \theta$
   (1) decreases, only   (3) decreases and then increases
   (2) increases, only   (4) increases and then decreases

6. What is the amplitude of the graph whose equation is $y = -4 \sin 2x$?

7. The exact value of $\tan \left(\text{Arc} \cos \dfrac{\sqrt{2}}{2} \right)$ is

   (1) 1   (2) $\sqrt{3}$ (3) -1 (4) $\dfrac{\pi}{4}$

8. For which value of x is $\tan (x + 20)°$ undefined?
   (1) -20 (2) 70   (3) 160   (4) 340

9. If $\cos (2x + 10°) = \sin (x + 20°)$, a value of x is
   (1) 20   (2) 30   (3) 40   (4) 60

10. If $f(x) = \cos \dfrac{x}{3} + \sin x$, then $f(\pi)$ equals

    (1) $\dfrac{3}{2}$ (2) $\dfrac{1}{2}$ (3) $-\dfrac{1}{2}$ (4) $\dfrac{\sqrt{3}}{2}$

11. What is the image of $(1, 0)$ after a counterclockwise rotation of $60°$?

    (1) $\left(\dfrac{1}{2}, \dfrac{\sqrt{3}}{2} \right)$ (2) $\left(\dfrac{\sqrt{3}}{2}, \dfrac{1}{2} \right)$ (3) $\left(\dfrac{1}{2}, -\dfrac{\sqrt{3}}{2} \right)$ (4) $\left(-\dfrac{\sqrt{3}}{2}, -\dfrac{1}{2} \right)$

12. (a) On the same set of axes, sketch and label the graphs of $y = \sin \frac{1}{2}x$ and $y = 2 \cos x$ as x varies from 0 to 2π radians.

(b) Using the same set of axes, sketch the reflection of $y = \sin \frac{1}{2}x$ in the line $y = -1$.

13. (a) On the same set of axes, sketch the graphs of the equations $y = \cos 2x$ and $y = \tan x$ in the domain $-\pi \le x \le \pi$.

(b) What is a line of symmetry of the graph of $y = \cos 2x$ as sketched in answer to part **(a)**?

ANSWERS TO SELECTED EXERCISES: CHAPTER 7

Section 7.1

1. (a) 0.5000   **(c)** 0.3881   **(e)** 0.3314
    (b) 1.0000   **(d)** 0.8258   **(f)** 1.0000

3. (a) 115°35′   **(b)** 66°22′   **(c)** 153°52′

4. (a) 29°30′   **(c)** 50°30′   **(e)** 26°40′
    (b) 68°20′   **(d)** 53°10′   **(f)** 38°40′

5. (a) $\cos R = \dfrac{12}{13}$, $\tan R = \dfrac{5}{12}$

    (b) $\sin S = \dfrac{12}{13}$, $\cos S = \dfrac{5}{13}$, $\tan S = \dfrac{12}{5}$

7. (a) $\sqrt{2}$ **(b)** $\sin A = \cos A = \dfrac{\sqrt{2}}{2}$, $\tan A = 1$

9. $\sin A = \dfrac{7}{25}$, $\cos A = \dfrac{24}{25}$, $\tan A = \dfrac{7}{24}$

11. 74.1   **13.** 48°10′

Section 7.2

1. (a) $\dfrac{\pi}{2}$ **(c)** $\dfrac{11\pi}{6}$ **(e)** $-\dfrac{5\pi}{4}$

    (b) $\dfrac{5\pi}{9}$ **(d)** $\dfrac{11\pi}{10}$ **(f)** $\dfrac{2\pi}{3}$

3. $\dfrac{2}{3}$

5. (a) 0.8391   **(b)** 1.0485   **(c)** 1.0619

6. (a) 71°40′   **(c)** 68°0′   **(e)** 50°30′
    (b) 30°30′   **(d)** 17°40′   **(f)** 72°40′

7. 6

9. $\sin \theta = \dfrac{\sqrt{5}}{3}$, $\cos \theta = -\dfrac{2}{3}$, $\tan \theta = -\dfrac{\sqrt{5}}{2}$

$$\csc \theta = \frac{3}{\sqrt{5}}, \sec \theta = -\frac{3}{2}, \cot \theta = -\frac{2}{\sqrt{5}}$$

11. $\cos \theta = -\frac{15}{17}$ **13.** 18   **15.** 45

16. (a) 0.5878   **(c)** −1.7321   **(e)** 2.4142
     (b) 0.9239   **(d)** −3.2361   **(f)** −2.1518

Section 7.3

1. $-\cos 75°$ **10.** -1 **19.** 1   **28.** 2

2. $\tan 70°$ **11.** $-\frac{\sqrt{3}}{2}$ **20.** $-\frac{2}{\sqrt{3}}$ **29.** -2

3. $-\sin 70°$ **12.** $\frac{1}{2}$ **21.** 45, 135   **30.** 3

4. $\csc 50°$ **13.** -2 **22.** 210, 330   **31.** 90, 270
5. $-\sin 60°$ **14.** 1   **23.** 135, 315   **32.** 0, 180

6. $-\cos 30°$ **15.** $-\frac{\sqrt{2}}{2}$ **24.** 150, 210   **33.** 270

7. $\tan 45°$ **16.** $-\frac{1}{\sqrt{3}}$ **25.** 30, 210   **34.** 135, 315

8. $-\sec 35°$ **17.** $-\frac{\sqrt{3}}{2}$ **26.** 60, 300   **35.** 60, 300

9. $\frac{\sqrt{3}}{2}$ **18.** $-\frac{\sqrt{3}}{2}$ **27.** 1

Section 7.4

1. (a) $y = 3 \cos x$ **(b)** $y = 3 \cos 2x$ **(c)** $y = 3 \cos \frac{1}{2}x$

2. (a) $y = 2 \sin x$ **(b)** $y = 2 \sin 2x$ **(c)** $y = 2 \sin \frac{1}{2}x$

3. (a) $y = 3$ **5.** -2 **8.** (3)   **11. (b)** 2
     (b) $y = 2$ **6.** 3   **9.** (2)   **12. (b)** *(1)* 3 *(2)* 4

4. (a) π **(b)** $\frac{\pi}{2}$ **7.** II   **10.** (3)   **13. (b)** 3

15.

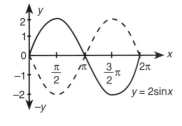

Section 7.5
1. (2)   **2. (b)** 3   **3. (b)** 1

Section 7.6
1. (a) 90.0°   **10. (a)** 135.3°   **19.** 90°   **28.** $\sqrt{7}$
   (b) 90° 0′   **(b)** 135° 20′

2. (a) 60.0°   **11.** −90°   **20.** 0   **29.** $-\dfrac{7}{24}$
   (b) 60° 0′

3. (a) 90.0°   **12.** 30°   **21.** $\dfrac{\sqrt{2}}{2}$ **30.** $\dfrac{\sqrt{5}}{3}$
   (b) 90° 0′

4. (a) −30.0°   **13.** −60°   **22.** 1   **31.** $\dfrac{1}{\sqrt{10}}$
   (b) −30° 0′

5. (a) 45.9°   **14.** 120°   **23.** $-\dfrac{1}{2}$ **32.** $\dfrac{13}{12}$
   (b) 45° 50′

6. (a) 25.2°   **15.** 45°   **24.** $\dfrac{3}{\sqrt{10}}$ **33.** $\dfrac{2}{\sqrt{3}}$
   (b) 25° 10′

7. (a) −270.0°   **16.** 60°   **25.** $\dfrac{12}{13}$ **34.** 60°
   (b) −270° 0′

8. (a) −30.0°   **17.** 90°   **26.** $\dfrac{4}{3}$ **35.** 1
   (b) −30. 0′

9. (a) −72.2°   **18.** 90°   **27.** 2   **36.** $-\dfrac{1}{2}$
   (b) −72° 10′

Regents Tune-Up: Chapter 7
1. 180   **4.** $\dfrac{\sqrt{3}}{4}$ **7.** (1)   **10.** (2)

2. $-\dfrac{4}{3}$ **5.** (2)   **8.** (2)   **11.** (1)

3. −sin 50°   **6.** 4   **9.** (1)

12.

13. (a)

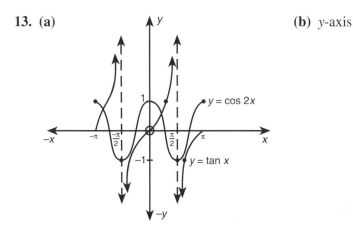

(b) y-axis

CHAPTER 8

TRIGONOMETRIC IDENTITIES, EQUATIONS, AND FORMULAS

8.1 USING QUOTIENT AND PYTHAGOREAN IDENTITIES

====== KEY IDEAS ======

An **identity** is an equation that is true for all possible replacements of the variable. Thus

$$x + 3 + x = 2x + 3$$

is an example of an identity. Several important trigonometric identities can be derived by working with a circle whose radius is 1.

Some trigonometric identities involve *squares* of trigonometric functions. The square of the sine function, for example, is written as $\sin^2 \theta$. Thus

$$(\sin \theta)(\sin \theta) = \sin^2 \theta.$$

Do not confuse $\sin^2 \theta$ with $\sin \theta^2$. The expression $\sin^2 \theta$ means that the function value is being squared, while $\sin \theta^2$ means that the measure of the angle is being squared.

Unit Circles and Identities

A **unit circle** is a circle whose radius is 1 and whose center is at the origin. Trigonometric functions of an angle have been defined in terms of *any* point $P(x, y)$ on the terminal side of the angle. If $P(x, y)$ is chosen so that it is the point at which the terminal side intersects the unit circle, as shown in Figure 8.1, then $OP = r = 1$, and

$$\cos \theta = \frac{x}{r} = \frac{x}{1} = x \quad \sin \theta = \frac{y}{r} = \frac{y}{1} = y.$$

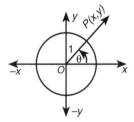

Figure 8.1 A Unit Circle

Thus each point on the unit circle has $\cos \theta$ as its x-coordinate, and $\sin \theta$ as its y-coordinate, that is,

$$P(x, y) = P(\cos \theta, \sin \theta).$$

Since tangent is defined as the quotient of y divided by x,

$$\tan \theta = \frac{y}{x} = \frac{\sin \theta}{\cos \theta}.$$

Also,

$$\cot \theta = \frac{x}{y} = \frac{\cos \theta}{\sin \theta}.$$

These relationships are known as the **quotient identities.**

===== **MATH FACTS** =====

QUOTIENT IDENTITIES

$\tan \theta = \dfrac{\sin \theta}{\cos \theta}$ $\cot \theta = \dfrac{\cos \theta}{\sin \theta}$

where $\cos \theta \neq 0$ where $\sin \theta \neq 0$

In a unit circle, $x^2 + y^2 = 1$. Replacing x by $\cos \theta$ and y by $\sin \theta$ produces the following **Pythagorean trigonometric identity**:

$$(\cos \theta)^2 + (\sin \theta)^2 = 1 \quad \text{or} \quad \sin^2 \theta + \cos^2 \theta = 1.$$

Dividing each term of $\sin^2 \theta + \cos^2 \theta = 1$ by either $\sin^2 \theta$ or $\cos^2 \theta$ produces two additional Pythagorean identities that are summarized in the table that follows. These identities are true for *any* angle θ. The Pythagorean identities are so important, and are needed so frequently, that they should be memorized.

===== **MATH FACTS** =====

PYTHAGOREAN IDENTITIES	EQUIVALENT FORMS
$\sin^2 \theta + \cos^2 \theta = 1$	$\sin^2 \theta = 1 - \cos^2 \theta$ or $\cos^2 \theta = 1 - \sin^2 \theta$
$\tan^2 \theta + 1 = \sec^2 \theta$	$\tan^2 \theta = \sec^2 \theta - 1$ or $1 = \sec^2 \theta - \tan^2 \theta$
$\cot^2 \theta + 1 = \csc^2 \theta$	$\cot^2 \theta = \csc^2 \theta - 1$ or $1 = \csc^2 \theta - \cot^2 \theta$

Examples

1. If $\cos = -\dfrac{5}{13}$ and $\angle x$ is in Quadrant III, use a Pythagorean or quotient to identity to find:

(a) $\sin x$ (b) $\tan x$

Solutions: (a) Use a form of the identity $\sin^2 x + \cos^2 x = 1$:

$$\sin^2 x = 1 - \cos^2 x = 1 - \left(-\frac{5}{13}\right)^2 = 1 - \frac{25}{169} = \frac{169 - 25}{169} = \frac{144}{169}.$$

If $\sin^2 x = \dfrac{144}{169}$, then $x = \pm\sqrt{\dfrac{144}{169}} = \pm\dfrac{12}{13}$. Since sine is negative in Quadrant III,

$$\sin x = -\frac{12}{13}.$$

(b) Using the quotient identity with $\sin x = -\dfrac{12}{13}$ and $\cos x = -\dfrac{5}{13}$ gives

$$\tan x = \frac{\sin x}{\cos x} = \left(-\frac{12}{13}\right) \div \left(-\frac{5}{13}\right) = \left(-\frac{12}{13}\right) \cdot \left(-\frac{13}{5}\right) = \frac{12}{5}.$$

2. Express in terms of sin or cos:

(a) $\sec x \cot x \sin^2 x$ (b) $\cos A (\sec A - \cos A)$

Solutions: (a) Replace $\sec x$ by the reciprocal of $\cos x$, and replace $\cot x$ by the quotient of $\cos x$ divided by $\sin x$:

$$\sec x \cot x \sin^2 x = \left(\frac{1}{\cos x}\right)\left(\frac{\cos x}{\sin x}\right)\sin^2 x = \frac{\sin^2 x}{\sin x} = \sin x.$$

(b) Use the distributive property and then simplify using reciprocal and Pythagorean identities.

$$\cos A (\sec A - \cos A) = \cos A \sec A - (\cos A)(\cos A)$$

$$= \cos A \left(\frac{1}{\cos A}\right) - \cos^2 A$$

$$= 1 - \cos^2 A$$

Since $\sin^2 A + \cos^2 A = 1$,
$\sin^2 A = 1 - \cos^2 A$: $= \sin^2 A$

3. If $\log \sin x = a$ and $\log \cos x = b$, express $\log \tan x$ in terms of a and b.

Solution: Begin by using the quotient identity:

$$\log \tan x = \log\left(\frac{\sin x}{\cos x}\right).$$

Use Quotient Law of Logs: $\quad = \log \sin x - \log \cos x$

Substitute given values: $\qquad = \boldsymbol{a - b}$

4. Express as a single trigonometric function:

$$\frac{\sin^2 A}{(\sec A - 1)(\sec A + 1)}.$$

Solution: Multiply the binomials in the denominator of the given fraction:

$$\frac{\sin^2 A}{(\sec A - 1)(\sec A + 1)} = \frac{\sin^2 A}{\sec^2 A - 1}$$

Since $1 + \tan^2 A = \sec^2 A$, $\sec^2 A - 1 = \tan^2 A$:

$$= \frac{\sin^2 A}{\tan^2 A}$$

Use quotient identity:

$$= \sin^2 A \div \left(\frac{\sin^2 A}{\cos^2 A}\right)$$

Invert and multiply:

$$= \sin^2 A \cdot \frac{\cos^2 A}{\sin^2 A}$$

Simplify:

$$\boldsymbol{= \cos^2 A}$$

Exercise Set 8.1

1–4. Use a Pythagorean identity to find the value of each indicated function.

1. If $\sin A = -\dfrac{3}{5}$ and $\angle A$ is in Quadrant IV, find $\cos A$.

2. If $\tan A = \dfrac{12}{5}$ and $\angle A$ is in Quadrant III, find $\sec A$.

3. If $\cot A = -\dfrac{9}{40}$ and $\angle A$ is in Quadrant II, find $\csc A$.

4. Show that $\dfrac{2\sin^2 x + 2\cos^2 x}{\sec x + \sec x}$ is equivalent to $\cos x$.

5–11. Use one or more identities to simplify each expression.

5. $\cot^2 A(1 - \cos^2 A)$

6. $\cos A(1 + \tan^2 A)$

7. $\dfrac{1}{\cos^2 A} - 1$

8. $\sin x(\csc^2 x - 1)$

9. $(1 - \cos^2 A)(\csc^2 A - 1)$

10. $(1 - \sin A)(1 - \sin A) \tan^2 A$

11. $\sin^2 A + \cos^2 A + \tan^2 A$

12–17. Express in simplest form in terms of sin x or cos x or both.

12. $\csc x \tan x$

13. $\dfrac{\cot x}{\csc x}$

14. $\dfrac{\tan^2 x + 1}{\cot^2 x + 1}$

15. $\dfrac{\tan x + \sec x}{1 + \sin x}$

16. $\dfrac{\sec x - \cos x}{\tan x}$

17. $\dfrac{2 \cot x}{1 + \cot^2 x}$

18. If $\log \sin x = a$ and $\log \cos x = b$, write in terms of a, b, or both a and b:
(a) $\log \sin^2 x$
(b) $\log (\sec^2 A - 1)$
(c) $\log \sec x$
(d) $\log (\cot^2 x + 1)$

19. If $\cos x \neq -1$, the fraction $\dfrac{\sin^2 x}{1 + \cos x}$ is equivalent to:
(1) $1 - \cos x$ (2) $-\cos x$ (3) $1 + \cos x$ (4) $\cos x - 1$

20. Show that the expression $\dfrac{\tan \theta \csc^2 \theta}{1 + \tan^2 \theta}$ can be reduced to $\cot \theta$.

21. Show that the expression $\dfrac{\sin \theta \tan \theta + \cos \theta}{\cos \theta}$ can be reduced to $\sec^2 \theta$.

22. Show that the expression $\dfrac{\sec x}{\cot x + \tan x}$ can be reduced to $\sin x$.

23. Show that, if x is an acute angle, $\tan x = \dfrac{\sin x}{\sqrt{1 - \sin^2 x}}$

8.2 SOLVING TRIGONOMETRIC EQUATIONS

$$\wedge$$
$$\text{KEY IDEAS}$$
$$\diagup\diagdown$$

Solving a trigonometric equation means finding the measures of the angles in a *specified* interval that make the trigonometric equation a true statement. For example, suppose that

$$\sin x = \frac{1}{2} \quad \text{and} \quad 0° \le x \le 360°.$$

Although $\sin 390° = \frac{1}{2}$, $x = 390°$ is *not* a solution since it is not between 0° and 360°.

When solving a trigonometric equation, treat the trigonometric function of the unknown angle as the variable and solve for it first.

Solving First-Degree Trigonometric Equations

In solving a first-degree algebraic equation, look to isolate the variable. Similarly, in solving a first-degree trigonometric equation, use familiar algebraic methods to isolate the trigonometric function.

Examples

1. Solve for x ($0° \le x \le 360°$): $2 \sin x + 1 = 0$.

Solution:	$2 \sin x + 1 = 0$
Solve for $\sin x$:	$2 \sin x = -1$
Since reference angle = 30°:	$\sin x = -\dfrac{1}{2}$
Sine is negative in	*Q$_{\text{III}}$: $x_1 = 210°$
Quadrants III and IV:	Q$_{\text{IV}}$: $x_2 = 330°$

In the interval $0° \le x < 360°$, the values of x that satisfy the given equation are **210°** and **330°**.

Note: The Roman numeral subscript that is one-half line down from "Q" indicates the quadrant in which the terminal side of the angle to its right lies. The roots are numbered sequentially as $x_1, x_2, x_3, \ldots$.

2. Solve for θ ($0° \leq \theta < 360°$): $|2 \cos \theta - 1| = 1$.

Solution: In general, if $|x| = d$, then $x = d$ or $x = -d$. In the given absolute-value equation, let $x = 2 \cos \theta - 1$ and $d = 1$. Hence

$$
\begin{array}{c|c}
2 \cos \theta - 1 = 1 \quad \text{or} & 2 \cos \theta - 1 = -1 \\
2 \cos \theta = 2 & 2 \cos \theta = 0 \\
\cos \theta = 1 & \cos \theta = 0 \\
\theta_1 = 0° & \theta_2 = 90° \\
& \theta_3 = 270°
\end{array}
$$

In the interval $0° \leq \theta < 360°$, the values of θ that satisfy the given equation are **0°**, **90°**, and **270°**.

Solving Quadratic Trigonometric Equations

Examples 3–5 illustrate that quadratic trigonometric equations are solved much like quadratic algebraic equations.

Examples

3. Solve for x ($0° \leq x < 360°$): $2 \sin^2 x + \sin x = 0$.

Solution: Solve for $\sin x$: $2 \sin^2 x - \sin x = 0$.

Factor $\sin x$: $\qquad\qquad\qquad\qquad \sin x\,(2 \sin x - 1) = 0$

$$
\begin{array}{c|c}
\sin x = 0 \quad \text{or} & 2 \sin x - 1 = 0 \\
x_1 = 0° & \sin x = \dfrac{1}{2} \\
x_2 = 180° & Q_I: x_3 = 30° \\
& Q_{II}: x_4 = 150°
\end{array}
$$

Hence, in the interval $0° \leq x < 360°$, the values of x that satisfy the given equation are **0°**, **30°**, **150°**, and **180°**.

4. Solve for x ($0° \leq x < 180°$): $4 \cos^2 x - 3 = 0$.

Solution: $\qquad\qquad\qquad 4 \cos^2 x - 3 = 0$

$$\cos^2 x = \frac{3}{4}$$

Take the square root of each side: $\qquad \cos x = \pm\sqrt{\dfrac{3}{4}} = \pm\dfrac{\sqrt{3}}{2}$

$$
\begin{array}{c|c}
\cos x = \dfrac{\sqrt{3}}{2} \quad \text{or} & \cos x = -\dfrac{\sqrt{3}}{2} \\
Q_I: x_1 = 30° & Q_{II}: x_3 = 150° \\
Q_{IV}: x_2 = 330° & Q_{III}: x_4 = 210°
\end{array}
$$

In the interval $0° \le x < 180°$, the values of x that satisfy the equation are **30°** and **150°**.

5. Solve for x to the *nearest tenth of a degree* $(0° \le x < 360°)$: $\tan^2 x = \tan x + 2$.

Solution: Write the quadratic equation in standard form and factor:

$$\tan^2 x - \tan x - 2 = 0$$
$$(\tan x + 1)(\tan x - 2) = 0$$

$\tan x + 1 = 0$	or	$\tan x - 2 = 0$
$\tan x = -1$		$\tan x = 2$
Q_{II}: $x_1 = 135°$		$x = \tan^{-1} 2$
Q_{IV}: $x_2 = 315°$		Using a scientific calculator,
		find x to the *nearest tenth of*
		a degree: 63.4°.
		Q_I: $x_3 = 63.4°$
		Q_{III}: x_4: = 243.4°

In the given interval $0° \le x < 360°$, the values of x to the *nearest tenth of a degree* that satisfy the given equation are **63.4°, 135°, 243.4°**, and **315°**.

Equations Requiring Substitutions

A trigonometric equation may include two different trigonometric functions. A reciprocal or Pythagorean trigonometric identity may permit one of these functions to be replaced so that an equivalent equation results that contains powers of the same trigonometric function.

Examples

6. For all values in the interval $0° \le x < 360°$ for which the functions are defined, solve $2 \cos x - 3 = 2 \sec x$.

Solution: The equation $2 \cos x - 3 = 2 \sec x$ includes the cosine and secant functions. Since these are reciprocal functions, $\sec x$ may be replaced by $\dfrac{1}{\cos x}$ $(\cos x \ne 0)$:

$$2 \cos x - 3 = 2 \sec x$$
$$2 \cos x - 3 = 2\left(\frac{1}{\cos x}\right)$$

To eliminate the fractional term, multiply each term of the equation by $\cos x$:

$$(\cos x)(2 \cos x) - 3 \cos x = \cancel{(\cos x)}\left(\frac{\overset{1}{\cancel{2}}}{\cancel{\cos x}}\right)$$

$$2 \cos^2 x - 3 \cos x = 2$$
$$2 \cos^2 x - 3 \cos x - 2 = 0$$
$$(2 \cos x + 1)(\cos x - 2) = 0$$

$$2 \cos x + 1 = 0 \qquad \text{or} \qquad \cos x - 2 = 0$$

$$\cos x = -\frac{1}{2} \qquad\qquad\qquad \cos x = 2$$

Q_{II}: $x_2 = 120°$ Since the maximum value of the cosine
Q_{III}: $x_2 = 240°$ function is 1, reject this root.

In the interval $0° \leq x < 360°$, the values of x that satisfy the given equation are **120°** and **240°**.

7. Solve for x to the *nearest 10 minutes* ($0° \leq x < 360°$):

$$3 \cos^2 x + 5 \sin x = 4.$$

Solution: The sine and cosine functions are related by the identity $\sin^2 x + \cos^2 x = 1$. When $\cos^2 x$ is replaced with $1 - \sin^2 x$ in the original equation, an equivalent equation results that contains only the sine function.

	$3 \cos^2 x + 5 \sin x = 4$
Replace $\cos^2 x$:	$3(1 - \sin^2 x) + 5 \sin^2 x = 4$
Use the distributive law:	$3 - 3 \sin^2 x + 5 \sin x = 4$
Simplify:	$-3 \sin^2 x + 5 \sin x - 1 = 0$
Multiply by -1:	$3 \sin^2 x - 5 \sin x + 1 = 0$

Since the quadratic equation cannot be factored, use the quadratic formula to solve for $\sin x$, where $a = 3$, $b = -5$, and $c = 1$:

$$\sin x = \frac{-b \pm \sqrt{b^2 - 4ac}}{2a}$$

$$= \frac{-(-5) \pm \sqrt{(-5)^2 - 4(3)(1)}}{2 \cdot 3}$$

$$= \frac{+5 \pm \sqrt{25 - 12}}{6}$$

$$= \frac{5 \pm \sqrt{13}}{6}$$

Since $\sqrt{13} \approx 3.60555$: $\sin x \approx \dfrac{5 \pm 3.60555}{6}$

$$\sin x \approx \frac{5 - 3.60555}{6} \quad \text{or} \quad \sin x \approx \frac{5 + 3.60555}{6}$$

$$\approx 0.2324 \qquad\qquad\qquad \approx 1.39343$$

$x \approx \sin^{-1} 0.2324$ Since the maximum value

Q$_\text{I}$: $x_1 \approx 13°30'$ of the sine function is 1,

Q$_\text{II}$: $x_2 \approx 166°30'$ reject this root.

In the interval $0° \leq x < 360°$, the values of x, correct to the *nearest 10 minutes*, that satisfy the given equation are **13°30′** and **166°30′**.

Exercise Set 8.2

1–12. Solve for x, *where* $0° \leq x < 360°$.

1. $2 \tan x + 2 = 0$

2. $4 \sin x + 5 = 5 \sin x + 4$

3. $|2 \sin x - 1| = 2$

4. $2 \sin^2 x - 1 = 0$

5. $|\tan x - 1| = 2$

6. $\tan^2 x - 3 = 0$

7. $4 \cos^2 x - 1 = 0$

8. $4 \sin^2 x - 3 = 0$

9. $2 \sin^2 x + \sin x = 1$

10. $3 \tan^2 x + \sqrt{3} \tan x = 0$

11. $\cos^2 x + 2 \cos x = 0$

12. $\sec^2 x = \sec x + 2$

13–18. Solve for x *($0° \leq x < 360°$) by making an appropriate substitution, using either a reciprocal or a Pythagorean identity.*

13. $2 \csc x + 3 = 2 \sin x$

14. $\csc^2 x + \cot x = 1$

15. $1 + 2 \cos x = \sec x$

16. $2 \sin^2 x - 3 \cos x = 3$

17. $2 \cos^2 x = 3(\sin x + 1)$

18. $2 \sec^2 x + \tan x = 5$

19–28. Solve for x *to the nearest 10 minutes, where* $0° \leq x < 360°$.

19. $3 \tan x + 4 = 0$

20. $5 \cos^2 x + \cos x = 0$

21. $3 \sin^2 x + 5 \sin x = 2$

22. $2 \cot^2 x + 5 \cot x + 3 = 0$

23. $\sin x + 2 = 3 \sin^2 x$

24. $3 \cos x + 1 = \sec x$

25. $2(\tan x - \cot x) + 3 = 0$

26. $2 \cos^2 x + 3 \cos x = 3$

27. $\cos^2 x = 4 \sin x + 2$

28. $\csc^2 x = 7 \csc x + 8$

29. Find, correct to the *nearest 10 minutes,* all values of x in the interval $0° \le x < 360$ that satisfy the equation

$$2 \tan^2 x - 5 \tan x = 2.$$

30. Find, correct to the *nearest tenth of a degree,* all values of x in the interval $0° \le x < 360°$ that satisfy the equation

$$\frac{3 \sin x}{6 \sin x + 1} = \frac{\csc x}{3}.$$

8.3 APPLYING THE SUM AND DIFFERENCE IDENTITIES

KEY IDEAS

Although $\sin (A + B) \ne \sin A + \sin B$, there are two identities that allow trigonometric functions of the sum or difference of two angles to be expressed in terms of combinations of trigonometric functions of the individual angles.

Formulas for Sin ($A \pm B$)

The sine of the sum or the difference of two angles can be expressed in terms of the sines and cosines of the individual angles.

MATH FACTS

SINE OF SUM OR DIFFERENCE

$$\sin (A + B) = \sin A \cos B + \cos A \sin B$$
$$\sin (A - B) = \sin A \cos B - \cos A \sin B$$

Examples

1. What is the exact value of $\sin 17° \cos 13° + \cos 17° \sin 13°$?

Solution: The given expression takes the form

$$\sin (A + B) = \sin A \cos B + \cos A \sin B,$$

where $A = 17°$ and $B = 13°$. Hence

$\sin 17° \cos 13° + \cos 17° \sin 13° = \sin (17° + 13°) = \sin 30° = \dfrac{1}{2}$.

2. Given: $\sin A = \dfrac{4}{5}$ and $\cos B = \dfrac{12}{13}$. If $\angle A$ is obtuse and $\angle B$ is acute, find the value of $\sin (A + B)$.

Solution: Before the identity for $\sin (A + B)$ can be used, the values of $\cos A$ and $\sin B$ must be determined.

Step 1: Find $\cos A$ by locating the reference triangle. Since

$$\sin A = \dfrac{4}{5} = \dfrac{y}{r}$$

and $\angle A$ lies in Quadrant II, let $y = 4$ and $r = 5$. The reference triangle is a *3-4-5* right triangle, where $x = -3$. Hence

$$\cos A = \dfrac{x}{r} = -\dfrac{3}{5}.$$

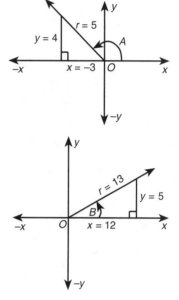

Step 2. Find $\sin B$ by locating the reference triangle. Since

$$\cos B = \dfrac{y}{r} = \dfrac{5}{13}.$$

Step 3: Evaluate the identity for $\sin (A + B)$.

$$\sin (A + B) = \sin A \cos B + \cos A \sin B$$
$$= \left(\dfrac{4}{5}\right)\left(\dfrac{12}{13}\right) + \left(-\dfrac{3}{5}\right)\left(\dfrac{5}{13}\right)$$
$$= \dfrac{48}{65} - \dfrac{15}{65}$$
$$= \dfrac{33}{65}$$

3. If $\cos x = a$, express the value of $\sin (270° - x)$ in terms of a.

Solution: Use the identity

$$\sin (A - B) = \sin A \cos B - \cos A \sin B,$$

where $A = 270°$ and $B = x$.

203

$$\sin (270 - x)° = \sin 270° \cos x - \cos 270° \sin x$$
$$= \quad (-1)(a) \quad - \quad 0 \cdot \sin x$$
$$= -a$$

Formulas for Cos (A ± B)

The cosine of the sum or the difference of two angles can be expressed in terms of the cosines and sines of the individual angles.

MATH FACTS

COSINE OF SUM OR DIFFERENCE

$$\cos (A + B) = \cos A \cos B - \sin A \sin B$$
$$\cos (A - B) = \cos A \cos B + \sin A \sin B$$

Examples

4. Using functions of 60° and 45°, express the value of cos 15° in radical form.

Solution: Since 60° – 45° = 15°, use the identity

$$\cos (A - B) \cos A \cos B + \sin A \sin B,$$

where $A = 60°$ and $B = 45°$.

$$\cos (60 - 45)° = \cos 60° \cos 45° + \sin 60° \cos 45°$$
$$= \left(\frac{1}{2}\right)\left(\frac{\sqrt{2}}{2}\right) \quad + \left(\frac{\sqrt{3}}{2}\right)\left(\frac{\sqrt{2}}{2}\right)$$
$$= \frac{\sqrt{2}}{4} \quad + \frac{\sqrt{6}}{4}$$
$$= \frac{\sqrt{2} + \sqrt{6}}{4}$$

5. If $\angle\theta$ is in Quadrant II and $\tan \theta = -\dfrac{4}{3}$, find the value of $\cos (180 + \theta)°$.

Solution: Use the identity

$$\cos (A + B) = \cos A \cos B - \sin A \sin B,$$

where $A = 180°$ and $B = \theta$. The values of cos θ and sin θ must be determined. Since

$$\tan \theta = -\frac{4}{3} = \frac{y}{x}$$

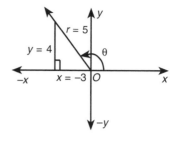

and $\angle \theta$ is in Quadrant II, let $x = -3$ and $y = 4$. The reference triangle is a *3-4-5* right triangle, where $r = 5$. Hence

$$\cos \theta = \frac{x}{r} = -\frac{3}{5} \quad \text{and} \quad \sin \theta = \frac{y}{r} = \frac{4}{5}.$$

Thus

$$\cos (180 + \theta)° = \cos 180° \cos \theta - \sin 180° \sin \theta$$

$$= (-1)\left(-\frac{3}{5}\right) - 0 \cdot \left(\frac{4}{5}\right)$$

$$= \frac{3}{5}$$

Formulas for Tan (*A* ± *B*)

The tangent of the sum or the difference of two angles can be expressed in terms of the tangents of the individual angles.

TANGENT OF SUM OR DIFFERENCE

$$\tan (A + B) = \frac{\tan A + \tan B}{1 - \tan A \tan B} \quad \tan (A - B) = \frac{\tan A - \tan B}{1 + \tan A \tan B}$$

Examples

6. If $\tan x = a$, express $\tan (-x)$ in terms of a.

Solution: Use the identity for $\tan (A - B)$, where $A = 0°$ and $B = x$.

$$\tan (A - B) = \frac{\tan A - \tan B}{1 + \tan A \tan B}$$

$$\tan (0 - x) = \frac{\tan 0 - \tan x}{1 + \tan 0 \tan x}$$

$$\tan (-x) = \frac{0 - \tan x}{1 + 0} = -\tan x = -a$$

7. If $\tan \theta = \dfrac{2}{3}$, find the value of $\tan (\theta + 45°)$.

Solution: Evaluate

$$\tan (A + B) = \frac{\tan A + \tan B}{1 - \tan A \tan B},$$

where $\tan A = \tan \theta = \dfrac{2}{3}$ and $\tan B = \tan 45° = 1$.

$$\tan (\theta + 45°) = \frac{\dfrac{2}{3} + 1}{1 - \left(\dfrac{2}{3}\right)(1)} = \frac{\dfrac{5}{3}}{\dfrac{1}{3}} = 5$$

Formulas for Sin (–x), Cos (–x), and Tan (–x)

In Example 6, it was shown that $\tan (-x) = -\tan x$. In a similar manner, reduction formulas for $\sin (-x)$ and $\cos (-x)$ can also be derived (see Exercise 6 below).

MATH FACTS

FUNCTIONS OF NEGATIVE ANGLES

$\sin (-x) = -\sin x \qquad \cos (-x) = \cos x \qquad \tan (-x) = -\tan x$

Exercise Set 8.3

1–4. Use an appropriate identity to find the exact value.

1. $\cos 34° \cos 26° - \sin 34° \sin 26°$

2. $\sin 50° \cos 5° - \cos 50° \sin 5°$

3. $\sin 75° \cos 15° + \cos 75° \sin 15°$

4. $\cos 80° \cos 20° + \sin 80° \sin 20°$

5. If $\tan x = \dfrac{1}{2}$ and $\tan y = \dfrac{2}{3}$, find the value of $\tan (x - y)$.

6. (a) Starting with the identity for $\sin (A - B)$, prove that $\sin (-x) = -\sin x$.
   (b) Starting with the identity for $\cos (A - B)$, prove that $\cos (-x) = \cos x$.

7. If $\sin A = \dfrac{5}{13}$, $\cos B = -\dfrac{4}{5}$, $\angle A$ is acute, and $\angle B$ is obtuse, find the numerical value of:
    (a) $\sin (A - B)$ (c) $\tan (45° - B)$
    (b) $\cos (A + B)$ (d) $\sec (A - B)$

8. If $\tan A = \dfrac{8}{15}$ and $\angle A$ terminates in Quadrant III, find the numerical value of:
    (a) $\sin (90° + A)$ (c) $\tan (A + 135°)$
    (b) $\cos (180° - A)$ (d) $\csc (270 - A)$

9. Using the identity for $\tan (A - B)$, show that $\tan 15° = 2 - \sqrt{3}$.

10. If $\tan (x + y) = 4$ and $\tan y = 2$, find the numerical value of $\tan x$.

11. If $\tan x = a$, express $\tan (45° - x)$ in terms of a.

12. Using functions of $45°$ and $30°$, express in radical form the value of:
    (a) $\sin 15°$ (b) $\cos 75°$ (c) $\tan 15°$ (d) $\tan 75°$

13. The expression $\cos (\pi + x) + \sin (\pi + x)$ equals:
    (1) $\cos x + \sin x$ (3) $- \cos x + \sin x$
    (2) $\cos x - \sin x$ (4) $- \cos x - \sin x$

14. The expression $\cos (270° + x)$ is equivalent to:
    (1) $\sin x$ (2) $-\sin x$ (3) $\cos x$ (4) $-\cos x$

15. The expression $\dfrac{\sin (90° + x)}{\sin (-x)}$ can be reduced to:
    (1) -1 (2) 1 (3) $-\cot x$ (4) $\cot x$

16. If $\sin A = \dfrac{3}{5}$, $\sin B = \dfrac{5}{13}$, and angles A and B are acute angles, what is the value of $\cos (A - B)$?
    (1) $-\dfrac{12}{65}$ (2) $\dfrac{16}{65}$ (3) $\dfrac{33}{65}$ (4) $\dfrac{63}{65}$

8.4 APPLYING THE DOUBLE-ANGLE IDENTITIES

∧
KEY IDEAS
∠ ∖

Letting $A = B$ in the identities for sin $(A + B)$, cos $(A + B)$, and tan $(A + B)$ produces the double-angle identities for sin $2A$, cos $2A$, and tan $2A$.

Formula for Sin 2A

Replacing $\angle B$ with $\angle A$ in the identity for sin $(A + B)$ yields the identity for sin $2A$.

MATH FACTS

SINE OF DOUBLE ANGLE

$$\sin 2A = 2 \sin A \cos A$$

Examples

1. Find the value of sin $2A$ if $\sin A = \dfrac{3}{5}$ and $\angle A$ is obtuse.

Solution: Since sin $2A = 2 \sin A \cos A$, the value of cos A is needed. Angle A terminates in Quadrant II with $\sin A = \dfrac{3}{5} = \dfrac{y}{r}$. The reference triangle is a *3-4-5* right triangle with $x = -4$. Hence $\cos A = -\dfrac{4}{5}$.

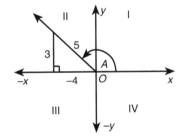

$$\sin 2A = 2 \sin A \cos A$$
$$= 2\left(\frac{3}{5}\right)\left(-\frac{4}{5}\right) = -\frac{24}{25}$$

2. If $\theta = \text{Arc tan } \dfrac{2}{\sqrt{5}}$, find the value of sin 2θ.

Solution: To evaluate the identity for sin 2θ, the values of sin θ and cos θ are needed. If $\theta = \text{Arc tan } \dfrac{2}{\sqrt{5}}$, then

$$\tan \theta = \frac{2}{\sqrt{5}} = \frac{y}{x}$$

and θ is in Quadrant I. Find the value of r by letting $x = \sqrt{5}$ and $y = 2$ in the Pythagorean relationship $x^2 + y^2 = r^2$:

$$(\sqrt{5})^2 + 2^2 = r^2$$
$$5 + 4 = r^2$$

Since $r^2 = 9$, $r = 3$. Hence

$$\sin \theta = \frac{y}{r} = \frac{2}{3}$$

and

$$\cos \theta = \frac{x}{r} = \frac{\sqrt{5}}{3}.$$

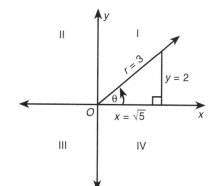

Thus,

$$\sin 2\theta = 2 \sin \theta \cos \theta = 2\left(\frac{2}{3}\right)\left(\frac{\sqrt{5}}{3}\right) = \frac{4\sqrt{5}}{9}.$$

Formula for Cos 2*A*

Replacing $\angle B$ with $\angle A$ in the identity for cos $(A + B)$ produces the identity

$$\cos 2A = \cos^2 A - \sin^2 A.$$

MATH FACTS

COSINE OF DOUBLE ANGLE

$$\cos 2A = \cos^2 A - \sin^2 A$$
or $\quad \cos 2A = 2 \cos^2 A - 1$
or $\quad \cos 2A = 1 - 2 \sin^2 A$

Examples

3. If $\angle x$ is in Quadrant II and $\sin x = 0.8$, find the value of $\cos 2x$.

Solution: Since the value of $\sin x$ is given, choose the form of the identity for $\cos 2x$ that involves only the sine function, that is, the third form, $\cos 2x = 1 - 2 \sin^2 x$.

$$\begin{aligned} \cos 2x = 1 - 2 \sin^2 x &= 1 - 2(0.8)^2 \\ &= 1 - 2(0.64) \\ &= 1 - 1.28 \\ &= \mathbf{-0.28} \end{aligned}$$

4. Show that the expression $\dfrac{\cos 2x}{\cos x + \sin x}$ is equivalent to $\cos x - \sin x$.

Solution: Choose the form of the identity for $\cos 2x$ that involves cosine and sine.

$$\frac{\cos 2x}{\cos x + \sin x} = \frac{\cos^2 x - \sin^2 x}{\cos x + \sin x}$$

Factor: $\qquad = \dfrac{\overset{1}{\cancel{(\cos x + \sin x)}}(\cos x - \sin x)}{\cancel{\cos x + \sin x}} = \mathbf{\cos x - \sin x}$

5. Solve for x ($0° \le x < 360°$): $\cos 2x - \cos x = 0$.

Solution: Since the equation contains $\cos x$, choose the form of the identity for $\cos 2x$ that is expressed only in terms of the cosine function.

$$\cos 2x - \cos x = 0$$

Replace $\cos 2x$ by $2 \cos^2 x - 1$: $\quad (2 \cos^2 x - 1) - \cos x = 0$

Put into standard form: $\qquad\qquad 2 \cos^2 x - \cos x - 1 = 0$

Factor: $\qquad\qquad\qquad\qquad (2 \cos x + 1)(\cos x - 1) = 0$

$$2 \cos x + 1 = 0 \qquad \text{or} \quad \cos x - 1 = 0$$

$$\cos x = -\frac{1}{2} \qquad\qquad \cos x = 1$$

$$\text{Q}_{\text{II}}: x_1 = 120° \qquad\qquad x_3 = 0°$$
$$\text{Q}_{\text{III}}: x_2 = 240°$$

In the interval $0° \le x < 360°$, the values of x that satisfy the equation are **0, 120°**, and **240°**.

Formula for Tan 2A

Replacing $\angle B$ with $\angle A$ in the identity for $\tan (A + B)$ produces the identity for $\tan 2A$.

MATH FACTS

TANGENT OF DOUBLE ANGLE

$$\tan 2A = \frac{2 \tan A}{1 - \tan^2 A}$$

Example

6. If $\tan A = 0.5$, find the value of $\tan 2A$.

Solution: $\tan 2A = \dfrac{2 \tan A}{1 - \tan^2 A} = \dfrac{2(0.5)}{1 - (0.5)^2}$

$$= \frac{1}{0.75} = 1 \div \frac{3}{4} = \frac{4}{3}.$$

Exercise Set 8.4

1. If $\cos x = \dfrac{15}{17}$ and $\angle x$ is acute, find the exact value.
   (a) $\sin 2x$ **(b)** $\cos 2x$ **(c)** $\tan 2x$

2. If $\tan x > 0$ and $\sin x = -\dfrac{24}{25}$, find the exact value.
   (a) $\sin 2x$ **(b)** $\cos 2x$ **(c)** $\tan 2x$

3. If $\tan x < 0$ and $\cos x = \dfrac{3}{\sqrt{13}}$, find the exact value.
   (a) $\sin 2x$ **(b)** $\cos 2x$ **(c)** $\tan 2x$

4. If $\csc \theta > 0$ and $\tan \theta = -\dfrac{1}{2}$, find the exact value.
   (a) $\sin 2\theta$ **(b)** $\cos 2x$ **(c)** $\tan 2\theta$

5. Solve for x, where $0° \le x < 360°$.
   (a) $\cos 2x - \sin x = 0$ **(d)** $\cos 2x = \sin 2x$
   (b) $\sin 2x + \sin x = 0$ **(e)** $\cos 2x - 3 \cos x = 1$
   (c) $\sin 2x + \sin (90° - x) = 0$ **(f)** $2 \sin 3x \cos 3x = 1$

6. Solve for θ to the *nearest 10 minutes,* where $0° \le \theta < 360°$.
   (a) $4 \cos 2\theta - 3 \sin \theta + 1 = 0$ **(b)** $2 \cos 2\theta = 7 \cos \theta$

7. Show that the expression $\dfrac{\sin 2A}{2 \tan A}$ is equivalent to $\cos^2 A$.

8. Show that the expression $(\cos x + \sin x)^2 - 1$ is equivalent to $\sin 2x$.

9. Show that the expression $\sin 2x \cot 2x + 1$ is equivalent to $2 \cos^2 x$.

10. Show that the expression $\sin x \sin 2x + \cos x \cos 2x$ is equivalent to $\cos x$.

11. Show that the expression $\dfrac{1 + \cos A + \cos 2A}{\sin A + \sin 2A}$ is equivalent to $\cot A$.

8.5 APPLYING THE HALF-ANGLE IDENTITIES

KEY IDEAS

Since $\angle A$ is two times as great as $\angle \dfrac{A}{2}$, the identity

$$\cos 2\theta = 1 - 2 \sin^2 \theta$$

is true when 2θ is replaced by A and θ is replaced by $\dfrac{A}{2}$. Solving for $\sin \dfrac{A}{2}$ gives

$$\sin \frac{A}{2} = \pm \sqrt{\frac{1 - \cos A}{2}}.$$

Similarly, the identity for $\cos \dfrac{A}{2}$ can be obtained from the identity

$$\cos 2\theta = 2 \cos^2 \theta - 1.$$

Formulas for $\text{Sin} \dfrac{A}{2}$, $\text{Cos} \dfrac{A}{2}$, and $\text{Tan} \dfrac{A}{2}$

The half-angle identities are summarized below. Notice that dividing the identity for $\sin \frac{A}{2}$ by the identity for $\cos \frac{A}{2}$ gives the identity for $\tan \frac{A}{2}$.

HALF-ANGLE IDENTITIES

$$\sin\frac{A}{2} = \pm\sqrt{\frac{1-\cos A}{2}}$$

$$\cos\frac{A}{2} = \pm\sqrt{\frac{1+\cos A}{2}}$$

$$\tan\frac{A}{2} = \pm\sqrt{\frac{1-\cos A}{1+\cos A}}$$

Each half-angle formula is expressed in terms of $\cos A$. The choice of a positive or negative sign in front of each radical depends on the quadrant in which $\angle\frac{A}{2}$ lies. For example, suppose that $0° \le A \le 360°$. If $\angle A$ lies in Quadrant IV, then $270° < A < 360°$. To determine the quadrant in which $\frac{A}{2}$ lies, divide each member of the inequality by 2. The result is

$$135° < \frac{A}{2} < 180°.$$

This means than $\frac{A}{2}$ lies in Quadrant II, so $\sin\frac{A}{2}$ is positive while $\cos\frac{A}{2}$ and $\tan\frac{A}{2}$ are negative.

Examples

1. If $\cos x = \dfrac{7}{8}$ and $\angle x$ is acute, find the value of $\sin\dfrac{x}{2}$.

Solution: $\sin\dfrac{x}{2} = \pm\sqrt{\dfrac{1-\cos x}{2}}$

$$= \pm\sqrt{\dfrac{1-\dfrac{7}{8}}{2}}$$

$$= \pm\sqrt{\dfrac{\dfrac{1}{8}}{2}} = \pm\sqrt{\dfrac{1}{16}} = \pm\dfrac{1}{4}$$

Since $\angle x$ is acute, $\dfrac{x}{2}$ is acute. Use the positive root. Then

$$\sin\frac{x}{2} = \frac{1}{4}.$$

2. If tan = $\dfrac{24}{7}$ and $\angle A$ ($0° \leq A < 360°$) lies in Quadrant III, find the value of cos $\dfrac{A}{2}$.

Solution: The value of cos A is needed to evaluate the half-angle identity for cosine. Since

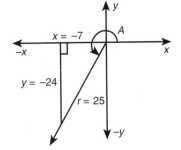

$$\tan A = \frac{24}{7} = \frac{y}{x}$$

and $\angle A$ lies in Quadrant III, let $x = -7$ and $y = -24$. Since $x^2 + y^2 = r^2$,

$$r = \sqrt{(-7)^2 + (-24)^2} = 25.$$

Thus,

$$\cos A = \frac{x}{r} = \frac{-7}{25}$$

$$\cos \frac{A}{2} = \pm\sqrt{\frac{1 + \cos A}{2}} = \pm\sqrt{\frac{1 + \left(\dfrac{-7}{25}\right)}{2}}$$

$$= \pm\sqrt{\frac{\dfrac{18}{25}}{2}}$$

$$= \pm\sqrt{\frac{1}{2}\left(\frac{18}{25}\right)}$$

$$\cos \frac{A}{2} = \pm\sqrt{\frac{9}{25}} = \pm\frac{3}{5}$$

If $\angle A$ is in Quadrant III, then $180° < A < 270°$, so that $90° < \dfrac{A}{2} < 135°$. Since $\dfrac{A}{2}$ lies in Quadrant II, where cosine is negative,

$$\cos \frac{A}{2} = -\frac{3}{5}.$$

3. If cos $A = -\dfrac{1}{10}$ and $\angle A$ is obtuse, find the exact value of tan $\dfrac{A}{2}$.

Solution:

$$\tan\frac{A}{2} = \pm\sqrt{\frac{1-\cos A}{1+\cos A}} = \pm\sqrt{\frac{1-\left(\dfrac{-1}{10}\right)}{1+\left(\dfrac{-1}{10}\right)}}$$

$$= \pm\sqrt{\frac{1+\dfrac{1}{10}}{1-\dfrac{1}{10}}} = \pm\sqrt{\frac{11}{10}\div\frac{9}{10}}$$

$$\tan\frac{A}{2} = \pm\sqrt{\frac{11}{9}} = \pm\frac{\sqrt{11}}{\sqrt{9}} = \pm\frac{\sqrt{11}}{3}$$

If $\angle A$ is obtuse, then $90° < A < 180°$. Hence $45° < \dfrac{A}{2} < 90°$. Since $\dfrac{A}{2}$ is acute, then tangent of $\dfrac{A}{2}$ is positive. Hence

$$\tan\frac{A}{2} = \frac{\sqrt{11}}{3}.$$

Exercise Set 8.5

1. If $\angle x$ $(0° \le x < 360°)$ terminates in Quadrant IV and $\cos x = 0.28$, find each value.

   (a) $\sin\dfrac{x}{2}$ (b) $\cos\dfrac{x}{2}$ (c) $\tan\dfrac{x}{2}$ (d) $\sec\dfrac{x}{2}$

2. If $\angle A$ is an acute angle and $\sin A = \dfrac{\sqrt{32}}{9}$, find each value.

   (a) $\sin\dfrac{A}{2}$ (b) $\cos\dfrac{A}{2}$ (c) $\tan\dfrac{A}{2}$ (d) $\csc\dfrac{A}{2}$

3. Find the value of $\cos\dfrac{A}{2}$ if $\angle A$ is acute and:

   (a) $\cos A = \dfrac{1}{7}$ (b) $\tan A = \dfrac{4}{3}$

4. Find the value of $\sin\dfrac{A}{2}$ if $\angle A$ $(0° \le A < 360°)$ terminates in Quadrant III and:

   (a) $\cos A = -0.62$ (b) $\sin A = -\dfrac{21}{29}$

5. Find the value of $\tan \dfrac{\theta}{2}$ if $\angle\theta$ ($0° \le \theta < 360°$) terminates in Quadrant IV and:

(a) $1 - \cos A = 0.2$ (b) $\cos 2A = \dfrac{-7}{9}$

6. If $\sin \dfrac{\theta}{2} = 0.4$ and $\angle\theta$ is obtuse, find the value of $\cos \theta$.

8.6 PROVING TRIGONOMETRIC IDENTITIES

$\wedge$
KEY IDEAS

The equation

$$2x + 1 = 9$$

is a *conditional equation* since it is true for only a particular value of the variable, namely, $x = 4$.

Since each side of the equation

$$x + 5 + x = 1 + 2x + 4$$

can be rewritten so that $2x + 5 = 2x + 5$, the original equation must be true for all possible values of x and is, therefore, an *identity*. This observation suggests a method that can be used to *prove* new trigonometric identities.

A Strategy for Proving Identities

To prove that a trigonometric equation is an identity, work on each side of the equation *separately* and show that the two sides can be made to look exactly alike. Start with the more complicated side of the equation, and express it in terms of sines and cosines, using the reciprocal and quotient identities. Working on the same side of the equation, you may need to do the following:

- Write a fraction in lowest terms, simplify a complex fraction, or combine fractions.
- Make a substitution, using another trigonometric identity.
- Perform some other algebraic operation that does not affect the other, less complicated side of the equation.

If the two sides of the equation still do not look alike, it may be helpful to transform the other side of the equation also, as illustrated in Example 1.

Examples

1. Prove that the following equation is an identity for all values of θ for which the expressions are defined:

$$\sec \theta - \cos \theta = \sin \theta \tan \theta.$$

Solution: To emphasize the importance of not performing operations that will affect both sides of the equation, draw a vertical boundary line below the equal sign. Express the left side in terms of sines and cosines, and then simplify.

$$\sec \theta - \cos \theta = \sin \theta \tan \theta$$

Use the reciprocal identity:	$\dfrac{1}{\cos \theta} - \cos \theta$	
Rewrite the second term, $\cos \theta$, as a fraction having $\cos \theta$ as its denominator:	$\dfrac{1}{\cos \theta} - \dfrac{\cos^2 \theta}{\cos \theta}$	
Add:	$\dfrac{1 - \cos^2 \theta}{\cos \theta}$	
Use the Pythagorean identity:	$\dfrac{\sin^2 \theta}{\cos \theta}$	$\sin \theta \tan \theta$
Change the right side to sines and cosines:	$\dfrac{\sin^2 \theta}{\cos \theta}$	$\sin \theta \left(\dfrac{\sin \theta}{\cos \theta} \right)$
Multiply on the right side:	$\dfrac{\sin^2 \theta}{\cos \theta}$ $=$	$\dfrac{\sin^2 \theta}{\cos \theta}.$

Hence **$\sec \theta - \cos \theta = \sin \theta \tan \theta$ is an identity.**

2. Prove that the following equation is an identity for all values of A for which the expressions are defined:

$$\sin 2A \cot A = 1 + \cos 2A.$$

Solution: On the left side of the given equation, express $\sin 2A$ and $\cot A$ in terms of $\sin A$ and $\cos A$, using the appropriate double-angle and quotient identities. In the right side of the equation, replace $\cos 2A$ with a form of the double-angle identity that makes the two sides look alike.

$$\sin 2A \cot A = 1 + \cos 2A$$

$$(2 \sin A \cos A)\,\frac{\cos A}{\sin A}$$

Use the identity on the
right side for cos 2A:

$2 \cos^2 A$	$1 + \cos 2A$
$2 \cos^2 A$	$1 + (2 \cos^2 A - 1)$
$2 \cos^2 A$	$= 2 \cos^2 A$

Hence **sin 2A cot A = 1 + cos 2A is an identity.**

3. Prove that the following equation is an identity for all values of x for which the expressions are defined:

$$\frac{\sec x + \csc x}{\tan x + \cot x} = \sin x + \cos x.$$

Solution: Since the right side of the given equation is already expressed in terms of sines and cosines, work only on the left side. Write the numerator in terms of sin x and cos x, using reciprocal identities. Change the denominator to sines and cosines, using the quotient identities.

$$\frac{\sec x + \csc x}{\tan x + \cot x} = \sin x + \cos x$$

Simplify the
complex fraction
by multiplying
its numerator
and denominator
by sin x cos x:

$$\frac{\dfrac{1}{\cos x} + \dfrac{1}{\sin x}}{\dfrac{\sin x}{\cos x} + \dfrac{\cos x}{\sin x}}$$

$$\frac{(\sin x \cos x)\left[\dfrac{1}{\cos x} + \dfrac{1}{\sin x}\right]}{(\sin x \cos x)\left[\dfrac{\sin x}{\cos x} + \dfrac{\cos x}{\sin x}\right]}$$

Multiply using the
distributive property:

$$\frac{\sin x + \cos x}{\sin^2 x + \cos^2 x}$$

Use the Pythagorean
identity:

$$\frac{\sin x + \cos x}{1}$$

$$\sin x + \cos x = \sin x + \cos x$$

Hence $\dfrac{\sec x + \csc x}{\tan x + \cot x}$ **= sin x + cos x is an identity.**

Exercise Set 8.6

1–15. Prove that each expression is an identity for all values of the angle(s) for which it is defined.

1. $\sin^2 A(1 + \tan^2 A) = \tan^2 A$

10. $\cot A - \dfrac{\cos 2A}{\sin A \cos A} = \tan A$

2. $\tan A(\csc A - \sin A) = \cos A$

11. $\dfrac{\sec A \sec B}{\tan A - \tan B} = \csc (A - B)$

3. $\dfrac{2 \cot A}{1 + \cot^2 A} = \sin 2A$

12. $\tan 2A = \dfrac{2}{\cot A - \tan A}$

4. $\dfrac{1 + \csc A}{\sec A} = \cos A + \cot A$

13. $\dfrac{1 + \tan^2 x}{1 - \cos^2 x} = \sec^2 x \csc^2 x$

5. $\tan A = \dfrac{\sin 2A}{1 + \cos 2A}$

14. $\dfrac{2}{\sec x} = \dfrac{2 - 2 \sin^2 x}{\cos x}$

6. $\dfrac{\sin 2A}{\sin A} - \dfrac{\cos 2A}{\cos A} = \sec A$

15. $\dfrac{\sin A}{1 - \cos A} + \dfrac{\sin A}{1 + \cos A} = 2 \csc A$

7. $\dfrac{2 \tan \theta}{1 + \tan^2 \theta} = \sin 2\theta$

16. $\dfrac{\sin (A + B) + \sin (A - B)}{\sin (A + B) - \sin (A - B)} = \dfrac{\tan A}{\tan B}$

8. $\dfrac{\cos^2 A}{\csc A - 1} = \dfrac{1 + \sin A}{\sin A}$

17. $\sec^2 x + \csc^2 x = (\tan x + \cot x)^2$

9. $\dfrac{(\cos x + \sin x)^2}{1 + \sin 2x} = \dfrac{\cos x \tan x}{\csc x}$

REGENTS TUNE-UP: CHAPTER 8

Each of the questions in this section has appeared on a previous Course III Regents Examination. Here is an opportunity for you to review Chapter 8 and, at the same time, prepare for the Course III Regents Examination.

---

1. Find a value of θ in the interval $0° \le \theta < 360°$ that satisfies the equation $\sin^2 \theta - \sin \theta - 2 = 0$.

2. For all values of A for which the expression is defined, $\dfrac{\cot A}{\csc A}$ is equivalent to
   (1) $\cos A$ (2) $\sin A$ (3) $\dfrac{1}{\cos A}$ (4) $\dfrac{1}{\sin A}$

3. If $\cos A = \dfrac{4}{5}$, find the positive value of $\tan \dfrac{A}{2}$.

4. What is the value of $\sin 210° \cos 30° - \cos 210° \sin 30°$?

5. If $\tan A = \dfrac{2}{3}$ and $\tan B = 3$, express $\tan (A - B)$ as a fraction in simplest form.

6. If $\sin x = \dfrac{5}{6}$, what is the value of $\cos 2x$?

7. If $\cos A = \dfrac{1}{2}$ and $\angle A$ is a positive acute angle, find the value of $\sin \dfrac{1}{2}A$.

8. The expression $\sin 2\theta \csc \theta$ is equivalent to
   (1) $\tan \theta$ (2) $\tan 2\theta$ (3) $2 \cos \theta$ (4) $2 \sin \theta$

9. If $\sin A = \dfrac{3}{5}$ and $\sin B = \dfrac{2}{3}$, and $\angle A$ and $\angle B$ are acute angles, what is the value of $\cos (A - B)$?
   (1) $-\dfrac{2}{3}$ (2) $\dfrac{4\sqrt{5}-6}{15}$ (3) $\dfrac{4\sqrt{5}+2}{5}$ (4) $\dfrac{4\sqrt{5}+6}{15}$

10. If $\tan x = -\dfrac{24}{7}$ and x is an angle in Quadrant II, find $\sin \dfrac{1}{2}x$.

11. **(a)** Find all values of θ in the interval $0° \le \theta < 360°$ that satisfy the equation $\cos 2\theta - \cos \theta = 0$.
    (b) For all values of 0 for which the expressions are defined, prove that the following is an identity:

    $$\frac{2 \sin^2 \theta}{\sin 2\theta} + \frac{1}{\tan \theta} = \sec \theta \csc \theta.$$

12. Find, to the *nearest degree,* all values of θ in the interval $0° \le \theta < 360°$ that satisfy the equation $7 \cos \theta + 1 = 6 \sec \theta$.

13. Find, to the *nearest degree,* all values of θ in the interval $0° \le \theta < 360°$ that satisfy the equation $\sec^2 \theta = 4 - 2 \tan \theta$.

14. **(a)** For all values of θ for which the expressions are defined, prove that the following is an identity:

    $$\frac{\cos 2\theta}{\sin \theta} + \sin \theta = \frac{\cot \theta}{\sec \theta}.$$

    (b) Solve for $\cos \theta$: $\cos \left(\dfrac{\theta}{2} \right) = \dfrac{\sqrt{5}}{4}$.

15. For all values of θ for which the expressions are defined, prove that the following is an identity:

    $$\frac{\sin 2\theta + \sin \theta}{\cos 2\theta + \cos \theta + 1} = \tan \theta.$$

16. Find, correct to the *nearest 10 minutes,* all values of x between $0°$ and $360°$ that satisfy the equation $2 \sin x + 4 \cos 2x = 3$.

ANSWERS TO SELECTED EXERCISES: CHAPTER 8

Section 8.1

1. $\dfrac{4}{5}$

2. $-\dfrac{13}{5}$

3. $\dfrac{41}{40}$

5. $\cos^2 A$

7. $\tan^2 A$

9. $\cos^2 A$

11. $\sec^2 A$

13. $\dfrac{\sin^2 x}{\cos^2 x}$

15. $\dfrac{1}{\cos x}$

17. $2 \sin x \cos x$

18. (a) $2a$ **(b)** $-b$
 (b) $2(a-b)$ **(d)** $-2a$
19. (1)

21. $\dfrac{\sin\theta\tan\theta+\cos\theta}{\cos\theta}=\dfrac{\sin\theta\tan\theta}{\cos\theta}+\dfrac{\cos\theta}{\cos\theta}$
$$=\tan^2\theta+1=\sec^2\theta$$

23. Since $\cos^2 x=1-\sin^2 x$ and $\angle x$ is acute, $\cos x=\sqrt{1-\sin^2 x}$. Hence

$$\tan x=\frac{\sin x}{\cos x}=\frac{\sin x}{\sqrt{1-\sin^2 x}}.$$

Section 8.2

1. $135°, 315°$
3. $210°, 330°$
5. $135°, 315°$
7. $60°, 120°, 240°, 300°$
9. $30°, 150°, 270°$
11. $90°, 270°$

13. $210°, 330°$
15. $60°, 180°, 300°$
17. $210°, 270°, 330°$
19. $124°50', 304°50'$
21. $19°30', 160°30'$
23. $90°, 221°50', 318°10$

25. $26°30', 116°30', 206°30', 296°30'$
27. $195°30', 344°30'$
29. $70°40', 160°40', 250°40', 340°40'$
30. $7.9°, 172.1°, 233.6°, 306.4°$

Section 8.3

1. $\dfrac{1}{2}$ **2.** $\dfrac{\sqrt{2}}{2}$ **3.** 1 **4.** $\dfrac{1}{2}$ **5.** $-\dfrac{1}{8}$

7. (a) $-\dfrac{56}{65}$ **(b)** $-\dfrac{63}{65}$ **(c)** 7 **(d)** $-\dfrac{65}{33}$

9. $\tan 15°=\tan(45°-30°)=\dfrac{\tan 45°-\tan 30°}{1+(\tan 45°)(\tan 30°)}=\dfrac{1-\dfrac{1}{\sqrt{3}}}{1+\dfrac{1}{\sqrt{3}}}=\dfrac{\sqrt{3}-1}{\sqrt{3}+1}$

$$=\frac{\sqrt{3}-1}{\sqrt{3}+1}\cdot\frac{\sqrt{3}-1}{\sqrt{3}-1}=\frac{4-2\sqrt{3}}{2}=2-\sqrt{3}.$$

11. $\dfrac{1-a}{1+a}$ **13.** (4)   **14.** (1)   **15.** (3)   **16.** (4)

Section 8.4

1. (a) $\dfrac{240}{289}$ **(b)** $\dfrac{161}{289}$ **(c)** $\dfrac{240}{161}$

3. (a) $-\dfrac{12}{13}$ **(b)** $\dfrac{5}{13}$ **(c)** $-\dfrac{12}{5}$

5. **(a)** 30°, 150°, 270°   **(d)** 22.5°, 112.5°, 202.5°, 292.5°
    (b) 0°, 120°, 180°, 240°   **(e)** 120°, 240°
    (c) 90°, 210°, 270°, 330°   **(f)** 15°
6. **(a)** 38°40′, 141°20′, 270°   **(b)** 104°30′, 255°30′

7. $\dfrac{\sin 2A}{2 \tan A} = \sin 2A \div 2 \tan A = 2 \sin A \cos A \times \dfrac{\cos A}{2 \sin A} = \cos^2 A$

9. $\sin 2x \cot 2x + 1 = (\sin 2x)\left(\dfrac{\cos 2x}{\sin 2x}\right) + 1 = \cos 2x + 1$

$\qquad = (2 \cos^2 x - 1) + 1 = 2 \cos^2 x$

11. $\dfrac{1 + \cos A + \cos 2A}{\sin A + \sin 2A} = \dfrac{1 + \cos A + 2 \cos^2 A - 1}{\sin A + 2 \sin A \cos A}$

$\qquad = \dfrac{\cos A(1 + 2 \cos A)}{\sin A(1 + 2 \cos A)} = \cot A$

Section 8.5

1. **(a)** 0.6   2. **(a)** $\dfrac{1}{3}$ 3. **(a)** $\dfrac{2}{\sqrt{7}}$ 5. **(a)** $-\dfrac{1}{3}$

   (b) −0.8   **(b)** $\dfrac{\sqrt{8}}{3}$ **(b)** $\dfrac{2}{\sqrt{5}}$ **(b)** $\dfrac{1}{\sqrt{2}}$

   (c) −0.75   **(c)** $\dfrac{1}{\sqrt{8}}$ 4. **(a)** 0.9   **(b)** $\dfrac{7}{\sqrt{58}}$ 6. −0.68

Section 8.6

1. $\sin^2 A(1 + \tan^2 A) = \sin^2 A(\sec^2 A) = \dfrac{\sin^2 A}{\cos^2 A} = \tan^2 A$

3. $\dfrac{2 \cot A}{1 + \cot^2 A} = \dfrac{2 \cot A}{\csc^2 A} = 2 \cot A \sin^2 A = 2 \dfrac{\cos A}{\sin A} \sin^2 A$

$\qquad = 2 \sin A \cos A = \sin 2A$

5. $\dfrac{\sin 2A}{1 + \cos 2A} = \dfrac{2 \sin A \cos A}{1 + (2 \cos^2 A - 1)} = \dfrac{2 \sin A \cos A}{2 \cos^2 A} = \dfrac{\sin A}{\cos A} = \tan A$

7. $\dfrac{2 \tan \theta}{1 + \tan^2 \theta} = \dfrac{2 \tan \theta}{\sec^2 \theta} = 2 \tan \theta \cos^2 \theta = 2 \dfrac{\sin \theta}{\cos \theta} \cos^2 \theta = 2 \sin \theta \cos \theta = \sin 2\theta$

9. Since $\dfrac{(\cos x + \sin x)^2}{1 + \sin 2x} = \dfrac{\cos^2 x + \sin^2 x + 2 \sin x \cos x}{1 + \sin 2x} = \dfrac{1 + \sin 2x}{1 + \sin 2x} = 1$

   and $\dfrac{\cos x \tan x}{\csc x} = (\cos x)\left(\dfrac{\sin x}{\cos x}\right)(\sin x) = 1,$

   then $\dfrac{(\cos x + \sin x)^2}{1 + \sin 2x} = \dfrac{\cos x \tan x}{\csc x}.$

11.

$$\frac{\sec A \sec B}{\tan A - \tan B} = \frac{\dfrac{1}{\cos A \cos B}}{\dfrac{\sin A}{\cos A} - \dfrac{\sin B}{\cos B}} = \frac{1}{\sin A \cos B - \sin B \cos A}$$

$$= \frac{1}{\sin(A - B)} = \csc(A - B)$$

13. $\dfrac{1 + \tan^2 x}{1 - \cos^2 x} = \dfrac{\sec^2 x}{\sin^2 x} = \sec^2 x \csc^2 x$

15. $\dfrac{\sin A}{1 - \cos A} + \dfrac{\sin A}{1 + \cos A} = \sin A\left[\dfrac{(1 + \cos A) + (1 - \cos A)}{(1 - \cos A)(1 + \cos A)}\right]$

$$= \frac{2 \sin A}{1 - \cos^2 A} = \frac{2 \sin A}{\sin^2 A} = \frac{2}{\sin A} = 2 \csc A$$

17. $(\tan x + \cot x)^2 = \tan^2 x + 2 \tan x \cot + \cot^2 x$
$$= \tan^2 x + 2 + \cot^2 x$$
$$= (\tan^2 x + 1) + (1 + \cot^2 x)$$
$$= \sec^2 \quad x \quad + \quad \csc^2 x$$

Regents Tune-Up: Chapter 8

1. $270°$ **3.** $\dfrac{1}{3}$ **5.** $-\dfrac{7}{9}$ **7.** $\dfrac{1}{2}$ **9.** (4)

2. (1)   **4.** 0 **6.** $-\dfrac{14}{36}$ **8.** (3)   **10.** $\dfrac{4}{5}$

11. (a) $0°, 120°, 240°$

(b) $\dfrac{2 \sin^2 \theta}{\sin 2\theta} + \dfrac{1}{\tan \theta} = \dfrac{2 \sin^2 \theta}{2 \sin \theta \cos \theta} + \dfrac{\cos \theta}{\sin \theta} = \dfrac{\sin \theta}{\cos \theta} + \dfrac{\cos \theta}{\sin \theta}$

$$= \frac{\sin^2 \theta + \cos^2 \theta}{\cos \theta \sin \theta} = \frac{1}{\cos \theta} \cdot \frac{1}{\sin \theta} = \sec \theta \csc \theta$$

12. $31°, 180°, 329°$ **13.** $45°, 108°, 225°, 288°$

14. (a) $\dfrac{\cos 2\theta}{\sin \theta} + \sin \theta = \dfrac{\cos 2\theta + \sin^2 \theta}{\sin \theta} = \dfrac{1 - 2 \sin^2 \theta + \sin^2 \theta}{\sin \theta}$

$$= \frac{1 - \sin^2 \theta}{\sin \theta} = \frac{\cos^2 \theta}{\sin \theta} = \frac{\cos \theta}{\sin \theta} \cos \theta$$

$$= \cot \theta \frac{1}{\sec \theta} = \frac{\cot \theta}{\sec \theta}$$

(b) $-\dfrac{3}{8}$

15. $\dfrac{\sin 2\theta + \sin \theta}{\cos 2\theta + \cos \theta + 1} = \dfrac{2 \sin \theta \cos \theta + \sin \theta}{2 \cos^2 \theta - 1 + \cos \theta + 1} = \dfrac{2 \sin \theta(\cos \theta + 1)}{2 \cos \theta(\cos \theta + 1)} = \tan \theta$

16. $30°, 150°, 194°30', 345°30'$

CHAPTER 9

SOLVING TRIANGLES

9.1 FINDING THE AREA OF A TRIANGLE, GIVEN SAS

KEY IDEAS

The **area** of a triangle is equal to one-half the product of the lengths of the base and the altitude drawn to that base. When the altitude is not given, trigonometry may be helpful in finding the altitude, which can then be used to find the area of the triangle.

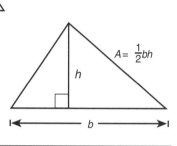

Area of a Triangle, Given SAS

In Figure 9.1, the area of $\triangle ABC$ may be expressed as $\frac{1}{2}bh$. In right triangle BDC, $\sin C = \frac{h}{a}$ or, equivalently, $h = a \sin C$. This means that h can be replaced by $a \sin C$ in the area formula:

$$\text{Area } \triangle ABC = \frac{1}{2}bh$$

$$= \frac{1}{2}b(a \sin C)$$

$$= \frac{1}{2}ab \sin C$$

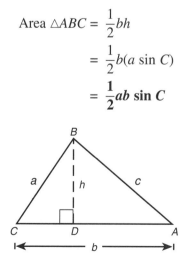

Figure 9.1 Finding the Area of a Triangle, Given SAS

MATH FACTS

AREA OF A TRIANGLE

The area of a triangle equals one-half the product of the lengths of any two sides and the sine of the included angle:

$$\text{Area } \triangle ABC = \frac{1}{2}ab \sin C = \frac{1}{2}ac \sin B = \frac{1}{2}bc \sin A$$

Examples

1. If $m\angle A = 150$, $b = 8$, and $c = 10$, find the area of $\triangle ABC$.

Solution: In $\triangle ABC$, b and c represent the lengths of a pair of adjacent sides and $\angle A$ is the included angle.

$$\text{Area} = \frac{1}{2}bc \sin A$$
$$= \frac{1}{2}(8)(10) \sin 150°$$
$$= 40 \sin 30°$$
$$= 40\left(\frac{1}{2}\right)$$
$$= 20$$

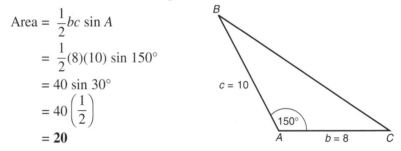

2. In parallelogram $ABCD$, $AB = 20$, $AD = 10$, and $m\angle A = 45$. Find the *exact* area of parallelogram $ABCD$.

Solution: The area of a parallelogram is equal to the product of the base and the altitude drawn to that base. In parallelogram $ABCD$, draw $\overline{DE}$ perpendicular to $\overline{AB}$, as shown in the accompanying diagram. In right triangle AED,

$$\sin 45° = \frac{DE}{10} \quad \text{or} \quad DE = 10 \sin 45°$$
$$DE = 10 \frac{\sqrt{2}}{2}$$
$$= 5\sqrt{2}$$

$$\text{Area} = \text{base} \times \text{altitude}$$
$$= AB \times DE$$
$$= 20 \times 5\sqrt{2}$$
$$= 100\sqrt{2}$$

Note: Since the *exact* area is required, the answer *must* be expressed in radical form. The problem could also have been solved by finding the sum of the areas of the two congruent triangles formed by drawing diagonal $\overline{DB}$.

3. Find the value of sin C if the area of $\triangle ABC$ is 15, $a = 5$, and $b = 10$.

Solution:

$$\text{Area} = \frac{1}{2}ab \sin C$$

$$15 = \frac{1}{2}(5)(10) \sin C$$

Multiply each side by 2: $\qquad 30 = 50 \sin C$

Divide by 50: $\qquad \dfrac{30}{50} = \sin C$

$$\sin C = \frac{3}{5} \text{ or } \mathbf{0.6}$$

Exercise Set 9.1

1. Find the area of $\triangle ABC$ if $b = 7$, $c = 12$, and $\angle A$ measures:
(**a**) 30°   (**b**) 45°   (**c**) 60°   (**d**) 90°   (**e**) 150°

2. Find, to the *neareast square inch,* the area of a triangle if the lengths of two sides are 10 inches and 20 inches and the measure of their included angle is:
(**a**) 28°   (**b**) 65°   (**c**) 100°   (**d**) 118°40′

3. Find the area of $\triangle DEF$ if $d = 4$, $e = 7$, and sin $F = 0.3$.

4. Find the value of sin C if the area of $\triangle ABC$ is 9, $a = 6$, and $b = 20$.

5. In parallelogram $ABCD$, $AB = 12$, $AD = 5$, and $m\angle A = 60$. Find the exact area of the parallelogram.

6. The length of each of the legs of an isosceles triangle is 6 inches, and the measure of each base angle is 75°. Find the area of the triangle, correct to the *nearest integer.*

7. The area of an isosceles triangle is 16 square units. If the measure of the vertex angle is 150, find the length of each leg of the triangle.

8. The area of an equilateral triangle is $25\sqrt{3}$. What is the length of a side of the triangle?

9. Find the measure of acute $\angle B$, correct to the *nearest 10 minutes,* if the area of $\triangle ABC$ is 8, $a = 3$, and $b = 10$.

9.2 SOLVING TRIANGLES: THE LAW OF SINES

=== KEY IDEAS ===

Solving a triangle means finding the measures of its unknown angles or sides by using other parts of the triangle whose measures are given.

The **Law of Sines** establishes a proportion involving the lengths of any two sides of a triangle and the *sines* of the angles opposite these sides. Thus, the Law of Sines is used when a relationship involving the measures of two sides and two angles of a triangle is needed.

Law of Sines

In any triangle the ratio of the lengths of any pair of sides is equal to the ratio of the sines of the angles opposite these sides.

=== MATH FACTS ===

LAW OF SINES

In $\triangle ABC$, each of the following proportions is true:

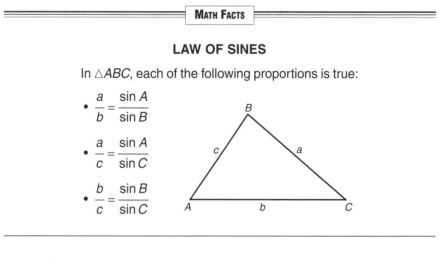

- $\dfrac{a}{b} = \dfrac{\sin A}{\sin B}$

- $\dfrac{a}{c} = \dfrac{\sin A}{\sin C}$

- $\dfrac{b}{c} = \dfrac{\sin B}{\sin C}$

Examples

1. In $\triangle ABC$, $a = 12$, $\sin A = 0.6$, and $\sin B = 0.4$. Find b.

Solution: Since SAA (**S**ide-**A**ngle-**A**ngle) is given, solve for b using the Law of Sines:

$$\frac{a}{b} = \frac{\sin A}{\sin B}$$

Cross-multiply: $b \sin A = a \sin B$
Substitute: $b(0.6) = 12(0.4)$

$$b = \frac{4.8}{0.6} = \mathbf{8.0}$$

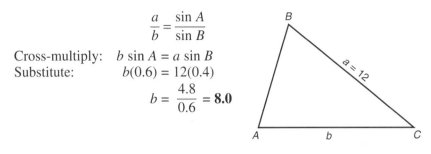

2. In $\triangle RST$, $r = 6$, $t = 9$, and $m\angle R = 30$. Find the value of $\sin T$.

Solution: Use Law of Sines: $\dfrac{r}{t} = \dfrac{\sin R}{\sin T}$

     Cross-multiply: $r \sin T = t \sin R$
     Substitute: $6 \sin T = 9 \sin 30°$

     Solve for $\sin T$: $\sin T = \dfrac{9}{6}(\sin 30°)$

$$= \frac{9}{6} \cdot \frac{1}{2}$$

$$= \frac{9}{12} \text{ or } \mathbf{0.75}$$

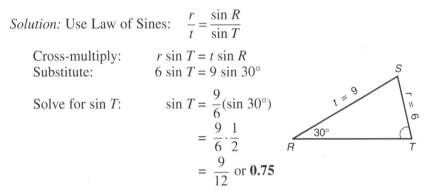

3. In $\triangle ABC$, $m\angle A = 59$, $m\angle B = 74$, and $b = 100$. Find c to the *nearest tenth*.

Solution: Solving for c using the Law of Sines requires knowledge of $m\angle C$. Since the sum of the measures of the angles of a triangle is 180,

   $m\angle C = 180 - (m\angle A + m\angle B)$
          $= 180 - (59 + 74)$
          $= 47$

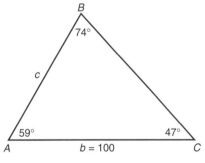

Now apply the Law of Sines: $\dfrac{b}{c} = \dfrac{\sin B}{\sin C}$

$$c \sin B = b \sin C$$
$$c \sin 74° = 100 \sin 47°$$
$$c \approx \frac{100(0.7314)}{0.9613} \approx 76.08$$

Thus, to the *nearest tenth*, $c = \mathbf{76.1}$.

4. In $\triangle ABC$, $\angle A$ measures $26°10'$, $a = 88.2$, $b = 100$, and $\angle B$ is acute. Find the measure of $\angle C$ correct to the *nearest 10 minutes*.

Solution: First solve for $\angle B$ using the Law of Sines.

$$\frac{a}{b} = \frac{\sin A}{\sin B}$$
$$a \sin B = b \sin A$$
$$88.2 \sin B = 100 \sin 26°10'$$
$$\sin B \approx \frac{100(0.4410)}{88.2} = \frac{44.1}{88.2} = 0.5$$

If $\sin B = 0.5$, then $\angle B$ is $30°$ or $150°$. It is given that $\angle B$ is acute, so $\angle B$ is $30°$. Since the sum of the measures of the angles of a triangle is $180°$,

$$\angle C = 180° - (26°10' + 30°)$$
Convert $1°$ to $60'$: $\quad = 179°60' - 56°10'$
$$= \mathbf{123°50'} \text{ to the } \textit{nearest 10 minutes.}$$

Solving "Double-Triangle" Problems

Sometimes two triangles overlap and have angles or sides in common. In order to apply a trigonometric relationship to one triangle, it may be necessary first to solve for a shared angle or common side by working in the other triangle.

Example

5. The angle of elevation from a ship at point A to the top of a lighthouse, point B, is $43°$. When the ship reaches point C, 300 meters closer to the lighthouse, the angle of elevation is $56°$. Find, to the *nearest meter*, the height, BD, of the lighthouse.

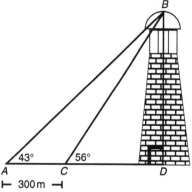

Solution: Reason "backwards": In right angle BDC, if the length of hypotenuse $\overline{BC}$ were known, BD could be determined by using the sine ratio. To solve for BC, use the Law of Sines in $\triangle ABC$. This requires finding the measure of another angle of this triangle.

230

Step 1: Find m$\angle ABC$. Since the measure of exterior angle DCB of $\triangle ABC$ is equal to the sum of the measures of the two nonadjacent angles of this triangle, m$\angle ABC + 43 = 56$. This means that m$\angle ABC = 13$.

Step 2: In $\triangle ABC$, find BC using the Law of Sines.

$$\frac{300}{BC} = \frac{\sin 13°}{\sin 43°} \quad \text{or} \quad BC \sin 13° = 300 \sin 43°$$

$$BC = \frac{300 \sin 43°}{\sin 13°}$$

$$\approx \frac{300(0.6820)}{0.2250} \approx 909.33$$

Step 3: In $\triangle BDC$, find BD using the sine ratio.

$$\sin 56° \approx \frac{BD}{909.33} \quad \text{or} \quad BD \approx 909.33(\sin 56°)$$

$$\approx 753.86874$$

$$\approx 754 \text{ to the } nearest\ meter$$

Exercise Set 9.2

1. In $\triangle ABC$, $a = 5$, $b = 9$, and $\sin A = 0.30$. Find the value of $\sin B$.

2. In $\triangle ABC$, $\sin A = \dfrac{2}{3}$, $\sin B = \dfrac{2}{5}$, and $a = 15$. Find b.

3. In $\triangle RST$, $\sin R = 0.36$, $r = 12$, and $s = 18$. Find the value of $\sin S$.

4. In $\triangle ABC$, $A = 30°$, $C = 105°$, and $b = 6$. Find a.

5. In $\triangle DEF$, $\sin D = 0.15$ and $\sin E = 0.60$. What is the ratio of side d to side e?

6. An ice skater starts from point A and skates in a straight line across a frozen lake to point B, which is 630 meters away. Then she skates directly to point C. If the measure of $\angle ABC$ is $47°30'$ and the measure of $\angle CAB$ is $31°20'$, find, to the *nearest meter,* the distance from C to A.

7. The measures of the angles of a triangle are in the ratio $2 : 3 : 4$. The shortest side of the triangle is 30 feet. Find, to the *nearest foot,* the length of the *longest* side.

8. The measures of two angles of a triangle are $46°40'$ and $58°30'$, and the length of the included side is 64.3 feet. Find, to the *nearest tenth of a foot,* the length of the *shortest* side of the triangle.

9. In $\triangle ABC$, the degree measure of $\angle A$ is $42°20'$, $a = 18$, $b = 25$, and $\angle B$ is acute. Find the measure of $\angle C$ to the *nearest 10 minutes*.

10. Just as a plane flies over a level fence joining two ground observation posts 4680 feet apart, it is spotted by observers at both posts. If the angles of elevation of the plane from the two posts at this moment are $72°20'$ and $51°50'$, respectively, find, to the *nearest 10 feet,* the height at which the plane is flying.

9.3 SOLVING TRIANGLES: THE LAW OF COSINES

═══════════════ **KEY IDEAS** ═══════════════

The **Law of Cosines** gives a relationship between the three sides of a triangle and the cosine of one of its angles. The Law of Cosines can be used to solve a triangle in which (1) the measures of any two sides and the included angle (*SAS*) are known or (2) the lengths of the three sides (*SSS*) are known.

Using the Law of Cosines, Given SAS

The Law of Cosines states that in *any* triangle the square of the length of one side is equal to the sum of the squares of the lengths of the other two sides minus twice the product of these two side lengths and the cosine of the included angle. The chart below gives three equivalent forms of the Law of Cosines.

Triangle	Given	To Find	Use Law of Cosines
	$b, \angle A, c$	a	$a^2 = b^2 + c^2 - 2bc \cos A$
	$a, \angle B, c$	b	$b^2 = a^2 + c^2 - 2ac \cos B$
	$a, \angle C, b$	c	$c^2 = a^2 + b^2 - 2ab \cos C$

The Law of Cosines formula simplifies to the Pythagorean theorem when it is used in a right triangle to find the length of the hypotenuse.

In Figure 9.2,

$$c^2 = a^2 + b^2 - 2ab \cos C$$
$$= a^2 + b^2 - 2ab \cos 90°$$
$$= a^2 + b^2 - 2ab(0)$$
$$= a^2 + b^2 - 0$$
$$c^2 = a^2 + b^2$$

Thus the Law of Cosines may be viewed as a generalization of the Pythagorean theorem. The Law of Cosines, unlike the Pythagorean theorem, can be applied to *any* triangle to find the length of a side, given the measures of the other two sides and the included angle (SAS).

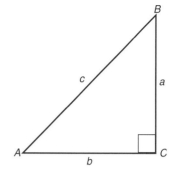

Figure 9.2 Using the Law of Cosines in a Right Triangle

Examples

1. In $\triangle ABC$, $a = 4$, $b = 5$, and $\cos C = \dfrac{1}{8}$. Find the length of side c.

Solution: $c^2 = a^2 + b^2 - 2ab \cos C$

$$= 4^2 + 5^2 - 2(4)(5)\left(\frac{1}{8}\right)$$

$$= 16 + 25 - \frac{40}{8}$$

$$= 36$$

$$c = \sqrt{36} = 6$$

2. In $\triangle RST$, $s = 3$, $t = 5$, and $m\angle R = 120$. Find the length of side r.

Solution: Since sides s and t and their included angle, R, are given, solve for r using the Law of Cosines:

$$r^2 = s^2 + t^2 - 2st \cos R$$
$$= 3^2 + 5^2 - 2(3)(5) \cos 120°$$
$$= 9 + 25 - 30(-\cos 60°)$$

$$= 34 - 30\left(-\frac{1}{2}\right)$$

$$= 34 + 15$$
$$= 49$$
$$r = \sqrt{49} = 7$$

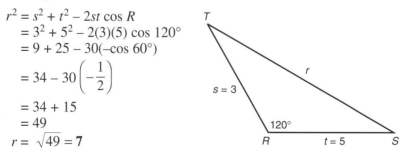

3. The lengths of two adjacent sides of parallelogram $ABCD$ are 16 centimeters and 20 centimeters. The measure of the angle between the two sides is 35°. Find, to the *nearest centimeter,* the length of the *longer* diagonal.

Solution: In parallelogram $ABCD$, let $AB = 16$, $AD = 20$, and $m\angle A = 35$. The longer diagonal of a parallelogram lies opposite the largest angle of the parallelogram. Since consecutive angles of a parallelogram are supplementary, $m\angle B = 180 - 35 = 145$. Hence $\overline{AC}$ is the longer diagonal of the parallelogram.

Let $x = AC$. Since opposite sides of a parallelogram have the same length, $BC = 20$. Find x by applying the Law of Cosines in $\triangle ABC$:

$$
\begin{aligned}
x^2 &= (AB)^2 + (BC)^2 - 2(AB)(BC)\cos 145° \\
&= 16^2 + 20^2 - 2(16)(20)(-\cos 35°) \\
&\approx 256 + 400 + 640(0.8192) \\
&\approx 1180.3 \\
x &\approx \sqrt{1180.3} \approx \mathbf{34} \text{ to the } \textit{nearest centimeter}
\end{aligned}
$$

Using the Law of Cosines, Given SSS

If the lengths of the three sides of $\triangle ABC$ are known (SSS), then any angle of the triangle can be solved for by using one of the following equivalent forms of the Law of Cosines:

$\cos A = \dfrac{b^2 + c^2 - a^2}{2bc}$	$\cos B = \dfrac{a^2 + c^2 - b^2}{2ac}$	$\cos C = \dfrac{a^2 + b^2 - c^2}{2ab}$

Example

4. In $\triangle ABC$, $a = 4$, $b = 8$, and $c = 5$. Find, correct to the *nearest degree,* the measure of the *largest* angle of the triangle.

Solution: In a triangle, the angle having the greatest measure lies opposite the side having the greatest length. Since $\angle B$ is the largest angle of $\triangle ABC$, choose the form of the Law of Cosines that solves for $\cos B$. Let $a = 4$, $b = 8$, and $c = 5$.

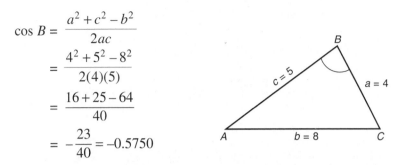

$$\cos B = \frac{a^2 + c^2 - b^2}{2ac}$$

$$= \frac{4^2 + 5^2 - 8^2}{2(4)(5)}$$

$$= \frac{16 + 25 - 64}{40}$$

$$= -\frac{23}{40} = -0.5750$$

Since cos B is negative, $\angle B$ is obtuse. The reference angle is the angle whose cosine is closest to 0.5750. Using a scientific calculator, find that this angle is 55°. Thus

$$\angle B = \cos^{-1}(-0.5750) = 180° - 55° = \textbf{125°}.$$

The chart that follows compares the situations in which the Law of Sines and the Law of Cosines are used.

Given	To Solve for...	Use...
Side-Side-Angle	Another angle	Law of Sines
Side-Angle-Angle	Another side	Law of Sines
Side-Angle-Side	The remaining side	Law of Cosines
Side-Side-Side	A specified angle	Law of Cosines

Exercise Set 9.3

1. In $\triangle ABC$, $b = 8$, $c = 6$, and $\cos A = \dfrac{17}{32}$. Find a.

2. In $\triangle ABC$, $a = 5$ and $b = 8$. Find c if $\angle C$ is:
   (a) 60°   **(b)** 90°   **(c)** 120°

3. In $\triangle DEF$, $d = 5$, $e = 7$, and $f = 8$. Find the value of the cosine of the *largest* angle of the triangle.

4. The lengths of the sides of a triangle are 7, 24, and 25. Find the value of the cosine of the *largest* angle of the triangle.

5. The lengths of the sides of a triangle are 6, 10, and 14. Find the value of the cosine of the *smallest* angle of the triangle.

6. In $\triangle ABC$, $a = \sqrt{19}$, $b = 3$, and $c = 2$. Find the measure of $\angle A$.

7. In $\triangle ABC$, $a = 5$ and $b = 6$. Express cos C in terms of side c.

8. From point P, tangent segments $\overline{PA}$ and $\overline{PB}$ are drawn to circle O in such a way that $\angle APB$ measures 120°. If the length of chord $\overline{AB}$ is 9, find the length of $\overline{PA}$.

9. The sides of a triangle have lengths 58, 92, and 124.
   (a) Find, to the *nearest ten minutes*, the *largest* angle of the triangle.
   (b) Find, to the *nearest integer*, the area of the triangle.

10. Points A and B are separated by an obstacle. To find the distance between them, a third point, C, is selected, which is 50 meters from A and 75 meters from B. If the measure of $\angle BAC$ is 120°40′, find, to the *nearest meter,* the distance from A to B.

11. The lengths of two consecutive sides of a parallelogram are 8 centimeters and 10 centimeters. If the length of the longer diagonal of the parallelogram is 14 centimeters, find, to the *nearest 10 minutes:*
   (a) the *largest* angle of the parallelogram
   (b) the angle formed by the longer side and the diagonal

12. Main Street and Park Avenue intersect at an angle of 74°. Mr. Jones lives on Main Street, 50 meters from the intersection, and Mr. Diaz lives on Park Avenue, 40 meters from the intersection. The triangle formed by the intersection and the houses is an acute triangle. Find, to the *nearest tenth of a meter,* the distance between the two houses.

13. A metal frame is constructed in the form of an isosceles trapezoid. Each base angle measures 73°30′, the length of the shorter base is 8.0 feet, and the length of each of the nonparallel sides is 5.0 feet. Find, to the *nearest tenth of a foot,* the length of a diagonal brace of this frame.

14. The lengths of two adjacent sides of a parallelogram are 50 and 80 inches. The length of the longer diagonal of the parallelogram is 100 inches.
   (a) Find, to the *nearest tenth of a degree,* the measure of the *largest* angle of the parallelogram.
   (b) Using the answer obtained in part (a), find, to the *nearest square inch,* the area of the parallelogram.

15. In the accompanying diagram, m$\angle C$ = 90, m$\angle CBD$ = 60, AB = 10, BC = 10, and AD = 15.
   (a) Find m$\angle A$ to the *nearest degree.*
   (b) Using the answer obtained in part (a), find the area of quadrilateral $ABCD$ to the *nearest square unit.*

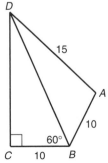

9.4 SOLVING TRIANGLES: MORE APPLICATIONS

$\bigwedge$
KEY IDEAS

In some situations, the sides of a triangle are also parts of a parallelogram. In other problems, the sides of a triangle are chords, secants, or tangents of a circle. In order to apply the Law of Sines or the Law of Cosines to these triangles, it may be necessary first to determine the measure of a part of the triangle, using geometric relationships found in parallelograms or circles.

Parallelogram of Forces

A single force that has the same effect as two forces acting simultaneously is called a **resultant force.** When the two forces form an acute or an obtuse angle, the resultant force can be represented by the diagonal of a parallelogram whose adjacent sides represent the two forces. Figure 9.3 shows two forces being applied at point A at an angle of 60°. If $\overline{AB}$
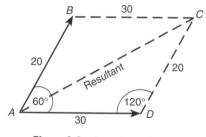

Figure 9.3   Resultant Force

is a 20-pound force and $\overline{AD}$ is a 30-pound force, then diagonal $\overline{AC}$ represents the resultant force.

Its magnitude can be determined by applying the Law of Cosines in $\triangle ADC$ (or $\triangle ABC$). Since opposite sides of a parallelogram are equal, $AB = DC = 20$. The measure of $\angle D$ is 120° since consecutive angles of a parallelogram are supplementary. Thus

$$(AC)^2 = (AD)^2 + (DC)^2 - 2(AD)(DC)\cos D$$
$$= (30)^2 + (20)^2 - 2(30)(20)\cos 120°$$
$$= 900 + 400 - 1200\left(-\frac{1}{2}\right)$$
$$= 1900$$
$$AC = \sqrt{1900} \approx 43.6 \text{ to the } \textit{nearest tenth}$$

Hence the magnitude of the resultant force is **43.6 pounds.**

Example 1 illustrates that is may be necessary to use the Law of Sines in solving a "parallelogram of forces" problem.

Example

1. Two forces of 437 pounds and 876 pounds act upon a body at an acute angle with each other. The angle between the resultant force and the 437-pound force is 41°10′. Find, to the *nearest 10 minutes,* the angle formed by the 437-pound and the 876-pound forces.

Solution: Draw parallelogram *ABCD*, where *AB* = 437, *AD* = 876, and the measure of ∠*CAB* = 41°10′. To find the measure of ∠*DAB*, let *x* = m∠*DAC*, so

$$∠DAB = 41°10′ + x.$$

In a parallelogram, opposite sides have the same measure as do alternate interior angles. Hence

$$BC = AD = 876$$

and

$$m∠BCA = m∠DAC = x.$$

To find *x*, apply the Law of Sines in △*ABC*. Then use your scientific calculator to help perform the calculations.

$$\sin x = \frac{437}{876} \times \sin 41°10′$$
$$\approx \frac{437}{876} \times \sin 41.167°$$
$$\approx 0.3284$$
$$x \approx \sin^{-1} 0.3284$$
$$\approx 19.17°$$
$$\approx 19°10′$$

Since ∠*DAB* = 41°10′ + 19°10′ = 60°20′, the angle formed by the two forces is **60°20′**, correct to the *nearest 10 minutes.*

Solving Triangles That Intersect Circles

Sometimes circle measurement relationships must be used before the Law of Sines or the Law of Cosines can be applied.

Example

2. In the accompanying diagram, $\overleftrightarrow{AB}$ is tangent to circle *O* at *B*, $\overleftrightarrow{AB}$ and $\overleftrightarrow{ADC}$ intersect at *A*, and chord $\overline{BC} \cong$ chord $\overline{CD}$. If m$\widehat{BD}$ = 60 and *BC* = 8, find the length of tangent segment $\overline{AB}$.

Solution: $\overline{AB}$ is a side of $\triangle ABC$ that can be solved for using the Law of Sines if SAA (side-angle-angle) is known. It is given that side $BC = 8$. Angle C is an inscribed angle, so

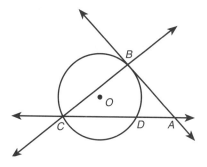

$$m\angle C = \frac{1}{2}(60) = 30.$$

The measure of $\angle A$ can be determined by first finding the measure of arc BC.

In a circle, congruent chords intercept equal arcs, so let

$$x = m\widehat{BC} = m\widehat{CD}.$$

Since the sum of the measures of the arcs of a circle is 360,

$$x + x + 60 = 360$$
$$2x = 300$$
$$m\widehat{BC} = x = 150$$

Angle A is formed by a tangent and a secant, so it is measured by one-half the difference of the measures of its intercepted arcs. Since $m\widehat{BC} = 150$ and $m\widehat{BD} = 60$,

$$m\angle A = \frac{1}{2}(150 - 60) = 45.$$

Applying the Law of Sines in $\triangle ABC$ gives

$$\frac{\sin A}{\sin C} = \frac{BC}{AB} \qquad \text{or} \qquad AB \sin A = BC \sin C$$
$$AB(\sin 45°) = 8 \sin 30°$$
$$AB\left(\frac{\sqrt{2}}{2}\right) = 8\left(\frac{1}{2}\right)$$
$$AB = \frac{2}{\sqrt{2}}(4) = \frac{8}{\sqrt{2}}$$

The length of tangent segment AB is $\dfrac{8}{\sqrt{2}}$ or, rationalizing the denominator,

$$AB = \frac{8}{\sqrt{2}} \cdot \frac{\sqrt{2}}{\sqrt{2}} = 4\sqrt{2}.$$

3. Using the diagram provided in Example 2, if $\widehat{BC} \cong \widehat{CD}$, $AB = 6$, and $AD = 4$, find:
(a) the length of: *(1)* $\overline{CD}$ *(2)* $\overline{BC}$ *(3)* $\overline{ADC}$
(b) $\angle A$ correct to the *nearest tenth of a degree*

Solutions: **(a)** If a tangent segment and a secant are drawn to a circle from the same point, then the square of the length of the tangent segment is equal to the product of the lengths of the secant segment and its external segment. Thus

$$(AD)(ADC) = (AB)^2$$
$$(4)(4 + CD) = (6)^2$$
$$4(4 + CD) = 36$$
$$4 + CD = 9$$
$$CD = 5$$

and

$$ADC = CD + AD = 5 + 4 = 9$$

If $CD = 5$, then BC also equals 5, since congruent arcs have equal chords. Thus

(1) $CD = 5$ *(2)* $BC = 5$ *(3)* $ADC = 9$

(b) In $\triangle ABC$, the lengths of the three sides are known, so the measure of $\angle A$ can be found by using the Law of Cosines.

$$(BC)^2 = (AB)^2 + (ADC)^2 - 2(AB)(ADC) \cos A$$
$$5^2 = 6^2 \quad + 9^2 \quad - 2(6)(9) \cos A$$
$$25 = 36 \quad + 81 \quad - 108 \cos A$$
$$25 = \quad 117 \quad - 108 \cos A$$
$$108 \cos A = 92$$

$$\angle A = \cos^{-1}\left(\frac{92}{108}\right)$$

$$= 31.6°, \text{ correct to the } \textit{nearest tenth of a degree}$$

Exercise Set 9.4

1. The resultant of a horizontal and a vertical force is a force of 200 pounds. If the resultant force makes an angle of 22° with the vertical force, and an angle of 38° with the horizontal force, find, to the *nearest pound,* the magnitude of the vertical force.

2. Two forces of 362 pounds and 529 pounds act upon a body at an acute angle with each other. The angle between the resultant and the 362-pound force is 35°40′. Find, to the *nearest 10 minutes,* the angle formed by the two given forces.

3. Two forces of 720 pounds and 640 pounds act upon a body at an angle of 42°40′ with each other. Find, to the *nearest 10 minutes,* the angle that the resultant force makes with the smaller force.

4. Two forces acting upon a body make an angle of 103°30′ with each other. The magnitude of the first force is 386 pounds. If the resultant makes an angle of 47°10′ with the first force, what is the magnitude of the resultant, to the nearest *tenth of a pound?*

5. Two forces of 70 pounds and 125 pounds act upon a body at an angle of 68° with each other. Find, to the *nearest 10 minutes,* the angle formed by the lines of action of the resultant and the larger force.

6. In Example 2, if $m\widehat{BC} = 170$, $m\widehat{BD} = 50$, $AD = 2$, and $CD = 6$, find the length of chord BC.

7–8. In circle O, $\overleftrightarrow{ADB}$ is a secant and $\overrightarrow{BC}$ is tangent at C.

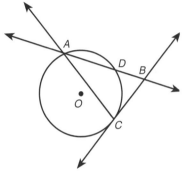

7. If $m\widehat{AD} : m\widehat{AC} : m\widehat{CD} = 2 : 7 : 3$ and $BC = 10$, find:
   (a) $\angle B$
   (b) AC correct to the *nearest tenth*

8. If $m\angle B = 45$, $BC = 12$, and $DB = 9$, find:
   (a) AB
   (b) AC correct to the *nearest tenth*
   (c) $\angle CAB$ correct to the *nearest degree*

Exercises 7 and 8

9–10. In circle O, $\overleftrightarrow{CDB}$ is a secant and $\overleftrightarrow{AB}$ is tangent at A.

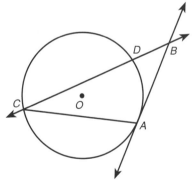

9. If $BD = 12$, $CD = 15$, and $m\widehat{AD} = 60$, find the measure of obtuse angle BAC correct to the *nearest 10 minutes.*

10. If $m\widehat{AD} = 60$, $m\widehat{CD} = 160$, $AB = 4$, and $BD = 2$, find:
   (a) CB
   (b) AC correct to the *nearest tenth*

Exercises 9 and 10

9.5 ANALYZING THE AMBIGUOUS CASE

When the dimensions $a = 2$, $b = 5$, and $\sin A = 0.6$ are given, the value of $\sin B$ can be found by using the Law of Sines as follows:

$$\frac{\sin A}{\sin B} = \frac{a}{b} \qquad \text{or} \qquad a \sin B = b \sin A$$

$$2 \sin B = 5(0.6)$$

$$\sin B = \frac{3.0}{2} = 1.5$$

Since the sine of an angle cannot be greater than 1, a triangle is not possible. For other choices of a, b, and $\sin A$, however, it may be possible to construct one or two triangles. Since side-side-angle dimensions produce no, one, or two triangles, the situation in which SSA (Side-Side-Angle) is given is called the **ambiguous case.**

The situations in which the given angle is acute (Case I) and not acute (Case II) are considered separately.

The Ambiguous Case Where Angle A < 90°

If the measures a and b of two sides and an opposite angle, A, are given, as shown in Figure 9.4, then the altitude (height) h of a possible triangle may be found by using the sine ratio:

$$\sin A = \frac{h}{b} \qquad \text{or} \qquad h = b \sin A.$$

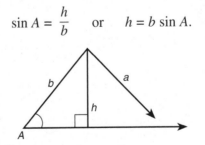

Figure 9.4 Ambiguous Case where $\angle A$ < 90°

A triangle can be constructed only if a, the side opposite the given acute angle, A, is at least as long as the altitude, h. The different situations are summarized in Tables 9.1 and 9.2.

TABLE 9.1 CASE I: ANGLE *A* IS ACUTE, AND THE SIDE OPPOSITE IS SHORTER THAN THE SIDE ADJACENT TO ∠*A*

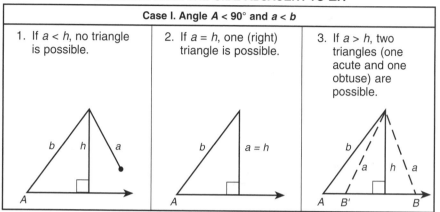

Case I. Angle *A* < 90° and *a* < *b*		
1. If *a* < *h*, no triangle is possible.	2. If *a* = *h*, one (right) triangle is possible.	3. If *a* > *h*, two triangles (one acute and one obtuse) are possible.

TABLE 9.2 CASE I (CONTINUED): ANGLE *A* IS ACUTE AND THE SIDE OPPOSITE HAS THE SAME OR GREATER LENGTH THAN THE SIDE ADJACENT TO ∠*A*

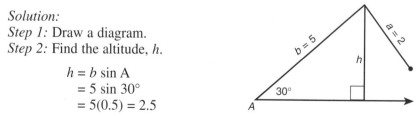

Case I. Angle *A* < 90° and *a* ≥ *b*
4. If *a* ≥ *b*, one triangle is possible.
If *a* = *b*, the triangle is isosceles.

Examples

1. If $a = 2$, $b = 5$, and m∠$A = 30$, how many distinct triangles can be constructed?

Solution:
Step 1: Draw a diagram.
Step 2: Find the altitude, *h*.

$$h = b \sin A$$
$$= 5 \sin 30°$$
$$= 5(0.5) = 2.5$$

Step 3: Compare *a* with *b* and *h*. Since $a < b$ and $a < h$, **no** triangle can be constructed having the given dimensions.

2. In $\triangle ABC$, if $a = 7$, $b = 10$, and m$\angle A = 37$, then $\angle B$:
(1) is an acute angle   (3) is a right angle
(2) is an obtuse angle   (4) is either an acute or an obtuse angle

Solution:
Step 1: Draw a diagram.
Step 2: Find the altitude, h.

$$h = b \sin A$$
$$= 10 \sin 37°$$
$$\approx 10(0.6018) \approx 6.02$$

Step 3: Compare a with b and h. Since $a < b$ and $a > h$, two triangles can be constructed. Thus $\angle B$ may be either an acute or an obtuse angle. The correct choice is **(4)**.

3. If $a = 7$, $b = 10$, and m$\angle B = 50$, how many distinct triangles can be constructed?

Solution: Here the given angle is B, and the side opposite it is b. Since $b > a$, the length of the side opposite acute angle B is longer than the side adjacent to $\angle B$. Thus exactly **one** triangle can be constructed.

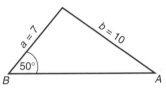

The Ambiguous Case Where Angle A ≥ 90°

Table 9.3 summarizes the number of possible triangles that can be constructed, given SSA (Side-Side-Angle), when the given angle is either an obtuse or a right angle.

TABLE 9.3 CASE II: ANGLE *A* IS NOT ACUTE

Case II: Angle *A* ≥ 90°	
1. If $a \le b$, no triangle is possible since the side opposite the greatest angle of a triangle must be its longest side.	2. If $a > b$, the side opposite the nonacute angle is longer than the adjacent side. Thus one triangle is possible.

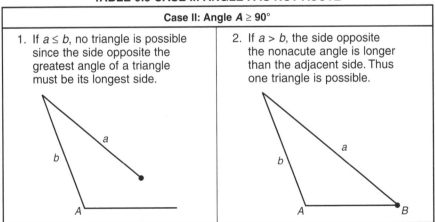

Example

4. If $r = 6$, $s = 5$, and m$\angle R = 100$, how many distinct triangles can be constructed?

Solution:
Step 1: Draw a diagram.
Step 2: Since the given angle is not acute, compare the side opposite with the side adjacent to the angle. Since r, the side opposite the obtuse angle, is longer than side s, **one** obtuse triangle can be constructed.

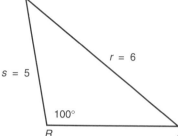

SUMMARY

Case I:	$A < 90°$ and $a < b$				$A < 90°$
	$a < h$	$a = h$	$a > h$	$a \geq b$	
Number of triangles:	0	1	2	1	

Case II:	$A \geq 90°$	
	$a \leq b$	$a > b$
Number of triangles	0	1

Exercise Set 9.5

1–5. Find the number of noncongruent triangles that can be constructed using the data provided in the accompanying table, where a *is the length of the side opposite $\angle A$ and* b *is the length of the side adjacent to $\angle A$.*

	A	a	b
1.	30°	8	10
2.	30°	5	4
3.	30°	4	9
4.	30°	4	9
5.	150°	6	7

6. If sin $A = 0.75$ and $b = 8$, for which value of a can two distinct triangles be constructed?
(1) 5   (2) 6   (3) 7   (4) 9

7. If $a = 5$ and $b = 10$, for which measure of $\angle A$ can two distinct triangles be constructed?
   (1) 20   (2) 30   (3) 45   (4) 120

8–10. In each case use the given data to determine the number of distinct triangles that can be constructed.

8. Given: $m\angle R = 100$, $r = 7$ and $s = 5$.

9. Given: $m\angle A = 43$, $a = 15$ and $b = 24$.

10. Given: $r = 7$, $s = 6$, and $m\angle R = 50$.

11–14. In each case, use the given data to determine whether it is possible to construct no triangle, two triangles, a right triangle, or an obtuse triangle.

11. Given: $\angle S = 100°$, $s = 8$, and $t = 9$.

12. Given: $\angle A = 34°20'$, $a = 57.0$, and $b = 100.0$.

13. Given: $\angle A = 40°10'$, $a = 12$, and $b = 20$.

14. Given: $\angle T = 30°$, $t = 4.6$, and $s = 9.2$.

15. Given: $\angle A = 60$, $a = 5\sqrt{2}$, and $b = 8$.

REGENTS TUNE-UP: CHAPTER 9

Each of the questions in this section has appeared on a previous Course III Regents Examination. Here is an opportunity for you to review Chapter 9 and, at the same time, prepare for the Course III Regents Examination.

1. In $\triangle ABC$, $a = 5$, $\sin A = \dfrac{1}{5}$, and $b = 4$. Find the value of $\sin B$.

2. In $\triangle ABC$, $b = 3$, $c = 4$, and $\angle A = 45°$. Expressed in simplest radical form, what is the area of $\triangle ABC$?

3. In $\triangle ABC$, $a = 2$, $b = 3$, and $c = 4$. What is the value of $\cos C$?

4. In $\triangle ABC$, if $\sin A = \dfrac{4}{5}$, $\sin B = \dfrac{3}{8}$, and $a = 24$, find b.

5. In $\triangle ABC$, $a = \sqrt{3}$, $b = \sqrt{3}$, and $m\angle C = 120$. Find C.

6. If $m\angle A = 30$, $a = 11$, and $b = 12$, the number of distinct triangles that can be constructed is:
   (1) 1   (2) 2   (3) 3   (4) 0

7. If $a = 5\sqrt{2}$, $b = 8$, and $m\angle A = 45$, how many distinct triangles can be constructed?
   (1) 1   (2) 2   (3) 3   (4) 0

8. The area of $\triangle ABC$ is 20. If $a = 10$ and $b = 8$, find the number of degrees in the measure of acute angle C.

9. If $m\angle A = 48$, $a = 7$, and $b = 9$, the number of distinct triangles that can be constructed is:
   (1) 1   (2) 2   (3) 3   (4) 0

10. The lengths of the sides of a triangular plot of land are 50, 80, and 100 meters.
    (a) Find, to the *nearest degree,* the measure of the *largest* angle of the triangle.
    (b) Using the answer obtain in part **(a)**, find, to the *nearest square meter,* the area of the triangle.

11. Two forces of 30 pounds and 40 pounds act upon a body, forming an acute angle with each other. The angle between the resultant and the 30-pound force is $35°10'$. Find, to the *nearest 10 minutes,* the angle between the two given forces.

12. In the accompanying diagram $\overleftrightarrow{DCFG}$ is tangent to circle O at F, $\overrightarrow{ECH}$ is a secant intersecting the circle at A and B, $m\widehat{AB} = 140$, and $m\widehat{AF} = 160$. If $FC = 10$, find AF to the *nearest tenth.*

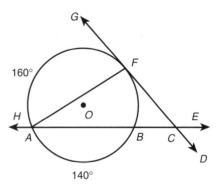

13. In the accompanying diagram, tangent $\overline{PB}$ and secant $\overline{PCA}$ are drawn to circle O, $AB = 8\sqrt{2}$, and $m\widehat{BC} : m\widehat{AC} : m\widehat{AB} = 3 : 4 : 5$.
   (a) Find the measure of:
       (1) $\widehat{BC}$ *(2)* $\angle PAB$ *(3)* $\angle APB$
   (b) Find the length of $\overline{PB}$.

14. The building lot shown in the accompanying diagram is shaped like an isosceles triangle with $AB = AC$ and $\angle BAC = 53°10'$. The area of the lot is 1 acre. Find the length, to the *nearest foot,* of each of the three sides. [1 acre = 43,560 square feet]

ANSWERS TO SELECTED EXERCISES: CHAPTER 9

Section 9.1

1. (a) 21	**(c)** $21\sqrt{3}$	**3.** 4.2	**7.** 8
(b) $21\sqrt{2}$	**(d)** 214.	**4.** 0.075	**8.** 8
2. (a) 47	**(c)** 98	**5.** $30\sqrt{3}$	**9.** 32°10′
(b) 91	**(d)** 88	**6.** 5.8	

Section 9.2

1. 0.54

2. 9

3. 0.54

4. $3\sqrt{2}$

5. $\dfrac{1}{4}$

6. 473

7. 46

8. 48.5

9. 68°20′

10. 4240

Section 9.3

1. $\sqrt{39}$

2. (a) 7

   (b) $\sqrt{89}$

   (c) $\sqrt{129}$

3. $\dfrac{1}{7}$

4. 0

5. $\dfrac{13}{14}$

6. 120°

7. $\dfrac{61-c^2}{60}$

8. $3\sqrt{3}$

9. (a) 109°30′

   (b) 2515

10. 38

11. (a) 101°30′ (b) 34°0′

12. 54.8

13. 11.0

14. (a) 97.9° (b) 3961

15. (a) 120° (b) 152

Section 9.4

1. 142

2. 59°10′

3. 25°40′

4. 451.0

5. 23°10′

6. $4\sqrt{3}$

7. (a) 60° (b) 11.1

8. (a) 16 (b) 25.9 (c) 19°

9. 131°20′ **10.** (a) 8 (b) 5.1

Section 9.5

1. 2

2. 1

3. 0

4. 1

5. 0

6. (3)

7. (4)

8. 1

9. 0

10. 1

11. No triangle

12. Two triangles

13. No triangle

14. A right triangle

15. No triangle

Regents Tune-Up: Chapter 9

1. $\dfrac{4}{25}$

2. $3\sqrt{2}$

3. −0.25

4. 11.25

5. 3

6. (2)

7. (2)

8. 30

9. (2)

10. (a) 98° (b) 1981

11. 60°50′

12. 15.3

13. (a) *(1)* 90°

     (2) 45°

     (3) 30°

   (b) 16

14. $AB = AC \approx 330$, $BC \approx 295$

PROBABILITY AND STATISTICS

CHAPTER 10

BERNOULLI EXPERIMENTS, THE BINOMIAL THEOREM, AND THE NORMAL CURVE

10.1 FINDING PROBABILITIES IN TWO-OUTCOME EXPERIMENTS

$$\bigwedge$$
=========== **KEY IDEAS** ===========
$$\diagup\underline{\quad}\diagdown$$

In tossing a coin there are two possible outcomes, head or tails. If a probability experiment that has exactly two possible outcomes is repeated, as in tossing a coin five times, it is called a **Bernoulli experiment.**

Each repetition of a Bernoulli experiment is called a *trial.* If a coin is flipped five times, then there are five trials. For each trial the concern is whether a particular outcome occurs or does not occur. If the probability of one of the outcomes occurring in a single trial is known, the probability that this outcome will occur *r* times in *n* trials can be easily determined.

Characteristics of a Bernoulli Experiment

A Bernoulli experiment has *n* identical trials such that all of the following are true:

- Each trial results in one of two possible outcomes. One of these outcomes is considered a "success," while the other is labeled a "failure."
- The *n* trials are *independent*. The outcome of one trial has no effect on the outcome of any other trial.
- The probability of a success in a single trial is usually denoted by the letter *p*, while the probability of a failure is represented by the letter *q*. Since the sum of the probabilities of the possible outcomes of any experiment is 1,

$$p + q = 1 \quad \text{or} \quad q = 1 - p.$$

- If there are *r* successes in *n* trials ($r \leq n$), there must be $n - r$ failures.

Obtaining *r* Successes, Followed by All Failures

Suppose a coin is weighted so that the probability of obtaining a head is $\frac{2}{3}$. If

$$p = P(\text{head}) = \frac{2}{3}, \quad \text{then} \quad q = P(\text{tail}) = 1 - p = \frac{1}{3}.$$

If this coin is tossed five times, the probability of obtaining a head on the first toss *followed by* four tails on subsequent tosses is calculated by multiplying the probability of the desired outcome occurring (head or tail) on each of the five trials:

$$\frac{2}{3} \cdot \frac{1}{3} \cdot \frac{1}{3} \cdot \frac{1}{3} \cdot \frac{1}{3} = \left(\frac{2}{3}\right)^1 \cdot \left(\frac{1}{3}\right)^4$$

The probability of obtaining a head on each of the first two tosses, *followed by* three tails, is

$$\frac{2}{3} \cdot \frac{2}{3} \cdot \frac{1}{3} \cdot \frac{1}{3} \cdot \frac{1}{3} = \left(\frac{2}{3}\right)^2 \cdot \left(\frac{1}{3}\right)^3.$$

Similarly, the probability of obtaining a head on each of the first three tosses, *followed by* two tails, is

$$\frac{2}{3} \cdot \frac{2}{3} \cdot \frac{2}{3} \cdot \frac{1}{3} \cdot \frac{1}{3} = \left(\frac{2}{3}\right)^3 \cdot \left(\frac{1}{3}\right)^2$$

Notice that on the right side of each of the preceding equations the power of $\frac{2}{3}$ ($= p$) represents the number of successes, the power of $\frac{1}{3}$ ($= q$) represents the number of failures, and the sum of the exponents equals the number of trials.

=============== | **MATH FACTS** | ===============

BERNOULLI EXPERIMENT WITH *r* SUCCESSES FIRST

$P(r$ successes, $n - r$ failures$) = p^r q^{n-r}$, where $p + q = 1$.

Example

1. In rolling a single die four times in succession, what is the probability of obtaining a 5 only on:
(a) the first roll?   **(b)** the first three rolls?

Solutions: **(a)** In the formula

$$P(r \text{ successes}) = p^r q^{n-r},$$

let $r = 1$, $n = 4$, $p = \dfrac{1}{6}$, and $q = 1 - \dfrac{1}{6} = \dfrac{5}{6}$. Then

$$P(\text{one } 5) = p^r q^{n-r} = \left(\frac{1}{6}\right)^1 \cdot \left(\frac{5}{6}\right)^3 = \frac{5^3}{6^4} = \frac{125}{1296}.$$

(b) Obtaining a 5 only on the first three rolls means that the fourth (last) roll is a "failure." Thus, since $r = 3$ and $n = 4$,

$$P(\text{three } 5\text{'s}) = p^r q^{n-r} = \left(\frac{1}{6}\right)^3 \cdot \left(\frac{5}{6}\right)^1 = \frac{5}{6^4} = \frac{5}{1296}.$$

Combination Notation

The number of different ways in which r things can be selected from a group of n things ($r \leq n$), without paying attention to the order in which the r things are selected, is represented by $_nC_r$. The notation $_nC_r$ is read as "the combination of n things taken r at a time," and can be evaluated using the formula

$$_nC_r = \frac{_nP_r}{r!} = \frac{n!}{r!(n-r)!}.$$

For example, to evaluate $_5C_3$, let $n = 5$ and $r = 3$; then

$$_5C_3 = \frac{5!}{3!(5-3)!} = \frac{5 \cdot 4 \cdot 3 \cdot 2 \cdot 1}{(3 \cdot 2 \cdot 1)(2 \cdot 1)} = \mathbf{10.}$$

Instead of using a complicated formula to figure out the number of combinations, you can use your scientific calculator. Since $_nC_r$ is usually printed above another calculator key, you will probably need to press the ⌷2nd⌷ function key before pressing the key that has $_nC_r$ printed above it. For example, to evaluate $_5C_3$, locate $_nC_r$ on your calculator and then key in

5   ⌷2nd⌷   ⌷$_nC_r$⌷   3   ⌷=⌷.

The display window now shows 10 since $_5C_3 = 10$.

MATH FACTS

EVALUATING COMBINATIONS

To evaluate $_nC_r$ for given values of n and r, key in:

n ⌷2nd⌷   ⌷$_nC_r$⌷ r ⌷=⌷.

If you remember the following relationships, you can often save time in evaluating combinations having the indicated form:

- $_nC_n = 1$ Example: $_5C_5 = 1$
- $_nC_0 = 1$ Example: $_5C_0 = 1$
- $_nC_1 = n$ Example: $_5C_1 = 5$

Obtaining r Successes in n Trials ($r \leq n$)

The r successes of a Bernoulli experiment need not occur consecutively in the first r trials. Within the n trials, the r successes ($r \leq n$) can be arranged in $_nC_r$ ways. Multiplying $_nC_r$ by $p^r q^{n-r}$ gives the probability of obtaining exactly r successes in any order within the n trials of a Bernoulli experiment.

For example, if the probability of winning a game is .7, then the probability of winning 3 out of 4 games is found by using the formula $_nC_r p^r q^{n-r}$, where $p = .7$, $q = .3$, $r = 3$, and $n = 4$:

$$P(\text{win } r \text{ out of } n \text{ games}) = {_nC_r}p^r q^{n-r}$$
$$P(\text{win 3 out of 4 games}) = {_4C_3}\,(.7)^3(.3)^{4-3}$$
$$= 4(.343)(.3)$$
$$= \mathbf{.4116}$$

MATH FACTS

BERNOULLI EXPERIMENT WITH r SUCCESSES IN n TRIALS

$P(r \text{ successes in } n \text{ Bernoulli trials}) = {_nC_r}p^r q^{n-r}$,

where

$$_nC_r = \frac{n!}{r!(n-r)!} \quad \text{and} \quad p + q = 1.$$

Examples

2. In a certain part of the country, the probability of rain on any day is $\frac{1}{5}$.
In the next 5 days, what is the probability that in that region it will rain:
(a) *exactly* 3 days   **(b)** *at least* 3 days   **(c)** *at most* 3 days

Solutions: This is a Bernoulli experiment in which there are two possible outcomes: (1) it rains or (2) it does not rain. Let $p = \frac{1}{5}$, $q = \frac{4}{5}$, and $n = 5$.
(a) Use the formula $_nC_r p^r q^{n-r}$, where $r = 3$.

$$P(\text{rains } exactly \text{ 3 days out of 5}) = {}_5C_3 \left(\frac{1}{5}\right)^3 \left(\frac{4}{5}\right)^2$$

$$= 10\left(\frac{1}{125}\right)\left(\frac{16}{25}\right)$$

$$= \frac{160}{3125}$$

(b) If it rains on *at least* 3 days, then it may rain on 3, 4, or 5 days. Hence the probability of rain on at least 3 days is the sum of the probabilities of rain on 3 days, 4 days, and 5 days.

$$P(\text{rains 3 days out of 5}) \quad = \frac{160}{3125}$$

$$P(\text{rains 4 days out of 5}) \quad = {}_5C_4 \left(\frac{1}{5}\right)^4 \left(\frac{4}{5}\right)^1$$

$$= 5\left(\frac{1}{625}\right)\left(\frac{4}{5}\right)$$

$$= \frac{20}{3125}$$

$$P(\text{rains 5 days out of 5}) \quad = {}_5C_5 \left(\frac{1}{5}\right)^5 \left(\frac{4}{5}\right)^0$$

$$= 1\left(\frac{1}{3125}\right)^1$$

$$= \frac{1}{3125}$$

Adding these probabilities gives the probability of rain on *at least* 3 days:

$$P(\text{rains } at\ least \text{ 3 days out of 5}) = \frac{160}{3125} + \frac{20}{3125} + \frac{1}{3125} = \frac{181}{3125}.$$

(c) If it rains on *at most* 3 days, then it may rain on 0, 1, 2, or 3 days. Hence the probability of rain on *at most* 3 days is the sum of the probability of rain on 0, 1, 2, and 3 days.

$$P(\text{rains 0 day out of 5}) \ = {}_5C_0 \left(\frac{1}{5}\right)^0 \left(\frac{4}{5}\right)^5 = \frac{1024}{3125}$$

$$P(\text{rains 1 day out of 5}) \ = {}_5C_1 \left(\frac{1}{5}\right)^1 \left(\frac{4}{5}\right)^4 = \frac{1280}{3125}$$

$$P(\text{rains 2 days out of 5}) = {}_5C_2 \left(\frac{1}{5}\right)^2 \left(\frac{4}{5}\right)^3 = \frac{640}{3125}$$

$$P(\text{rains 3 days out of 5}) = \frac{160}{3125}$$

Adding these probabilities gives the probability of rain on *at most* 3 days:

$$P(\text{rains } at\ most \text{ 3 days}) = \frac{1024}{3125} + \frac{1280}{3125} + \frac{640}{3125} + \frac{160}{3125} = \mathbf{\frac{3104}{3125}}.$$

3. Circle O is divided into four regions, as shown in the accompanying diagram, with $\overline{ROS}$ a diameter. A fair spinner is placed at O.

(a) If the spinner is spun once, determine the probability that the spinner will stop in region:

    (1) A   *(2) C*   *(3) D*

(b) If the spinner is spun three times, what is the probability that the spinner will stop in region D:

    (1) exactly twice?   *(2) at least* twice?   *(3) at most* twice?

Solutions: **(a)** The fractional parts of the area of circle O that are contained in regions A, C, and D represent the probabilities that the spinner will land in these regions.

Since region A has a central angle of 60°, it has $\dfrac{60°}{360°}$ or $\dfrac{1}{6}$ of the area of circle O.

Since $\overline{ROS}$ is a diameter, region C has a central angle of $180° - 45° = 135°$ and region D has a central angle of $180° - 60° = 120°$. Hence region C has $\dfrac{135°}{360°} = \dfrac{3}{8}$ of the area of circle O, while region D has $\dfrac{120°}{360°} = \dfrac{1}{3}$ of the area of circle O.

Thus

$$(1)\ P(A) = \frac{1}{6} \qquad (2)\ P(C) = \frac{3}{8} \qquad (3)\ P(D) = \frac{1}{3}.$$

(b) This is a Bernoulli experiment in which there are two possible outcomes: the spinner stops in region D, or the spinner does not stop in region D. Since $P(D) = \dfrac{1}{3}$, let $p = \dfrac{1}{3}$ and $q = \dfrac{2}{3}$.

(1) $P(\text{stops in } D\ r \text{ times out of } n \text{ spins}) = {}_nC_r p^r q^{n-r}$. To find the probability that the spinner will stop in region D exactly two times in three spins, let $r = 2$ and $n = 3$.

$$P(\text{stops in } D \textit{ exactly } \text{twice}) = {}_3C_2\left(\frac{1}{3}\right)^2\left(\frac{2}{3}\right)^1$$

$$= 3\left(\frac{1}{9}\right)\left(\frac{2}{3}\right)$$

$$= \frac{6}{27}$$

(2) If the spinner stops in region D at least twice in three spins, then it may stop in region D two or three times. Hence the probability that the spinner will stop in region D at least twice is the sum of the probabilities that it will stop in region D exactly two times and exactly three times. In part *(1)*, the probability that the spinner will stop in region D exactly two times was found to be $\dfrac{6}{27}$.

$$P(\text{stops in } D \text{ two times}) = \frac{6}{27}$$

$$P(\text{stops in } D \text{ three times}) = {_3C_3}\left(\frac{1}{3}\right)^3\left(\frac{2}{3}\right)^0 = \frac{1}{27}$$

Adding these probabilities gives the probability that the spinner will stop in region D *at least* twice:

$$P(\text{stops in } D \text{ at least twice}) = \frac{6}{27} + \frac{1}{27} = \frac{7}{27}.$$

(3) <u>Method 1:</u> Stopping in region D *at most* twice in three spins means stopping in region D two or fewer times. The probability that the spinner will stop in region D at most twice is, therefore, the sum of the probabilities that it will stop in region D no time, exactly one time, and exactly two times.

$$P(\text{stops in } D \text{ no time}) = {_3C_0}\left(\frac{1}{3}\right)^0\left(\frac{2}{3}\right)^3 = \frac{8}{27}$$

$$P(\text{stops in } D \text{ one time}) = {_3C_1}\left(\frac{1}{3}\right)^1\left(\frac{2}{3}\right)^2 = \frac{12}{27}$$

$$P(\text{stops in } D \text{ two times}) = \frac{6}{27}$$

Adding these probabilities gives the probability that the spinner will stop in region D *at most* two times:

$$P(\text{stops in } D \text{ at most twice}) = \frac{8}{27} + \frac{12}{27} + \frac{6}{27} = \frac{26}{27}.$$

<u>Method 2:</u> Stopping in region D *at most* twice in three spins is equivalent to not stopping in region D three times. From part *(2)*, the probability that the spinner will stop in region D three times is $\dfrac{1}{27}$, so the probability that it will not stop in D three times is $1 - \dfrac{1}{27}$ or $\dfrac{26}{27}$. Hence

P(stops in D *at most* twice) = P(*not* stopping in D three times)

$$= \frac{26}{27}$$

Exercise Set 10.1

1. A fair coin is tossed three times. Find the probability of obtaining:
   (a) exactly two heads
   (b) exactly one tail
   (c) at least two heads

2. The probability of winning a game is $\frac{1}{3}$, and the probability of losing a game is $\frac{2}{3}$. If five games are played, find the probability of winning:
   (a) exactly two games
   (b) at most one game
   (c) not more than two games

3. A coin is weighted so that the probability of obtaining a head is four times as great as the probability of obtaining a tail. If the coin is tossed four times, find the probability of obtaining:
   (a) exactly four heads   (c) at most one head
   (b) an equal number of heads and tails   (d) at least one head

4. A quiz consists of five True or False questions. If a student answers each question by randomly writing True or False, what is the probability that the student will answer more questions correctly than incorrectly?

5. A circular region is divided into three sections and labeled as shown in the accompanying diagram. If the spinner is spun five times, what is the probability that:
   (a) it will land on the black section exactly two times?
   (b) it will land on either the blue or red section each time?

6. A certain part of the country has a 70% chance of rain each day. Find the probability that this area will have:
   (a) *no* rain on the next 3 consecutive days
   (b) *exactly* 5 rainy days in 1 week
   (c) *at most* 2 days of rain in 1 week
   (d) *at least* 6 days of rain in 1 week

7. A quiz consists of five multiple-choice questions. Each question has four choices. If a student answers each question by randomly selecting one of the four choices, what is the probability that the student will:
(a) answer each question correctly?
(b) answer the first two questions correctly and the next three questions incorrectly?
(c) receive a grade of at least 80%?

8. The receivable channels on a TV set are indicated on the channel selector shown in the accompanying diagram. If the probability of selecting each channel is the same, find the probability of choosing:
(a) *exactly* two even-numbered channels on three random selections
(b) *at least* two odd-numbered channels on three random selections

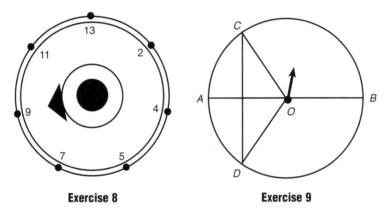

Exercise 8   Exercise 9

9. In the accompanying diagram of circle O, diameter $\overline{AB}$ is perpendicular to chord $\overline{CD}$ and $m\angle AOC = 60$. A fair spinner is placed at O. Determine the probability that the spinner will stop:
(a) in region BOC in one spin
(b) in region AOD in one spin
(c) in region BOC *at least* twice in three spins
(d) in region AOC *at most* once in three spins

10. Regular pentagon *ABCDE* is inscribed in circle *O* and divided into three regions as shown in the accompanying diagram. A fair spinner is placed at *O*.

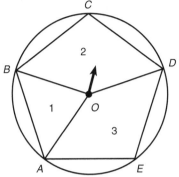

(a) If the spinner is spun once, determine the probability that it will stop:

    (1) in region 1   *(2)* in region 2

    (3) in region 3

(b) If the spinner is spun three times, determine the probability that it will stop:

    (1) in region 2 *exactly* once

    (2) in region 2 at *least* twice

    (3) in region 1 *no more than* once

    (4) in each of the three regions

10.2 EXPANDING $(a + b)^n$

KEY IDEAS

A binomial such as $(a + b)^5$ may be expanded by repeated multiplication, using $(a + b)$ as a factor five times:

$$(a + b)^5 = a^5 + 5a^4b + 10a^3b^2 + 10a^2b^3 + 5ab^4 + b^5.$$

Notice that there are $5 + 1$ or 6 terms. For any positive integer exponent, expanding $(a + b)^n$ will always produce a series of $n + 1$ terms involving powers of *a* and *b*. These expansions follow a pattern that can be represented by an algebraic formula called the **binomial theorem.**

Binomial Theorem

In the expansion of $(a + b)^5$, the numerical coefficients of the terms can be represented using combinations:

$$(a + b)^5 = 1a^5 + 5a^4b + 10a^3b^2 + 10a^2b^3 + 5ab^4 + 1b^5$$

$$= {}_5C_0a^5 + {}_5C_1a^4b + {}_5C_2a^3b^2 + {}_5C_3a^2b^3 + {}_5C_4ab^4 + {}_5C_5b^5$$

Notice that the numerical coefficient of the first and the last terms is 1; that is, ${}_5C_0 = {}_5C_5 = 1$. Also observe that the series of terms consists of descending powers of *a* and ascending powers of *b* so that:

- the first term is a^5 and the last term is b^5;
- the sum of the exponents in each term is 5.

The binomial theorem describes this pattern for *any* positive integer n.

MATH FACTS

BINOMIAL THEOREM

$$(a + b)^n = {}_nC_0\,a^n + {}_nC_1\,a^{n-1}b + {}_nC_2\,a^{n-2}b^2 +$$
$${}_nC_3\,a^{n-3}b^3 + \dots + {}_nC_{n-1}ab^{n-1} + {}_nC_n b^n$$

Example 1 shows how the binomial theorem can be used to expand a power of a binomial of the form $(a + b)^n$ by substituting values into a formula, rather than performing repeated multiplications of the binomial.

Example

1. Expand $(3x - y)^4$ using the binomial theorem.

Solution: For $n = 4$, the binomial theorem states:

$$(a + b)^4 = {}_4C_0a^4 + {}_4C_1a^3b + {}_4C_2a^2b^2 + {}_4C_3ab^3 + {}_4C_4b^4.$$

Let $x = 3x$ and $b = -y$. Then

$$(3x - y)^4 = {}_4C_0(3x)^4 + {}_4C_1(3x)^3(-y) + {}_4C_2(3x)^2(-y)^2$$
$$+ {}_4C_3(3x)(-y)^3 + {}_4C_4(-y)^4$$

Simplify, and substitute ${}_4C_0 = {}_4C_4 = 1$, ${}_4C_1 = 4$, ${}_4C_2 = 6$, and ${}_4C_3 = 4$:

$$(3x - y)^4 = (1)(81x^4) + (4)(27x^3)(-y) + (6)(9x^2)(y^2)$$
$$+ (4)(3x)(-y^3) + (1)(y^4)$$
$$= 81x^4 - 108x^3y + 54x^2y^2 - 12\,xy^3 + y^4$$

Writing the *k*th Term

Sometimes the only thing you want to know about the power of a binomial is what a particular term looks like. Specific terms in a binomial expansion of the form $(a + b)^n$ are identified by their position numbers in the series. For example, since the expansion of $(a + b)^5$ is as follows:

First	*Second*	*Third*	*Fourth*	*Fifth*	*Sixth*
term	*term*	*term*	*term*	*term*	*term*

$${}_5C_0a^5 + {}_5C_1a^4b + {}_5C_2a^3b^2 + {}_5C_3a^2b^3 + {}_5C_4ab^4 + {}_5C_5b^5$$

the third term is ${}_5C_2a^3b^2$. Observe that in the expansion of $(a + b)^n$:

- The numerical coefficient of the kth term is $_nC_{k-1}$. For example, the numerical coefficient of the **third** term is $_5C_{3-1} = {_5C_2}$.
- The exponent of b in the kth term is $k - 1$, and the exponent of a is $n - (k - 1)$. For example, in the **third** term the exponent of b is $3 - 1 = 2$, and the exponent of a is $5 - (3 - 1) = 5 - 2 = 3$.
- In each term the sum of the exponents of a and b is n. In the first term the power of b is 0, and in the last term the power of a is 0.

MATH FACTS

kTH TERM OF $(a + b)^n$

$$k\text{th term} = {_nC_{k-1}}a^{n-(k-1)}b^{k-1}$$

For example, the second term in the expansion of $(3x - y)^4$ may be found by letting $a = 3x$, $b = -y$, $n = 4$, and $k = 2$:

$$\begin{aligned}
\text{second term} &= {_4C_{2-1}}(3x)^{4-(2-1)}(-y)^{2-1} \\
&= (4)(3x)^3(-y)^1 \\
&= (4)(27x^3)(-y) \\
&= -108x^3y
\end{aligned}$$

Examples

2. What is the middle term in the expansion of $(x - 2y)^4$?

Solution: Since the expansion of $(a + b)^n$ consists of $n + 1$ terms, the expansion of $(x - 2y)^4$ has $4 + 1$ or 5 terms. The middle term is the third term. To find the third term let $a = x$, $b = -2y$, $n = 4$, and $k = 3$:

$$\begin{aligned}
{_nC_{k-1}}a^{n-(k-1)}b^{k-1} &= {_4C_{3-1}}x^{4-(3-1)}(-2y)^{3-1} \\
&= {_4C_2}x^2(-2y)^2 \\
&= 6x^2(4y^2) = 24x^2y^2
\end{aligned}$$

3. What is the numerical coefficient of the term that contains x^5y^4 in the expansion of $(x + yi)^9$, where $i = \sqrt{-1}$?

Solution: The first term contains x^9, the second term contains x^8y, the third term contains x^7y^2, the fourth term contains x^6y^3, and the *fifth* term contains x^5y^4. Let $a = x$, $b = yi$, $n = 9$, and $k = 4$:

$$\begin{aligned}
{_nC_{k-1}}a^{n-(k-1)}b^{k-1} &= {_9C_{5-1}}x^{9-(5-1)}(yi)^{5-1} \\
&= 126x^5y^4i^4
\end{aligned}$$

Since $i^4 = 1$, the fifth term is $126x^5y^4$. The numerical coefficient of the term that contains x^5y^4 is **126**.

Exercise Set 10.2

1–4. Use the binomial theorem to write each expansion.

1. $(x + y)^4$ **2.** $(2r - s)$ **3.** $(p - 3q)^4$ **4.** $\left(2x + \dfrac{y}{3}\right)^5$

5–8. Find the third term in each expansion.

5. $(p + q)^8$ **6.** $(2y - x)^5$ **7.** $(3x - 5y)^6$ **8.** $(1 - \sin x)^7$

9–12. Find the fourth term in each expansion.

9. $(x - 2)^7$ **10.** $(1 + y)^5$ **11.** $\left(a - \dfrac{b}{2}\right)^6$ **12.** $(a + bi)^8$

13–15. Find the fifth term in each expansion.

13. $(r - 2s)^5$ **14.** $(3 - k)^8$ **15.** $(a + bi)^7$

16. What is the numerical coefficient of the term x^4y^2 in the expansion of $(x + y)^6$?

17. What is the numerical coefficient of the term c^5 in the expansion of:

     (a) $(b - 2c)^5$ **(b)** $\left(b + \dfrac{c}{3}\right)^6$

18–21. In the expansion of each of the following binomials, find:

     (a) the middle term   **(b)** the next-to-last term

18. $(\sin x - \cos x)^6$ **19.** $\left(10 - \dfrac{x}{2}\right)^4$

20. $(p - 2q)^8$ **21.** $(a - bi)^{10}$ $[i = \sqrt{-1}]$

10.3 COMPARING STATISTICAL MEASURES

$$\bigwedge$$
KEY IDEAS

Much of statistics is concerned with finding ways to describe how the individual numbers in a set are distributed in value.

The *mean, median,* and *mode* are measures of **central tendency** since they indicate how the data values are grouped about some central value.

The *range, mean, absolute deviation, variance,* and *standard deviation* are measures of **dispersion** since they indicate whether the data are spread out or are clustered together.

Since no single statistical measure describes a set of data values completely, when analyzing data you need to look at measures of dispersion as well as measures of central tendency.

Statistics

Statistics is the branch of mathematics that deals with collecting, organizing, displaying, and interpreting data. Data are facts and figures. Numerical data may be referred to as values, scores, measures, or observations.

Subscripted Variables

Sometimes it is convenient to use a single variable, say x, to represent an entire list of data values. An individual data value in the list may be named by writing x followed by a number, called a subscript, that represents its position in the list. For example, the first data value in a list is called x_1 (read as "x sub 1"), the second data value is called x_2, and so forth. Notice that the subscript is written to the right of the variable, one-half line down from it.

Variables such as x_1 and x_2 are called *subscripted variables.* If $x = \{15, 7, 4, 13, 11\}$, then

$$x_1 = 15, \quad x_2 = 7, \quad x_3 = 4, \quad x_4 = 13, \quad \text{and} \quad x_5 = 11.$$

Sigma Notation

Many of the formulas used in statistics involve finding the sum of a series of numbers. The symbol Σ is the capital Greek letter *sigma* and indicates that the sum of whatever follows should be taken. In the summation $\sum\limits_{i=1}^{5} x_i$, i is called the *index variable*, 1 is the *lower limit* (first value for i), and 5 is the *upper limit* (last value for i). Thus, $\sum\limits_{i=1}^{5} x_i$ represents the sum of the values of x_i as i increases from 1 to 5, in steps of 1:

$$\sum_{i=1}^{5} x_i = x_1 + x_2 + x_3 + x_4 + x_5$$
$$= 15 + 7 + 4 + 13 + 11 = 50$$

Here are some additional facts about summation notation that you should know:

- The index variable may start at a whole number different from 1.

    Example: $\sum\limits_{i=1}^{5} x_i = x_3 + x_4 + x_5$

- If a constant factor appears inside the summation sign, it may be "passed through it."

    Example: $\sum\limits_{i=1}^{5} 2x_i = 2 \sum\limits_{i=1}^{5} x_i$
    $$= 2(x_1 + x_2 + x_3 + x_4 + x_5)$$

- The index variable may be used to represent the terms to be added.

    Example: $\sum\limits_{i=1}^{5} i^2 = 1^2 + 2^2 + 3^2 + 4^2 + 5^2$
    $$= 1 + 4 + 9 + 16 + 25$$
    $$= 55$$

Example

1. Evaluate:

(a) $\sum\limits_{k=1}^{3} (2k-1)^2$ (b) $\sum\limits_{n=3}^{4} \frac{1}{7}(2^n)$ (c) $\sum\limits_{p=1}^{3} 64^{\frac{1}{p}}$

Solutions: (a) The summation symbol tells you to evaluate and then accumulate terms of the form $(2k-1)^2$ for $k = 1$, 2, and 3.

$$\sum_{k=1}^{3} (2k-1)^2 = (2 \cdot 1 - 1)^2 + (2 \cdot 2 - 1)^2 + (2 \cdot 3 - 1)^2$$

$$\begin{aligned}
&= (2-1)^2 && + (4-1)^2 && + (6-1)^2 \\
&= 1^2 && + 3^2 && + 5^2 \\
&= 1 && + 9 && + 25 \\
&= \mathbf{35}
\end{aligned}$$

(b) Since the starting value of the index variable is 3, the summation symbol tells you to evaluate and then accumulate terms of the form $\frac{1}{7}(2^n)$ for $n = 3, 4,$ and 5.

$$\sum_{n=3}^{5} \frac{1}{7}(2^n) = \frac{1}{7} \sum_{n=3}^{5} 2^n$$

$$= \frac{1}{7}(2^3 + 2^4 + 2^5)$$

$$= \frac{1}{7}(8 + 16 + 32)$$

$$= \frac{1}{7}(56) = 8$$

(c) $\sum_{p=1}^{3} 64^{\frac{1}{p}} = 64^{\frac{1}{1}} + 64^{\frac{1}{2}} + 64^{\frac{1}{3}}$

$$= 64 + 8 \quad + 4$$
$$= \mathbf{76}$$

Mean, Median, and Mode

The **mean** (average) of a set of data values is the sum of the values divided by the number of values. Thus, if subscripted variables of the form x_i represent the individual data values, $\bar{x}$ (read as "x bar") is commonly used to represent the mean.

If there are n data values, then

$$\text{Mean} = \bar{x} = \frac{1}{n} \sum_{i=1}^{n} x_i = \frac{1}{n} (x_1 + x_2 + x_3 + \cdots + x_n).$$

If $x = \{15, 7, 4, 13, 1\}$, then

$$\bar{x} = \frac{1}{5}(15 + 7 + 4 + 13 + 1) = \frac{1}{5}(50) = \mathbf{10.}$$

The **median** of a set of data values is the middle value when the numbers are arranged in size order. To find the median of $\{15, 7, 4, 13, 1\}$, arrange the numbers is ascending (or descending) order: $\{1, 4, 7, 13, 15\}$. The median is **7**, since 7 is the middle value of the set.

When an ordered data set has an even number of data values, the median is found by taking the average of the two middle values. The median of $\{6, 17, 18, 22, 23, 31\}$ is **20**, since 20 is the average of 18 and 22.

The **mode** is the most frequent occurring data value in a set of observations. The mode of $\{2, 3, 1, 2, 4, 3, 5, 6, 2, 5\}$ is **2**, since 2 appears more times than any other value in the list.

Measures of Dispersion

Consider the two sets of numbers:

$$A = \{49, 53, 51, 55\} \quad \text{and} \quad B = \{1, 2, 5, 200\}.$$

The mean of each set is 52. For set A, the mean of 52 is fairly representative of the members of the set. The same is not true, however, for set B since each of its measures varies greatly from the mean of 52. Since it is useful to know whether the mean is a representative data value, additional statistical measures must be introduced that indicate the extent to which the individual data values are scattered or dispersed about the mean. Statistics that measure this type of variability are called **measures of dispersion.**

The simplest measure of dispersion is the *range*. The **range** of a set of numbers is the difference between the largest and the smallest numbers of the set. The range of the set 1, 2, 5, 200 is 199 since $200 - 1 = 199$. When the range is relatively large, the value of the mean *may* be distorted.

Variance

The deviation from the mean of the data value x_i is the amount by which that value differs from the mean. The **variance** of a set of numbers is the average of the squares of the deviations from the mean. The variance of 1, 2, 5, 200 can be calculated using the formula $\dfrac{1}{n} \sum_{i=1}^{n} (x_i - \bar{x})^2$ as follows:

$$\begin{aligned}
\text{Variance} &= \frac{1}{4}[(1-52)^2 + (2-52)^2 + (5-52)^2 + (200-52)^2] \\
&= \frac{1}{4}[(-51)^2 + (-50)^2 + (-47)^2 + (148)^2] \\
&= \frac{1}{4}[2,601 + 2,500 + 2,209 + 21,904] \\
&= \frac{29,214}{4} = \mathbf{7303.5}
\end{aligned}$$

By *squaring* each deviation from the mean, the variance formula prevents the mean deviations from summing to zero. The squaring process, however, tends to exaggerate the size of the variance in comparison to the values of the individual data items it is describing. The next measure of dispersion attempts to correct this weakness.

Standard Deviation

The **standard deviation** of a set of numbers is defined as the square root of the variance. The standard deviation is the most widely used measure of dispersion. The letter *s* or σ (the lower-case Greek letter sigma) is commonly used to represent the standard deviation. Sometimes the standard deviation is abbreviated as S.D.

If the variance of the set 1, 2, 5, 200 is 7303.5, then the standard deviation is $\sqrt{7303.5} = 85.5$, rounded to the nearest tenth. Since the standard deviation is considerably greater than the mean of 52, you would suspect that the data values are widely scattered, rather than clustered about the mean.

Although the standard deviation σ of a set of *n* data values can be found using the formula

$$\sigma = \sqrt{\frac{1}{n}\sum_{i=1}^{n}(\bar{x} - x_i)^2},$$

the calculations may be lengthy and error-prone. After a set of data values has been entered and stored in your scientific calculator, the mean and standard deviation of those values can be easily obtained by pressing a couple of keys. If you are using a Casio scientific calculator, you will need to have the calculator in the SD (*Statistical Data*) mode before entering data values. Once the calculator is in the SD mode, you can accumulate data values by pressing the $\boxed{\text{M+}}$ key after each new value is entered.

Here is a procedure for finding the mean and standard deviation of 1, 2, 5, and 200 that will work for many Casio calculators:

- Press the DATA entry key after entering each of the data values, as in

  1 $\boxed{\text{M+}}$ 2 $\boxed{\text{M+}}$ 5 $\boxed{\text{M+}}$ 200 $\boxed{\text{M+}}$

- Find the mean by pressing the $\boxed{\text{SHIFT}}$ key and then pressing the key that has $\bar{x}$ printed directly above it.
- Find the standard deviation by pressing the $\boxed{\text{SHIFT}}$ key and then pressing the key that has $x\sigma_n$ printed directly above it.

If you are using a Texas Instruments calculator, you can follow a similar procedure by using the $\boxed{\Sigma+}$ key instead of the $\boxed{\text{M+}}$ key. Since not all calculators work in the same way, you may need to read the manual that came with your calculator.

Example

2. On a certain civil service examination, the grades of five people were 71, 73, 74, 86, and 96. Find:
(a) the mean grade
(b) the standard deviation to the *nearest tenth*
(c) the percentage of the total scores that fall within one standard deviation of the mean

Solutions: Using your scientific calculator, enter and accumulate the five data values.

(a) Press the ⎡2nd⎤ function key, and then press the key that has $\bar{x}$ printed directly above it. The mean grade is **8.0**.

(b) Press the ⎡2nd⎤ function key, and then press the key that has σ printed directly above it. The standard deviation, correct to the *nearest tenth*, is **9.6**.

(c) One standard deviation to the left of the mean is $80 - 9.6 = 70.4$, and one standard deviation to the right of the mean is $80 + 9.6 = 89.6$. Four out of five grades are between 70.4 and 89.6. Only 96 is not in this interval.

Hence $\dfrac{4}{5}$ or **80%** of the grades fall within one standard deviation of the mean.

Exercise Set 10.3

1–6. Evaluate.

1. $\displaystyle\sum_{k=1}^{4} \sqrt{2}k^3$

3. $\displaystyle\sum_{k=1}^{5} (k-1)^2$

5. $\displaystyle\sum_{k=1}^{3} \left(\frac{3^k}{k}\right)$

2. $\displaystyle\sum_{k=1}^{5} (k^2-1)$

4. $\displaystyle\sum_{n=2}^{4} (n-n^2)$

6. $\displaystyle\sum_{k=0}^{3} \left(\frac{k}{k+1}\right)$

7–12. Find the numerical value.

7. $\displaystyle\sum_{k=1}^{4} \sin\frac{k\pi}{2}$

9. $\displaystyle\sum_{k=0}^{4} \sin\frac{k\pi}{4}$

11. $\displaystyle\sum_{p=0}^{3} \log 10^p$

8. $\displaystyle\sum_{k=0}^{4} \left(\cos\frac{k\pi}{2}\right)^2$

10. $\displaystyle\sum_{k=1}^{3} \cos\frac{\pi}{k}$

12. $\displaystyle\sum_{n=1}^{4} 4^{\frac{n}{2}}$

13. Simplify:

(a) $\displaystyle\sum_{n=0}^{4} i^n$ and (b) $\displaystyle\sum_{n=37}^{40} i^n$, where $i = \sqrt{-1}$

14. If $\log x = a$, express $\displaystyle\sum_{k=1}^{4} \log x^k$ in simplest form in terms of a.

15. Find the value of $\displaystyle\sum_{k=2}^{5} {}_7C_{k+1}$.

16. On a math test, five students received the following scores: 96, 79, 100, 88, and 82.
   (a) Find the mean.
   (b) Find the standard deviation of these scores.
   (c) What percentage of the total scores fall within one standard deviation of the mean?

17. A high school football team scored the following numbers of points during the ten-game season: 19, 20, 21, 27, 29, 29, 34, 40, 40, 41.
   (a) Find:
       (1) the median   *(2)* the mean
       (3) the standard deviation to the *nearest hundredth*
   (b) What percentage of the total scores fall within one standard deviation of the mean?

18. Given the following ten scores: 61, 65, 65, 65, 67, 69, 71, 74, 75, 78. For these scores, find:
   (a) the mode   **(c)** the mean
   (b) the median   **(d)** the standard deviation to the *nearest tenth*

10.4 GROUPING DATA

KEY IDEAS

The number of times that a particular value x_i is repeated in a set is called its **frequency** and is denoted as f_i. If a number appears only once, its frequency is 1.

Organizing data values by listing them in a table with their frequencies often simplifies statistical computations.

Interpreting Frequency Tables

Table 10.1 shows members of the set of data values 3.0, 3.0, 4.0, 4.0, 4.0, 5.0, 5.0, 5.0, 5.0, 5.0, organized according to their frequencies. Thus:

$x_1 = 3.0$ and $f_1 = 2$
$x_2 = 4.0$ and $f_2 = 3$
$x_3 = 5.0$ and $f_3 = 5$

TABLE 10.1 DATA VALUES AND FREQUENCIES

x_i Score	f_i Frequency
3.0	2
4.0	3
5.0	5

Since

$$\Sigma f_i = f_1 + f_2 + f_3 = 10,$$

Σf_i represents the total number of data values in the sample.

Examples

1. Using Table 10.1, find:
(a) the median   **(b)** the mean

Solutions: **(a)** Since $\Sigma f_i = 10$, there are 10 scores. The two "middle" scores are the fifth and sixth scores in the table. Since the fifth score is 4.0 and the sixth score is 5.0, the median is $\dfrac{4.0+5.0}{2} = $ **4.5.**

(b) Method 1: Divide the sum of the 10 data values by 10:

$$\bar{x} = \frac{\Sigma f_i x_i}{\Sigma f_i} = \frac{2(3.0)+3(4.0)+5(5.0)}{2+3+5} = \frac{43}{10} = \mathbf{4.3}$$

Method 2: Using your scientific calculator, enter and accumulate the 10 data values. Press the ⎡2nd⎤ function key, and then press the key that has $\bar{x}$ printed directly above it. The mean is **4.3.**

2. Using the accompanying set of grouped data, find:
(a) the sum of the data values
(b) the mean
(c) the standard deviation correct to the *nearest tenth*
(d) the probability that a measure selected at random will fall within one standard deviation of the mean

x_i Measure	f_i Frequency
50	4
58	4
62	3
64	6
65	2
68	1

Solutions: **(a)** Using your scientific calculator, enter and accumulate the 20 data values. If you have a Casio calculator, you can quickly enter the same data value more than once by repeatedly pressing the ⎡M+⎤ key. For example, to enter 50 four times, make sure the Casio calculator is in the SD mode and then key in

50 ⎡M+⎤ ⎡M+⎤ ⎡M+⎤ ⎡M+⎤.

You can find the sum of the statistical data values stored in many Casio calculators by pressing the recall ⎡RCL⎤ key followed by the number ⎡2⎤ key. The display shows 1200 and Σx in the corner of the window. Since $\Sigma x = 1200$, the sum of the 20 data values entered is **1200.**

Some scientific calculators have a frequency ⎡FRQ⎤ key that allows you to enter the number of times that a data value occurs in the set. For example, if you have a Texas Instruments calculator with a [FRQ] key, you can enter 50 four times by using this key sequence:

$$50 \quad \boxed{\text{2nd}} \quad \boxed{\text{FRQ}} \quad 4 \quad \boxed{\Sigma+}.$$

You can find the sum of the statistical data values stored in a Texas Instruments calculator by pressing the [2nd] function key followed by the key that has Σx printed directly above it. If you need help in learning the statistical features of the calculator you are using, check the instruction booklet for that calculator.

(b) To find the mean, press the [2nd] function key and then press the key that has $\bar{x}$ printed directly above it. The mean is **60.**

(c) To find the standard deviation, press the [2nd] function key and then press the key that has σ printed directly above it. The standard deviation, correct to the *nearest tenth,* is **5.6.**

(d) $P(\text{any } x_i \text{ is within } 1.\text{S.D.}) = \dfrac{\text{Number of } x_i \text{ within 1 S.D.}}{\text{Total number of measures}}$

Since the mean is 60 and the standard deviation is approximately 5.6, you need to find the number of measures that are between $60 - 5.6$ and $60 + 5.6$ or, equivalently, between 54.4 and 65.6. The data values and their corresponding frequencies that fall in this interval are as follows:

$$x_2 = 58, f_2 = 4; \quad x_3 = 62, f_3 = 3; \quad x_4 = 64, f_4 = 6; \quad x_5 = 65, f_5 = 2.$$

The total number of data values that fall within one standard deviation of the mean is

$$f_2 + f_3 + f_4 + f_5 = 4 + 3 + 6 + 2 = 15$$

Since the total number of measures is 20,

$$P(x_i \text{ is within 1 S.D.}) = \frac{15}{20} = \frac{3}{4}.$$

Exercise Set 10.4

1–3. For each set of measurements, find:

(a) the median

(b) the mean to the
  nearest tenth

(c) the standard deviation to the *nearest tenth*

(d) the probability that a measure picked at random will fall within one standard deviation of the mean

1.

x_i	f_i
60	1
75	7
80	3
90	4

2.

x_i	f_i
91	2
96	3
105	6
111	3
113	4

3.

x_i	f_i
56	4
58	3
60	1
61	5
62	7

4. The accompanying table shows the grades of 20 students on a Course III class exam.
  (a) Find, to the *nearest tenth*, the standard deviation.
  (b) Which statement is true for this set of data?
    (1) median > mode
    (2) median = mode
    (3) median < mode
  (c) What is the probability that a score selected at random lies within one standard deviation of the mean?

Score	Frequency
72	6
76	5
84	7
88	2

10.5 WORKING WITH NORMAL CURVES

KEY IDEAS

If each of the different heights of the students in your school is plotted against the corresponding number of students at each height, a curve that is approximately bell-shaped will most likely result. Many real-life data, when graphed, follow a bell-shaped curve.

   If you know that a set of data "fits" a bell-shaped, or *normal,* curve, you can draw conclusions about how far the data are from the mean.

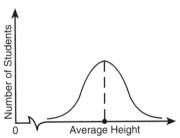

Normal Curves

A bell-shaped curve is actually the graph of a complicated mathematical function that is studied in more advanced statistics courses. The graph of this function is called a **normal curve.** A normal curve is symmetric with respect to the vertical line $x = \bar{x}$. If a set of data values, such as the scores on a test, fits a normal curve, then the numbers of these data values that fall within one, two, and three standard deviations of the mean can be predicted, as shown in Figure 10.1.

Figure 10.1 A Normal Curve

Since 68% of the data values or scores fall within one standard deviation of the mean, 34% fall on either side of (one standard deviation away from) the mean. Since the normal curve is symmetric about the vertical line $x = \bar{x}$, the mean and the median coincide. Hence 50% of the data values are found on either side of the mean.

When a large number of plotted data points closely approximate the bell shape of a normal curve, the data are said to be *approximately* **normally distributed.** When data are *assumed* to be normally distributed, the relationships summarized in Table 10.2 can be used to draw conclusions concerning the approximate numbers of data scores that are one, two, and three standard deviations from the mean.

TABLE 10.2 NORMALLY DISTRIBUTED SCORES [σ REPRESENTS THE STANDARD DEVIATION (S.D.)]

Interval	Interval Length	Contains...
$\bar{x} - \sigma$ to $\bar{x} + \sigma$	2σ	68% of all scores
$\bar{x} - 2\sigma$ to $\bar{x} + 2\sigma$	4σ	95% of all scores
$\bar{x} - 3\sigma$ to $\bar{x} + 3\sigma$	6σ	99% of all scores

Examples

1. A set of test scores that follows a bell curve has a mean of 65 and a standard deviation of 5.
(a) Approximately what percent of the scores fall between 55 and 75?
(b) If 1000 students took the test, about how many students scored between 60 and 70?

Solutions: **(a)** If one standard deviation is 5, then an interval of two standard deviations is 10. Since 65 – 10 = 55 and 65 + 10 = 75, the interval 55 to 75 represents *two* standard deviations on either side of the mean of 65.

Since the data follow a bell curve, you can expect approximately 95% of the test scores to fall between 55 and 75.

(b) Since 65 – 5 = 60 and 65 + 5 = 70, the interval 60 to 70 represents one standard deviation about the mean of 65. Hence about 68% of the test scores fall between 60 and 70.

If 1000 students took the test, then approximately 68% × 1000 or **680** students had scores between 60 and 70.

2. On a quiz, the mean score is 25 and the standard deviation is 2.3. Which score could be expected to occur less than 5% of the time?
(1) 20   (2) 28   (3) 23   (4) 24

Solution: If it is assumed that the scores are normally distributed, 95% of them are expected to fall within two standard deviations of the mean, so scores that are *more than* two standard deviations from the mean are expected to occur less than 5% of the time. Since an interval of two standard deviations is 2 × 2.3 = 4.6, look in the choices for a score that differs from the mean of 25 by more than 4.6. The score of 20, choice (1), is the only value given that is more than 4.6 units from 25.

The correct choice is **(1)**.

3. On an exam, 95% of the scores ranged between 74 and 84. If the scores are approximately normally distributed and the mean is 79, find the standard deviation.

Solution: The length of the interval from 74 and 84 is 10 points. Since 95% of normally distributed scores fall within two standard deviations of the mean, the length of the interval from 74 to 79 is 2σ and from 79 to 84 is another 2σ. Thus, the length of the interval 74 to 84 is a total of 4σ.

$$4\sigma = 10$$
$$\sigma = \frac{10}{4} = \mathbf{2.5}$$

4. The scores on a standardized exam have a mean of 78 and a standard deviation of 3.5. If a normal distribution of scores is assumed, a student's score of 86 would rank:

(1) below the 75th percentile
(2) between the 75th and 85th percentiles
(3) above the 95th percentile
(4) between the 95th and 85th percentiles

Solution: Since two standard deviations represent $2 \times 3.5 = 7$ points, a score of 85 is two standard deviations to the *right* of the mean of 78. Although 95% of the scores fall within two standard deviations of *either side* of the mean, half this amount (47.5%) falls to the *right* of the mean.

In a normal distribution 50% of the scores fall to the *left* of the mean. This means that a total of approximately 50% + 47.7%, or 97.5%, of the scores will be less than or equal to 85. A score of 86 is, therefore, above the 95th percentile.

The correct choice is **(3)**.

Exercise Set 10.5

1. Approximately what percent of normally distributed scores fall between 70 and 90 if the mean is 80 and the standard deviation is:
(a) 10?   **(b)** 5?   **(c)** 3.3?

2. A set of standardized test scores has a mean of 73 and a standard deviation of 7.
(a) Approximately what percent of the scores fall between 66 and 80?
(b) If 1000 students took the test, about how many students scored between:
  (1) 66 and 80?   *(2)* 73 and 80?   *(3)* 59 and 87?

3. On a quiz, the mean score is 72 and the standard deviation is 3.4. Which score could be expected to occur *less than* 5% of the time?
(1) 65   (2) 67   (3) 72   (4) 78

4. The scores on an exam are normally distributed with a mean of 77. Find the standard deviation if the interval from 71 to 83 contains:
(a) 68% of the scores   **(b)** 95% of the scores   **(c)** 99% of the scores

5. Which of the following statements about a normal distribution is *always* true?
(1) the mean = the median   (3) the mean > the median
(2) the mean < median   (4) the variance > the standard
                                          deviation

6. In the following diagram, the shaded area represents approximately
95% of the scores on a standard
test. If these scores ranged from
52 to 96, which of the following
could be the standard deviation?
(1) 11   (3) 76
(2) 22   (4) 44

7. A student scores 84 on a standardized exam. The mean for the exam is
75, and the standard deviation is 4. If a normal distribution of scores is
assumed, how does this student rank?
(1) below the 75th percentile   (3) above the 95th percentile
(2) between the 75th and 85th   (4) between the 85th and
     percentiles   95th percentiles

8. Answer question 7 if the student scores 80.

9. The mean for a standardized exam is 81, and the standard deviation is
6. If the scores are normally distributed, approximately what percentile
corresponds to each of the following grades?
(a) 81   **(b)** 75   **(c)** 93   **(d)** 87

10. For a standardized test whose scores are normally distributed, if the
mean is 20 and the standard deviation is 2.6, which score will occur
less than 5% of the time?
(1) 25.1   (2) 22.6   (3) 18.7   (4) 14.6

Each of the questions in this section has appeared on a previous Course III Regents Examination. Here is an opportunity for you to review Chapter 10 and, at the same time, prepare for the Course III Regents Examination.

1. Evaluate $\displaystyle\sum_{k=2}^{4}(4-k^2)$.

2. The test scores for five students were 59, 60, 63, 76, and 87. How many points greater than the median is the mean?

3. The mean of a normally distributed set of data is 52, and the standard deviation is 4. Approximately 95% of all cases will lie between which measures?
   (1) 44 and 52   (2) 44 and 60   (3) 48 and 56   (4) 52 and 64

4. What is the last term of the expansion of $(2x - 3y)^4$?

5. A fair coin is tossed ten times, and a head appears each time. What is the probability that on the next three tosses of the coin exactly two heads will appear?

6. If the probability of winning a game is $\dfrac{1}{4}$, find the probability of winning at least three games out of four.

7. What is the seventh term in the expansion of $(2x - y)^7$?

8. (a) Find, to the *nearest tenth,* the standard deviation for the accompanying data.
   (b) The given data do *not* form a normal distribution. If a measure is selected at random from the given data, what is the probability that it will differ from the mean by less than one standard deviation?

Measure (x_i)	Frequency (f_i)
20	4
21	2
24	5
26	3
30	6

9. An electronic game contains nine keys. Four of the keys have numerals, and five have symbols. Each key is equally likely to be presesed on each move.

1	2	∧
3	4	∨
—	<	>

(a) Find:

    (1) P(4)   *(2)* P(numeral key)   *(3)* P(symbol key)

(b) Find the probability of pressing:

    (1) exactly two numeral keys on three random presses

    (2) at least two symbol keys on three random presses

10. In the accompanying diagram, the circle is divided into four sections as shown, and

$$m\widehat{AB} : m\widehat{BC} : m\widehat{CD} : m\widehat{DA} = 3 : 4 : 2 : 1$$

(a) If the spinner is spun once, find:

    (1) P(red)   *(2)* P(green)

(b) Determine the probability of obtaining:

    (1) exactly two greens in three spins

    (2) at least three reds in four spins

    (3) at most two yellows in three spins

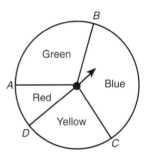

ANSWERS TO SELECTED EXERCISES: CHAPTER 10

Section 10.1

1. (a) $\dfrac{3}{8}$ **(b)** $\dfrac{3}{8}$ **(c)** $\dfrac{4}{8}$ **7. (a)** $\dfrac{1}{1024}$ **(b)** $\dfrac{27}{1024}$ **(c)** $\dfrac{16}{1024}$

2. (a) $\dfrac{80}{243}$ **(b)** $\dfrac{112}{243}$ **(c)** $\dfrac{192}{243}$ **8. (a)** $\dfrac{60}{343}$ **(b)** $\dfrac{275}{343}$

3. (a) $\dfrac{256}{625}$ **(c)** $\dfrac{17}{625}$ **9. (a)** $\dfrac{1}{3}$ **(c)** $\dfrac{7}{27}$

    (b) $\dfrac{96}{625}$ **(d)** $\dfrac{624}{625}$ **(b)** $\dfrac{1}{6}$ **(d)** $\dfrac{200}{216}$

4. $\dfrac{16}{32}$ **10. (a)** *(1)* $\dfrac{1}{5}$ *(2)* $\dfrac{2}{5}$ *(3)* $\dfrac{2}{5}$

5. (a) $\dfrac{270}{1024}$ **(b)** $\dfrac{243}{1024}$ **(b)** *(1)* $\dfrac{54}{125}$ *(3)* $\dfrac{112}{125}$

6. (a) $\dfrac{27}{1000}$ **(c)** $\dfrac{287{,}955}{10^7}$ *(2)* $\dfrac{44}{125}$ *(4)* $\dfrac{24}{125}$

    (b) $\dfrac{16{,}966}{10^7}$ **(d)** $\dfrac{3{,}294{,}172}{10^7}$

Section 10.2

1. $x^4 + 4x^3y + 6x^2y^2 + 4xy^3 + y^4$
3. $p^4 - 12p^3q + 54p^2q^2 - 108pq^3 + 81q^4$
5. $28p^6q^2$ **13.** $80rs^4$ **19. (a)** $-150x^2$
7. $30{,}375x^4y^2$ **15.** $35a^3b^4$ **(b)** $-5x^3$
9. $-280x^4$ **17. (a)** -32 **21. (a)** $-252a^5b^5i$
11. $-\dfrac{20}{8}a^3b^3$ **(b)** $\dfrac{6}{243}bc^5$ **(b)** $-19ab^9i$

Section 10.3

1. $100\sqrt{2}$ **7.** 0 **13. (a)** 1 **17. (a)** *(1)* 29
2. 50 **8.** 3 **(b)** 0 *(2)* 30
3. 30 **9.** $1+\sqrt{2}$ **14.** $10a$ *(3)* 8.06
4. -20 **10.** $-\dfrac{1}{2}$ **15.** 98 **(b)** 40%
5. $\dfrac{33}{2}$ **11.** 6 **16. (a)** 89 **18. (a)** 65 **(c)** 69
                (b) 8 **(b)** 68 **(d)** 5.1
6. $\dfrac{23}{12}$ **12.** 30 **(c)** 60%

Section 10.4

1. (a) 75 **2. (a)** 105 **3. (a)** 61 **4. (a)** 5.8
   (b) 79 **(b)** 104.7 **(b)** 59.9 **(b)** (3)
   (c) 8 **(c)** 7.4 **(c)** 2.3 **(c)** $\dfrac{12}{20}$
   (d) $\dfrac{10}{15}$ **(d)** $\dfrac{9}{18}$ **(d)** $\dfrac{16}{20}$

Section 10.5

1. (a) 68% **(b)** 95% **(c)** 99%
2. (a) 68%
   (b) *(1)* 680 *(2)* 340 *(3)* 950
3. (1)
4. (a) 6 **(b)** 3 **(c)** 2
5. (1) **6.** (1) **7.** (3) **8.** (4)
9. (a) 50 **(b)** 16 **(c)** 95 **(d)** 84
10. (4)

Regents Tune-Up: Chapter 10

1. -17

2. 6

3. (2)

4. $81y^4$

5. $\dfrac{3}{8}$

6. $\dfrac{13}{256}$

7. $14xy^6$

8. **(a)** 3.8

    (b) $\dfrac{8}{20}$

9. (a) *(1)* $\dfrac{1}{9}$ *(2)* $\dfrac{4}{9}$ *(3)* $\dfrac{5}{9}$

    (b) *(1)* $\dfrac{240}{729}$ *(2)* $\dfrac{425}{729}$

10. (a) *(1)* $\dfrac{1}{10}$ *(2)* $\dfrac{3}{10}$

    (b) *(1)* $\dfrac{189}{1000}$ *(3)* $\dfrac{124}{125}$

          (2) $\dfrac{37}{10000}$

GLOSSARY

Abscissa The x-coordinate of a point in the coordinate plane.

Absolute value The absolute value of a number x, denoted by $|x|$, is its distance from zero on the number line. Thus, $|x|$ always represents a nonnegative number.

Acute angle An angle whose degree measure is greater than 0 but less than 90.

Acute triangle A triangle that contains three acute angles.

Additive inverse The opposite of a number. The additive inverse of a number x is $-x$ since $x + (-x) = 0$.

Altitude A segment that is perpendicular to the side to which it is drawn.

Ambiguous case The case in which the measures of two sides and an angle that is not included between the two sides are given. These measures may determine one triangle, two triangles, or no triangle.

Amplitude The amplitude of functions of the form $y = a \sin bx$ and $y = a \cos bx$ refers to their maximum height, which is $|a|$.

Angle The union of two rays that have the same endpoint.

Angle of depression The angle formed by a horizontal line of vision and the line of sight an object is viewed beneath the horizontal line of vision.

Angle of elevation The angle formed by a horizontal line of vision and the line of sight an object is viewed above the horizontal line of vision.

Antilogarithm The antilogarithm of a given number x is the number N whose logarithm is x. Thus, the antilogarithm of 2 is 100 since $\log 100 = 2$.

Arc A part of a circle. If the degree measure of the arc is less than 180, the arc is a **minor** arc. If the degree measure of the arc is greater than 180, the arc is a **major** arc. A **semicircle** is an arc whose degree measure is 180.

Arc cos x or Cos^{-1} x The angle A whose cosine is x, where $0° \le A \le 180°$.

arc cos x or cos^{-1} x An angle whose cosine is x, where the angle is not restricted in value.

Arc sin x or Sin^{-1} x The angle A whose sine is x, where $-90° \le A \le 90°$.

arc sin x or sin^{-1} x An angle whose sine is x, where the angle is not restricted in value.

Arc tan x or Tan^{-1} x The angle A whose tangent is x, where $-90° < A < 90°$.

arc tan x or tan^{-1} x An angle whose tangent is x, where the angle is not restricted in value.

Area of a triangle The number of square units enclosed by the triangle that can be computed by one of these two formulas: (1) Area $= \frac{1}{2} bh$ where b is a side of the triangle, called the base, and h is the altitude drawn to that side; (2) Area $= \frac{1}{2} ab$ $\sin C$ where a and b are the lengths of any two sides of the triangle and C is the angle of the triangle formed by those two sides.

Associative property The mathematical law that states that how three numbers are grouped when they are added or multiplied does not matter.

Asymptote A line is a horizontal asymptote if a graph approaches it but does not intersect it as x increases or decreases without bound.

Average See **Mean.**

Bernoulli experiment The repetition of a simple probability experiment having exactly two possible outcomes, a fixed number of times under identical conditions so that the outcome of any one experiment, called a *trial,* does not affect the outcome of any other trial.

Binomial A polynomial with two unlike terms, as in $3x + 2y$.

Binomial theorem A formula that tells how to expand a binomial of the form $(a + b)^n$ without performing repeated multiplications, as in
$(a + b)^3 = {}_3C_0a^3 + {}_3C_1a^{3-1}\,b^1 + {}_3C_2a^{3-2}\,b^2 + {}_3C_3a^{3-3}b^3$
$\qquad = a^3 + 3a^2b + 3ab^2 + b^3$

Central angle An angle whose vertex is the center of a circle and whose sides are radii.

Characteristic The integer part of a common logarithm.

Chord A line segment whose endpoints are points on a circle.

Circle The set of points (x, y) in a plane that are a fixed distance r from a given point (h, k), called the *center*. Thus, $(x - h)^2 + (y - k)^2 = r^2$.

Combination A subset of a set of objects in which order is not considered.

Combination formula The combination of n objects taken r at a time, denoted by ${}_nC_r$, is given by the formula ${}_nC_r = \dfrac{{}_nP_r}{r!} = \dfrac{n!}{r!(n-r)!}$

Common logarithm A logarithm whose base is 10.

Commutative property The mathematical law that states that the order in which two numbers are added or multiplied does not matter.

Complementary angles Two angles whose degree measures add up to 90.

Complex fraction A fraction that contains other fractions in its numerator, its denominator, or both its numerator and its denominator.

Composition of functions The composition of function f followed by function g is a new function, denoted by g ∘ f, consisting of the set of function values g(f(x)), provided that f(x) is in the domain of g.

Composition of transformations A sequence of transformations in which the image of one transformation is used as the preimage for a second transformation.

Congruent angles (or sides) Angles (sides) that have the same measure. The symbol for congruence is ≅.

Conjugate pair The sum and difference of the same two terms, as in $a + b$ and $a - b$.

Constant A quantity that is fixed in value. In the equation $y = x + 3$, x and y are variables and 3 is a constant.

Coordinate The real number that corresponds to the position of a point on a number line.

Coordinate plane The region formed by a horizontal number line and a vertical number line intersecting at their zero points.

Cosecant The reciprocal of the sine function.

Cosine ratio In a right triangle, the ratio of the length of the leg that is adjacent to a given acute angle to the length of the hypotenuse. If an angle is in standard position, the cosine ratio is $\dfrac{x}{r}$, where $P(x, y)$ is an arbitrary point on the terminal ray of the angle and $r = \sqrt{x^2 + y^2}$.

Cotangent The reciprocal of the tangent function.

Coterminal angles Angles in standard position whose terminal rays coincide.

Degree A unit of angle measure that is defined as 1/360 of one complete rotation of a ray about its vertex. For conversion of degrees to radians, and of radians to degrees, see **Radian.**

Degree of a monomial The sum of the exponents of the variable factors.

Degree of a polynomial The greatest degree of the monomial terms.

Dependent variable For a function of the form $y = f(x)$, y is the dependent variable.

Diameter A chord of a circle that contains the center of the circle.

Dilation A transformation in which a figure is enlarged or reduced based on a center and a scale factor.

Direct isometry An isometry that preserves orientation.

Discriminant The quantity $b^2 - 4ac$ that is underneath the radical sign in the quadratic formula.

Distributive property of multiplication over addition For any real numbers a, b, and c, $a(b + c) = ab + ac$ and $(b + c)\, a = ba + ca$.

Domain of a relation The set of all possible first members of the ordered pairs that comprise a relation.

Domain of a variable The set of all possible replacements for a variable.

Equation A statement that two quantities have the same value.

Equivalent equations Two equations that have the same solution set. Thus, $2x = 6$ and $x = 3$ are equivalent equations.

Ellipse An oval curve an equation of which is $ax^2 + by^2 = c$, where a, b, and c have the same sign and $a \neq b$.

Event A particular subset of outcomes from the set of all possible outcomes of a probability experiment. In flipping a coin, one event is getting a head; another event is getting a tail.

Exponent In x^n, the number n is the exponent and tells the number of times the base x is used as a factor in a product. Thus, $x^3 = (x)(x)(x)$.

Exponential equation An equation in which the variable appears in an exponent.

Exponential function A function of the form $y = b^x$, where b is a positive constant that is not equal to 1.

Extremes In the proportion $\dfrac{a}{b} = \dfrac{c}{d}$, the terms a and d are the extremes.

Factor A number or variable that is being multiplied in a product.

Factorial n For any positive integer n, factorial n is denoted by $n!$ and is defined as the product of consecutive integers from n to 1. Thus, $5! = 5 \cdot 4 \cdot 3 \cdot 2 \cdot 1 = 120$.

Factoring The process by which a number or polynomial is written as the product of two or more terms.

Factoring completely Factoring a number or polynomial into its prime factors.

Failure In a two-outcome probability experiment, the outcome that is not a "success" is a "failure."

FOIL The rule for multiplying two binomials horizontally by forming the sum of the products of the first terms (F), the outer terms (O), the inner terms (I), and the last terms (L) of each binomial.

Frequency The number of times a data value occurs or the number of full cycles the graph of a trigonometric function completes in an interval of 2π radians.

Function A relation in which no two ordered pairs have the same first member but different second members.

Fundamental counting principle If event A can occur in m ways and event B can occur in n ways, then both events can occur in m times n ways.

Glide reflection The composite of a line reflection and a translation whose direction is parallel to the reflecting line.

Greatest common factor (GCF) The GCF of two or more monomials is the monomial with the greatest coefficient and the variable factors of the greatest degree that are common to all the given monomials. Thus, the GCF of $8a^2b$ and $20ab^2$ is $4ab$.

Half-turn A rotation in which the angle of rotation is $180°$.

Horizontal-line test If no horizontal line intersects the graph of a function in more than one point, the graph represents a one-to-one function.

Hyperbola A curve that consists of two branches, an equation of which is $ax^2 + by^2 = c$, where a and b have opposite signs and $c \neq 0$. A special type of hyperbola, called an *equilateral* or *rectangular hyperbola*, has the equation $xy = k$, where $k \neq 0$.

Hypotenuse The side of a right triangle that is opposite to the right angle.

Image In a geometric transformation, the point or figure that corresponds to the original point or figure.

Imaginary number A number of the form $a + bi$, where b is a nonzero real number and i is the imaginary unit.

Imaginary unit The number denoted by i, where $i = \sqrt{-1}$.

Independent variable For a function of the form $y = f(x)$, x is the independent variable.

Index The number k in the radical expression $\sqrt[k]{x}$, which tells what root of x is to be taken. In a square root radical the index is omitted and is understood to be 2.

Inequality A sentence that uses an inequality relation such as < (is less than), ≤ (is less than or equal to), > (is greater than), ≥ (is greater than or equal to), or ≠ (is unequal to).

Initial side The side of an angle in standard position that remains fixed on the positive x-axis.

Inscribed angle An angle whose vertex is a point on a circle and whose sides are chords.

Integer A number from the set {...–3, –2, –1, 0, 1, 2, 3,...}.

Inverse variation A set of ordered pairs in which the product of the first and second members of each pair is the same nonzero number. Thus, if y varies indirectly as x, then $xy = k$, where k is a nonzero number called the constant of variation.

Irrational number A number that cannot be expressed as the quotient of two integers.

Isometry A transformation that preserves distance.

Isosceles triangle A triangle in which two sides have the same length. The unequal side is called the **base** and the equal sides are called **legs.** The angle formed by the legs is called the **vertex angle.**

Law of Cosines In a triangle, the square of the length of any side is equal to the sum of the squares of the lengths of the other two sides minus twice the product of the lengths of these sides and the cosine of the included angle.

Law of Sines In a triangle the lengths of any two sides have the same ratio as the sines of the angles opposite these sides.

Leg of a right triangle Either of the two sides of a right triangle that is not opposite the right angle.

Linear equation An equation in which the greatest exponent of a variable is 1. A linear equation in two variables can be put into the form $Ax + By = C$, where A, B, and C are constants and A and B are not both zero.

Line reflection A transformation in which each point P that is not on line ℓ is paired with a point P' on the opposite side of line ℓ so that line ℓ is the perpendicular bisector of $\overline{PP'}$. If P is on line ℓ, then P is paired with itself.

Line symmetry A figure has line symmetry when a line ℓ divides the figure into two parts such that each part is the reflection of the other part in line ℓ.

Logarithm of x An exponent that represents the power to which a given base must be raised to produce a positive number x. Thus, $\log_2 8$ is 3 since $2^3 = 8$.

Major arc An arc whose degree measure is greater than 180.

Mantissa The decimal part of a common logarithm.

Mapping A relation in which each member of one set is paired with exactly one member of a second set.

Mean (Average) The value obtained when the sum of a set of n data values is divided by n.

Means In the proportion $\frac{a}{b} = \frac{c}{d}$, the terms b and c are the means.

Median The middle value when the numbers in a set of data values are arranged in size order.

Median of a triangle A line segment whose endpoints are a vertex of the triangle and the midpoint of the opposite side.

Minor arc An arc whose degree measure is less than 180.

Mode The value that occurs most frequently in a given set of data.

Monomial A number, a variable, or the product of a number and a variable, as in $3x^2y$.

Multiplicative inverse The reciprocal of a nonzero number.

Negative angle An angle in standard position whose terminal ray rotates in a clockwise direction.

Normal curve A bell-shaped curve that describes a distribution of data values in which approximately 68 percent of the values fall within one standard deviation of the mean, 95 percent fall within two standard deviations of the mean, and 99 percent fall within three standard deviations of the mean.

Obtuse angle An angle whose degree measure is greater than 90 but less than 180.

Obtuse triangle A triangle that contains an obtuse angle.

One-to-one function A function in which no two ordered pairs have the same value of y but different values of x.

Ordered pair Two numbers that are written in a definite order.

Ordinate The y-coordinate of a point in the coordinate place.

Origin The zero point on a number line.

Outcome A possible result in a probability experiment.

Perfect square A rational number whose square root is rational, as in 25 or $\frac{9}{16}$.

Period The period of a sine, cosine, or tangent curve is the number of degrees or radians needed for the curve to complete one full cycle. The period of functions of the form $y = a$ sin bx and $y = a$ cos bx is $\frac{2\pi}{|b|}$.

Permutation An ordered arrangement of objects.

Point symmetry A figure has point symmetry if, after it has been rotated 180°, the image coincides with the original figure.

Polygon A simple closed curve whose sides are line segments.

Polynomial A monomial or the sum or difference of two or more monomials, as in $3x + 2y$.

Positive angle An angle in standard position whose terminal ray rotates in a counter-clockwise direction.

Power A number written with an exponent.

Preimage If under a certain transformation A' is the image of A, then A is the preimage of A'.

Prime factorization The factorization of a polynomial into factors each of which is divisible only by itself and 1 (or −1).

Probability of an event The number of ways in which the event can occur divided by the total number of possible outcomes.

Proportion An equation that states that two ratios are equal. In the proportion $\frac{a}{b} = \frac{c}{d}$, the product of the means equals the product of the extremes: $b \cdot c = a \cdot d$.

Pythagorean theorem The square of the length of the hypotenuse of a right triangle is equal to the sum of the squares of the lengths of the legs of the triangle.

Quadrant One of four rectangular regions into which the coordinate plane is divided.

Quadrantal angle An angle in standard position whose terminal ray coincides with a coordinate axis.

Quadratic equation An equation that can be put into the form $ax^2 + bx + c = 0$, provided that $a \neq 0$.

Quadratic formula The roots of the quadratic equation $ax^2 + bx + c = 0$ are given by the formula $x = \frac{-b \pm \sqrt{b^2 - 4ac}}{2a}$ $(a \neq 0)$.

Quadratic polynomial A polynomial whose degree is 2.

Quadrilateral A polygon with four sides.

Radian The measure of a central angle of a circle that intercepts an arc whose length equals the radius of the circle. To change from degrees to radians, multiply the number of degrees by $\frac{\pi}{180°}$. To change from radians to degrees, multiply the number of radians by $\frac{180°}{\pi}$.

Radical equation An equation in which the variable appears underneath the radical sign.

Radical (square root) sign The symbol $\sqrt{}$, which denotes the positive square root of a nonnegative number.

Radicand The expression that appears underneath a radical sign.

Range (1) The set of all possible second members of the ordered pairs that comprise a relation. (2) In a set of numerical data values, the difference between the greatest and smallest values.

Ratio A comparison of two numbers by division. The ratio of a to b is the fraction $\frac{a}{b}$, provided that $b \neq 0$.

Rational number A number that can be written in the form $\frac{a}{b}$, where a and b are integers and $b \neq 0$. Decimals in which a set of digits endlessly repeat, such as $0.25000...$ $\left(=\frac{1}{4}\right)$ and $0.33333...$ $\left(=\frac{1}{3}\right)$, represent rational numbers.

Real number A number that is a member of the set that consists of all rational and irrational numbers.

Reference angle When an angle is placed in standard position, the acute angle formed by the terminal ray and the x-axis.

Relation A set of ordered pairs.

Replacement set The set of values that a variable may have.

Right angle An angle whose degree measure is 90.

Right triangle A triangle that contains a right angle.

Root A number that makes an equation a true statement.

Rotation A transformation in which a point or figure is moved about a fixed point a given number of degrees.

Rotational symmetry A figure has rotational symmetry if it can be rotated more than $0°$ but less than $360°$ so that the image coincides with the original figure.

Scalene triangle A triangle in which the three sides have different lengths.

Secant The reciprocal of the cosine function.

Secant line A line that intersects a circle in two different points.

Semicircle An arc whose degree measure is 180.

Sigma (lower case) The Greek letter σ, which represents standard deviation.

Sigma (upper case) The Greek letter Σ, which indicates a summation of terms.

Similar figures Figures that have the same shape. Two triangles are similar if two pairs of corresponding angles have the same degree measure.

Sine ratio In a right triangle, the ratio of the length of the leg that is opposite a given acute angle to the length of the hypotenuse. If an angle is in standard position, the sine ratio is $\frac{y}{r}$, where $P(x, y)$ is an arbitrary point on the terminal ray of the angle and $r = \sqrt{x^2 + y^2}$.

Solution Any value from the replacement set of a variable that makes an open sentence true.

Solution set The collection of all values from the replacement set of a variable that make an open sentence true.

Square root The square root of a non-negative number n is one of two identical numbers whose products is n. Thus, 3 and -3 are the two square roots of 9 since $3 \times 3 = 9$ and $(-3) \times (-3) = 9$. The symbol $\sqrt{9}$ represents the principal or positive square root of 9, so $\sqrt{9} = 3$ because $3 \times 3 = 9$.

Standard deviation The square root of the variance.

Standard position An angle whose vertex is fixed at the origin and whose initial side coincides with the positive x-axis.

Success Any favorable outcome of a probability experiment.

Supplementary angles Two angles whose degree measures add up to 180.

System of equations A set of equations whose solution is the set of values that make all of the equations true at the same time.

Tangent line A line that intersects a circle in exactly one point.

Tangent ratio In a right triangle, the ratio of the length of the leg that is opposite a given acute angle to the length of the leg that is adjacent to that angle. If an angle is in standard position, the tangent ratio is $\frac{y}{x}(x \neq 0)$, where $P(x, y)$ is an arbitrary point on the terminal ray of the angle.

Terminal ray The side of an angle in standard position that rotates about the origin.

Theorem A mathematical generalization that can be proved.

Transformation A one-to-one mapping whose domain and range are the set of all points in the plane.

Translation A transformation in which each point of a figure is moved the same distance and in the same direction.

Trinomial A polynomial with three unlike terms, as in $x^2 - 3x + 5$.

Unit circle A circle whose radius is 1.

Variance The sum of the squares of the differences between all of the individual data values and the mean, divided by the number of data values.

Vertical-line test If no vertical line intersects a graph in more than one point, the graph represents a function.

REGENTS EXAMINATION
FORMULAS

To The Student Reader: *The following set of formulas is provided in the New York State Regents Examination question booklet so that you do not have to memorize these formulas for this examination. Your teacher, however, may require you to memorize the formulas for class tests.*

Formulas

Pythagorean and Quotient Identities

$$\sin^2 A + \cos^2 A = 1$$
$$\tan^2 A + 1 = \sec^2 A$$
$$\cot^2 A + 1 = \csc^2 A$$

$$\tan A = \frac{\sin A}{\cos A}$$

$$\cot A = \frac{\cos A}{\sin A}$$

Functions of the Sum of Two Angles

$$\sin (A + B) = \sin A \cos B + \cos A \sin B$$
$$\cos (A + B) = \cos A \cos B - \sin A \sin B$$

$$\tan (A + B) = \frac{\tan A + \tan B}{1 - \tan A \tan B}$$

Functions of the Difference of Two Angles

$$\sin (A - B) = \sin A \cos B - \cos A \sin B$$
$$\cos (A - B) = \cos A \cos B + \sin A \sin B$$

$$\tan (A - B) = \frac{\tan A - \tan B}{1 + \tan A \tan B}$$

Law of Sines

$$\frac{a}{\sin A} = \frac{b}{\sin B} = \frac{c}{\sin C}$$

Law of Cosines

$$a^2 = b^2 + c^2 - 2bc \cos A$$

Functions of the Double Angle

$$\sin 2A = 2 \sin A \cos A$$
$$\cos 2A = \cos^2 A - \sin^2 A$$
$$\cos 2A = 2 \cos^2 A - 1$$
$$\cos 2A = 1 - 2 \sin^2 A$$

$$\tan 2A = \frac{2 \tan A}{1 - \tan^2 A}$$

Functions of the Half Angle

$$\sin \tfrac{1}{2}A = \pm \sqrt{\frac{1 - \cos A}{2}}$$

$$\cos \tfrac{1}{2}A = \pm \sqrt{\frac{1 + \cos A}{2}}$$

$$\tan \tfrac{1}{2}A = \pm \sqrt{\frac{1 - \cos A}{1 + \cos A}}$$

Area of Triangle

$$K = \tfrac{1}{2}ab \sin C$$

Standard Deviation

$$S.D. = \sqrt{\frac{1}{n} \sum_{i=1}^{n} (x_i - \bar{x})^2}$$

REGENTS EXAMINATION

EXAMINATION AUGUST 1996 SEQUENTIAL MATH III

Part I

Answer 30 questions from this part. Each correct answer will receive 2 credits. No partial credit will be allowed. Write your answers in the spaces provided on the separate answer sheet. Where applicable, answers may be left in terms of π or in radical form.

1 In the accompanying diagram, $\overline{AB}$ and $\overline{AC}$ are tangents to circle O, and chord $\overline{BC}$ is drawn. If $m\angle ABC = 72$, what is $m\angle A$?

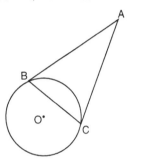

2 Express the product in simplest form:

$$\frac{a^2 - 9}{a^2 - 3a} \cdot \frac{a^2 + a}{a + 3}$$

3 Express 225° in radian measure.

4 Solve for x: $\sqrt{2x - 2} - 2 = 0$

5 If the transformation $T_{(x,y)}$ maps point $A(1,-3)$ onto point $A'(-4,8)$, what is the value of x?

6 A set of boys' heights is distributed normally with a mean of 58 inches and a standard deviation of 2 inches. Expressed in inches, between which two heights should 95% of the heights fall?

7 If $\sin A > 0$ and $\sec A < 0$, in which quadrant does the terminal side of $\angle A$ lie?

8 In which quadrant does the sum of $3 + 2i$ and $-4 - 5i$ lie?

9 Solve for x: $2^{x+2} = 4^{x-1}$

10 In $\triangle CAT$, $a = 4$, $c = 5$, and $\cos T = \frac{1}{8}$. What is the length of t?

11 Evaluate: $\displaystyle\sum_{k=3}^{7} (3k + 2)$

12 Express $\dfrac{5}{2 - i}$ in simplest $a + bi$ form.

13 Solve for y: $y^{-\frac{1}{2}} = \frac{1}{3}$

14 In $\triangle ABC$, $a = 6$, $b = 7$, and $m\angle B = 30$. Find $\sin A$.

15 Solve for all values of x: $|3x - 2| = 16$

Directions (16–35): For *each* question chosen, write on the separate answer sheet the *numeral* preceding the word or expression that best completes the statement or answers the question.

16 In the accompanying figure of circle O, $m\angle ABC = 38$.

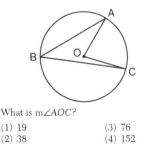

What is $m\angle AOC$?

(1) 19   (3) 76
(2) 38   (4) 152

289

17 In a circle, diameter $\overline{AB}$ is perpendicular to chord $\overline{CD}$ at L. Which statement will always be true about this circle?

(1) $CL = LD$ (3) $(CL) \times (LD) = AB$
(2) $AL > LB$ (4) $BL > LA$

18 After which transformation of $\triangle ABC$ could the image $\triangle A'B'C'$ *not* have the same area?

(1) translation   (3) point reflection
(2) rotation   (4) dilation

19 The expression $\sin 50° \cos 40° + \cos 50° \sin 40°$ is equivalent to

(1) $\sin 10°$ (3) $\sin 90°$
(2) $\cos 10°$ (4) $\cos 90°$

20 If $\log_b x = y$, then $\log_b x^2$ is

(1) $y + 2$ (3) $y - 2$
(2) $2y$ (4) y

21 Which graph represents an inverse variation between all values of x and y?

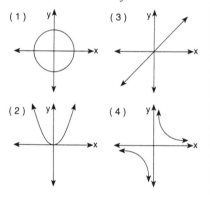

22 The graph of any function and the graph of its inverse are symmetric with respect to the

(1) x-axis
(2) y-axis
(3) graph of the equation $y = -x$
(4) graph of the equation $y = x$

23 If $m\angle B = 60$, $a = 6$, and $c = 10$, what is the area of $\triangle ABC$?

(1) 15   (3) $15\sqrt{3}$
(2) 30   (4) $30\sqrt{3}$

24 What is the period of the equation $y = -6 \sin 2x$?

(1) $-\frac{2}{6}$ (3) 2π
(2) -6π (4) π

25 The expression $\dfrac{1 + \cos 2x}{\sin 2x}$ is equivalent to

(1) $\tan x$ (3) $-\sin x$
(2) $\cot x$ (4) $-\cos x$

26 If $f(x) = 4 \cos 3x$, what is the value of $f\left(\frac{\pi}{4}\right)$?

(1) $-\sqrt{2}$ (3) 135
(2) $-2\sqrt{2}$ (4) 4

27 For which value of θ is the fraction $\dfrac{6}{\cos \theta}$ undefined?

(1) $0°$ (3) $60°$
(2) $30°$ (4) $90°$

28 Which equation has roots of $3 + \sqrt{2}$ and $3 - \sqrt{2}$?

(1) $x^2 + 6x + 7 = 0$ (3) $x^2 - 7x - 4 = 0$
(2) $x^2 - 6x + 7 = 0$ (4) $x^2 - 7x + 6 = 0$

29 In basketball, Nicole makes 4 baskets for every 10 shots. If she takes 3 shots, what is the probability that *exactly* 2 of them will be baskets?

(1) 0.288   (3) 0.600
(2) 0.432   (4) 0.960

30 When two resistors are connected in a parallel circuit, the total resistance is $\underline{\quad \dfrac{1}{\frac{1}{R_1} + \frac{1}{R_2}} \quad}$. This complex fraction is equivalent to

(1) $R_1 + R_2$ (3) $R_1 R_2$
(2) $\dfrac{R_1 + R_2}{R_1 R_2}$ (4) $\dfrac{R_1 R_2}{R_1 + R_2}$

31 Which graph represents the inequality $x^2 - 4 > 0$?

(1)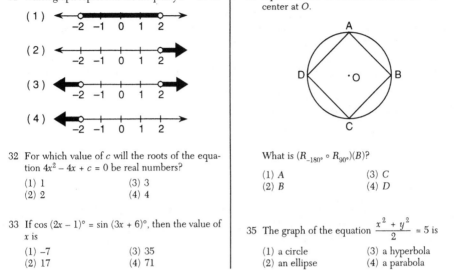

(2)

(3)

(4)

32 For which value of c will the roots of the equation $4x^2 - 4x + c = 0$ be real numbers?

(1) 1   (3) 3
(2) 2   (4) 4

33 If $\cos (2x - 1)° = \sin (3x + 6)°$, then the value of x is

(1) −7   (3) 35
(2) 17   (4) 71

34 Square $ABCD$ is inscribed in a circle with the center at O.

What is $(R_{-180°} \circ R_{90°})(B)$?

(1) A (3) C
(2) B (4) D

35 The graph of the equation $\dfrac{x^2 + y^2}{2} = 5$ is

(1) a circle   (3) a hyperbola
(2) an ellipse   (4) a parabola

Part II

Answer four questions from this part. Clearly indicate the necessary steps, including appropriate formula substitutions, diagrams, graphs, charts, etc. Calculations that may be obtained by mental arithmetic or the calculator do not need to be shown.

36 In the accompanying diagram, $\overrightarrow{PA}$ is tangent to circle O at point A, secant $\overline{PBD}$ intersects diameter $\overline{AC}$ at point E, chord $\overline{AB}$ is drawn, $m\angle P = 40$, and $m\overset{\frown}{CD}:m\overset{\frown}{DA} = 1:8$.

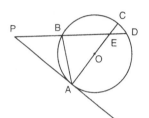

Find:

a $m\overset{\frown}{DA}$

b $m\overset{\frown}{AB}$

c $m\angle BEA$

d $m\angle BAC$

e $m\angle PBA$

37 a Solve for x: $x + \sqrt{2x - 1} = 8$

b Solve for y: $\dfrac{y}{y - 1} = \dfrac{8}{y} + \dfrac{1}{y - 1}$

38 a Find, to the *nearest degree*, all values of x in the interval $0° \le x < 360°$ that satisfy the equation $2 \sin^2 x = 1 + \sin x$.

b For all values of x for which the expression is defined, prove that the following is an identity:

$$\cot x = \frac{\sin 2x}{1 - \cos 2x}$$

39 a On graph paper, sketch the graph of the equation $y = \tan x$ in the interval $0 \le x \le 2\pi$. [4]

b On the same set of axes, sketch the graph of the equation $y = 2 \sin x$ in the interval $0 \le x \le 2\pi$.

c Use the graphs sketched in parts a and b to determine *one* value of x in the interval $0 \le x \le 2\pi$ that satisfies the equation $\tan x = 2 \sin x$.

40 Two forces act on a body at an angle of 100°. The forces are 30 pounds and 40 pounds.

a Find the magnitude of the resultant force to the *nearest tenth* of a pound.

b Find the angle formed by the greater of the two forces and the resultant force to the *nearest degree*.

41 a On the same set of axes, sketch and label the graphs of the equations $xy = 8$ and $y = \log_2 x$ in the interval $-6 \le x \le 6$.

b Using the graphs sketched in part a, find an integer value of x for which $\log_2 x > \dfrac{8}{x}$.

42 a The probability of a biased coin coming up heads is $\frac{3}{4}$.

(1) When the coin is flipped three times, what is the probability of *at least* two heads?

(2) When the coin is flipped four times, what is the probability of *at most* one head?

b Find the standard deviation, to the *nearest hundredth*, for the following test scores:

100, 99, 99, 97, 96, 96, 95, 94, 93, 91

EXAMINATION JANUARY 1997 SEQUENTIAL MATH III

Part I

Answer 30 questions from this part. Each correct answer will receive 2 credits. No partial credit will be allowed. Write your answers in the spaces provided on the separate answer sheet. Where applicable, answers may be left in terms of π or in radical form.

1 In the accompanying diagram, $\overline{AB}$ is tangent to circle O at B and $\overline{ACD}$ is a secant. If $AB = 9$ and $AD = 27$, find AC.

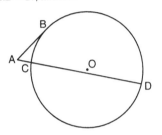

2 In terms of i, express in simplest form:

$$\sqrt{-64} - 3\sqrt{-4}$$

3 In $\triangle ABC$, $\sin A = \frac{2}{3}$, $\sin B = \frac{4}{5}$, and side $a = 20$. Find side b.

4 In the accompanying diagram, $\overline{CD}$ is tangent to circle O at B, AO and BO are radii, and chord $\overline{AB}$ is drawn. If m$\angle AOB = 108$, find m$\angle ABD$.

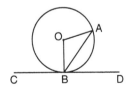

5 Solve for y: $\dfrac{4}{5y - 3} = \dfrac{2}{3y + 4}$

6 Solve for y: $3^{y+1} = 9^{y-1}$

7 Express 1.2π radians in degrees.

8 In which quadrant does the graph of the sum of $(-3 - 5i)$ and $(2 + 4i)$ lie?

9 Evaluate: $\displaystyle\sum_{n=1}^{3} (2n - 1)$

10 If $f(x) = x - 3$ and $g(x) = x^2$, what is the value of $(f \circ g)(2)$?

11 In $\triangle ABC$, $a = 8$, $b = 9$, and $\cos C = \frac{2}{3}$. Find c.

12 In a normal distribution, 68% of the scores fall between 72 and 86 and the mean is 79. What is the standard deviation?

13 In a circle with a radius of 4 centimeters, what is the number of radians in the central angle that intercepts an arc of 8 centimeters?

14 If x varies inversely as y, and $x = 9$ when $y = 8$, find x when $y = 12$.

Directions (15–35): For *each* question chosen, write on the separate answer sheet the *numeral* preceding the word or expression that best completes the statement or answers the question.

15 If $f(x) = 3^x$, then $f(-2)$ equals
(1) $\frac{1}{9}$ (3) -6
(2) 9 (4) -9

16 The expression $\dfrac{\cot \theta}{\csc \theta}$ is equivalent to

(1) $\dfrac{\cos \theta}{\sin^2 \theta}$ (3) $\tan \theta$
(2) $\sin \theta$ (4) $\cos \theta$

293

17 In the accompanying diagram of circle O, the measure of $\overset{\frown}{RS}$ is 64°.

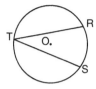

What is m∠RTS?

(1) 32 (3) 96
(2) 64 (4) 128

18 If sin A > 0 and (sin A)(cos A) < 0, in which quadrant does ∠A terminate?

(1) I (3) III
(2) II (4) IV

19 The solution set of the inequality $|x - 3| < 5$ is

(1) $\{x < 8 \text{ and } x < -2\}$
(2) $\{x < 8 \text{ or } x < -2\}$
(3) $\{x < 8 \text{ and } x > -2\}$
(4) $\{x > 8 \text{ or } x < -2\}$

20 For which value of x is $f(x) = \frac{\sin x}{\cos x}$ undefined?

(1) 0 (3) $\frac{\pi}{2}$

(2) $\frac{\pi}{4}$ (4) π

21 The expression cos 80° cos 20° − sin 80° sin 20° is equivalent to

(1) cos 60° (3) sin 100°
(2) cos 100° (4) sin 60°

22 Which statement is true about the roots of the equation $\sqrt{x^2 - 5x + 5} = 1$?

(1) The only root is 1.
(2) The only root is 4.
(3) Both 1 and 4 are roots.
(4) Neither 1 nor 4 is a root.

23 If the coordinates of P are (−2,7), what are the coordinates of $(D_2 \circ r_{y=x})(P)$?

(1) (4,−14) (3) (−4,14)
(2) (−14,4) (4) (14,−4)

24 Which graph represents the equation $\frac{x^2}{4} + \frac{y^2}{4} = 1$?

25 What is the period of the graph of the equation $y = a \sin bx$?

(1) $\frac{2\pi}{a}$ (3) a

(2) $\frac{2\pi}{b}$ (4) b

26 What is the product of the roots of the equation $2x^2 - x - 2 = 0$?

(1) 1 (3) −1
(2) 2 (4) −2

27 What is the image of $A(5,2)$ under $R_{90°}$?

(1) (−5,2) (3) (2,5)
(2) (5,−2) (4) (−2,5)

28 The set {0,1,−1} is closed under the operation of

(1) addition (3) subtraction
(2) multiplication (4) division

29 If sin $(x + 20°)$ = cos x, the value of x is

(1) 35° (3) 55°
(2) 45° (4) 70°

30 The probability of Gordon's team winning any given game in a 5-game series is 0.3. What is the probability that Gordon's team will win *exactly* 2 games in the series?

(1) $(0.3)^2(0.7)^3$ (3) $10(0.3)^2(0.7)^3$
(2) $5(0.3)^3(0.7)^2$ (4) $5(0.3)^2(0.7)$

31 What is the solution set of the inequality $x^2 - 3x - 10 > 0$?

(1) $\{x \mid -2 < x < 5\}$ (3) $\{x \mid x < -5 \text{ or } x > 2\}$
(2) $\{x \mid -5 < x < 2\}$ (4) $\{x \mid x < -2 \text{ or } x > 5\}$

32 What is the middle term in the expansion of $(3x - 2y)^4$?

(1) $-6x^2y^2$ (3) $-216x^2y^2$
(2) $36x^2y^2$ (4) $216x^2y^2$

33 If the graphs of the equations $y = \log_3 x$ and $y = 2$ are drawn on the same set of axes, they will intersect where x is equal to

(1) 1   (3) 3
(2) 2   (4) 9

34 An obtuse angle of a parallelogram has a measure of 150°. If the sides of the parallelogram measure 10 and 12 centimeters, what is the area of the parallelogram?

(1) 30 cm^2 (3) $60\sqrt{2}$ cm^2

(2) 60 cm^2 (4) $60\sqrt{3}$ cm^2

35 The accompanying diagram shows a sketch of a quadratic function, f(x).

What is the nature of the roots of the quadratic equation $f(x) = 0$?

(1) imaginary
(2) real, rational, and equal
(3) real, rational, and unequal
(4) real, irrational, and unequal

Part II

Answer four questions from this part. Clearly indicate the necessary steps, including appropriate formula substitutions, diagrams, graphs, charts, etc. Calculations that may be obtained by mental arithmetic or the calculator do not need to be shown.

36 *a* Solve for x and express the roots in terms of i:

$$\frac{x + 3}{3} + \frac{x + 3}{x} = 2$$

b Solve for x and express the roots in simplest $a + bi$ form:
$$x^2 = 6x - 10$$

37 *a* Find, to the *nearest degree*, all values of θ in the interval $0° \le \theta < 360°$ that satisfy the equation $3 \sin^2 \theta - \sin \theta - 2 = 0$.

b Solve for x to the *nearest tenth*:
$$5^x = 30$$

38 *a* On the same set of axes, sketch and label the graphs of the equations $y = -2 \sin x$ and $y = \cos 2x$ as x varies from 0 to 2π radians.

b Using the graphs sketched in part *a*, determine the number of points in the interval $0 \le x \le 2\pi$ that satisfy the equation $\cos 2x = -2 \sin x$.

39 *a* The table below shows the set of score data for an English examination.

x_i	f_i
100	2
90	3
80	6
70	5
60	4

Find the standard deviation of these scores to the *nearest tenth*. [4]

b In the accompanying diagram, a regular hexagon with a spinner is divided into six equal areas labeled with a letter or a number.

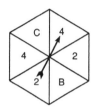

If the spinner is spun four times, find the probability that it will land in a

(1) numbered area *at most* one time [3]
(2) lettered area *at least* three times [3]

40 *a* Express in simplest form:

$$\frac{1 - \frac{1}{x}}{\frac{1}{x^2} - \frac{1}{x}} \quad [5]$$

b For all values of x for which the expressions are defined, prove the following is an identity:

$$\frac{\cos 2x}{\sin x} + \frac{\sin 2x}{\cos x} = \csc x \quad [5]$$

41 In the accompanying diagram of circle O, $\triangle ABC$ is formed by tangent $\overline{AB}$, secant $\overline{BDC}$, and chord $\overline{AC}$; $\overline{CA} \cong \overline{CD}$; $m\widehat{AC} = 140$; and $AC = 10$.

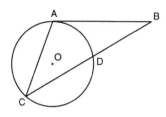

Find:

a $m\widehat{AD}$ [2]
b $m\angle B$ [2]
c AB to the *nearest tenth* [6]

42 *a* On your answer paper, copy and complete the table for the values of y for the equation $y = \log_2 x$. [4]

x	$\frac{1}{4}$	$\frac{1}{2}$	1	2	4
y					

b On graph paper, using the completed table, draw the graph of the equation $y = \log_2 x$ for the interval $\frac{1}{4} \le x \le 4$. Label the graph *b*. [2]

c On the same set of axes, reflect the graph drawn in part *b* in the *y*-axis and label it *c*. [2]

d On the same set of axes, reflect the graph drawn in part *b* in the line $y = x$ and label it *d*. [2]

EXAMINATION JUNE 1997 SEQUENTIAL MATH III

Part I

Answer 30 questions from this part. Each correct answer will receive 2 credits. No partial credit will be allowed. Write your answers in the spaces provided on the separate answer sheet. Where applicable, answers may be left in terms of π or in radical form.

1 Express 240° in radian measure.

2 In $\triangle ABC$, $a = 12$, $\sin A = 0.45$, and $\sin B = 0.15$. Find b.

3 Find the value of $\sum\limits_{k=1}^{3} (3k - 5)$.

4 Solve for x: $4^{(3x+5)} = 16$

5 Express the sum of $\sqrt{-64}$ and $3\sqrt{-4}$ as a monomial in terms of i.

6 Solve for all values of x: $|2x + 5| = 7$

7 What will be the amplitude of the image of the curve $y = 2 \sin 3x$ after a dilation of scale factor 2?

8 What is the solution of the equation $\sqrt{5x - 9} - 3 = 1$?

9 In the interval $90° \le \theta \le 180°$, find the value of θ that satisfies the equation $2 \sin \theta - 1 = 0$.

10 Express in simplest form: $\dfrac{1}{\dfrac{1}{a} + \dfrac{1}{b}}$

11 If $f(x) = x^0 + x^{\frac{2}{3}} + x^{-\frac{2}{3}}$, find f(8).

12 When the sum of $4 + 5i$ and $-3 - 7i$ is represented graphically, in which quadrant does the sum lie?

13 In the accompanying diagram, $\overline{AP}$ is a tangent and $\overline{PBC}$ is a secant to circle O. If $PC = 12$ and $BC = 9$, find the length of $\overline{AP}$.

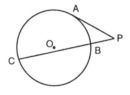

14 Circle O has a radius of 10. Find the length of an arc subtended by a central angle measuring 1.5 radians.

15 If $f(x) = 5x - 2$ and $g(x) = \sqrt[3]{x}$, evaluate $(f \circ g)(-8)$.

Directions (16–35): For *each* question chosen, write on the separate answer sheet the *numeral* preceding the word or expression that best completes the statement or answers the question.

16 For which value of x is the expression $\dfrac{1}{1 - \cos x}$ undefined?

(1) 90° (3) 270°
(2) 180° (4) 360°

17 The expression $\log \sqrt{\dfrac{x}{y}}$ is equivalent to

(1) $\frac{1}{2}(\log x - \log y)$ (3) $\frac{1}{2} \log x - \log y$
(2) $\log \frac{1}{2}x - \log \frac{1}{2}y$ (4) $\log \frac{1}{2}x - \log y$

18 If $f(x) = \cos 3x + \sin x$, then $f\left(\dfrac{\pi}{2}\right)$ equals

(1) 1 (3) −1
(2) 2 (4) 0

297

19 Expressed in $a + bi$ form, $(1 + 3i)^2$ is equivalent to

(1) $10 + 6i$

(2) $-8 + 6i$

(3) $10 - 6i$

(4) $-8 - 6i$

20 The expression $\dfrac{\tan \theta}{\sec \theta}$ is equivalent to

(1) $\cot \theta$

(2) $\csc \theta$

(3) $\cos \theta$

(4) $\sin \theta$

21 Which equation is represented by the graph below?

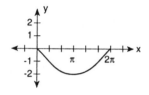

(1) $y = -2 \sin \frac{1}{2}x$

(2) $y = -\frac{1}{2} \sin 2x$

(3) $y = \frac{1}{2} \sin 2x$

(4) $y = 2 \sin \frac{1}{2}x$

22 Expressed in $a + bi$ form, $\dfrac{5}{3 + i}$ is equivalent to

(1) $\frac{15}{8} - \frac{5}{8}i$

(2) $\frac{5}{3} - 5i$

(3) $\frac{3}{2} - \frac{1}{2}i$

(4) $15 - 5i$

23 Gordon tosses a fair die six times. What is the probability that he will toss *exactly* two 5's?

(1) $_6C_5 \left(\frac{5}{6}\right)^2 \left(\frac{1}{6}\right)^4$

(2) $_6C_2 \left(\frac{5}{6}\right)^2 \left(\frac{1}{6}\right)^4$

(3) $_6C_5 \left(\frac{1}{6}\right)^2 \left(\frac{5}{6}\right)^4$

(4) $_6C_2 \left(\frac{1}{6}\right)^2 \left(\frac{5}{6}\right)^4$

24 If $\sin \theta$ is negative and $\cot \theta$ is positive, in which quadrant does θ terminate?

(1) I

(2) II

(3) III

(4) IV

25 The domain of the equation $y = \dfrac{1}{(x - 1)^2}$ is all real numbers

(1) greater than 1

(2) except 1

(3) less than 1

(4) except 1 and -1

26 In the accompanying diagram, about 68% of the scores fall within the shaded area, which is symmetric about the mean, $\bar{x}$. The distribution is normal and the scores in the shaded area range from 50 to 80.

What is the standard deviation of the scores in this distribution?

(1) $7\frac{1}{2}$

(2) 15

(3) 30

(4) 65

27 The expression $2 \sin 30° \cos 30°$ has the same value as

(1) $\sin 15°$

(2) $\cos 60°$

(3) $\sin 60°$

(4) $\cos 15°$

28 In the accompanying diagram of a unit circle, the ordered pair (x,y) represents the point where the terminal side of θ intersects the unit circle.

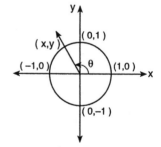

If $m\angle\theta = 120$, what is the value of x in simplest form?

(1) $-\frac{\sqrt{3}}{2}$

(2) $\frac{\sqrt{3}}{2}$

(3) $-\frac{1}{2}$

(4) $\frac{1}{2}$

29 In $\triangle ABC$, side a is twice as long as side b and $m\angle C = 30$. In terms of b, the area of $\triangle ABC$ is
(1) $0.25\,b^2$ (3) $0.866\,b^2$
(2) $0.5\,b^2$ (4) b^2

30 Which quadratic equation has roots $3 + i$ and $3 - i$?
(1) $x^2 - 6x + 10 = 0$ (3) $x^2 - 6x + 8 = 0$
(2) $x^2 + 6x - 10 = 0$ (4) $x^2 + 6x - 8 = 0$

31 Which is the fourth term in the expansion of $(\cos x + 3)^5$?
(1) $90 \cos^2 x$ (3) $90 \cos^3 x$
(2) $270 \cos^2 x$ (4) $270 \cos^3 x$

32 The graph of the equation $y = \frac{6}{x}$ forms
(1) a hyperbola   (3) a parabola
(2) an ellipse   (4) a straight line

33 The roots of the equation $-3x^2 = 5x + 4$ are
(1) real, rational, and unequal
(2) real, irrational, and unequal
(3) real, rational, and equal
(4) imaginary

34 Which equation does *not* represent a function?
(1) $y = 4$ (3) $y = x - 4$
(2) $y = x^2 - 4$ (4) $x^2 + y^2 = 4$

35 If the point $(2,-5)$ is reflected in the line $y = x$, then the image is
(1) $(5,-2)$ (3) $(-5,2)$
(2) $(-2,5)$ (4) $(-5,-2)$

Part II

Answer four questions from this part. Clearly indicate the necessary steps, including appropriate formula substitutions, diagrams, graphs, charts, etc. Calculations that may be obtained by mental arithmetic or the calculator do not need to be shown.

36 *a* On the same set of axes, sketch and label the graphs of the equations $y = 2 \cos x$ and $y = \sin \frac{1}{2}x$ in the interval $-\pi \le x \le \pi$.

   b Using the graphs drawn in part *a*, determine the number of values in the interval $-\pi \le x \le \pi$ that satisfy the equation $\sin \frac{1}{2}x = 2 \cos x$.

37 In the accompanying diagram, isosceles triangle *ABC* is inscribed in circle *O*, and vertex angle *BAC* measures 40°. Tangent $\overline{PC}$, secant $\overline{PBA}$, and diameters $\overline{BD}$ and $\overline{AE}$ are drawn.

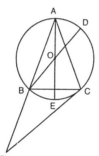

Find:
   a m$\widehat{BC}$
   b m$\angle ABD$
   c m$\angle DOE$
   d m$\angle P$
   e m$\angle ACP$

38 Find, to the *nearest ten minutes* or *nearest tenth of a degree*, all values of x in the interval $0° \le x < 360°$ that satisfy the equation $2 \sin 2x + \cos x = 0$.

39 *a* Find the standard deviation, to the *nearest hundredth*, for the following measurements:

   24,28,29,30,30,31,32,32,32,33,35,36

   b A circle that is partitioned into five equal sectors has a spinner. The colors of the sectors are red, orange, yellow, blue, and green. If four spins are made, find the probability that the spinner will land in the green sector

   (1) on *exactly* two spins
   (2) on *at least* three spins

40 *a* Express in simplest form:
   $$\frac{3y + 15}{25 - y^2} + \frac{2}{y - 5}$$

   b Solve for x and express the roots in simplest $a + bi$ form:
   $$2 + \frac{5}{x^2} = \frac{6}{x}$$

41 In $\triangle ABC$, $AB = 14$, $AC = 20$, and m$\angle CAB = 49$.
   a Find the length of $\overline{BC}$ to the *nearest tenth*. [6]

   b Using the results from part *a*, find m$\angle C$ to the *nearest degree*.

42 Given: $f = \{(x,y) \mid y = \log_2 x\}$
   a On graph paper, sketch and label the graph of the function f. [3]

   b Write a mathematical explanation of how to form the inverse of function f.

   c On the same set of axes, sketch and label the graph of the function f^{-1}, the inverse of f. [3]

   d Write an equation for f^{-1}.

EXAMINATION JANUARY 1998 SEQUENTIAL MATH III

Part I

Answer 30 questions from this part. Each correct answer will receive 2 credits. No partial credit will be allowed. Write your answers in the spaces provided on the separate answer sheet. Where applicable, answers may be left in terms of π or in radical form.

1 Express the sum of $\sqrt{-25}$ and $2\sqrt{-9}$ as a monomial in terms of i.

2 In $\triangle ABC$, $b = 6$, $c = 3$, and $\sin B = 0.4$. Find the value of $\sin C$.

3 An angle that measures $\frac{7\pi}{4}$ radians is in standard position. In which quadrant does its terminal side lie?

4 In the accompanying diagram, segments $\overline{RS}$, $\overline{ST}$, and $\overline{TR}$ are tangent to circle O at A, B, and C, respectively. If $SB = 3$, $BT = 5$, and $TR = 13$, what is the measure of $\overline{RS}$?

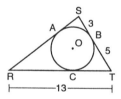

5 Solve for x: $\quad \sqrt{5x + 2} - 3 = 0$

6 Evaluate: $\quad \sum_{k=1}^{4} (k + 2)^3$

7 If $f(x) = (16x)^0 + x^{\frac{2}{3}}$, find $f(64)$.

8 Express in simplest form: $\quad \dfrac{\dfrac{x}{y} - \dfrac{y}{x}}{\dfrac{1}{y} + \dfrac{1}{x}}$

9 Find the image of $A(4,-2)$ under the transformation $r_{y=x}$.

10 Solve for y: $\quad 2^{(y-3)} = \frac{1}{16}$

11 If a fair coin is tossed five times, what is the probability of tossing *exactly* three heads?

12 If $f(x) = 2 \sin^2 x + \sin x + 1$, find the value of $f\left(\frac{\pi}{6}\right)$.

13 Find $m\angle\theta$ in the interval $180° \le \theta \le 270°$ that satisfies the equation $2 \cos \theta + 1 = 0$.

14 In the accompanying table, y varies inversely as x. What is the value of m?

x	2	4	m
y	18	9	3

15 In the accompanying diagram, tangent $\overline{CD}$ and secant $\overline{CBA}$ are drawn to circle O from external point C. If $DC = 4$ and $AB = 6$, find the length of $\overline{BC}$.

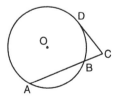

16 Write a single translation that is equivalent to $T_{3,-1}$ followed by $T_{-5,5}$.

301

17 Express the product of $4 - 3i$ and $2 + i$ in simplest $a + bi$ form.

18 If $\log_x \frac{1}{4} = -2$, find x.

Directions (19–35): For *each* question chosen, write on the separate answer sheet the *numeral* preceding the word or expression that best completes the statement or answers the question.

19 Sin 50° cos 30° + cos 50° sin 30° is equivalent to

(1) cos 80°   (3) cos 20°
(2) sin 20°   (4) sin 80°

20 If $f(x) = x - 3$ and $g(x) = x^3$, then $f(g(3))$ is

(1) 0   (3) 24
(2) 6   (4) 30

21 Which curve has only one line of symmetry?

(1) a circle   (3) a parabola
(2) an ellipse   (4) a hyperbola

22 Which equation is represented in the accompanying graph?

(1) $y = 2 \sin 2x$ (3) $y = 2 \sin \frac{1}{2}x$
(2) $y = \frac{1}{2} \sin \frac{1}{2}x$ (4) $y = \frac{1}{2} \sin 2x$

23 The solution set of $|x - 3| > 5$ is

(1) $\{x < 8 \text{ and } x < -2\}$ (3) $\{x < 8 \text{ and } x > -2\}$
(2) $\{x < 8 \text{ or } x < -2\}$ (4) $\{x > 8 \text{ or } x < -2\}$

24 The graph of the equation $y = 10^x$ lies entirely in Quadrants

(1) I and II   (3) I and IV
(2) II and III   (4) III and IV

25 Which graph of a relation is also a function?

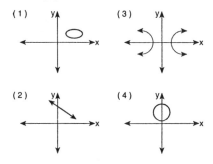

26 If $\theta = \text{Arc cos } \frac{\sqrt{2}}{2}$, what is the value of tan θ?

(1) 1   (3) $\frac{1}{\sqrt{2}}$
(2) $\sqrt{2}$ (4) $\frac{1}{2}$

27 If tan $\theta < 0$ and csc $\theta > 0$, in which quadrant does θ terminate?

(1) I   (3) III
(2) II   (4) IV

28 In the accompanying diagram of a unit circle, the ordered pair (x,y) represents the point where the terminal side of θ intersects the unit circle.

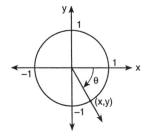

If $\theta = -\frac{\pi}{3}$, what is the value of y?

(1) $-\frac{\sqrt{3}}{2}$ (3) $-\sqrt{3}$
(2) $-\frac{\sqrt{2}}{2}$ (4) $-\frac{1}{2}$

29 What is the fourth term in the expansion of $(x - 2y)^5$?

(1) $80x^2y^3$ (3) $-80x^2y^3$

(2) $80xy^4$ (4) $-80xy^4$

30 The heights of a group of 1000 women are normally distributed. The mean height of the group is 170 centimeters (cm) with a standard deviation of 10 cm. What is the best approximation of the number of women between 170 cm and 180 cm tall?

(1) 950   (3) 340

(2) 680   (4) 170

31 For which value of x is $f(x)$ undefined if $f(x) = \dfrac{\cos x}{1 - \cos 2x}$?

(1) 1   (3) $\frac{\pi}{2}$

(2) $\frac{1}{2}$ (4) π

32 The graph of the equation $xy = -8$ is

(1) an ellipse   (3) a circle

(2) a hyperbola   (4) a parabola

33 The solution of $x^2 - 3x < 0$ is

(1) $0 < x < 3$ (3) $x < 0$ or $x > 3$

(2) $x > 3$ (4) $x < 0$

34 If $m\angle A = 45$, $AB = 10$, and $BC = 8$, the greatest number of distinct triangles that can be constructed is

(1) 1   (3) 3

(2) 2   (4) 0

35 In $\triangle ABC$, $a = 8$, $b = 9$, and $m\angle C = 135$. What is the area of $\triangle ABC$?

(1) 18   (3) $18\sqrt{2}$

(2) 36   (4) $36\sqrt{2}$

Part II

Answer four questions from this part. Clearly indicate the necessary steps, including appropriate formula substitutions, diagrams, graphs, charts, etc. Calculations that may be obtained by mental arithmetic or the calculator do not need to be shown.

36 *a* On the same set of axes, sketch and label the graphs of the equations $y = \cos 2x$ and $y = -2 \sin x$ in the interval $0 \le x \le 2\pi$.

   b Using the graphs sketched in part *a*, determine the number of values of x in the interval $0 \le x \le 2\pi$ that satisfy the equation $-2 \sin x - \cos 2x = 3$.

37 Find all positive values of θ less than 360° that satisfy the equation $2 \cos 2\theta - 3 \sin \theta = 1$. Express your answers to the *nearest ten minutes* or *nearest tenth of a degree*.

38 *a* Given: $r = 2 - i$ and $s = 4 + 3i$

     (1) On graph paper, draw and label the graphs of these complex numbers.

     (2) On the same set of axes, graph the sum of r and s as drawn in part *a*(1) and label it *t*.

     (3) On the same set of axes, draw the image of *t* after a counterclockwise rotation of 90° and label it *t'*.

   b Express the roots of the equation $2x + \dfrac{5}{x} = 2$ in simplest $a + bi$ form.

39 In the accompanying diagram of circle O, chord $\overline{AB}$ is parallel to diameter $\overline{EC}$, secant $\overline{PBD}$ intersects $\overline{EC}$ at F, tangent $\overline{PA}$ is drawn, $m\widehat{AB} = m\widehat{BC}$, and $m\widehat{CD} = 80$.

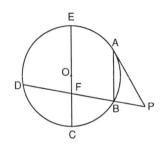

Find:

a $m\widehat{AE}$

b $m\angle ABD$

c $m\angle DFC$

d $m\angle P$

e $m\angle PAB$

40 a Solve for all values of x:

$$\frac{2x}{x+3} + \frac{3}{x-3} = \frac{8}{x^2 - 9}$$

b If $\log_b R = 0.75$ and $\log_b S = 0.25$, find the value of

(1) $\log_b R^2 S$

(2) $\log_b \dfrac{\sqrt[3]{R}}{RS}$

41 In $\triangle ABC$, $a = 6$, $b = 7$, and $c = 10$.

a Find the measure of angle A to the *nearest ten minutes* or *nearest tenth of a degree*.

b Using the result from part a, find the area of $\triangle ABC$ to the *nearest tenth*.

42 The table below shows the scores on a writing test in an English class.

x_i	f_i
95	4
85	13
75	11
70	6
65	2

a Using the accompanying set of data, find both the mean and the standard deviation to the *nearest tenth*.

b What is the number of scores that fall within one standard deviation of the mean ($\bar{x} \pm 1\sigma$)?

c Find, to the *nearest tenth*, the percentage of scores in this set of data that are within one standard deviation of the mean.

d What is the number of scores that fall within two standard deviations of the mean ($\bar{x} \pm 2\sigma$)?

e Find the percentage of scores in this set of data that are within two standard deviations of the mean.

ANSWERS TO REGENTS EXAMINATIONS

AUGUST 1996

1. 36
2. $a + 1$
3. $\frac{5\pi}{4}$
4. 3
5. -5
6. 54 and 62
7. II
8. III
9. 4
10. 6
11. 85
12. $2 + i$
13. 9
14. $\frac{3}{7}$

15. $6, -\frac{14}{3}$
16. 3
17. 1
18. 4
19. 3
20. 2
21. 4
22. 4
23. 3
24. 4
25. 2
26. 2
27. 4
28. 2

29. 1
30. 4
31. 3
32. 1
33. 2
34. 3
35. 1
36. a 160
   b 80
   c 50
   d 50
   e 100
37. a 5
   b 8

38. a 90, 210, 330
39. c 0 or π or 2π
   or $\frac{\pi}{3}$ or $\frac{5\pi}{3}$
40. a 45.6
   b 40
41. b 5 or 6
42. a (1) $\frac{54}{64}$
    (2) $\frac{13}{256}$
   b 2.72

JANUARY 1997

1. 3
2. $2i$
3. 24
4. 54
5. -11
6. 3
7. 216
8. III
9. 9
10. 1
11. 7
12. 7
13. 2

14. 6
15. 1
16. 4
17. 1
18. 2
19. 3
20. 3
21. 2
22. 3
23. 4
24. 1
25. 2
26. 3

27. 4
28. 2
29. 1
30. 3
31. 4
32. 4
33. 4
34. 2
35. 1
36. a ±3i
   b 3 ± i
37. a 90, 222, 318
   b 2.1

38. b 2
39. a 12.3
   b (1) $\frac{48}{81}$
    (2) $\frac{9}{81}$
40. a $-x$
41. a 80
   b 30
   c 12.9
42. a

x	$\frac{1}{4}$	$\frac{1}{2}$	1	2	4
y	-2	-1	0	1	2

ANSWERS TO REGENTS EXAMINATIONS

JUNE 1997

1. $\frac{4\pi}{3}$
2. 4
3. 3
4. -1
5. $14i$
6. $-6, 1$
7. 4
8. 5
9. $150°$
10. $\frac{ab}{b+a}$
11. $5\frac{1}{4}$
12. IV
13. 6
14. 15

15. -12
16. 4
17. 1
18. 1
19. 2
20. 4
21. 1
22. 3
23. 4
24. 3
25. 2
26. 2
27. 3
28. 3

29. 2
30. 1
31. 2
32. 1
33. 4
34. 4
35. 3
36. b 2
37. a 80
  b 20
  c 140
  d 30
  e 110

38. $90°, 194.5, 270°, 345.5°$
      or
  $90°, 194.30', 270°, 345.30'$
39. a 3.06
  b (1) $\frac{96}{625}$
    (2) $\frac{17}{625}$
40. a $\frac{1}{5-y}$
  b $\frac{3}{2} \pm \frac{1}{2}i$
41. a 15.1
  b 44
42. b Reflect the function in $y = x$
      or
  Interchange the x's and y's
      or
  An equivalent statement
  d $y = 2^x$
      or
  $x = \log_2 y$

JANUARY 1998

1. $11i$
2. 0.2
3. IV
4. 11
5. $\frac{7}{5}$
6. 432
7. 17
8. $x - y$
9. $(-2,4)$
10. -1
11. $\frac{10}{32}$
12. 2
13. 240
14. 12

15. 2
16. $T_{-2,4}$
17. $11 - 2i$
18. 2
19. 4
20. 3
21. 3
22. 4
23. 4
24. 1
25. 2
26. 1
27. 2
28. 1

29. 3
30. 3
31. 4
32. 2
33. 1
34. 2
35. 3
36. b 1
37. 14.5, 165.5, 270
    or
  14°30', 165°30', 270°
38. b $\frac{1}{2} \pm \frac{3}{2}i$
39. a 60
  b 80
  c 100
  d 50
  e 30

40. a $\frac{1}{2}, 1$
  b (1) 1.75
  b (2) -0.75
41. a 36.2 *or* 36°10'
  b 20.7
42. a $\bar{x} = 79.4$, $\sigma = 8.4$
  b 24
  c 66.7
  d 36
  e 100

INDEX

half-angle identity for, 213
inverse of, 182
sum and difference identities
for, 204
Cotangent function, 163–164
Coterminal angles, 160

Dependent variable, 63
Diameter, 127
Difference of two squares, 8
Dilations, 75
Direct isometry, 86
Discriminant, 51
Division
of algebraic fractions, 13
of complex numbers, 50
of radicals, 24–25
Domain, 62
Double angle identities, 208, 209,
211

Ellipse, 68
Equations
absolute value, 30
exponential, 116–117
fractional, 36–37
logarithmic, 111
quadratic, 52–53
radical, 38–39
trigonometric, 197–200
with rational exponents, 39–40
Equidistant chords, 128
Exponential
equations, 116–117
functions, 103
Exponents, 1–2
Extraneous roots, 36

Factoring, 8–10
Fields, 43–44
Fractions
complex, 18–19

operations with, 10, 12–16
Fractional equations, 36–37
Fractional exponents, 5
Frequency
of a data item, 269
of a trigonometric function, 174
Function, 62
composite, 69–70
domain and range, 62
inverse, 89
notation, 64
one-to-one, 90
trigonometric, 164
Functions of negative angles, 160

Glide reflections, 85
Graphs
of complex numbers, 45–46
of exponential functions,
103–104
of logarithmic functions, 104
of quadratic relations, 67–68
of trigonometric functions,
174, 180

Half-angle identities, 213
Half-turn, 80
Horizontal line test, 91
Hyperbola, 68, 94–95

Identities
double angle, 208–211
half angle, 212–213
proving, 216–218
Pythagorean, 193
quotient, 193
reciprocal, 163
sum and difference, 202–205
Imaginary numbers
operations with, 48–50
powers of, 46
Independent variable, 63